METROPOLIS

MARTIN-GROPIUS-BAU

Exhibition organizers

Christos M. Joachimides
Norman Rosenthal

Martin-Gropius-Bau, Berlin
20 April – 21 July 1991

ZEITGEIST
Gesellschaft zur Förderung
der Künste in Berlin e.V.

Board
Hartmut Ackermeier
Friedrich Weber
Gerhard Raab

The exhibition was made possible
through a generous subvention from the
Stiftung Deutsche Klassenlotterie, Berlin.

Individual projects have been additionally
supported by
Philip Morris GmbH
The Japan Foundation

INTERNATIONAL ART EXHIBITION BERLIN 1991

METROPOLIS

Edited by
Christos M. Joachimides
and
Norman Rosenthal

Rizzoli
NEW YORK

CATALOGUE

Coordinating editor
Wolfgang Max Faust

Editorial staff
Gerti Fietzek
Michael Glasmeier

Editorial assistant
Margarete Lauer

House editor
Robert Williams

Cover design by
Soukoup Krauss, Frankfurt/M.,
Anja Nienstedt, Berlin,
based on a photograph
by Jochen Littkemann, Berlin

Produced by
Dr. Cantz'sche Druckerei
Ostfildern 1 near Stuttgart
Lithography by
System-Repro, Filderstadt 1
Typeset by
Weyhing GmbH, Stuttgart
Bound by
G. Lachenmaier, Reutlingen

The German-language version of this publication is
copyright © 1991 by Edition Cantz, Stuttgart.

First published in the United States of America in 1991
by
RIZZOLI INTERNATIONAL PUBLICATIONS, INC.
300 Park Avenue South, New York, NY 10010

EXHIBITION

Administration
Robert Unger

Office manager
Tina Aujesky

Project assistants
Thomas Büsch, Karola Gräßlin, Julian Scholl

Press officer
Bernhard Ingelmann

Secretarial assistants
Barbara Herold, Caroline Schneider

Additional staff
Susanne Ackers, Andreas Binder, Brigitte Crockett,
Juana Corona, Flora Fischer, Ute Lindner

Conservation
Christiane Altmann, Roland Enge

Technical organization
Jürg Steiner
and Museumstechnik GmbH
Managing director
Sybille Fanelsa
Technical manager
Thomas Kupferstein
Lighting
Uwe Kolb
Installation team
Andreas Baumann, Wolfgang Heigl,
Frauke Hellweg, Bernd Manzke, Udo Miltner,
Andreas Neumann, Andreas Piontkowitz,
Bernard Poirier, Volker Schöverling,
Jean Baptiste Trystram, Werner Voßmann

Transport
Hasenkamp, Berlin

Insurance
ABP Behrens & Partner

ISBN 0-8478-1363-0 / Library of Congress Cataloging – in – Publication Number: LC 91-52610 / Printed in Germany

CONTENTS

LENDERS TO THE EXHIBITION

Bonnefantenmuseum, Maastricht
Des Moines Art Center, Des Moines, Iowa
Hirshhorn Museum and Sculpture Garden, Washington, D.C.
Kunsthaus Zürich
Musée d'Art Contemporain de Lyon
The Museum of Contemporary Art, Los Angeles
Vancouver Art Gallery
Zentrum für Kunst und Medientechnologie Karlsruhe – Museum für Gegenwartskunst

Air de Paris, Nice
Brooke Alexander Gallery, New York
Galleria Lucio Amelio, Naples
American Fine Arts Co., New York
Thomas Ammann, Zürich
Frida Baranek
Galerie Beaubourg, Marianne + Pierre Nahon, Paris
Mickey/Larry Beyer, Cleveland, Ohio
Galerie Bruno Bischofberger, Zurich
Mary Boone Gallery, New York
Galerie Daniel Buchholz, Cologne
Jean-Marc Bustamante
Pedro Cabrita Reis
Collection Antoine Candau
Leo Castelli Gallery, New York
Collection Bruno e Fortuna Condi, Naples
Paula Cooper Gallery, New York
Ascan Crone, Hamburg
Leopold von Diergardt
The Eli Broad Family Foundation, Santa Monica, California
Gerald S. Elliott, Chicago, Illinois
Jo + Marlies Eyck, Wijlre
Jan Fabre
Milton Fine
Emily Fisher Landau, New York
Katharina Fritsch
Laure Genillard Gallery, London

Gilbert & George
Barbara Gladstone Gallery, New York
Jay Gorney Modern Art, New York
Ulrich Görlich
Rainer Görß
Studio Guenzani, Milan
Agnes Gund, New York
Galerie Max Hetzler, Cologne
Gary Hill
The Oliver Hoffmann Collection
Jenny Holzer
Galerie Ghislaine Hussenot, Paris
Cristina Iglesias
Collection Issinger, Berlin
Jablonka Galerie, Cologne
Jänner Galerie, Vienna
Galerie Johnen & Schöttle, Cologne
Galerie Isabella Kacprzak, Cologne
Kazuo Kenmochi
Jon Kessler
Galerie Jule Kewenig, Frechen / Bachem
Galerie Bernd Klüser, Munich
Imi Knoebel
Jeff Koons
Jannis Kounellis
The Kouri Collection
Attila Kovács
Collection J. Lagerwey, The Netherlands
Galerie Yvon Lambert, Paris
Lambert Art Collection, Geneva
George Lappas
Otis Laubert
Stuart Levy Gallery, New York
Galleria Locus Solus, Genoa
Luhring Augustine Gallery, New York
La Máquina Española, Madrid
Collection Achille e Ida Maramotti Albinea, Reggio Emilia, Italy
Gerhard Merz
Metro Pictures, New York
Olaf Metzel

Yasumasa Morimura
The Mottahedan Collection
Juan Muñoz
Galerie Christan Nagel, Cologne
Galerie 1900 – 2000, Paris
Galerie Nordenhake, Stockholm
Marcel Odenbach
Galerie Pedro Oliveira, Oporto
Reiner Opoku, Cologne
The Pace Gallery, New York
Galerie Peter Pakesch, Vienna
Franz Paludetto, Turin
Galería Marga Paz, Madrid
Collection Francesco Pellizzi
Dmitri Prigov
The Rivendell Collection
Frederic Roos Collection, Switzerland
Edward Ruscha
Collection Sanders, Amsterdam
Julian Schnabel
Karsten Schubert Ltd., London
Gaby + Wilhelm Schürmann, Aachen
Collection Francesco Serao, Naples
Fundação de Serralves, Oporto
Collection Tony Shafrazi, New York
Cindy Sherman
Sonnabend Gallery, New York
Collection Dr. Reiner Speck, Cologne
Gian Enzo Sperone, Rome
Monika Sprüth Galerie, Cologne
Galleria Christian Stein, Milan
Haim Steinbach
Stux Gallery, New York
Galerie Tanit, Munich/Cologne
Collection Tubacex
Galerie Sophia Ungers, Cologne
Waddington Galleries, London
Galerie Michael Werner, Cologne/ New York
Thea Westreich, New York
Wewerka & Weiss Galerie, Berlin
Bill Woodrow
Christopher Wool

← METROPOLIS: installations in the atrium, Martin-Gropius-Bau. Photograph: Werner Zellien, Berlin

Christos M. Joachimides Norman Rosenthal

Acknowledgements

An exhibition of this size and organizational complexity could only have been realized with the extraordinary degree of help we have received from all those involved.

Particular thanks are due to the Stiftung Deutsche Klassenlotterie, Berlin. Its generous financial support has made possible the realization of the exhibition.

In the Berlin Senate, Department of Cultural Affairs, inparticularly in the person of Karl Sticht, we found from the outset a cooperative partnership which energetically supported this project.

We are most appreciative of the cooperative willingness of the Berlinische Galerie, particularly Prof. Jörn Merkert and Dr. Ursula Prinz.

Our greatest thanks, however, are due to the artists who, inspired by the idea and conception of this exhibition and the extraordinary Martin-Gropius-Bau have made such substantial contributions to the exhibition.

Furthermore, the organizers are grateful to all the lenders who through their great generousity have made so many significant works of art available. Equally to all those who in so many different ways and with understanding and enthusiasm have contributed suggestions, help and encouragement. We particularly would like to mention:

Helge Achenbach, Düsseldorf; Lucio Amelio, Naples; Paul Andriesse, Amsterdam; Heiner Bastian, Berlin; Peter Bianchi, Bratislava; Bildhauerwerkstätten Berlin: Werner Ahrens; Paula Cooper, New York; Maria Corral, Madrid; Diego Cortez, New York; Ascan Crone, Hamburg; Mark Deweer, Zweregem-Otegem; Goethe Institut São Paulo: Klaus Vetter; Bärbel Gräßlin, Frankfurt/M.; Walter Grasskamp, Everswinkel; Roger de Grey, London; Loránd Hegyi, Budapest; Max Hetzler, Cologne; Damian Hirst, London; Justizvollzugsanstalt Tegel, Berlin; Günter Schmidt-Fich; Jule Kewenig, Cologne; Katerina Koskina, Athens; Willy Ludwig, Berlin; Gerd Harry Lybke, Leipzig; Casimiro Xavier de Mendonça, São Paulo; Jürgen H. Meyer, Düsseldorf; Museum für Verkehr und Technik Berlin: Ulrich Kubisch; Fumio Nanjo, Tokyo; Franz Paludetto, Turin; Anne Rider, London; Michael Schulz, Berlin; Luis Serpa, Lisbon; Ingrid Sischy, New York; Rainer Sonntag, Berlin; Reiner Speck, Cologne; Staatsbibliothek Preußischer Kulturbesitz Berlin: Siegfried Detemple; Jörg-Ingo Weber, Berlin; Klaus Werner, Leipzig; Emeline Wick, London; Heribert Wuttke, Rheinbach; Donald Young, Chicago.

We are most thankful to our authors for their knowledgeable and informative contributions. They have made the catalogue into a lively forum for the discussion of art today and for important aspects of intellectual discourse in a rapidly changing world. That this is so, owes much to the inspiration und energetic involvement of our coordinating editor Wolfgang Max Faust.

We are also equally grateful to the publishing house Edition Cantz, Stuttgart, especially to Bernd Barde and Dr. Ulrike Bleicker, who have produced this beautiful publication that accompanies the exhibition. We were encouraged by the confidence shown by Rizzoli International Publications, New York, inparticularly Alfredo de Marzio and Charles Miers, in publishing the English language version of the catalogue.

Last but not least we wish to express our deep thanks to all our collaborators who have worked in the METROPOLIS office and in the Martin-Gropius-Bau. Their tireless involvement and boundless enthusiasm have alone made the realization of this project possible.

METROPOLIS: installations in the atrium, Martin-Gropius-Bau. Photograph: Werner Zellien, Berlin

Christos M. Joachimides

The Eye Low on the Horizon

Nine years after 'Zeitgeist', ten years after 'A New Spirit in Painting', we – in a quite different artistic and historical situation – intend METROPOLIS to focus on art at the beginning of the Nineties.

The previous exhibitions addressed art as it presented itself in the early Eighties, not least as a result of the great painting explosion on both sides of the Atlantic.

At the beginning of this decade we are faced with new questions – of a political, social and media-conditioned nature – and they demand new answers from artists. We now see before us art in a period of radical change, a kaleidoscope of different artistic approaches, formal positions and differentiated attitudes.

Art using photography occupies an important place in the exhibition. This involves not just photographs, but works of art created by photographic means derived from the visual arts tradition. Painting remains, of course, of equal importance – whether abstract or figurative, whether as an image reflecting the media, or as an image reflecting other images.

Large-scale, three-dimensional works are a focal point of the exhibition: sculptures and installations shaped by a poetically hermetic image of the world, and also objects, paintings and environments resulting from an intensive confrontation with Pop Art. They are markers indicating an artistic will to occupy space, and so transform it into a stage for a new creative freedom. Strategies for this are various – from the mystification of material to existential soundings of the human condition, from narrative associational bridges to distorted reconstructions of an 'as-if' reality. The medium itself is not so important for these artists – particularly as they often work with various media in parallel; they are much more concerned with the attitudes conveyed.

And yet, ancestry can be traced. The poetic, alchemistic spirit of Marcel Duchamp is stealing over the horizon of this young generation that has been moving into the public eye since the mid-Eighties. A noticeable feature of art in this century is the imaginary pendulum swinging between two poles – between Picasso and Duchamp. If 1981 was Picasso's hour, Duchamp's time has come in 1991.

This exhibition grew out of an intensive dialogue between ourselves and the artists involved. A more lucid picture of today's art and its situation slowly emerged from a fog of expressive information, as a result of repeated studio visits in many countries, discussions, and meetings with many of the participating artists in Berlin at the Martin-Gropius-Bau.

One thing we established easily as we researched our exhibition is that as far as the image of art presented today is concerned, there are two obvious points of culmination drawing artistic events to themselves like magnets: New York, and the area around Cologne. But an exhibition taking place in Berlin in 1991 would not be just if it did not try hard to identify the authentic events in the visual arts to be found today behind the gates, recently thrown open, of Eastern Europe. Finding these out is extremely difficult. Sparse and barely functioning channels of communication and information often considerably impeded our investigations and attempts to determine precisely what constitutes the current situation. Despite all this METROPOLIS intends to introduce a number of East European artists whose work we found to be interesting and multi-layered, which we hope will give authentic information on creativity and the state of art in societies subject to considerable upheaval.

The exhibition contains work by two generations of artists. In order better to understand more recent art as it presents itself today, we are also showing work by those artists of the older generation whose œuvre stands as a model for the present. They give the exhibition a necessary art-historical perspective.

The exhibition also asks questions. What can art tell us about late twentieth century society – are its features symptomatic, connotative, parallel? Has the role of the artist in society perhaps changed more than the role of art, and, if so, is that due in part to the spectacular events that so fundamentally changed the art market in the Eighties?

The title of the exhibition – METROPOLIS – looks at the present, remembers a great past, and attempts to point at the future.

The contemplation of the present involves the looking at art today. We see an art arising from the canyons of Manhattan, from industrial premises in Cologne or Düsseldorf, from the warehouses of East London – an art that finds its stimuli in friction with cities, by ironizing metropolitan life to the utmost, or by dissecting second-hand reality communicated by the media and reassembling it by artistic means. It filters and encodes this experience of the world by conceptual attitudes within the various media to which it lays claim, whereby beauty and violence, sexuality and objectification, freedom and isolation indicate the human spectrum in the context of this art.

Our memories are of Berlin in the early decades of this century, when it was a crucial intersection point for Modernism between Paris and Moscow, Milan and Stockholm – a scene of discussion, comparison and contradiction, a great stage, the laboratory of the young century's artistic ideas and utopias.

As for the future: Berlin is transforming itself after the upheavals of the last eighteen months, which changed Germany and Europe fundamentally; it can once more become a place where paths of mind and spirit can cross, a place in which new and radical change can emerge.

Since the *Demoiselles d'Avignon*, Modernism has become more and more hermetic, more and more encoded, accessible to fewer and fewer people – this is also true, incidentally, of modern music. Works of art are not immediately comprehendible, and the laborious unravelling of codes is often necessary in order properly to understand the structure and canons upon which they are based.

I see the exhibition – an independent medium of expression in its own right – as a way to develop strategies for getting over this hurdle in the history of ideas: strategies of portrayal, presentation, confrontational dialogue, surprise. Repose and tension, concentration and acceleration involved in order to make works of art themselves.

Here we can see an analogy with work in the theatre and the task of the director. Our aim is to make this complex, encoded art more easily accessible to a larger audience. Sensual curiosity should be aroused, so that the first epidermal experience changes into an intellectual and spiritual thirst for knowledge that stimulates and encourages a more profound concern with the works of art themselves.

This exhibition should also be perceived as a score. A score that contains, for example, elements of John Cage's 'random theory'. The Martin-Gropius-Bau is ideal for this: the visitor is offered the opportunity of finding at least six or seven possible routes through the exhibition. And on his chosen route he is confronted by either crescendos or diminuendos. He passes through meditative zones and sharp-edged areas. Musicality, indeed rhythm, should surely be crucial features of exhibition presentation. Often it is a cryptic, scarcely visible element that makes an exhibition start to 'chime'. Our task is to make each visitor's progress through the exhibition a rich experience.

If we see art as training for the imagination, as the point where reflection acquires apparently contradictory, provocative forms, where consensus-troubling questions provide a reaction to a world that already has a handy answer for everything, then METROPOLIS is the laboratory, a witches' kitchen, of a creative freedom that can signal a return to Utopia at the beginning of the last decade of this waning century – a century that even now leaves open all questions about where art is coming from and going to, an art that from the outset presented a manifesto for changing the world.

Translated from the German by Michael Robinson

Norman Rosenthal

The Principle of Restlessness

The proposition that art comes from art is common-place, yet, when confronted with the new, this is not always apparent, particularly to an audience traditionally suspicious of art. Even within the context of so-called radical art, the 'art world' invariably tends to like what it already knows. Art, and the perception of what it might be, has a lot to do with recognition and expectation. The discourse about art, which, after all, can only truly take place through the medium of the exhibition (for what is the purpose of a work of art other than to be exhibited?), should contribute towards refining that process of recognition so as to achieve, perhaps, some kind of consensus among its audience.

The traditions of art in the West in the twentieth century have certainly been diverse. This is not the place to rehearse them, except to intimate that the history of art, whether perceived from the point of view of Expressionism (hot) or cerebral conceptualism, for example Cubism (cold), has renewed itself in countless subjective, but not necessarily arbitrary, ways, thus decisively enriching our culture. In the last decade there has been too much talk of art existing in a state of Post-Modernism, as though the age of modern art is somehow over, and the experiments of Picasso, Kandinsky or De Chirico, for example, are no longer relevant for the art of today, any more than are Raphael's frescoes or Rembrandt's self-portraits. Yet, those artists of earlier centuries can contribute to a discussion of our present situation. The purpose of studying the art of the past is to help the old survive, and even to feel contemporary. The obverse of this is to place the art of today within a tradition, and to try and make clear its roots in a past discourse that needs to be shown to have some relevance. Otherwise it deserves to be consigned to oblivion, which, in the end, is the fate of most art production.

The problem for those presenting an exhibition of new art, is not so much one of defining originality –

whatever that might be – but to point towards a possible future, and ensure that the gates into the paradise of art that Kandinsky imagined, remain well and truly open. De Chirico wrote in 1919 of 'a European era like ours, that carries with it the enormous weight of infinite civilizations and the maturity of so many spiritual and fateful periods that produces an art that in certain aspects resembles that of the restlessness of myth'.[1] A function of art, and of contemporary art in particular – and of contemporary literature, music, film, etc – is to replace myth, perhaps even religion, not merely to describe it. For if old art can be explained by academics in terms of its subject-matter, technique and social and historical context, then contemporary art should remain elusive, lost in mysterious rites. The explication for a dead hare (Beuys), for igloos (Mario Merz), sacks of coal (Kounellis), or a *Lightning Field* (Walter de Maria) – an arbitrary allusion to the subject-matter of, by now, well-known contemporary sculpture – remains more useful, and thus beautiful, by being a spectacular assault on our subconscious. Connections and juxtapositions do not need instant explanation. Indeed, in our era, when explanation is all and belief, at least superficially, seems to play a very small part, perhaps art's most useful role is to preserve sophisticated codes of belief. Possibly, the more inexplicable a work of art remains, the more multi-layered its range of meanings, the more valid and useful it becomes to the viewer. It is precisely the lack of an obvious moral tone that gives art its dynamism and force, and suggests, or at least gives hope for – even if false hope – the creation of new work. And when the falseness of such principles of hope become all the more apparent, when the world of art finds itself flooded by epigones and imitators of the successful modes of representation that at any one moment appear supreme, it becomes, once again, a time for innovation and discussion, particularly in a world dominated by information systems that somehow can act both as a barrier and as a stimulation to the development of authentic forms of visual expression.

In 1910 it was still possible in Europe for authentic and totally opposed styles of art to survive side by side and hold a place in the discourse of art. Parisian Cubism could legitimately contrast itself with the metaphysical obsessions of Turin, and with the expressive colour developments taking place in' Dresden, Berlin and Munich. Within Germany itself the spiritual and technical strategies were quite different in each city: the *genius loci* was then a major factor within the structure of modern art. Subsequently, increased communication systems began to influence the development of an international style and, not for the first time in the history of art, imperialistic commands were issued; in this case they came first from Paris, and then from New York. Old codes were always being broken by new subversions, which in turn became new orthodoxies. Thus, after about 1960, Abstract Expressionism established itself as a new international style, to be followed by Pop Art, Conceptual and Minimal art, and most recently by a figurative expressionism that, at first, seemed to indicate that 'the artists' studios are full of paintpots again',[2] producing a wonderful illusion of endless creative vitality everywhere. It was none the worse for being an illusion, for all constellations of artists are by definition illusory, but they are valid at the moment of belief. They then remain as beautiful and enriching moments within the collective memory of world art. Meanwhile, the individual artist must doggedly pursue his own course.

That was ten years ago. As we enter the last decade of this tumultuous century, however, which now demands its artistic as well as political reassessment – above all, concerning the question of progress – the crucial question seems once more to be about individuality. After decades of conflicting dogmas, it might be useful to question whether or not a return to a new individuality is possible, a particular eclecticism within overall creativity that allows personal mythologies, both political and aesthetic, to impose themselves on our mental landscape of the visual arts.

In fact, several modes of art actively suggest themselves as models that might define the tradition, and therefore the legitimacy, of art practice today. Some might hesitate to speak of fathers and grandfathers of art, but Western art, surely, might be described as a Tree of Jesse, a dream of an earthly paradise, or, perhaps, as a series of gardens full of seductive delights that succeed one another, but rarely, if ever, reach an ultimate flowering. Three artists above all define the positions and possibilities of art today. Two of these fathers of art – one European, the other American – are Joseph Beuys and

Marcel Duchamp, *Étant Donnés*, 1946–1966

Marcel Duchamp, *Étant Donnés*, 1946–1966

Andy Warhol, the high priests of contemporary art practice. The grandfather is Marcel Duchamp, the European who made his home in America, and whose work, it can be argued, is the point of origin of so much serious American art of this century. The paradox is that Duchamp, both as man and artist, attempted every possible strategy to place himself outside the styles, the 'isms' of art.

The embracing influence of Duchamp's three major works, the *Nude Descending a Staircase*, *The Large Glass* and *Étant Donnés*, is everywhere in this exhibition. His *Nude Descending a Staircase* was a consciously created 'masterpiece' that broke the decidedly unerotic conventions of Cubism, which preferred the still-life, the portrait and the pure landscape to any suggestion of illicit or even seductive behaviour. It is erotic charge that alone connects these three works, each so utterly different in technique and appearance. Each inevitably allows an intensification and an increased explicitness that, paradoxically, increases the mystification and frustration, making one feel that, for all the explanations offered, we can never really get to the bottom of the mystery. The door of *Étant Donnés* remains firmly closed. We are merely permitted to put our eye to the peep-hole, and never more than one person at a time is ever able to witness the work of art. The particular viewing-point is prescribed even more precisely than that of a painting: if it is a three-dimensional sculpture, it conforms to none of the normal criteria, for one cannot walk around it. Nor can it be described by that unsatisfactory term 'environment', for it is not possible for the spectator to be part of it. It might best be described as theatre, or rather, a peep-show that aspires to the condition of art. This breaching of convention, 'I have forced myself to contradict myself in order to avoid conforming to my own taste',[3] rules out, as far as possible, the question of style, of which, like a fingerprint or handwriting, each artist of substance is somehow a prisoner. There can be no doubting the artistic authenticity and originality of *Étant Donnés*. Of course, Duchamp made it easy for us; it might be less obvious were the piece not so clearly presented within the context of the rest of his *œuvre* in the Museum at Philadelphia. Given its location, its subtle, paradoxical mental and physical structures define it as a model on

Joseph Beuys, *Hirschdenkmäler*, 1982, *Zeitgeist* exhibition

which so much contemporary art has been dependent, from Neo-Dada to that of the present.

The desire to make art strongly contrasts with the desire to escape from its history. To attempt objectivity, and to make general what is fundamentally private and/or erotic, has determined a vital path that cannot be eliminated. The piece of furniture (Artschwager), the gas lamp (Kounellis), the cinematographic panorama (Ruscha), arouse in us memories that stimulate the imagination within the context of art, and make connection with the 'given' ('étant donnés') panopticon of Philadelphia.

But beyond the private nature of Duchamp's investigations and quasi-scientific experiments, come the social and even religious dimension that, in an exemplary way, Joseph Beuys brought to the making of art. He, too, defined an art that took many diverse physical forms and opened up endless new possibilities for making art: 'The extended concept of art is no theory, but a way of proceeding which says that the inner eye is much more crucial than the external images developing in any way. The precondition for good outward pictures, that are also hung in museums, is that the inner image, the structure of thought, of imagination, of feeling, provide the quality which you must have of a balanced picture. In this way I bring the picture back to its place of origin... In the beginning was the word. The word is a form.'[4]

For Beuys, the reality of art was the charge that he brought to the materials he used, whether organic or inorganic, whether fat, wax, food or plants, metal, felt, batteries, or the tools of the sculptural studio gathered together to make the sculpture *Hirschdenkmäler* (Stag monuments), shown at the *Zeitgeist* exhibition in 1982. It is these charges that have within them the inner symbolic strength to change, or, at least, the possibility of changing, the current order of life for the better. Art, in that sense, is always a diagram, sometimes it is only a drawing, which enables the transformation to take place. Works of art are fundamental 'Richtkräfte' (Directive forces), serving as models for the mind, indicators that offer the hope for life on this planet to continue through the medium of art. This is not, however, to deny the erotic charge with which Beuys's work is filled. His drawings, for instance those in *the Secret Block for a Secret Person in Ireland*, are filled with the most astonishing sculptural and erotically charged representations of women and of himself, that in no way deny – on the contrary, they elevate – the individual's right – his or her necessity of self-expression – down to the most secret, even illicit, action that through the context of art is made legitimate and 'beautiful'.

Indeed, the life force, the organic poetry with which Beuys invested his own unique systems of expression, without question made the continuity of art possible, exactly because of its clear links with crucial moments of art, literature, and metaphysical knowledge systems of the past, with Leonardo da Vinci, Goethe and Rudolf Steiner – all creative individuals of imagination, who strove, often within the context of war and destruction, to make the creative and the positive grow. If the function of art is to enrich our lives and to clear the ground through transformation and catharsis, images of war, poverty and disease – all of which are still so prevalent in our world today – and which are constantly taking on new and negative 'creative' forms themselves, are vital sources of both subject-matter and materiality for the artist. 'Zeige deine Wunde' (Show your wound), declared Beuys as the subject of one of his most powerful environments, and this quasi-religious injunction is, perhaps, a further pointer to the role of the contemporary artist, who, through his or her own dreams and obsessions, can most creatively give art its vital therapeutic, even healing value. It was through his creative behaviour, which ranged from excessive narcissism to the representation of extreme humility, that Beuys, whose work so demonstratively was made up of both, ultimately is able to survive. Beuys preferred largely to reject traditional forms, painting and sculpture, for alternative materials: 'Der Fehler fängt schon an, wenn einer sich anschickt, Keilrahmen und Leinwand zu kaufen' (the mistake starts as soon as one goes out to buy a stretcher and canvas). Even rubbish in the street, as in the action *Ausfegen* (Street sweeping, 1972), was potential material for making art. It is this theatricality that is just one of the many points of contact with *Étant Donnés* – those props that enable art to take place off-stage and within the art gallery, and which have a natural force preserving them from banality, making them attractively mysterious, and investing them with the aesthetic dimension. 'The silence of Marcel Duchamp is overrated', declared Beuys in 1964. Maybe this critique was based on the assumption that the older master had given up art for chess (the existence of *Étant Donnés* was not known at the time), but it belies the affinities that ultimately existed between these two key figures, who have been so decisive in making space for the art of our time. Of the creative act, Duchamp wrote in 1957 that it exists between 'the two poles of creation of art: the artist on one hand, and on the other the spectator who later becomes the posterity'.[5]

That Duchamp should refer to art in a social, or rather societal, way is, perhaps, surprising and it was probably meant in a somewhat different way to Beuys. But it is what also links him to that other father figure of the art of our time, Andy Warhol. The persona of Warhol never seemed to suggest social critique, rather it implied

Joseph Beuys, *Ausfegen*, Berlin 1972

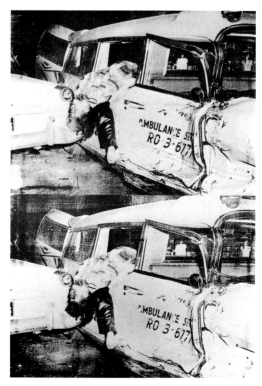

Andy Warhol, *Ambulance Disaster Two Times,* 1963

the idea of society, a life that took place on one level at least at the parties and expensive restaurants of a world of glamour: 'We went back to the hotel to meet Joseph Beuys and then we had dinner with Beuys and his family at some family Italian restaurant. He was sweet. Really a lot of fun'.[6] Of course, that was true as well, and just as Beuys's work is not only a social critique but is also full of humour and self-deprecation (an essential part of all art activity), so Warhol (if one prefers to believe the message of his astonishing large and extensive output, rather than the evidence of the society columns) suggests a critical and objective stance concerning everyday things, and the extraordinary ability, like Beuys, to make them beautiful. The images and objects of everyday life – the soup can, the Coca-Cola bottle, the Brillo box, the cliché icons of the media (Marilyn, Liz, Jackie and a host of others), the disasters of contemporary society (the car crash, the suicide, the race mob, the funeral, the execution chamber, the atomic bomb, the criminal, the politicians and the dollar bills) were all transferred with the precision and skill of Goya into therapeutic and aesthetic objects, every bit as powerful and suggestive for further art strategies as the expanded theory and practice

of art that Beuys, from a different perspective, was able to suggest. The concern with consumer culture, the ability to transform it into elite objects (which, paradoxically, are available more or less to everyone), was in one sense the opposite stategy from Beuys, who sought, from a position of elite culture to move (with mixed success) towards a more democratic cultural position (The Organization for Direct Democracy; 7,000 Oaks). But, in fact, the positions were closer than might be imagined. Beuys referred to his studio as a workshop; Warhol described his factory as a place 'where you build things. This is where I make or build my work. In my art work hand painting would take much too long and anyway that is not the age we live in. Mechanical means are *today* and using them I can get more art to more people. Art should be for everyone'.[7]

The positions of Beuys, Warhol and Duchamp are ultimately not far from one other; collectively they inform many of those positions taken up by many younger artists today and are manifest in this exhibition. The art object as a commodity, as a subject for endless and entertaining gossip (as it has been from time immemorial) as well as for serious discourse – essentially all brought about through Warhol's work – made the jump to aesthetic validity on a scale way beyond that of Duchamp's own ready-mades. Of course, both Beuys and Warhol worked within a cultural context that informed the positions they took, the one with Fluxus, the other with Pop Art; both were movements that somehow appeared momentarily redundant within the expansive painting movements of the late Seventies and early Eighties. If artists today seem to be receiving signals from both Fluxus and Pop Art, they are also informed by developments that occurred in the intervening years, years that witnessed an extraordinary explosion of artistic activity on both sides of the Atlantic, both among artists and their audiences. Minimal and Conceptual art, *arte povera* and art forms using every possible technique and medium – photography, video, performance, as well as sculpture and painting – are all present today. There are strategies that assert ever more radical possibilities for making paintings (Georg Baselitz), and support the continuity of European discourse in terms of Classical myth (Jannis Kounellis); the conflicts and constraints of freedom in an urban society are transcended by Gilbert & George; and there is the cathartic description of mutation and deformation of the environmental and mental psyche (Bruce Nauman), the very American combination of matter of factness and surreal possibilities of assemblage (Artschwager), and further ambiguity between matter-of-factness and transcendent mystery that suggest the possibility of the best paintings still having to be made (Richter and Ruscha). All these positions invented over the last thirty years (and there are surely others) are highly suggestive to a new generation of artists that is itself rapidly establishing its place in that continuum of art to which we have addressed ourselves, and which were all in their day relatively marginal to the concerns of art criticism and perception, when measured against many of their contemporaries.

The world of cultural criticism, beset with theories of post-modernity and deconstruction, is, as Habermas has pointed out, ultimately 'insensitive to the highly ambivalent context of cultural and social modernity'.[8] To look at and to contemplate artists in relation to one another, as, for instance, in this exhibition we have chosen to relate within the atrium of the Martin-Gropius-Bau the work of Ian Hamilton Finlay, Jonathan Borofsky, Jan Fabre and Mike and Doug Starn, is surely not only to ask why, but to celebrate the continuing alchemical possibilities of art, to suggest beautiful mysteries, to pose riddles without answers with contemporary relevance, to manufacture a *Wunderkammer* as a solace, an escape, as well as a commentary on death and disease and the general futility of existence that, nonetheless, is destined continually to celebrate birth and the creative life.

1 Quoted in Massimo Carra (ed.) *Metaphysical Art*, London, 1971, p. 88
2 C. M. Joachimides in *A New Spirit in Painting*, catalogue, Royal Academy of Arts, London, 1981, p. 14
3 Quoted in *Étant Donnés* – Reflections on a new work, Philadelphia Museum of Art, 1987, p. 13
4 Friedhelm Mennekes, *Beuys on Christ, A Position in Dialogue*, Stuttgart, 1989, p. 62
5 Michel Sanouillet and Elmer Peterson, *The Writings of Marcel Duchamp*, New York, 1989, p. 138
6 Pat Hackett (ed.) *The Andy Warhol Diaries* 1989, p. 275
7 Quoted by Benjamin Buchloh in *Andy Warhol, A Retrospective*, The Museum of Modern Art, New York, 1989, p. 40
8 Jürgen Habermas, *The Philosophical Discourse on Modernity*, Cambridge, Mass., 1989, p. 338

Wolfgang Max Faust

Metropolis and the Art of Our Time

Artificiality dominates present-day metropolitan life: it is a life shaped by the needs of the information media. Its reality increasingly reveals itself to be a staged and simulated reality. A second Nature has supplanted the first, usurping the place of direct experience. In a world totally ruled by its communications, this second Nature reinterprets time and space. The ubiquitous eye of the electronic media transcends all spatial limitations, and its implied message is that 'everything' is there to be seen. And so the visible and the image virtually coalesce. Boundaries between fact and fiction become fluid. Even the real starts to look like a representation of the possible. The all-encompassing view annihilates distance. Events in space are reduced to a perpetual Here; and in the dimension of time this Here is matched by a Now.

The extension into space has its temporal counterpart in the expansion of the present. Formerly, the present was a point on an evolutionary line, clearly defined in relation to past and future; now it has changed into a 'perpetual present', including both past and future within itself and activating the present dimension within them. The whole idea of Utopia is being rethought. It is beginning to approximate to 'Atopia': the act of embarking on a polymorphous present in which contradictions are not denied and incompatibilities are tolerated.

This is a situation full of ambivalence. In a consumer society, the 'Here and Now' manifests itself above all in the structures of the entertainment industry, in which, in accordance with the dictates of the market, all aspects of life feature as present stimuli. Perceiving merges with forgetting. In such a situation, the empty, consumption-oriented individual is the ideal interlocutor.

But there is another aspect to this expansion of the present. It manifests itself as an all-absorbing instant: as the intense experience of a 'fulfilled present' that defines its value precisely in terms of the absence of a past and a future. This is a form of experience largely alien to Western civilization, whose obsession with progress, evolution and futurity has never left much room for the dignity of the present moment. The mind-altering experience of accepting that 'it is what it is' has consistently been undervalued or negated. Now this experience looms ever larger, reinforcing our age's preoccupation with living in the present.

Art Today

Contemporary art, at the outset of the last decade of this century, encompasses all the aspects just described. Art is marked by metropolitan life, and also by the dominance of the information media. A consumer society that defines almost every part of life in market terms is something so consistently this-worldly as to connect – through the act of consumption – with the expansion of the present. Art, too, is reinterpreting the idea of Utopia – as held by successive avant-gardes in the history of Modernism – to present a variety of coexisting focuses of experience.

Contemporary art is not a unified movement, fixated on specific media or sharply defined artistic concepts. In place of unity we see multiplicity: a range of distinct but commensurate positions. And what all these have in common is that the aspects of art they offer are laden with past experience. However unequivocally these contemporary artworks may belong to 'Now', they still constantly refer back to radical changes and reformulations that took place earlier in the twentieth century. This is what makes contemporary art so perplexing. It is art about the possibility of art; it directs the eye to itself and at the same time insists on making the eye look beyond.

Art looks at art history; but it also sets its sights on relations with politics, culture and economics. Contemporary art can be seen in terms of two forces, one centrifugal and one centripetal; and this gives rise to two questions. First, what actually counts as art? Second, how is art to overstep its own boundaries? The interaction of artist, artwork and society defines new parameters: and it is these that govern the specific identity of today's art.

Historical Background

The historical process that emerges is one that began in the late eighteenth century and still continues today. In the first phase of the process, art emancipated itself from its previous subjection to religious and social criteria. Thereafter, until the middle of the nineteenth century, an 'aesthetic of the artist' prevailed. Works of art were embodiments of human autonomy and self-determination: they expressed the freedom of the individual. In the second half of the nineteenth century the dominant artistic ethos changed. The work itself, as an autonomous object, came to occupy the central focus of attention; the new governing principle was an 'aesthetic of the work'.

This aesthetic retained its validity well into the second half of the twentieth century. Successive avant-gardes discovered a variety of new justifications for art, expanding the definition of art itself through a series of fresh starts, revolutions and innovations. Extreme positions were reached, which served to stake out the limits of what art can be. Two dominant tendencies emerged. One referred the work, as an autonomous formulation, to an existential level of experience. Its aim was to communicate 'The Spiritual in Art': to make the unconscious communicable, and to 'speak of mysteries through mysteries'. The other tendency concentrated on the material reality of the work of art, making the work refer back to itself and to its own material, colour and form.

What both tendencies had in common was the attempt to use the individual work of art to convey something never known before. Art derived its unique significance from innovation, authenticity, autonomy.

As alienation grew within society, art was an intimation of possible freedom. Interpreted as a 'social antithesis of society' (Adorno), art took on a Utopian aspect, pointing beyond existing reality.

Art and the Aesthetic of Context

Both the artistic conceptions defined above, the 'aesthetic of the artist' and the 'aesthetic of the work', still exist today. But since the mid-century a new shift has begun, a progressive reinterpretation of art itself within the contemporary world. Increasingly, the context in which art appears has come to define its meaning. From a number of viewpoints, ideas of modern art formerly taken for granted have now started to be called into question. The very idea of 'The New', which persisted through successive generations of artists, is losing its validity. With the realization that to a large extent the realm of The New has already been staked out, there are signs of a shift from successive to coexistent artistic positions. Past artistic discoveries have become points of reference for an art that recombines and develops existing artistic ideologies. It is an attitude marked by a combination of involvement and detachment. The critique blends with the affirmation.

However, this revision of Modernism is not simply a continuation of the innovations of the past: it is a reinterpretation of the essence of art itself. Art no longer refers to an unrealized future; it now focuses on the experience of 'Here and Now'.

What once unfolded as a diachronic succession of events now reverts to a synchronic level, on which networks and chains of connections, coincidences and contrasts become visible. This is what gives contemporary art its protean form: its ability both to enrich itself from the past and to absorb formative factors from its own context in the present.

Of these contextual factors – as they emerged in the course of the 1980s – one of the most vital is the economic one: the art market. In the decade just past, art attained greater popularity than ever before. Commercial success led to the emergence of an international art industry backed by modern techniques of reproduction and communication, which made information about art universally accessible. At the same time, an extensive network of galleries and exhibition venues came into being. A multitude of publications bestowed legitimacy on contemporary art. Commentary and reproduction became the governing factors in the public – and commercial – response to art.

Árt's status as a commodity – previously an incidental aspect – now became one of its major parameters. And this, in turn, reinforced art's growing tendency to refer to its context. As a result, two new factors have emerged to modify the perception of art. The first is that art today – even the individual work of art – is closely bound to economic factors and is experienced through forms of mediation and reproduction. The second is that a tension exists between this mediated experience and the direct perception of the work on the spot. Indirect and direct experience thus require to be taken in relation to each other. And this reinforces the experience of art as context.

Exhibitions

The defining qualities of contemporary art – diversity, the context aesthetic, art about the possibility of art – also govern the forms of its presentation in exhibitions. These have become many-layered experiences that can no longer afford to limit themselves to a single category of art. They embody the awareness that any presentation of art creates an interpretative framework within which the art itself is perceived. Exhibitions create discourses and dialogues. They point to the agreements and disagreements between different artistic formulations.

Exhibitions are also highly relevant to the media transmission that nowadays presides over the public experience of art; for they, by contrast, afford the experience of art on the spot, 'Here and Now'. Not only does the discourse of the exhibition itself relate to each visitor's individual mode of reading the work; at the same time the exhibition promotes art's tendency to pursue 'immediacy of experience'. Radical concentration on the individual work, and associative connection between works, set in train a dynamic process that continues beyond the confines of the exhibition itself.

A Panorama of Pictures

In the present 'Optical Age', pictures in art make reference both to their own tradition and, simultaneously, to the worlds of imagery that surround them. A displacement has taken place: 'pictures' in art are no longer exclusively 'paintings'. Other media – and photography above all – have come to be included as a matter of course. The result is an array of definitions of the picture that correspond to its various possibilities.

The picture as a painting about painting is an enquiry into the essence of paint and the nature of the specific experience that it communicates (Baselitz). Here figuration (Dokoupil, Kovács, Sarmento) meets abstraction (Richter, Davenport); and gesture (Richter) and monochrome (Knoebel) join forces. Some works, by charging the picture with elements of language, go beyond painting (Schnabel, Ruscha, Wool).

When references to history, everyday culture, religion and politics find their way into the work, pictures begin to speak (Schnabel, Ruscha, Halley). It becomes clear that pictures today no longer define themselves in terms of establishing and promoting 'style'; instead, they represent the freedom to put into a picture anything that can become pictorial (Daniëls, Kuitca, Sarmento).

This is a freedom that also entails an element of doubt. Accordingly, alongside attempts to give the picture a spiritual dimension, we find works that proclaim total aesthetic indifference (Oehlen). The promise of a higher meaning, such as will make the picture into an existential experience (Bleckner), is countered by works that deliberately play games with banality (Prince). Pictures thus reveal their dependence on decisions that stem from specific concepts. And one of those decisions is that of the choice of medium.

In particular, the coexistence of painting and photography directs attention to the significance of that particular choice. The technique of photography accentuates what is impossible to convey in painting; painting gives a name to what the photograph cannot show. However, what emerges from this tension is not all-out conflict but a dialogue about the possibility of picture-making. For even those contemporary artists who work with the photographic medium insert it into complex pictorial conceptions.

The picture as a depiction of seen reality – defined by the artist's eye and presented through a specific technique – turns out to be a form of interpretation in itself (Ruff, Förg, Bustamante). In its exclusive reference to reality, the photograph shows what has been made of this reality in pictorial terms (Clegg & Guttmann, Fischli/Weiss, Görlich). This opens the prospect of linking photography with such themes as politics, culture and media aesthetics (Wall, Sherman). The staged photograph and the montage carry this one step further and mark the transition from depiction to sign: the coining of a pictorial language of metaphor that unites seen reality with fiction (Gilbert & George, Morimura).

A panorama of pictures has emerged that interweaves – here and now – both with the history of pictures and with the picture-content of our everyday life. It sets out to make present-day experience visible; to convey interpreted reality to the eye. This process of making visible is not restricted to pictures, as is shown by those artists who regard pictures as only *one* among several possible modes of working. They broaden their perspectives to other media and modes of creativity.

Sculptures and objects supply their pictures with parallels and counterpoints, expansions and concentrations (Artschwager, West, Förg, Trockel, Guzmán, Zakharov).

The Language of Objects

One important characteristic of 1990s art is its 'made' quality. The experience of artificiality, which metropolitan life generally imparts, shows itself in art as a conjunction between conception and appearance. Art does not 'grow naturally': it emerges from a stock of concepts. And so, in three-dimensional work as elsewhere, the most varied traditions within twentieth-century art persist and coexist, ranging from autonomous sculpture to the integration of everyday articles into art.

Both in the making and in the showing of these works there is a strong emphasis on their quality as 'objects': an aspect that links making with showing. One favoured current option is the abstract sculpture that draws attention to its own form and its self-referential

use of material (Baranek, Iglesias). The aesthetic experience that clings to these objects is one of silence and visual concentration. The eye takes in the relationships between heaviness and lightness, open and closed forms, compactness and fragility.

In contemporary art this same experience is noticeably often found in conjunction with other aspects of sculpture. Figurative elements (Gober, Muñoz), quotations from architecture (Cavenago, Cabrita Reis), references to the world of objects (Mike and Doug Starn, Bałka, Whiteread), enrich the silence with narrative elements. And so the hermetic enclosure inherent in abstract sculpture begins to become elusive. Intermediate forms appear, linking the world of art with contexts that lie outside it. The viewer's associative capacity is stimulated, and he is provoked into 'reading' the connections.

Wherever contemporary sculpture operates in 'in-between' areas, it makes constant reference to everyday objects. Numerous works look like transmogrified pieces of furniture (Artschwager, Armleder, Mucha, West), or like references to consumer and leisure interests (Koons, Borofsky, Perrin), or like quotations from retail display techniques (Steinbach). The Duchampian tradition of the Readymade is revived, but its intention is redefined. This is no longer a matter of integrating an everyday object into art and thereby making it into art. The attitude implied is rather the reverse: an artwork juxtaposed with an article of consumption is a reference to the consumption of art.

In a society in which almost all social relationships are market-mediated, art too becomes a market phenomenon. Warhol's message is being reformulated. The question is this: To what extent has art become a commodity among other commodities? To what extent has the perception of art been reduced to a single act of consumption with no consequences? There is a disturbing aspect to this. All the qualities traditionally associated with art – autonomy, authenticity, innovation – emerge in this light as aspects of a specific consumer attitude: one that, in dealing with art, assumes a freedom that its own economic involvements render highly conditional.

This shift in values is counterbalanced by a number of contemporary works that associate art with an existential dimension (Nauman). These are works in which art is a means of communicating profound experiences through a metaphorical language of objects. The work of art as a glyph of cosmic understanding is a reference to a silent realm of awareness that cannot be conveyed in any other language. Its reference is to the present moment; but it concurrently refers to archetypal experiences. The 'made' quality of the work of art speaks of artistic creation as a defining activity of the human race. The issue here is the necessity of art, and the position it can occupy in the present.

Spaces and Installations

In an exhibition, paintings and sculptures assert their quality of presence; but it is installations and spatial works above all that aim at direct experience and include the viewer. Walking around the works forms a connection with the spatial context. Seeing them from a number of perspectives turns perception into a process. By embracing this added dimension, the works reinforce the value of immediate experience: something that no photographic reproduction can ever replace. Many artists respond to this quality by making works specific to the space in which they are shown: works that point to the exhibition as the place of aesthetic experience.

This turns the relationship between work and space into a complex web of semantics. Occupied by the work, the space sets itself apart from other spaces and defines itself as 'art space'. This entitles the work inside it to make a statement as to the nature of art. Metaphysical dimensions are opened up, which lend the work a spiritual aura (Byars). At the same time, the space is enabled to give visible embodiment to ideas about art. What is being 'shown' is a definition of art; its implications are made palpable to the senses through the configuration of the space (Gerhard Merz).

Works of this kind are self-referential, pointing to the nature of art itself; others, however, go beyond the thematic bounds of art. Allusions to the history of civilization and ideas are incorporated, linking the art of today with elements of its genesis: desire for order and closeness to violence (Finlay). Other works may be described as three-dimensional allegories, verging on theatricality (Fabre, Prigov, Borofsky, Kaufmann, Lappas). These are historical tableaux in which the protagonist, the visitor to the exhibition, launches into an action for which he must, as it were, write his own script. The work thus points to something beyond itself. It supplies props, of a cryptic nature. It makes a visionary conjunction between myth and contemporary civilization (Kounellis); it combines quotations from cultural history with elements of social criticism (Kelley).

The ability of everyday objects to fit into new contexts in art space is shown by installations that combine discarded objects, scrap technology, chance finds and garbage to create new ensembles (Noland, Laubert, Kessler). The unregarded object, barely noticed and soon outworn, thus becomes the focus of attention. The way in which objects are ordered within the artwork points far beyond art (Woodrow). What orders them in everyday life (Fritsch)? What structures, what values, what interests do they embody?

Art as a response to the consumer society (Metzel) becomes a stimulus to reflection on social relationships. What affinities and disparities exist between art and daily life? What can the art experience do to make us see daily life through different eyes? Works of art provide no definitive answers to these questions. They voice no forthright critique. Their structure is an open one, and its aim is the emergence of consciousness. The viewer must find the answer for himself. This reference back to the viewer involves him in art space as a participant. He discovers that the perception of art is a process in which he is active.

This process quality is especially clear in video installations. The moving image introduces the dimension of time into the work; it also points to the way in which reality is filtered through the media in present-day life. The insertion of the electronically generated picture into complex arrangements of objects is a way of combining stasis with motion, setting the evanescent image against the enduring object. The appearance and disappearance of the images catch the eye. The passing of time becomes perceptible. The works operate in real time, on the analogy of experimental and surveillance installations (Nauman, Hill); or else they present time as repeated, assembled, manipulated (Odenbach, Viola). The images on the screen are non-material; and so a virtual reality takes shape. This is relevant to the act of seeing itself. For even the image seen 'in the eye' is evanescent and momentary: there is no holding it. A dialogue arises between human 'artificiality' and human nature.

The Present

Art today – pictures, sculptures, installations, spaces – presents us with a multiple field of experience. It does not define itself restrictively; it is not exclusively self-referential. This is no 'artificial paradise of art'. It reaches out into a variety of contexts and absorbs their implications. It looks back to its own history (Richter, Baselitz); it displays its own economic entanglements with the consumer society (Steinbach, Noland, Herold); it addresses the public with political statements (Holzer); it speaks of the yearning for beauty (Merz); it finds images for destruction and violence (Nauman, Görß, Kelley, Kenmochi). It juxtaposes hope and resignation, optimism and doubt. In place of the harmony of a sole definition of art – as manifested in styles, 'isms' or set media – it espouses pluralism, on principle.

This relates art to the present-day experience of reality; now that the grand ideologies are gone, there is a prospect that politics and society may be changed through the coexistence of divergent positions. Art is not one 'system' among many. Nor does it exist in splendid isolation. Its network of affinities is what gives it its crucial topical importance: art becomes part of reality and combines with other realities.

Translated from the German by David Britt

Achille Bonito Oliva

Ars Metropolis

In recent years the creative output of artists has been dominated by a particular way of seeing, a phenomenological approach that resulted in the recovery of the use of everyday objects and materials as Process Art and the re-use of compositional techniques and styles, which in turn marked the *felice inattualita* freshness of painting and sculpture. A refinement of this approach by the *transvanguardia calda* has come about through a disenchantment with, and rejection of, ideologies – a reaction that can be seen to have taken place across the cultural spectrum. It has allowed artists to overcome their fear of employing unfashionable instruments of expression, precisely because faith in the value of pure experimentation has been superseded by the judging of works of art by the intensity of their effects. The outset of the 1990s has seen a further refinement of this approach, a refinement that is quintessentially urban. This is the direct effect of the expansion of the metropolis or megapolis, with all its contradictions and divisions. Today, a kind of 'urban art' has the upper hand. In short, artists have adopted a fragmentational and precarious approach that is not restricted to privileged perspectives, and which permits the work of art to acquire a range of expressive meanings, richness of themes and a complexity that is truly experimental, in the sense that it attempts stylistic interweavings and occasionally employs multi-media elements.

Art does not rewrite its own history, it is not a work of retrospection that continues along lines in which its formal effects have already been realized; instead, it explores new ground and other decontextualizing 'languages' with respect to its historical position. In effect, the 'system' of art, which includes artist, critic, gallery owner, collector, museum, the mass media and the public, has become the niche in which the work of art is created, and as such it has made the creative experience radically urban. The initial validating identity of the work of art acquires an additional cultural value, a value that since the 1960s has been determined by the support of the international art world.

As I postulated in *Arte e sistema dell'arte* (1973), each movement and its artists are subject to a rigorous method of observation that functions in terms of selection and reception, and these elements are technologically up-dated by the received traditional notions of art's immortality. With the increasingly mass-produced nature of our environmental world, and in a society in which access to culture is determined by the industrial system, the downward lines of pressure have the major hand and impose an art that is initially and principally interpreted through a *poetiche d'insieme*. These form both the protective niche itself and the lens through which the presence of the artist and his work is perceived.

Art has now become a kind of 'super art', one which is freely disseminated throughout Europe and North America, filtered and modified by the strong presence of other cultural determinants besides those of the artist. The domineering power of money has shattered the idealistic situation in which art itself was once considered and assessed. If there was a dichotomy – with culture (art and criticism) on the one hand, and economics (the art market and collectors) on the other – this has now been overturned. These (now binary) forces interact in a dialectic that influences the ways in which a work of art might be judged. Specialized production now includes artistic production, defining boundaries that are no longer solely economic (the market) nor those of culture's technical organization (the museum).

Just as the natural elements of still-life paintings in the seventeenth century were salvaged from an uncontaminated context close to man, in the 1990s the objects assembled or featured in works of art are extrapolated from that 'other place' of industrial production, which has formed around man a contextual setting that, if artificial, is nevertheless present. Here, today, the heightened simulation of reality is still continued, through the value the artist himself places on formal elaboration, which enables him to solicit a quite different response from the beholder of his work.

Now, obviously, it is possible to explain the approach more easily than the work that results, which involves constructing a vocabulary that overcomes the chaos that is the disseminated, multiple presence of everyday objects. The approach, exactly suited to the world in and for which such art is produced, necessitates a creative anxiety on the part of the artist, which not only imparts meaning and formal value to the work but also indicates how and where this anxiety originates. The approach can also involve a conversion, in this case that of the gaze of the beholder (who is often the collector or consumer of art), so that the work of art is examined with the same kind of respect given other cultural objects – a way of looking that is quite distinct from the way the everyday original is observed. So it is that the creative approach is also bound up with the social ritual of art consumption, which is traditionally practised through a sense of contemplative awe. Art today brings with it a way of seeing that is able to address the work of art as someting removed from the banality of the mass-produced 'original'. For this to occur the artist must be able to ensure that in the process of turning the everyday object into an art-object of cultural fetishism, it takes on a transcending power. Its heightened reality signifies that a rhetorical approach has been adopted that does not mean emphasizing the everyday object itself, but seeks in fact to encompass the work of art with a means of recognition furnished by the psychological investment of the beholder, according to his own personal, social, moral and political identity. Today's artists do this, conscious of a fetishism dictated by conventions in which art remains anchored to beauty and is vouchsafed the value of a unique message delivered from a radical position. Now that works of art are realized through the use of everyday elements, as a result they are tied to their own inevitable duplication. And artists also have to bear in mind the paradox that art, even in its present form, sparks off powerful emotional reactions to the object represented.

As we approach the year 2000, art, re-established in its frame, seems resolutely fixed to highlighting the ghostly, abstracted essence of everyday objects. Precisely because these objects are condemned to a process of consumption and obsolescence, the works of art themselves are charged with that fact. This way of illustrating the fact can be assimilated within the styles of representation bequeathed by art's own history. The need for abstraction by past artists can be compared to the situation today, in which objects of consumption have been emptied of any essence by the processes of mass production; both European and American artists have responded to this by widening their field of action, to bring within the frame of art images of the objects of consumption and consumption itself – the ultimate act of inter-social relations between man and reality.

Undoubtedly, consumerism tends also to establish a fundamental condition that finds within the standardization of life's essential patterns its inevitable conclusion. Today's artist undramatically becomes the model of subjectivity by choosing not to escape from a real and concrete relationship with the world. Thus the object of consumption becomes the model for a work of art, the formation of which is encoded with meanings drawn from the outside world. This enhances the 'model' within the frame of art, producing an objectification that has no precedent, in the sense of allowing meaning to charge the otherwise inert object within the frame. This 'everyday inertia' carried into the frame of art seems to imply the inertia of the everyday of the original object. Such is the way the artist establishes a kind of link between himself and the world around him, a link between his own expressive wishes and the measurable dynamics of the outside world. In this phase, the artist's effort to find a suitably heightened reality is performed by moving towards the kind of work in which this is expressed through everyday objects. The paradoxical result is the establishment of a 'super-objectivity of the subject', the unveiling of an impersonal style able to communicate on the same wavelength as other contemporary art as well as on that of society itself. The meaning subordinate to European and American neo-objectification underlines the heightened realism or hyper-realism of a style that wants to make itself known, that wants to arrive at art's final phase of consumption – contemplation.

The dismantling of ideology in the 1980s in the West, as well as the consequences of various attempts made in Yugoslavia, Poland and Hungary in the 1950s and Czechoslovakia in the 1960s, produced a catalyst able to initiate debate that serves also as a retrospective on the entire socialist system in Eastern Europe in the person of the Soviet Union's Gorbachev. Today, a correspondence can be found between the West and East. In the West there is the progress towards a post-industrial civilization and a post-modern culture that stands beyond the simple optimism in production that so damaged its economies over recent decades. In the East a morbid collapse of ideology functions in the same way, in as much as it is able to destroy conceptual models of behaviour. In both cases we are involved in a discussion on the value of planning – a culture concerned with the predictions given by a faith invested in the future, and a culture concerned with the linear progress of history in the direction of a discredited idea of progress. In both cases there is the problem of a present that requires solutions applicable to the results of the brief moment that is the recent past. In this way a sort of correspondence is set up between the passage through culture and through art from the conditions of an ideal 'positive utopia' to be superimposed on the world, to the conditions of a 'negative utopia' circumscribed by the flagrant value of elaborated thought and the completed work, outside the dream of a mythical 'somewhere else' where culture and art would be the source of motivation.

It is accepted by today's artists that neo-objectification must establish itself within art's present 'system'. Artists must try to develop a vocabulary that allows them to penetrate that which is inert in the everyday world, rather than to attempt (impossibly) to alter it. The first approach exposes the artist's actual condition. He does not want to deny the reality of the present but, in fact, intends to communicate with it by employing an approach, a vocabulary and materials that far from being negative and insulating are comprehensive and legible, and an affirmative corroboration of his own 'sweet project'. This is possible precisely because the artist feels validated by the super-objectivity of his work, by the hyper-reality of a vocabulary that, far from destroying the object, respects its everyday inertness. Such a condition determines, in fact, the super-objective representation of it, which in turn testifies to its ability to face up to a relationship with the world on the side of specific production.

Following the *transavanguardia calda* of the 1980s, the *transavanguardia fredda* (i.e. 'cold') defends the rule of art and the super-objective subjectivity of the artist, which is capable – where it is affirmed that 'art is what it is' – of elevating itself or its own role through formulating a vocabulary that is within art's own history, indeed within history more generally. If Nietzsche had prophesied the transformation of the world into a fairy-tale and of narrative into truths without foundation, Heidegger would surely have confirmed their inevitable destiny. We live, in fact, in times of rhetoric: just as art is now talked about in the everyday language of the shop window, so there is the frame's own power of persuasion, which implies it is both exposed and protected, offered and held back, is for use and yet for contemplation. Long before Warhol there was Baudelaire, the founding father of 1855 – the year of the Exposition Universelle in Paris. The poet took note of the new objectification of art, which acquired the indifferent characteristics of and the same status as merchandise. Baudelaire's proposal was to make art an entirely commercial product. From then until now, the transparent ritual of an art able to work its way through its own system by means of a rule of super-objectivity – (a form of merchandise that enjoys the privilege of holding the symbolic centre of a market that has by now itself passed from poetry to prose with startling clarity and without any sense of nostalgia) – has continued to increase.

Art, in its ability to 'prophesy' the past through the re-telling of history, had already seen the fall of the Berlin Wall, and through this the overcoming of the ideology that underpinned it. As was the case in the cultural world at the end of the Austrian Empire, the subject became less and less significant in the great unfolding story of the world; its voice was extinguished as a result of a historical exhaustion. Thus, in the modern world with the collapse of the Russian Empire, a kind of posthumous subject (thanks to its private narcissism) has spoken through the *transavanguardia calda*, and now continues to express its painterly and sculptural neo-objectivity throught the *transavan-guardia fredda.*

In the course of the last hundred years the artist has moved justifiably slowly and, as a consequence, individually, with a sense of purpose that is not hedonistic and is, in fact, accompanied by a fair baggage of constructive ethics. This does not mean that an abstract notion of optimism concerning history needs to be embraced once again, regardless of a desire to retain the distinction between art and other forms of production. Productivity is art when it is able at the outset to define its own context, to declare its own internal logic.

The artists of the 1990s accept the value of a 'negative utopia' in a positive way, with forms able to depict the possibility of an 'ordered severity' within the meaningful grid of the work, but without the ulterior presumption of their being able to impose it on a disordered world. The end of the Russian Empire puts artistic production back into the centre of things, the only form able to represent the uprooting and disordered movement of ideas. As was the case with the Austrian Empire's demise, we have a vast and truly international panorama intervening in this historical situation. Within such a panorama artists produce meaningful systems, while affected by deconstruction, recycling, movement, contamination and eclecticism. The same dualities are implied in technology's use of visual effects: the video clip synthesizes meanings that have been purged of the utopian tensions given them by the avant-garde.

To repair the subject from behind the objectivity of the work does not signify that an erasure has been carried out. With regard to the last hundred years, if we have ever had the advantage of an acquired lucidity that enables us to look stoically at the future, and to look without yearning for an exalted past, it is now. The last decade of the twentieth century thus opens on a scenario that no longer oscillates between the dichotomies of art and life, capitalism and communism, creativity and ideology or nature and history. If anything, a new conflict looms – that of North and South, of riches and poverty. The old oppositions by now have been absorbed by the cultural anthropology of post-modern man. This term has also become one that is no longer set in opposition to the modern. If

anything, it outlines the position of a culture that, through computerized forms of memory, can range across a massively enlarged territory, one without spatial or temporal boundaries. Here, two- and three-dimensional images can be formed, bearing both the abstract and the figurative.

Obviously, the international generation of the 1990s will, by the year 2000, entrust to the neo-objectivity of art its intensely creative potential for uniting memory and meaningful style, experimentation and representation, ornamentation and communication, the collective poetry of art's history and the personal prose of the everyday material itself. Ironic neutrality seems to be contained within these already international artists, which are sure to be seen by society – not necessarily by the naked eye, but (preferably) by the photographic lens, obliging the works to pass through the caudal pitchfork of the metal detector, as if at an airport. Urban art tends to recognize as its own contextual space a sort of 'global state', which, as Ernst Jünger affirms, already exists for technology. Where a centre does not exist, there is a field that is continually under pressure at its margins. A 'constellational' world – according to Norbert Elias's definition – is well represented in art by the double polarity of the 'hot' and 'cold' *transavanguardia.* Creativity is now expressed without the hegemony of a powerful vocabulary or the prevalent influence of a single market. Geographically, art will tend to turn towards an ambiguous strategy of movement and confirmation, similar to the physical law of Continental drift, through which the distance between them is narrowed until catastrophe is broached by the collision of 'lands' still separated by 'waters': *art* versus the second millenium. This movement will probably lead towards the growth of a communal process of the visual reorganization of peoples who, though geographically separated, are brought more closely together by means of satellite communications. At the same time, this reorganization of images, in so far as it concerns art, will lead to a short-circuit between local and international 'codes'. This will in part be brought about by the prevalent form of art – one going against that of the second millenium, and spurred on by the speed of circulation of various visual codes between Europe, America, Africa, Asia and Oceania. A wide range of contextually present styles will function in a single context, a context in which artists will act and interact. In this situation, the old ideology of the Cold War (East and West) will no longer exist around the year 2000 and, instead, there will be the healthy conflict of Cold Peace (North and South): communication will become one of bearing value – that of art and of the means it has of showing itself.

Art, in the case of *transavanguardia fredda,* has now become a movement tied to the world of merchandise as a product of post-industrial society. It thus remains a protected presence, a fragment, of which – paradoxically – nothing is missing; it participates in the great puzzle that is the world. The epigraph could well be from Goethe: 'The difficult and the good are the material of art. To see the difficult treated easily gives us an idea of the impossible.'

Translated from the Italian by Vittoria Di Palma

Christoph Tannert

Reality in the Foreground

The process of German unification – as seen from the perspective of an Eastern art world go-between – begins in the middle of an every-day routine.

One morning (it must have been around the beginning of March 1990), I am standing in my local grocery store. The cashiers are thinking aloud about grandiose schemes, for example, whether or not the store should be turned into a private stock company, or if they should make taxpayers put up the bill instead of submitting to state-dictated rationalization plans. I ask for some bread rolls, the good old kind, five pfennigs apiece – but there aren't any more, not even 'under the counter'. Why? 'bako', they say – that's the former state-owned baking enterprise – 'bako's bit the dust!' That, for me, was the end of the GDR. These days, of course, I have a choice: I can buy sawdust rolls from West Germany, or I can buy none at all. Now I like to start my day by thinking about Cronenberg's horror movie *Shivers,* and that takes care of grocery-shopping stress.

And yet it takes the news of the termination of a line of aluminium cutlery that's been produced for the past thirty years to make one realize just how sweeping all the changes really are. Just think of what it stood for, that humble, easily bent, easily broken aluminium cutlery: it was proof of the limited autarchy of a social system, the symbol of that system's meagre application of resources that cost so much to buy; it attested to the constitutionally prescribed uniformity of cafeterias and school kitchens, cheap inns and vacation hotels; it stood for a culture of poverty that survived long after those first real years of need after the war, a culture as familiar to us all as the flimsy money in our pockets that was made from the same raw material.[1]

The author of this melancholy reminiscence is the young poet Durs Grünbein. I've spent many an evening at his place over the years. To save money we'd go over to

a soup kitchen called the *Löffelerbse* in the Berlin neighbourhood of Prenzlauer Berg. Many of our other artist friends were regulars there too. A sad farewell! I cry with them. No more table decorations with heroic slogans; and gone too are the Heroes of Labour from the adjacent tables, our Harvest Captains, our Honoured Railroaders of the People, all those Diligent Helpers from the Fighting Reserves of the Party, not to mention the 'pacemaker brigades' with their 'flaglets' along the parade routes. Where are they now, those culture functionaries, those Vigilant Watchers Over The Spiritual-Cultural Life Of The Working Class And The Allied Classes Of The Remaining Population? Whatever happened to the outstanding folk art collectives, their sponsorship brigades and the associated woodworking cooperatives and intarsia clubs? A band from Karl-Chemnitz-Stadt,[2] *The Violin Collective,* is one of the few institutions still bearing its socialist honorary title with pride; a well thought-out ideological conception and participation in many a workers' festival gave it the courage to forge musical-operative leadership in the field of German dance music. But who will follow them? Who knows the tribulations that exist in the post-socialist plane? Who will name names? (Questions by a groping, white-collar proletarian.)

Nothing is as it was, and yet everything is the same. The culture functionaries from the old days have jobs in the *Treuhandanstalt* (the company overseeing the privatization of GDR industry), or are now chief consultants in the Berlin Offices of outfits with names like 'Nuhan Koizai Shimbun Culture Inc.'. They are founding new art associations for the protection of a faded cultural heritage; they are even hawking GDR art at the Cologne Art Fair. How come? Because it is impossible to cut the umbilical cord between corporate headquarters, salon art, and the order-issuing classes of the cultural gerontocrats in the East. Why, I ask, are the media reporting, *ad nauseum,* all the same worn-out stuff about the official artists from the GDR? Because the corporate heads in East and West have a tender longing for the facile easel painting, for the pictorial epic as historical chronicle, for the perspectives of ardent national self-examination, for expressive gushes of lava and blood and mannerist time-tunnel excursions *à la* Tübke. Naturally, the old-new mercantilism is playing a role – not to mention the low risks for money-launderers, and the Hong Kong-style pragmatism – yes indeed, Berlin is turning into a real world capital: 'the Mongols are already striking their tents along the Müggelsee…'[3] Heiner Müller has seen the day. Gallerists with 'Eastern experience' (which makes it sound as if they are veterans of some campaign) have doubled their turnover in the past few months. The pictures they sell once decorated socialist initiation temples and also accompanied Schalck-Golodkowski – responsible for raising foreign currency for the GDR by illegal methods – on his trips. The hip professional (West) decorates his dentist's practice with works that were swept from walls by the people's anger in the East.

Standstill and Change

It would seem that all standards are 'in transit'. Actually, though, not much has changed in German heads. It was to be expected that the pious slogans of the Leipzig Autumn ultimately would not be enough to work off the huge amounts of fear and rage stored up in the course of forty years of East German life, and that the rest of the steam would be unloaded on the country's streets. Now those dammed-up feelings find their release in street fights or through attacks by car drivers on the rest of the population. The aggressive dullness that, in the East, frequently falls below general standards of good behaviour, has mixed with the euphoric yeah-saying of the yuppie generation in the West to touch off a booming cross-border trade in techniques for blocking independent thinking and genuine communication. Meanwhile, the political experimenters are fiddling around with their Jacob's ladders and selling 'freedom of choice' as respiratory equipment. But no one is humming along. (The corners of those mouths in East German faces were

never very mobile in those days.) But after all, who wouldn't go crazy with rage in a situation like this?

One year on from the opening of the Berlin Wall, all the conditions for the production of art in East Germany have been changed – but the art itself has hardly changed at all. This is not a bad sign, for it shows that art's own laws are not too sensitive to changes in politics. The cultural functionaries of the old GDR used to demand just that from their official art, a certain breathless quality that they called 'contemporary awareness': frescoes by Arno Mohr, Walter Womacka and Willi Neubert, or decorations on East Berlin's Palace of the Republic with paintings by Ronald Paris, Werner Tübke, Bernhard Heisig, Willi Sitte, Hans Vent, Wolfgang Mattheuer, Günther Brendel and others. And yet the artists of the internal emigration, and even their fearless young counterparts of the 1980s, consistently refused to be bought off, and largely rejected the corrupting offers. There was never any direct resistance among those artists who were members of the Artists' Union. Activists of the political opposition, however, stuck out their necks and made up for the moral courage lacking in the others. I never once met an artist-dissident of the type whose existence the Western media were always trying to conjure up. Those artists who turned their backs on the slogans of the day, following, instead, art's inner voice, have so far avoided adjusting to the new market pressure. If, though, there really are drastic rises in rents and other costs of living, as expected in 1991 – what then?

Watching the old art-school directors and their former followers in the Party whine self-righteously about their days in power is unbearable. It is macabre to watch former comrades beat their breasts in front of the TV cameras – and then continue to stay in office. By claiming that they at least painted 'critical' pictures (as Bernhard Heisig likes to say), they do their best to get on the side of the people with their hands clean. One is left wondering why the SED would have tried to build up the state with a bunch of so-called 'problem pictures'. Criticism was allowed so long as it was articulated from the 'standpoint of the working class', i.e., it was reserved for people who were members of the system. The idea that factional struggles within the Party (for this 'criticism' was never more than that) could ever possibly be equated with the situation of existential powerlessness from which non-conformists painted their pictures, amounts to a crippling of art and is a farce for every viewer. In the GDR, where art was constantly misused in order to provide a means for the indoctrination and education of the population (even when there was high-sounding talk of the 'dialogic picture'), theories and their creative manifestations took on a value they never had in the West. One had the impression that the custodians of Socialist Realism still believed in the propaganda of Catholic iconography and Protestant texts, as if they were still living in the seventeenth century. The censorship of art was considered crucial to the survival of the system.

Today, comparisons between East and West leave one with the impression that people in the non-capitalist countries still believe in the immediacy of artistic expression, while their counterparts in the West are coming to terms with the loss of utopia, in whatever forms this may have taken. And yet conservatism, state Catholicism, nationalism and resistance to new communicative systems also exist in Eastern Europe. At the same time there are plenty of glowing utopias – dreams of the manifestation of the real freedom of the recipient in and through art – to be found between Chicago and Cologne. My own assumptions are based on the permanent cross-fertilization of the systems, on the overlapping and reciprocal influences of the apparently separate consumer worlds and cultural industries, and to this extent they are also based on an interpenetration of attitudes towards the world and art. The notion that Eastern Europe was a hermetically sealed ghetto for artists is a fairy-tale that corresponds to the desire by old and new Stalinists to protect themselves from outside influence, but that scarcely existed in reality. There are drastic differences between the individual countries of Eastern Europe in respect of cultural exchange with Western Europe. Poland and Hungary proved much more flexible than the GDR – the reasons why are well-known. And yet, particularly in realms outside of state control, the dialogues that took place incrementally promoted a sort of spiritual 'networking' that, hitherto, has received scant attention. In view of this fact, it makes little sense to speak of a 'need for catching up' in aesthetic experience when we are debating about Eastern Europe. Arguments that ignore the coincidence of the non-coincident run the risk of further cementing a concept of art centred exclusively on Western Europe.

The West in the East – The East in the West

The advance of the Western European and American entertainment industries into Eastern Europe has had a profound influence on mass culture in the East for twenty-five years – an influence that has not left art unaffected. However, because of the scant attention given in either the East or West to the relationship between high culture and low culture, the linkage between Western and Eastern European art did not become apparent. And yet the eagerness of Eastern artists for dialogue has found little resonance in the West. Previously separate currency systems, and the lack of market structures in Eastern Europe were also a barrier. After the political changes brought about by *perestroika* in the USSR, the West expected an inrush of beneficial, exotic powers from the East. A 'crisis of meaning' in the West – the result of speechlessness and surplus – had nourished hopes for a mythographic renewal from the East. And yet this renewing force failed to materialize, at least not as some neatly labelled refill package. This may have had something to do with the fact that the Soviet art that became known in the West during this time (the various shades of *sotsart* of the 1970s and 1980s) follows very different structural patterns than, for example, the installations and conceptual work of such artists as Ilya Kabakov, Aleksandr Brodskiy, Illya Utkin, Andrej Filippov and Yelena Yelagina, or the sci-fi/dada experiments of the *Populyarnaya Mechanika* group; one might also think of avant-garde movements in the Baltic Republics... Incidentally, the exhibition possibilities for non-conformists have not seriously improved even under the Gorbachov thaw.

'The light is out and we're waiting for someone to come and fix it':[4] this is Ilya Kabakov's answer to the social crisis in the East and the general crisis of meaning, with all its dormant ideological and stylistic movements, in the West. A new spirituality is beginning to make itself felt throughout the world. Kabakov refuses to be a prophet, and yet his atmospheric spaces create physical experiences, his use of texts are spiritual stimuli that update the mythic component of human experience. This is why Kabakov (like the Soviet film-makers after Andrej Tarkovskiy, who were also belatedly discovered in the West), continues to fascinate Western Europeans and Americans anew from project to project. It is the result of our own ignorance when we fail to take notice of the work of those Eastern Europeans who never observed a division of art into 'East and West', and who also had no need for banal confrontations for the sake of self-determination. The cross-pollination of cultures is promoted not by making comparison between the art of different countries, but rather by the acknowledgment of each artist as an international figuration, as it were, engaged in an urgent search for a complex presence. Artists are tourists, and the circulation of their products in the market is a fact. At the same time, economic factors are by no means necessary constituents of their public presence. This is shown by the widespread existence of self-help projects by artists, unified by their rejection of ideologies and the power of money. Whether this can be seen as a more old-fashioned form of rejection, as opposed to a more contemporary rejection of the artist's rôle as outsider and the embrace of Post-Modern advertising strategies, may be decided by the results. Today, in a world where rich and poor are moving farther and farther apart, some artists are consciously siding with those whose funds are scant and influence on the economy non-existent. The slowdown of the world economy will also inevitably rein in the unbelievable over-evaluation of art as an investment factor, not to mention the exaggerated sense of self-worth of the art critics and their estimates of their own abilities to manipulate the 'value increases' of an artwork.

Most of the GDR artists are continuing to work in their old manner even under the new conditions – the traditionalists as well as those more concerned with expanding the horizons of style. And I estimate that this process will last at least a further ten years. A restless urge to express oneself, to be able to exhibit free from external interference and outside of the museums, has taken hold of the underground scene in the East. The feeling of finding oneself in a situation of upheaval, amid temporary chaos and legal vacua, still holds some traces of enthusiasm. Self-determination and independence

remain the driving forces of these micro-activites churning up the cultural soil. Theories of isolation, of survival through withdrawal, continue to reside, like some silent and defining memory, in the fiction of a humanistic culture bearing traces of an idiosyncratic Marxism. Because the official rejection of Marx and Engels in the former GDR has dragged down Adorno, Marcuse, Habermas, Brecht and Tucholsky along with the GDR itself, those who place their hopes in the idea of a 'Third Way' insist upon slowing down the whole affair of German-German absorption. While opposition of this sort was once forced to remain underground, today it has become public, with sympathizers in the parties of the leftist and 'alternative' spectrum. And yet their influence on social conditions is meagre. The cunning diversity of their strategies is quite effective, however, when it is a matter of guaranteeing the mobility of the cultural memory. To this extent it would be wrong to speak of these operations, which are, after all, helping to build up grassroot political sensibilities, as an act of mourning.

The democratization of East Germany has created cultural conditions that encourage counter-proposals for high and, especially, mass culture (even as they remain permanently infected by it) – proposals that take root in a multi-media linkage of artistic potential that has long been popular in the GDR. German unification has been followed by a rapid fusion of subcultures in East and West, developing, in the process, a functioning system that is at its most visible in Berlin. The results of police actions to clear squatter's buildings have meant that a project as quirky as the 'Bookstore for GDR Literature' (formerly Mainzer Strasse, East Berlin) continues to exist on the basis of distinct independence from local conditions despite many a police search. A restless existence, more in time than at some permanent location, has secured its survival. The vague conditions of ownership of many buildings in East Berlin have proved to be of help for vagabond culture. While the formerly state-supported art of the GDR now attempts to woo the banks, the unofficial scene is going on the offensive by bundling energies frayed between East and West. The newly founded Druckhaus Galrev ('a publishing house the other way around'),[5] whose members include Sasha Anderson, Bert Papenfuss, Stefan Döring, Rainer Schedlinski, Michael Thulin and other writers of an almost unknown, clandestine GDR literature, is setting out to claim its place in the poetry market.

As far as GDR culture is concerned, the aim should not be to preserve institutions, but, rather, to protect and stabilize moral attitudes. It is naturally worth noting that the non-conformists of yesterday have been rather ill-disposed of late. Which might be fine if we could only see them acting that way in groups, instead of as lonely individuals.

November 1990

Translated from the German by Christian Caryl

1 Durs Grünbein: 'Nach dem Fest', in *Abriss der Ariadnefabrik*, ed. Andreas Koziol and Rainer Schedlinski (Berlin, 1990), p. 309.
2 In 1990 the residents of Karl-Marx-Stadt voted in a referendum to change the name of their city back to Chemnitz – as it was known in the pre-Communist era.
3 Heiner Müller: 'Stalingrad interessiert mich mehr als Bonn', *Literatur Konkret* (Hamburg), 15 (1990/91), p. 69.
4 Ilya Kabakov in the *Boston Phoenix* (9 November 1990), § iii, p. 13.
5 'Galrev' is the inversion of the German word 'Verlag' (publishing house).

Boris Groys

Moscow Conceptualism,
or The Representation of the Sacred

The West's increased attention in recent years to art from Eastern Europe – and from Soviet Russia in particular – has led to intense discussion about the extent to which the art of those countries authenticates or expresses their national identities. That such a discussion should develop at precisely this time is puzzling, yet symptomatic. It is puzzling because of its inner contradiction to the currently dominant forms of discourse about art. Within the broadly Post-Modernist direction taken by contemporary art criticism, authenticity, identity, authorial intention, originality and other related concepts have been subjected to critical enquiry and deconstruction. The entire strategy of contemporary art theory aims at giving equal status to – even, perhaps, to the point of privileging – the copy, the simulacrum, the reproduction, *vis-à-vis* traditional notions of the authenticity of the original. This strategy is not focused on the individual and the original authorship of art, but rather on art's social and semiotic function within distinct cultural contexts, and the differences that arise as a result of the multiplicity of available readings. The consumption of art thus becomes more important than its production, for it is consumption that constantly changes the meanings and uses of artistic form. The traditional Modernist appeal to authenticity and identity is usually characterized within Post-Modern theory as yet another consumerist illusion.

All of these theoretical positions vanish more or less without trace, however, when the discussion turns to Russian art, from which critics automatically begin to demand originality and authenticity in the most traditional senses of these terms. This is probably an expression of the hidden conviction that the bias to the secondary – to reproduction – and to the means of mass information is found only in the West and, therefore, that the critique of the original and the authentic

is purely Western, and thus an original and authentic practice. On the other hand, however, this practice exists against the background of a distinct nostalgia for the original, a nostalgia freshly aroused each time contact is re-established with the art of those countries or regions considered to be non-Western. Russia, however, despite numerous attempts by many of its own writers and thinkers to prove the contrary, is not a country whose cultural origins are non-Western. All the elements of its artistic heritage – from the icons of Christianity and the historical or socially critical painting of the Enlightenment, through to Marxism and the avant-garde – are firmly within the European cultural tradition. It is true that in Russia all of these forms and styles were different in many ways from parallel developments in the West. One can, in fact, put it this way: if things Western were used in the West in a Western way, and if things Eastern were used in the East in an Eastern way, then Russia, because of its medial position between East and West, tended to use things Western in an Eastern way, and things Eastern in a Western way. And here Russia provides, perhaps, only the earliest example of a cultural phenomenon now being repeated in almost all non-Western countries.

At the same time, Soviet art becomes *art* – in the contemporary, Western, secularizing sense of the word – only once it crosses beyond the borders of the Soviet state: within the state, at least until recently, works of Soviet art were objects of a neo-sacred cult, elevated to a position similar to that held by art in earlier religions. But if the sacred forms of the past really were authentic, and, therefore, were able to preserve their originality even as they passed through later processes of secularization and aestheticization, the new Soviet cult used forms already secularized by Western culture. What took place was essentially a process of the secondary neo-sacralization of art: all Soviet culture serves as a gigantic monument to its own kind of ready-made aesthetic, within which objects and processes of contemporary culture – such as Marxism, scientific progress, or the conquest of space – are used in an Eastern way, that is to say, in a neo-sacred fashion.

This is the reason why in Russia, Post-Modern art and theory have enjoyed such success since the early 1970s. Attention to the consumption and use of art offered the Russian artist the possibility of articulating the specifics of his own cultural situation without him being pressurized by demands for authenticity or originality. Under Soviet control, Russia has generally been a country of consumption par excellence, although this fact is rarely acknowledged beyond its own borders. In our day the consumption of things is usually associated with their commercialization, but Bataille has already demonstrated that the contemporary annihilation of things by means of their commercialized consumption had its correspondence in earlier times, with their direct annihilation taking place within the framework of sacred actions, ritualized warfare, or aspirations toward prestige and glory. Precisely this type of sacralized and purely destructive consumption of things and people was characteristic of the Soviet Union after the creation within itself of a new sacred cult formed around the Western imports of Marxism and the ideology of industrialization.

Consumption and Cult

Today, there is a fair degree of understanding in the West about the development of that art best known as 'Moscow Conceptualism', which, at least from the early 1970s, began to concern itself with the recovery of this cult, even while anticipating, at that early stage, its eventual dissolution. The novelty of the Russian situation is shown by the traces of destructive consumption this cult has left behind in contemporary Western cultural artefacts. Here the 'Easternness' of Russia is used in an entirely Western way as an aesthetic value and potential good for export: new Russian art exports to the West the very same forms it took from the West in earlier times – but perverted and destroyed in the intervening

period by their use within Russia. At first, this reconstruction of the Soviet cult was mostly perceived – particularly within the country itself – as destructive irony. Today, as in the work of Ilya Kabakov, Vitali Komar and Alexander Melamid, Erik Bulatov or Dmitri Prigov, this art became virtually the only monument to those distant times. Such is the situation of any art of our age that is involved with analyses of the phenomena of mass culture. While this culture still reigns, such art is perceived as a critique of that culture, but once it has disappeared – and the forms of mass culture always disappear quickly – the art itself is revealed as its salvation, by fixing it in the space of historical memory.

The orientation of Moscow Conceptualism towards the consumer, the market, and export potential contradicts the intentions that have lain behind all Russian art of the past few decades. As far back as the early 1920s, the Russian avant-garde called for the artist, as the producer of art, to rule over the consumer – or, to put it another way, for a total artistic restructuring of the world. At the same time, however, the ultimate act of creation was understood to be an act of ultimate destruction. The symbol for this was Malevich's *Black Square* – a sign of pure nothingness. Socialist Realism spoke out against this 'nihilism' of the avant-garde with the demand 'to use, for socialist construction and for socialist education of the masses, all the best conceived of by mankind in the realm of art since the beginning of its history'. Here, culture is viewed *de facto* in purely consumerist and utilitarian terms: the other (that is, the consumer) has been vanquished by the avant-garde. The production of all art that has, in fact, lost its potential consumer is itself transformed into the consumption of everything historically created, into the pure manifestation of will to power.

The art market in the Soviet Union began to be liquidated around the middle of the 1930s: art ceased to be a commodity geared to consumer taste. All artistic activity was subordinated to one body – the Union of Soviet Artists. This Union controlled exhibitions and publishing, the system of art education, even the purchase of artworks with state funds. One can see how this led to the realization of an authentic artistic utopia: artists bought works from one another, criticized one another, displayed their own work, and so on – all in complete independence from the tastes or interests of the public. For a complete personal realization of this utopia, one simply developed one's career within the Artists' Union. At the same time, any artistic activity outside of the Artists' Union was forbidden: to be involved in any form of capitalist trading was not in keeping with the socialist economic system, nor with the corresponding extra-economic understanding of culture. One result of this entirely narcissistic culture was the inflated production of portraits of Lenin and other symbols of power, which, thanks to their overproduction, lost all value.

The unofficial art that arose at the end of the 1950s (after the death of Stalin) was not an integrated part of the system controlled by the Artists' Union. Viewed as an attempt to introduce Western market conditions into the Soviet ideological economy, it was persecuted accordingly. Today, a well-trained eye is needed when examining the works produced over recent decades by official and unofficial artists if one is to understand why their creators ended up in different camps. Marxism was formulated in the cultural context prevailing in the second half of the nineteenth century, and for this reason it is understandable why contemporaneous cultural forms were sacralized along with it: every development that took place after Marxism had become established was either Marxism, or it was reactionary decadence. And this is the source of the distinctive stylistic unity of Stalinist culture. But the detoxification that followed in the 1950s was itself succeeded by a phase of complicated strategic manœuvres – modified forms of Cézannism, Magic Realism, Symbolism, Expressionism, even Photorealism and a variant of Post-Modernism involving quotations from classicism, all of which appeared in the official camp; while abstract art, Minimalism, Conceptualism and Post-Conceptualism and radical forms of Surrealism became part of the unofficial camp. Throughout all this, the artists themselves were doubtless aware of the consequences of each choice. The choices they made, therefore, were never the result of 'internal necessity', as the Modernist myth would have it; rather, each was a strategy wholly determined by a political situation that had little in common with the original aims of, for example, Cézannism or Minimalism.

The Transformation of Art

As a result, all the basic codes of twentieth-century art in Soviet Russia underwent a profound transformation. Thus, for example, despite the fact that unofficial art maintained the kind of underground existence that even the most radical avant-garde artistic circle of the turn of the century might have envied, Soviet unofficial artists knew from the very outset in the 1950s that Modernism had already triumphed in the West, and therefore, that their own position was radically different from that of the avant-garde: Soviet unofficial artists did not talk about overthrowing established norms, but rather about restoring them in a country in which a path that was at once too original and too provincial had been followed; in other words, they talked about how to join up with the outside world's artistic traditions. Here it must be added that many of the artists of the unofficial culture, who were completely isolated, also grounded their art in various neo-sacral myths that more or less referred to orthodox religious tradition: within the atheist Soviet state, any reference to religious tradition was a sign of opposition – yet one more major difference from the situation of avant-garde art in the West. From its very beginning, therefore, Moscow Conceptualism was thoroughly imbued with the sacred – from sacralized official ideology to the private, unofficial sacralized artistic ideologies. As a result, it was only natural that Conceptualism in Russia – unlike in the West, where it responded at one time to the language of science and logic, and later to the problems of commercialization and the representation of the sexual – concentrated its attention on the codes of representation of the sacred in contemporary culture. In its own way, Moscow Conceptualism dealt with the neo-secularization of Soviet neo-sacredness.

Thus Komar & Melamid, working within *sotsart*, analysed the official Soviet myth; Erik Bulatov examined the ways this myth functioned in everyday life; and Ilya Kabakov dealt, above all, with the sacralization of the artistic gesture itself in official as well as in unofficial culture. To the same extent that official culture began to break down, Moscow Conceptualism increasingly moved on to analyse the neo-sacred itself, outside of its concretization within the framework of Soviet Marxism. Thus Dmitri Prigov, for example, creates texts and installations that involve certain ecstatic conditions summoned up by ideological-artistic intoxication; Andrey Monastyrski works with various forms of Zen Buddhist and Christian neo-sacredness, combining them with the symbolism of Eastern (Chinese and Korean) Marxism; the Medical Hermeneutics group works with the theory of Sublimation – according to which art is created from certain special, quasi-sacred psychic conditons related to shamanism – and analyses the codes within which these conditions are represented in art.

At the same time, work with the mechanisms of sacralization does not mean, for Moscow Conceptualism, either identification with these mechanisms or with their criticism in the spirit of 'demythologization'. The neo-sacred in any or all of its forms today comprises the secularized artefacts of mass culture and artistic tradition. In this respect, Western artists are essentially in the same position as their Soviet counterparts. Every artist today creates his own myth, his own code, his own closed system of objects and meanings – in essence, his own sacred space. But for this the artist first needs to shatter outside collective or individual myths in order to create his own from their fragments. Any contemporary art is thus simultaneously critical and mythographic; it resists totalitarianism even as it makes private use of the mechanisms of collective neo-sacredness. The tools used for the destruction and demythologization of the sacred are discovered to be those instruments necessary for a new sacralization. Complete secularization or commercialization, precisely like complete sacralization, is impossible: the aestheticizing consumption of art is never fully emancipated from its sacred utilization.

The Post-Modern ideology of infinite criticism, interpretation, deconstruction, desire, dialogue, textuality and so forth is itself not only subversive; in its appeal to the infinite it automatically gives birth to a new world of the sacred.

This ambiguity deeply embedded in today's artistic (and cultural) situation is not always recognized sufficiently clearly, however. As a result, it has led to the characteristic confrontation in contemporary art between the search for new sacredness to the exclusion of all criticism, and consistent criticism to the exclusion of all sacralization, a confrontation in which both sides display the same familiar *naïveté* regarding their unambiguous positions. Moscow Conceptualism aims at thematizing precisely this ambiguity. Its primary model here is, of course, the fate of official Soviet Marxism, which was transformed from a critique of ideology into a sacralized ideology just at the moment it formed the historical space of its own victory – the triumph of socialism in one country. But the same fate befalls any other critique that creates for itself its own space in the totality of its texts, artistic objects and so forth.

The criticism of myth is itself mythogenic. Desacralization itself has sacralizing power, for those who study the history of religions understand the phenomenon of transfer – how the sacred aura is passed to anyone nearing its source, regardless of whether the recipient's original quest was undertaken as a form of piety or with sacrilegious intentions. The logic of the sacred blurs many borders, among them the border dividing the authentic from the secondary. Moscow Conceptualism merely shows this blurring of borders in action when it transforms reflections of a specifically Soviet type of consumption of culture into a method of artistic production.

Translated from the Russian by Christian Caryl

Jeffrey Deitch

The Art Industry

How will art history remember the 1980s? Will it be for the straw paintings of Anselm Kiefer? The plate paintings of Julian Schnabel? The stainless-steel bunny of Jeff Koons? Or could it be that the past decade will be best remembered not for its art, but for its art market? It is quite possible that the image of a painting being auctioned off for $ 50,000,000 is having more impact on how art is perceived and understood today than the actual art the decade produced.

The last ten years have seen contemporary art pass from the margins of the mainstream economy into a thriving sector of the global consumer culture. Art has become media-ized and monetized; it has assumed the clear economic function that it had only to a minimal extent throughout the hundred-year history of the avant-garde. The art marketplace has developed from a kind of cottage industry into a complex communications system, with a much broader cultural and economic role than simply the buying and selling of objects. The infrastructure that has developed to present, transport, sell, interpret and preserve art has transformed the traditional art world into something that now can only be called the art industry.

This Warholization of art may endure as the most lasting artistic contribution of the 1980s, redefining the way art is understood both by its audience and by artists themselves. A new, broader view of art history is recognizing that such developments as the beginning of the trade in paintings as independent objects of art during the Renaissance, have an importance parallel to contemporaneous formal innovations, such as the invention of single-point perspective. The 1980s may turn out to be one of those periods in which the transformation of art's cultural and economic role has had a more lasting impact than the formal and conceptual innovations within art itself.

Successive generations of artists and critics have grappled with the question of the role of art in the age of mechanical reproduction. While several critical journals still seem to be devoted to pondering this issue, circumstances have moved far beyond the 1930s model. Now the issue is to understand the work of art in the age of art investment funds, art as corporate image enhancement, and art as the centrepiece of real estate development schemes. We are now in an environment where shares in works of art are syndicated to hundreds of small investors by Japanese brokerage firms, where one million people will buy tickets through Ticketron for a two-hour 'blockbuster' exhibition viewing-slot, and where one of the world's most prestigious modern art museums rents out its collection.

What is the 'art industry'? Certain elements of it, such as the international auction houses and the emergence as celebrities of even neophyte art dealers and collectors, have received so much coverage they hardly need to be further discussed. But the emergence of the art industry means much more than just an increasingly powerful art market and expanded media coverage. It is very enlightening, and also quite surprising, to try to outline its various aspects, before examining its scope, its structure and its growing influence. What follows is a description of seven new trends, all of which are part of the convergence of developments that have transformed the art world into the art industry.

Art as Investment

Certainly the most spectacular aspect of the 1980s art boom has been the art-as-investment phenomenon. It has, ironically, been responsible for perhaps the greatest expansion ever of the art audience. The art market was virtually annexed by the financial press, which made front-page news of a field formerly relegated to the back columns of the 'leisure section'. In a world where money is the measure of value, the enormous prices realized for works of art caused people to start to take notice. The message of such innovations as the Salomon Brothers index, which measured the performance of art against stocks, bonds, gold, and other financial assets, was that art was important and worth paying attention to. By the end of the 1980s, the type of cultured individual who ten years before would have been conversant with the latest movies but hardly aware of contemporary art, was likely not only to have heard of some of the leading younger artists, but actually to have bought some of their work.

From an art-critical point of view, what is especially interesting about the art-as-investment approach is the way the art market has functioned as a communications system to dramatically expand the public's consciousness of art. The marketplace has served as a much more efficient communications channel than the traditional channels of museum exhibitions and art publications. A further fascinating aspect of the phenomenon of art investment is how auction prices have come to be understood by the broader audience as a measure not only of monetary value, but of critical esteem. Since traditional measures of quality are so intangible and difficult to understand, the auction price hierarchy has come to be accepted, even by some insiders, as a critical hierarchy as well. Increasingly, auction results, as well as critical articles and museum exhibitions, are establishing the broad consensus of quality.

In addition to its effect on how art is understood, the art-as-investment enterprise has fueled the creation of a whole new infrastructure of journals, consultants, private curators, warehousing concerns and other specialists intent on servicing the new investment buyer. In cities such as New York or Paris, the art industry now provides jobs for hundreds of people, and in terms of its economic importance competes with fashion, advertising and other style-conscious industries.

Some observers feel that the current slowdown in the art market will dismantle the notion of art as an investment, bringing back a more 'pure' form of art appreciation. The excessive art market speculation of the late 1980s has now abated, but the same monetary hierachy that fueled artists' reputations is now operating in reverse. Certain artists whose auction prices fell dramatically during the past year have seen their critical reputations hammered by the media.

The naive perception that art prices would keep climbing forever will be replaced by a more sober, realistic attitude, but the altered consciousness of art caused by the promotion of art as an investment is likely to have a permanent effect. When the art market was at the margins of the economy, it was fairly isolated from the general economic cycles. Now the whole apparatus of the art market has grown so large and so interconnected with the rest of the economy that it will begin to experience the same boom and bust cycles that affect almost every other industry.

Art as the Impetus to Economic Development – Particularly Real Estate Development

Virtually every sophisticated city in the world now has its Soho-type district – a community that, like the original in New York, has developed around the few pioneering artists and galleries responsible for sparking the transformation of a decaying neighbourhood into a mecca for fashion and chic restaurants. This Soho-ization of former marginal urban areas is now so widespread, it is difficult to remember that this trend began little more than fifteen years ago. The original Soho-type developments evolved naturally and haphazardly before mainstream real estate developers really caught on to what was happening. Now Soho-ization is something that real estate interests and city planning authorities try to manufacture. Unlike the Marais in Paris, or downtown Santa Monica in California, where Soho-like districts have developed naturally as part of a reurbanization process, 'arts districts' in many communities, particularly in the USA, have a packaged, artificial quality.

Sometimes, art-as-economic-development projects are rather simple and small scale, for example the shopping mall in Santa Monica that reserved a retail space for its own Museum of Art. Other projects are extremely complex and ambitious, such as the Los Angeles mixed use development that has the Museum of Contemporary Art as its centrepiece. In Japan, several golf courses have clubhouses filled with expensive art, and major pieces of sculpture have been placed around the fairways in order to attract new members. The idea is that members will enjoy the benefits of the financial appreciation of their club's art in addition to enjoying its aesthetic qualities and aura of prestige. Who twenty years ago would have thought that the display of advanced art would help to rent office space, lure customers to clothing boutiques, and even assist the sale of golf-club memberships?

The typical Soho-ized district includes one or more airy New Age-style restaurants modelled on Soho's original, artist-operated 'Food', as well as a complement of boutiques which have somehow been grafted onto the experience of viewing contemporary art. The large white-painted, renovated loft space typical of Soho and Soho-type districts has also become part of the art experience, and at least two whole generations of artists have made their work with this kind of space in mind.

The ultimate extension of art as the centrepiece of economic development is the Mass Moca scheme for North Adams, an ailing community in western Massachusetts. The project calls for the creation of an advanced art super museum, with vast converted factory spaces housing large-scale works, surrounded by shops, restaurants and a hotel. The object is not only to create a major centre for art, but also to generate a major economic turnaround for North Adams. The concept is that the art will draw enough people to fill the restaurants and the hotel, providing jobs and contributing to a general economic revival of the community.

Art as Corporate Image Enhancement

The art of using art to enhance a corporation's image has by now become almost a science. Several powerful firms and numerous individual consultants have made a business of counselling corporations on how to use art to perform a host of public-, employee- and investor-relations functions. Several major multinational corporations, such as Philip Morris with its memorable slogan – 'it takes art to make a company great', have made art central to their public profile. Corporate arts policies range from the idealistic modernist art-in-the-workplace model to sophisticated strategies for manipulating public opinion through art sponsorship.

Hans Haacke's influential works exploring the fuller implications of the art patronage of Mobil, Philip Morris, and other multinationals have made art's audience more aware of how corporate support is motivated by something far more complex than simply good corporate citizenship and disinterested giving. Corporate arts patronage is no longer a kind of personal hobby of the chairman. Companies use sophisticated market research and hire professional arts policy managers to shape results-orientated arts support programmes. The government affairs officers of numerous corporations have become skilled at the use of arts patronage as a means to set up opportunities for their top executives to socialize with government officials. The late Armand Hammer was a master of this kind of art politics power brokerage.

Another kind of corporate arts patronage involves the use of a collection to enhance a company's image for creativity and innovation. Perhaps the most brilliant example of this strategy has been the Saatchi Collection in London which, in addition to its enormous influence on the art world of the 1980s, played an important role in building Saatchi and Saatchi's creative reputation. The recent dispersal of large sections of the collection and the concurrent decline of the agency's fortunes have changed the way the whole enterprise was originally understood, but it remains an extraordinary model of how to link advanced art with a perception of business creativity.

Some critics had expected the aura of the art work to disappear in the age of mechanical reproduction, but the ironic result is that the media age has made the aura of the work of art more powerful than ever. A substantial part of the art industry is, in fact, built around the merchandising of this aura.

Art as Consumer Marketing

One of the marketing trends of the 1980s was the packaging of this artistic aura by practitioners of upscale consumer marketing. The success of the Absolut Vodka advertising campaign, and the use of artists such as Francesco Clemente as models for fashion houses, has shown the allure of advanced art for the advanced consumer. As with other aspects of the art industry, the most innovative applications of art as consumer marketing have been developed in Japan. Japan did not have the same tradition of art for art's sake as the West, for the Japanese generally viewed art as something aligned to architecture, craft or decoration. It is, therefore, not surprising that Japan has been in the forefront of new hybrid approaches which merge art into the upscale consumer experience. The Seibu chain of department stores has been the most innovative in integrating art into their merchandising programme. Their Sezon Museum of Art serves as a focus for their advertising and promotion, bringing thousands of people into their store, in which an entire floor is devoted to a series of galleries and art-related boutiques.

Art is embraced by merchandisers as the next step beyond fashion, a kind of conceptual product that can be marketed like the campaigns of Calvin Klein, Ralph Lauren and Guess Jeans, in which an image rather than a material object is sold. The cutting edge of marketing is the attempt to sell not consumer goods, but a consumer experience. The merchandiser need not sell the art itself, only its aura.

We are entering an era in which the technology behind most consumer products has become so universal that the offerings of competing manufactures have become more or less equal. The most sophisticated corporations are learning that if potential buyers find competing models made by different manufacturers pretty much the same, they are likely to buy the product made by the company whose culture and personality are perceived to be the most interesting. The next stage of consumer marketing may be an effort by the best run companies to use art and culture to develop corporate personalities that will give consumers the kind of warm feelings that will induce them to buy their products.

Art as Political Marketing

Politicians in several countries have learned that the support of contemporary art and the use of art to spark tourism and economic development is very good politics. Jack Lang is, of course, the symbol of this new kind of advanced art politics. The French government has found that state support of the arts is now the fourth most popular issue with its electorate; more support of the arts means more votes.

The Spanish government has also made the support of contemporary art a major priority, and Spain's new profile as an art centre has served to symbolize the new dynamism and creativity of Spanish culture and industry. The government's support of the Arco art fair, as well as its support of numerous new museums and exhibitions, has helped to develop a new business sector and attract a more sophisticated kind of tourism.

The Soviet government has used contemporary art in a different way, pushing the promotion of its vanguard artists not only as a means to earn hard currency but, more importantly, as a symbol to show that the Soviet Union is open for business as well as open to free expression. Sotheby's Moscow auction of contemporary art held in the summer of 1988 was an extraordinary representation of the new Soviet attitude. It is particularly interesting to see how art that was intended to be radical and anti-establishment has been drawn into a marketing scheme to support the public image and economic development programme of the state. It is ironic that the American government has caved in to reactionary elements, and is now curbing its support of contemporary art and its commitment to free expression at the same time that the Soviet Union is using art as political capital.

Art as the Ultimate Consumer Goods

The art of recreational shopping has by now become one of our society's primary cultural activities, ranking with watching television and listening to pop music. One of the most fascinating things about observing the development of art collecting during the past decade was to see it become, for some of the newer buyers, the ultimate form of shopping. Art is perhaps the ideal post-industrial product. It is aesthetic and conceptual, not something that everyone requires in order to fill a material need. For the sophisticated consumer who already owns virtually everything he or she needs to be comfortable, and who already has been sated by fashion, objects of art are the ultimate consumer goods. Collecting, or shopping, for art has developed into the highest level of consumer experience, with the elegance of the galleries, the excitement of the auctions and the glamour of international travel to exhibitions delivering the ultimate in consumer gratification.

In contrast, serious art collecting remains the challenging and time-consuming pursuit it has always been, something restricted to the small number of people with the aptitude and willingness to learn. The novel phenomenon described here refers to the new, more superficial, involvement with art collecting that has characterized much of the growth of the 1980s art market. In addition to the small circle of traditional collectors, we now have a wide new audience of art consumers, a development with broad implications for the future of the art wold.

The Development of a New Form of Meta-Art Midway Between Art and Entertainment

Laurie Anderson, Talking Heads, Madonna and a surprising amount of what is on MTV, have fulfilled the dream of many 1970s performance artists of delivering advanced art, or at least a derivative of it, to a broad audience. Teenagers around the world are now absorbing through television the kind of material that previously one would have had to go to an avant-garde performance space to see. A number of the directors of MTV music videos are from the art world milieu, and on occasion they have produced material as challenging as the most sophisticated video art. An advanced sensibility that twenty years ago one couldn't have imagined going mainstream, is now a standard part of the average teenager's acculturation.

Madonna's career is a good example of how a kind of meta-art sensibility has begun to penetrate mainstream entertainment. Madonna first emerged in New York's East Village performance scene in the early 1980s and she has retained elements of the performance art approach. Her performing persona has some fascinating parallels to the work of a number of advanced artists.

This fusion between art and entertainment is probably only just beginning; it is likely to become one of the most interesting artistic arenas of the 1990s. The many new media delivery systems, such as cable and satellite

TV and cheap video rental shops, have circumvented the middlebrow fare of the established TV networks as well as opening up the possibility of the broad availability of advanced programming. This new meta-art will not only circumvent the traditional TV networks, but may circumvent the traditional art world as well. As things develop, and especially as new computer graphics and simulation techniques open up a whole new arena of meta-art, traditional measures of artistic quality will be severely challenged.

Art as a Profession

One of the most direct and tangible results of the transformation of the art world into the art industry has been the way the change in circumstances has forced artists into approaching art more and more as a profession. Becoming an artist is still not the same as becoming a doctor or a lawyer, but the demands of the market, the media and the museums have required that successful artists spend an inordinate amount of their time simply taking care of business. Many artists have found it necessary to reorganize their studios into businesslike premises, with book-keepers, receptionists and secretaries in addition to assistants to help fabricate the work. The artist whose work is in demand sometimes finds a large part of the day filled with meetings and telephone conversations regarding forthcoming exhibitions, commissions and media coverage.

The enormous growth of the commercial, curatorial and critical superstructure during the past decade has also created a new body of hundreds of non-artist art professionals, all demanding the artist's time. The enterprise of making it as an artist now encompasses hours spent trying to figure out who influences who in the art network, and hours spent cultivating these new art professionals – who all need something to sell, exhibit or write about. A whole new class of very professional, very hip, but somewhat uninspired artists has emerged. These people have studied the preferences and gauged the influence of the talked-about new critics, curators and gallery directors, and make a profession out of creating products for this new structure.

The 'artist as job' syndrome has had an especially strong effect on students and younger artists who sometimes spend as much effort trying to learn how the system works as they do making art. The supposed route to art-world success has become well-known and well-travelled: one of the right schools, a job as an assistant to a famous artist, cultivation of the critics and gallerists whom one meets while working for the famous artist… It was only a short time ago that aspiring artists rarely expected even to make a living from their art, let alone make it into a business.

It is debatable whether or not the new atmosphere of art as a profession has had any effect on creativity. Whether or not it has had any effect on artistic quality, it certainly has begun to change one's conception of what it means to be an artist. There are some observers who feel that the 1990s will be about art reverting back to being more about a state of mind than a profession. But with additional new galleries and museums opening every year, and an expansion of the art network to eastern Europe, south-east Asia, and other new territories, it is difficult to see how the professional demands on artists will lessen.

Advanced art, which only twenty years ago seemed completely alien and in complete opposition to the mainstream economy, ironically has become the basis for the perfect post-industrial industry. Art is perhaps the ideal product for a global consumer economy increasingly oriented toward commerce in images, symbols and information. It is not to be assumed, however, that art is going to lose its special qualities and be swallowed up by materialism as it becomes more integrated into the consumer economy. Paradoxically, post-industrial society may actually be becoming less, rather than more, materialistic. As the fulfilment of basic material needs and comforts is taken more and more for granted in the post-industrialized countries, the consumer is becoming increasingly interested in buying a product's aesthetic, symbolic or spiritual attributes, rather than in buying the material product itself.

Advertising now gives much less emphasis to such qualities as 'long lasting' or 'labour-saving', benefits eagerly sought after in the earlier, industrial age. Some of the most advanced advertising no longer even shows the manufactured product, displaying only its manufactured

aura. An ad for an English car might show only a romantic vision of the English countryside, while one for blue jeans might reveal only the face of a model with seductive eyes. In either case, it is no longer the physical product that is being sold. What the consumer is buying is its perceived symbolic qualities. We are seeing the devolopment of what could be called a post-materialistic society in which art may have a much more important role than it ever did.

The art industry is becoming one of the new industries built around global micromarkets. The age of mass manufacturing and even mass media is coming to a close and is being replaced by the manufacturing of smaller lots and the production of more focused programming, targeted toward specific market segments. The integration of computerized customer-preference information into the manufacturing process, and just-in-time inventory management are making mass-marketing obsolete. The new computerized manufacturing technology and the development of new, more focused, media delivery systems mean that specialized products can be sold globally to targeted specialized markets. A product no longer needs to be watered down to fit the preferences of the largest possible number of people in order to be sold worldwide. The marketing channels and media delivery systems already exist, so that even advanced art can be marketed globally without compromising its edge to the specialized audience that understands it. A product no longer needs to 'go mass' in order to reach a vast global market.

The issue of artists entering into an engagement with the consumer economy might at first seem like a betrayal of all that modernism stood for, a sell-out to the bourgeois values that the modern movement fought against. Rather than a betrayal of modernism, however, it is perhaps more like an exploitation of its victory. The burgeoning of youth culture, from Elvis Presley in the 1950s to the flower children in the 1960s, was the final push in the gradual process that saw modernism evolve into a kind of classless global consumer culture, overwhelming the old bourgeois establishment. The new global consumer culture of rock music, sexually liberated fashion, clean, functional design, and other derivatives of the modern spirit is, ironically, a large part of modernism's heritage. The consumer culture has by now absorbed the art world to such an extent that the artist no longer has much of a choice as to whether or not he or she enters and engages in it. He or she is already part of it.

Is this all a disaster for true art, or could it even be an unexpected fulfilment of the utopian Bauhaus dream? Could the engagement by contemporary artists with the communications and entertainment industries be today's equivalent to Kandinsky's ceramics, Rietveld's chairs, and Rodchenko's billboards? The Bauhaus, De Stijl, and Productionist movements promoted the integration of modern art and design into the mass manufacturing processes of the industrial age. Perhaps the continuation of that vision is to integrate today's art into advertising, entertainment, and consumer merchandis-ing – its economic equivalents in the post-industrial age. Today's widely accessible art and culture markets can be viewed as the realization of the egalitarian modernist ideal of bringing art to the people.

The central artistic dilemma of the next decade will probably not be abstraction versus figuration, or expressionism versus conceptualism. The dilemma will be the extent to which artists choose either to embrace or walk away from their new roles as prime actors in the global post-industrial economy. Will artists take advantage of their new position to reach a wider audience? Or will they try to isolate themselves from the pull of the consumer culture, and retreat into a kind of art sanctuary?

SOMETIMES SCIENCE ADVANCES FASTER THAN IT SHOULD

IF YOU'RE CONSIDERED USELESS NO ONE WILL FEED YOU ANYMORE

HANDS ON YOUR BREAST CAN KEEP YOUR HEART BEATING

THE MOST PROFOUND THINGS ARE INEXPRESSIBLE

SOMEDAYS YOU WAKE AND IMMEDIATELY START TO WORRY, NOTHING IN
PARTICULAR IS WRONG, IT'S JUST THE SUSPICION THAT FORCES ARE
ALIGNING QUICKLY AND THERE WILL BE TROUBLE.

THERE'S A FINE LINE BETWEEN INFORMATION AND PROPAGANDA

IF YOUR CLOTHES CATCH ON FIRE, DROP DOWN IMMEDIATELY, ROLL UP
IN A BLANKET, COAT OR RUG TO SMOTHER THE FLAMES, REMOVE ALL
SMOLDERING CLOTHING AND CALL A DOCTOR OR AMBULANCE.

LACK OF CHARISMA CAN BE FATAL

ROMANTIC LOVE WAS INVENTED TO MANIPULATE WOMEN

IF YOU ARE NOT POLITICAL YOUR PERSONAL LIFE SHOULD BE EXEMPLARY

GO WHERE PEOPLE SLEEP AND SEE IF THEY'RE SAFE

YOU SHOULD LIMIT THE NUMBER OF TIMES YOU ACT AGAINST YOUR
NATURE, LIKE SLEEPING WITH PEOPLE YOU HATE.
IT'S INTERESTING TO TEST YOUR CAPABILITIES FOR A WHILE BUT TOO MUCH
WILL CAUSE DAMAGE.

TORTURE IS BARBARIC

YOU ONLY CAN UNDERSTAND SOMEONE OF YOUR OWN SEX

IN A DREAM YOU SAW A WAY TO SURVIVE AND YOU WERE FULL OF JOY

THE FUTURE IS STUPID

DIE FAST AND QUIET WHEN THEY INTERROGATE YOU OR LIVE SO LONG THAT
THEY ARE ASHAMED TO HURT YOU ANYMORE

EATING TOO MUCH IS CRIMINAL

PROTECT ME FROM WHAT I WANT

SAVOUR KINDNESS BECAUSE CRUELTY IS ALWAYS POSSIBLE LATER

USE WHAT IS DOMINANT IN A CULTURE TO CHANGE IT QUICKLY

WHEN YOU'RE ON THE VERGE OF DETERMINING THAT YOU DON'T LIKE
SOMEONE IT'S AWFUL WHEN HE SMILES AND HIS TEETH LOOK ABSOLUTELY
EVEN AND FALSE.

THE IDEA OF TRANSCENDENCE IS USED TO OBSCURE OPPRESSION

WITH ALL THE HOLES IN YOU ALREADY, THERE'S NO REASON TO DEFINE THE
OUTSIDE ENVIRONMENT AS ALIEN

YOU ARE SO COMPLEX THAT YOU DON'T ALWAYS RESPOND TO DANGER

SEX DIFFERENCES ARE HERE TO STAY

THERE IS A PERIOD WHEN IT IS CLEAR THAT YOU HAVE GONE WRONG BUT
YOU CONTINUE. SOMETIMES THERE IS A LUXURIOUS AMOUNT OF TIME
BEFORE ANYTHING BAD HAPPENS.

WHAT A SHOCK WHEN THEY TELL YOU IT WON'T HURT AND YOU ALMOST
TURN INSIDE OUT WHEN THEY BEGIN.

MONEY CREATES TASTE

THE SMALLEST THING CAN MAKE SOMEBODY SEXUALLY UNAPPEALING.
A MISPLACED MOLE OR A PARTICULAR HAIR PATTERN CAN DO IT.
THERE'S NO REASON FOR THIS BUT IT'S JUST AS WELL.

STUPID PEOPLE SHOULDN'T BREED

SOMEONE WANTS TO CUT A HOLE IN YOU AND FUCK YOU THROUGH IT,
BUDDY.

THE WORLD OPERATES ACCORDING TO DISCOVERABLE LAWS

TRUE FREEDOM IS FRIGHTFUL

THE ONLY WAY TO BE PURE IS TO STAY BY YOURSELF

THE MOUTH IS INTERESTING BECAUSE IT'S ONE OF THOSE PLACES WHERE THE
DRY OUTSIDE MOVES TOWARD THE SLIPPERY INSIDE.

WAR IS A PURIFICATION RITE

THERE'S NO REASON TO SLEEP CURLED UP AND BENT.
IT'S NOT COMFORTABLE, IT'S NOT GOOD FOR YOU, AND IT DOESN'T
PROTECT YOU FROM DANGER. IF YOU'RE WORRIED ABOUT AN ATTACK
YOU SHOULD STAY AWAKE OR SLEEP LIGHTLY WITH LIMBS UNFURLED
FOR ACTION.

YOU HAVE TO HURT OTHERS TO BE EXTRAORDINARY.

Vilém Flusser

The Status of Images

Most of the pictures in this exhibition are paintings and photographs, that is to say, they are 'still' pictures. But the world of visual effects surrounding us today consists, to a large extent, of moving (animated and serial) and plangent images. So what status have these 'still' pictures within broader visual trends and the general pictorial cacophony? The most obvious answer is that they are islands of contemplation towards which we row against a raging current – in order on their calm shores to collect our thoughts. But this is an answer that deserves some critical attention; it should not be glibly accepted.

Let us imagine we are trying to explain in turn to a person from Magdalenian Lascaux and from Medician Florence that some of today's pictures actually *move*. This would lead to misunderstandings: the person from Lascaux would think such pictures must wander from cave to cave, while the person from Florence would claim that his pictures have been moving since the time artists began painting on canvas instead of on the walls of rooms. For this reason we would have to add that today's picture-frames have remained just as fixed as those of old, and that, in this literal sense of the word, their *status* has not changed considerably: they are still *stationary* objects. It is the spectacle visible *within* the frame that has started to move; such images are no longer frozen scenes but moving events. The person from Lascaux would conclude that the moving shadows in our pictures are similar to those cast by his camp-fire onto the walls of his cave. We would then have to explain that our shadows are coloured, and that they not only move along the surface of the 'wall', but also appear to emerge from within the rock and then return to it. The Florentine might venture the suggestion that such pictures are actually windows. To this we would have to reply that in such pictures not only does the depicted scene move, as in a window, but also that the observer's eye can approach or distance itself from the scene.

In order to make the confusion complete, we could add that these moving pictures can also be heard. Initially, both the person from Lascaux and the Florentine would understand this to mean the noise that is produced when transporting the pictures from cave to cave or from church to church. They would later infer that the moving shadows tell of the mystery of the realm of shadows. We, in turn, would have to explain that the moving figures in the picture talk, laugh and sing, that the thunder crashes and that raindrops splatter. Most importantly, and unexpectedly, we would have to explain that the entire pictorial sequence is immersed in others, one of which consists of musical tones. Having learned this, both would probably claim (the person from Lascaux confidently, the Florentine with hesitation) that such pictures must be alternative realities.

With this, of course, we could not agree. We would be compelled to point out that these kinds of pictures do indeed possess visual and aural qualities, but cannot be smelled or tasted. Most importantly, however, we would point out that we cannot actually bump into the pictured figures. This counter-argument would not be accepted by either of them. The person from Lascaux would claim that other realities exist parallel to that of our conscious experience – the world of dreams or the realm of the dead, for example – and he would ascribe our moving pictures to these other realities. In the meantime, the Florentine might say that our account has persuaded him: he has begun to believe in our picture technology, and is convinced that the future will bring the creation of pictures that can be smelled, tasted and even felt. We would have to agree with them both. And, to complicate matters, we would also have to tell them that we are now just beginning to hear and to see hitherto invisible and inaudible phenomena in our pictures – such as algorithms, objects curved into the fourth dimension, or vibrations beyond the normal power of our senses. Upon hearing this, both of them would probably declare that, if in our shoes, they would henceforth look only at such pictures, and disregard the comparatively dull, empirical world.

Here we would have to admit that this is already the case. People actually spend most of their time sitting in front of that relatively stationary picture-frame in order to stare at it. How, the two would then ask, are the pictures presented to the seated viewer? The answer would horrify them both. For we would have to explain that the things pictured are not actually in the same place where the people are sitting, but in a location inaccessible to them; and that the pictures are transmitted from that inaccessible place to those who want to see them. The horror of the two questioners would be twofold. First: when the moving pictures are transmitted from an inaccessible place into the relatively stationary frame, then they move as a whole – everything inside them moves as well. It is a double-movement in which the content of the picture moves differently from the picture as a whole. Second: during one of these transmissions, many seated people are staring through many picture-frames into the same picture at the same moment, and looking through that same picture at the same inaccessible place. And there, at that place, all the gazes meet, but without them meeting each other. How horrible it is that all of these people see the same thing, and yet remain blind to one other for precisely this reason. In view of the hellish twist bringing about such blindness, neither of our visitors from the past would probably want to stay with us much longer.

The Flood of Images

We would probably prefer to go with them to escape the blinding and deafening flood of images, and to enjoy the pictures of the early Renaissance, or of early cattle and horses. But such a trip could not be successful. For wherever we go, we are accompanied by a flood of blinding and deafening pictures streaming forth from the equipment we have dragged along. These devices that accompany us everywhere no longer have to dangle *in front* of our stomachs: we already have them *in* our stomachs, where they click, roll and wind. We are at the mercy of the plangent flood of images.

We cannot row against the pictorial current towards the good, old pictures. Instead, if we wish to avoid drowning, we must either try to row faster than the current or to head to one side or the other in the hope of finding a place to tie up. Since we can no longer manufacture the good, old pictures, we must either create moving and plangent images that are much newer than those that surround us, or else we must manufacture 'still'

pictures that stand apart from the flood. But such an assertion cannot simply be made; it must also be reinforced. First, we must provide plausible reasons for why there can be no going back to the good, old pictures. Then we must describe how the pictures that threaten to drown us can be overcome in technical, aesthetic and existential terms. And, finally, we must explain how (indeed, whether or not it is possible at all) to produce 'still' pictures that can save us from their moving and plangent counterparts.

The good, old pictures were created whenever someone stood back from an object in order to see it, and to make that which was seen accessible to others. This step back from the objective into the subjective, and the subsequent turn toward the inter-subjective is an extraordinarily complicated gesture, and the two historical examples already invoked can be used to illustrate it. The person at Lascaux saw his object – a horse, for example – from his subjective standpoint. This was a fleeting and private view, and it had to be recorded and published in order for others to participate in it. To do this, the person at Lascaux coded what he had seen into symbols, and then transferred these symbols to the wall of the cave by means of clay paint and a flat-bladed tool. Anyone who knew the code could approach the wall, decode the view and receive the message. The gesture of the Florentine differed from this in only one respect. The object to which the Florentine referred was not equally objective, for it was already impregnated with a prior subjectivity – a Biblical scene, for example. This meant that the code into which the Florentine translated his view consisted of a set of already existing symbols, to which he added some of his own. In other words, the picture in Lascaux is prehistoric, and can easily be deciphered by each viewer according to his own method; the Florentine's picture is historical, and one has to know the story in order to be able to decipher it.

Pictures can no longer be created in this way. Since Descartes, science has distanced itself from the objective and, following the invention of photography, science has created devices to record and codify that which is seen. If we describe the complicated gesture of image-making with the word 'imagination', then we must note that modern science and technology have attempted to perfect the imagination by putting it into machines. This means that no human being is capable of competing with the machines. In fact, the situation is even more complicated than this. Whenever we view an image in Lascaux or Florence, we assume the standpoint of our machines, because our entire world-view is shaped by them. For this reason we receive (i. e. we decode) the old pictures according to the modern world-view: by means of devices.

The Telematic Information Society

Because we are prevented either from escaping the flood of images or returning to the old pictures, we can only attempt to move forward to new images. There are three aspects that make the flood of images so horrible: they are manufactured at a site inaccessible to their recipients; they standardize the view of all recipients, making them blind to one other in the process; and they appear more real than all the another information we receive through other media (including our senses). The first observation indicates that we stand in front of the images without *responsibility*, i. e., we are incapable of any response. The second, that we are being robbed of the ability to speak – of our individuality, or of our capacity for human contact. And the third, that we owe most of our experiences, knowledge, judgements and decisions to images, and that we are thus existentially dependent on them. If we take a closer look at the situation, we will notice that none of these three horrifying qualities lie in the images themselves, but rather in the way they are structured in order to reach their recipients. The horror lies in the 'structure of communication', or – to put it more simply – in the material and/or immaterial cables. If we could switch the cables, the horror would be remedied. But the images would also be changed as a result.

The type of informational structure that dominates at present can be simply described in the following terms: the images are manufactured by a 'sender', and disseminated from there in bundles to 'recipients' along cables that transmit only in one direction – to the recipient. This means that the recipients are 'irresponsible' because the cables do not transmit their responses. It also means that all recipients receive the same message, and thus have the same views; that they do not see one another because the cables cannot be interconnected; and that the images are received as realities because the structure of the circuit rules out criticism of the

images. If one were to re-route the images into an interconnected system of reversible cables, the horror would be banished. Every recipient would be capable of response – and thus be 'responsible' – because he would be a sender at the same time, and thus an active participant in image production. The images would be sent into each node of the network, thus enabling each recipient to have a different view from any one of the other recipients linked to him. All participants would be constantly connected in a dialogue. And this dialogue would mean that the reality content of the images would be subject to constant criticism. Switching the bundled images into networks and making the cables reversible would lead to something called a 'telematic information society'.

Several observations must be added here. First of all, the horrifying method of switching outlined above can handle not only moving and plangent images, but also information coded in very different ways. What we have here called 'bundled switching' began with printing – notably that of newspapers and magazines – and is equally characteristic of the dissemination of 'still' photos and radio sounds. Secondly, the interconnection of reversible cables is not a utopia; such approaches have been used at least since the creation of postal systems, and have attained near perfection in telephone and telegraph networks. And yet the reversible interconnection of computer terminals and plotters had to happen before moving, plangent pictures could be added. At the same time, although the 'bundled switching' method is already centuries old, and although the creation of information networks has been going on for a long time, it is only now that the full impact of the idea has become apparent: namely, in the idea that moving and plangent images from cinema and television can be converted into interconnected, synthetic computer images.

To witness the immense transformation created by this change, we need only to look at young people today, as they sit in front of their terminals and look at the pictures they create there interactively. This new generation of image producers and image consumers, who appear on the threshold of the new century, is actually overcoming the horrible assault on responsibility, individuality and creativity by leaping forward out of the flood of images. This generation is creating a new social structure, and with it a new structure of reality. And the new, synthetic images that render abstract ideas visible and audible and which are created in the course of the new, creative dialogue, are not only aesthetically, but also ontologically and epistemologically, incapable of comparison either with the good, old pictures or the images currently bombarding us.

'Still' Pictures

But this leap forward out of the flood of images and into the next century is not the only option available to us, now that technology has cut off all avenues of retreat to the pictures of the past. There is yet another way out, namely the creation of 'still' pictures cunningly designed to outsmart the image-making devices. In order for us to understand this seemingly simple, but actually extremely complicated, way out of the visual cacophony into contemplative silence, we must first consider the meanings of the words 'device' and 'cunning'.

Devices are technological mechanisms, and technology is the application of scientific knowledge to phenomena. Scientific knowledge is knowledge that has been acquired at a distance from phenomena according to a certain methodology. 'Devices' can thus be defined as mechanisms that reverse this scientific distance from the phenomena by technical means. In other words, devices are mechanisms that turn the abstract into the concrete; mathematical equations are turned into pictures, for example, as in the case of cameras. Equations from optics, chemistry, mechanics and similar fields are made visible by means of cameras. Or, to put it another way, the phenomena from which the equations have been abstracted, appear in concrete form in photographs.

This overly abbreviated account demonstrates that all technical images produced by means of devices, such as photographs (and all those that follow), are the structural opposite of old pictures. Old pictures are subjective abstractions of phenomena, while technical images are the concrete expressions of objective abstractions. This reversal explains most of the misunderstandings that occur upon receipt of the technical images – above all, the misunderstanding that regards images produced by technical means as 'objective pictures of the environment'. Photographs, films, videos and virtually all technical images are produced by devices that codify objective knowledge according to a particular programme. Only someone who knows this code can actually decode such pictures. Because knowledge of the code presumes certain scientific knowledge, the 'normal' recipient is illiterate in respect to these pictures. The television viewer knows virtually nothing about the rules of electronics, optics and acoustics upon which the device is based, and for this reason he does not decode the pictures; instead, he simply assumes them to be objectively correct.

In spite of this general visual illiteracy (or precisely because of it), the technologically mediated view of things becomes authoritative. All of us see the world as if we were constantly looking at it through a camera. Although the objectivity of scientific knowledge as it is concretely expressed in devices may have come under question from various quarters, such questions do not always reach the recipient of images and sounds. For this reason, we can say that the horrors of the flood of images described here could be surmounted by anyone able to outsmart, by means of cunning, the devices creating the flood.

'Cunning' (Ger. *List*) is best defined by a detour through Latin and Greek. Latin has the word *ars*, which also means roughly 'agility, flexibility', as applied to a wrist, for example. Related to the noun *ars* is the verb 'to articulate' meaning 'to state something clearly', but also, in a figurative sense, 'to turn and twist one's hand'. *Ars* is most commonly translated as 'art', but one should not forget this associated meaning of agility. The Greek equivalent of *ars* is *techné*. And *techné* can be related to *mechané* in the sense of flexibility or nimbleness in manual work; hence also *mechané techné*. The origin of *mechané*, in turn, is the ancient root *magh*, which has left its imprint on German with the words *Macht* ('power') and *mögen* ('to be able'). The entire context becomes clear when Odysseus, the planner of the Trojan Horse, is described as *polyméchanos*, which designates him as an inventor and translates as the 'cunning one' or 'resourceful one'.

Devices are cunningly constructed mechanisms. They are machines; they function mechanically; they are machinations: they are in short, technical. Devices are artificial. And precisely because they are cunning, mechanical, technical – and hence artificial, they can be outsmarted by the cunning use of art, by 'artfulness'. Those involved today in the creation of 'still' pictures are being artful in just this way, although they might not always be conscious of it. Every 'still' picture created today, regardless of the method used and regardless of its ultimate intention, is an attempt to outfox the devices. Such a picture refuses to be disseminated in bundles, because it is structurally opposed to the device. The artful dodgers who create such images amid the flood of pictures, and who steadfastly manage to keep them out of the flood, deserve the name of 'artist' in its real sense, namely as 'cunning reversers and twisters' of the devices spewing out the horrible flood of images.

Strategies of Photography

The vast majority of photographs (and there are countless numbers of them) testifies to the aims implicit in the camera. Such pictures have been cunningly (that is, technologically) produced in order to create an appearance of objectivity in the recipient. Such photos could actually have been produced without the involvement of a photographer by means of a self-timer, for their actual producers are the technicians who have designed the cameras and the industry that has employed the technicians. This is especially obvious in the case of so-called amateur photos. The amateur photographer has done nothing that is different from the operation of the self-timer; he has simply followed the increasingly easy to understand user's instructions. But most of the so-called art photographs belong to this type of image as well. The art photographer is trying to get something from the camera that has never been obtained from it before – 'original' pictures. But, given enough time, the self-timer will do the same. The self-timer, moreover, can take photographs far more quickly than can art photographers.

And yet, there is a small number of photographs that express precisely the opposite aim. In this case an attempt is made, by outsmarting the cunning camera, to force the device to do something for which it was not designed. The intention of the people who take such photographs is to create pictures that run at right-angles to the flood of images, pictures that force the device to function contrary to the level of advance of its own technology. The exhibition and the viewing of such pictures create an island in the ocean of images, an island that is not only a refuge, but also a base for attempts to bring the devices back under control.

But here a new question arises: why should photographs, rather than other technical images such as videos or holograms, lend themselves to being outsmarted in this way? At first glance this would seem to be the wrong question, for is the world not filled with exhibitions of technical images that attempt to outsmart the devices in precisely this way? Closer examination, however, confirms the correctness of the question. All image-making devices other than the photo camera have yet to be fully evaluated; they still harbour some surprises for their users. The same is true of the movie camera: it is still possible to make experimental films. And all of the exhibitions mentioned above are devoted to such experiments with devices. But the photo camera has been exhausted, if not rendered obsolete, and many photographers now speak of the approaching end of the medium. If someone today takes 'experimental photographs', he does so precisely because he has not understood that the 'obsolete camera' no longer has anything to offer for purposes of experimentation. Instead, he should direct his efforts towards outsmarting a device that, because it is fully automated, continues to spew out more and more millions of pictures.

There is yet another explanation of why it is that photographs in particular are good for outsmarting technology. Photo cameras, like all their successors, are image-making devices, and photographs are images that can be duplicated and disseminated according to methods similar to those used for all other technical images. But photos are 'still', and cling to a surface, while all other technical images are either animated, or accompanied by sound; some even break into the third dimension and take on volume. For this reason, at first glance photographs resemble 'old' pictures, and in fact there are images from the era before devices (such as lithographs) that comprise a bridge between the 'old' pictures and photographs. By attempting to outsmart the photo camera, therefore, the camera is compelled, strangely enough, to operate contrary to its implicit programme and is forced to create something like an old picture. The people who produce such photographs are, therefore, attempting to force a device back to the level of Lascaux.

Pictures Transcending Devices

There is a great temptation to extend this view to those pictures that are presently being produced without the aid of devices, in ways that have remained little changed since the time of Lascaux. From the perspective taken here, which regards the present status of pictures primarily as a flood created by devices, such pictures look like escape attempts that seem to point in the same direction as the photographic works. One should, however, try to resist this interpretation – and not because of those official critics who deny that the history of pictures since Lascaux (or at least since the beginning of our civilization) has been brought to its logical conclusion by the invention of image-making devices. While they concede such devices may have influenced image-making, in essence these critics extend to the nineteenth and twentieth centuries a history of the fine arts designed for the seventeenth and the eighteenth centuries. Distinctions are made between tendencies and styles, and paintings of the present are judged according to similar aesthetic criteria as, say, paintings of the Baroque era. If this critical approach aspires to consistency, it must dispute the 'pictorial' status of technical images, or at least assert that they are not 'art'. It must then explain the fact that, since the invention of the devices, 'actual' pictures have been increasingly banished from everyday life; that they have become more and more elitist; and that it has become more and more difficult for society to decode them. Regardless of the official critique, though, we do not have to see non-technical images merely as an 'escape attempt' – as a move toward something 'reactionary'.

For it is clear that the non-technical pictures produced today are different from the old ones. Today's images are not the continuation of history. They have been produced in the awareness that technical images have assumed many of the tasks that once had to be performed by the old pictures. The producers of non-technical images are looking for gaps left open by the devices; they are trying to do what the devices are incapable of doing. For this reason, it is misleading (and, to image-makers, offensive) to consider these images as just another link in a chain of pictures that goes back for thousands of years. This chain was broken by the invention of the photo camera – even if not all the painters of the nineteenth and twentieth centuries have conceded this, and continued (and continue) to paint as if photography and film had never been invented. At present, however, the producers of non-technical images seem quite aware of the task that faces them.

The inventors of image-making devices intended to shift imagination from man to machines, and they did this for two reasons: first, to achieve a more effective imagination; and second, to lead man to a new and different power of perception. Both aims have not only been achieved, but exceeded. The imagination functioning in technical images is so powerful that we not only regard these images as reality, but also live within their functions. The new power of perception, namely the ability to use devices to turn even the most abstract concepts (such as algorithms) into pictures, is enabling us to experience knowledge as images, and thus to experience it aesthetically. And yet, not all human imaginative capacities can be replaced by devices. That which is irreplaceable can be shown by those images being created at present by non-technical means.

The burden placed upon such images is immense. It is not a matter of filling gaps and replacing the devices, but, on the contrary, a matter of revealing what it is that makes the human imagination unique – that which is irreplaceable and cannot be simulated. Only a few people are making serious attempts at present to show the limits of what the devices can produce, for in order to do this one must have first come to a full appreciation of the possibilities such devices have. (Most people blithely claim that their actions could not be performed as well by machines, even though it is often shown that exactly the opposite is true.) The few people who are prepared to fully exploit the capabilities of devices in order to surpass them are the non-technical image-makers. It is according to such criteria, and not to those of official art criticism, that such pictures should be judged if we want to do justice to them in the context of the flood of images: pictures that transcend the devices.

We can say that these images, like photographs, are produced in order to outsmart the devices. And yet these are distinct strategies, two opposing lines of cunning. Photographic works are created in order to compel devices to perform a task for which they are not programmed. Non-technical images are made to show the limits of the devices, and thus to transcend them. Both kinds of images are still, and this stillness is the quiet before, and after, the storm.

Translated from the German by Christian Caryl

Dietmar Kamper

The Four Boundaries of Seeing

Dedicated to the blind photographer Evgen Bavčar

At present, nothing seems more certain than the triumph of the eye over the human senses: the image machines are running at full speed; old and new visual media are relentlessly competing; more and more of the existing world is coming into view. The visual age has reached its culmination. But at the same time, however, certain doubts have arisen – the superfluity of visual information may well be leading to a reversal of its function. The horizon of experience is already literally clogged by images, with some commentators speaking of 'ocular tyranny', others of 'torture by images'.[1] Even as it reaches its zenith, the concept of the power of the eye over the world is turning out to have certain weaknesses. In this respect, one question might give us pause for thought: What have we done by creating images that go beyond all accustomed boundaries? A new and frightening invisibility is present precisely in the domain of the visible. Objects are displaying a conspicuous resistance to their retention in the hands of human beings. The world of phenomena, formerly a concern of unmediated certainty, has been deeply undermined. And the image itself has become subjected to a process of fragmentation whose effects were once ascribed only to reality. The time has come to take stock. What will it cost to privilege the eye to a point where its pre-eminence is undisputed? To extend the visual images until they fuse with the real and expand to infinitude – to a point where the space of the other will no longer remain in the reciprocal game between the self and other?

Whoever attempts to take stock will immediately find himself caught up in radical ambiguities. Such ambiguities cannot be avoided, even by the practiced critic of appearances. Speaking about images is only possible in dissent. Neither criticism nor affirmation of current processes comes closer to resolving the issue – but such a purpose may well be served by a mode of thought that does not shy away from performative self-contradiction. Elsewhere I have portrayed the current effort to be 'in the picture' as the only thoroughly human revolution of meaning and the senses, and in so doing have performed an ultimately unbearable affirmation *contre cœur*.[2] Here the argument shall once again be presented in the form of an exaggeration, but this time stressed in the negative, in order to take into account the 'hell of images' (Abel Gance), without forgetting that we can only hope to remedy the confusion inspired by strictly ambivalent facts if we are willing to embrace contradictory positions.

Let us start our stocktaking with Leonardo da Vinci and his praise of the eyes, his eulogy to the visual faculty that is man's only recompense for the misery of his existence:

The eye in which the beauty of the cosmos is reflected for the viewer is of such excellence, that whoever suffers the loss of the same shall be robbed of the notion of all those works of nature whose sight allows the soul to find contentment in the dungeon of the human body.... And he who loses his eyes, leaves his soul in a dark prison, where one must abandon every hope of once again seeing the sun, the light of the world....

Certainly there is no one who would not be more willing to lose his hearing or his sense of smell than to lose his eye: the loss of hearing means conceding the loss of all those sciences that are resolved in words, and only because of this would one prefer this loss to that of the beauty of the world that lies in the natural as well as accidental surfaces of the bodies reflected in the human eye.[3]

These sentences may be read as a prophetic statement that predetermines an entire age. As opposed to medieval hearing, which was oriented to the word (or more precisely the voice) of God, painting now came to be regarded as *the* science of the new age. Leonardo still thought in terms of a certain unity of perception, art and science, and hoped for reward through the beauty of the cosmos, an ordered apprehension of the universe. Essentially, painting outlined a process that would find its completion in the approaching conquest of space and the apparently unlimited expansion of the visual through new modes of observation: namely, the privileging of the eye as the guiding sense of orientation, a role that survives to this day. Today, however, as suggested above, this notion of the eye as guide suffers increasing setbacks. The methodical efforts to achieve a form of perception that would be protected against mistakes by a monitoring gaze have resulted in assurances that comprise, together and *en masse,* an arsenal of rigid abstractions. And yet these endless efforts proved unsuccessful. Few beautiful surfaces remain, and an enduring joy of vision has not come to pass. The eyes have remained so extraordinarily vulnerable to deception, that one must remember to balance the bright, well-lit side of the story with its dark, night side: on the one hand, the controlling power's victory by means of seeing and being seen, and on the other, a history of the eye's suffering, a steadfast passion that culminates with the highest point of ocular power. This can be illustrated through a consideration of the four boundaries of seeing.

These boundaries did not simply exist: they came into being as the result of history's most ambitious attempt to overcome borders with the eye. In this sense they represent boundaries in the extreme, which are probably insurmountable precisely because they originate in the desire to surmount. As far as we know, this is the first time that an enlightened mankind has found itself in such a position – liberated from religion's visual taboos to a greater extent than ever before, and alone with itself, and with the results of its efforts to create a world of its own through images. This not only inspired successes, but also illusions and delusions that quickly led to panic when attempts to illuminate them were subsequently made, thus blocking, whether in panicked flight forward or back, the path to a more sober approach. One must attempt to comprehend in stages. New areas of thought are opened up wherever old orders collapse, and time is gained amid the ruined bastions of traditional knowledge.

The First Boundary: The Crescendo of the Invisible

It is impossible to expand the circle of the visible without – at the same time – increasing that which is invisible. The more light, the more shadow. This effect runs counter to the intention of the European Enlightenment – a contradiction exemplified by the way that a gaze can be dazzled into blindness by excessive light.

The old realm of the invisible still exists today. In fact, far more of the invisible than the visible can still be seen. Behind those surfaces on which the gaze can rest lie entire worlds of space that cannot be seen. Vision cannot reach this realm of the invisible, although attempts to do so have been made time and again over the past five hundred years. Seeing remains superficial; it remains on the surface. The depth of the world is not for the eye. And when vision does penetrate, the surfaces merely increase, and with them the superficies and superficialities. The visual age has offered proof of this *ex negativo*. Its slogan, 'to make visible all that is invisible', is deceptive in a twofold sense. It did not move any closer to the old realms of the invisible; and, indeed, it produced new ones. Seeing has its own specific blindness: the more that is visible, the more there is that becomes invisible. This, of course, means growth. And the more precisely the traditional fronts become defined, the more powerless becomes the human eye against the new type of invisibility that has been created in the course of its enthronement: the abstract world of numbers and figures, of formulae and equations.

Entirely new ghosts and monsters were created on the margins of the visible, calculable world. These images were accompanied by anti-images whose full impact is yet to be seen. To this extent, Goya's *Capricho 43,* the famous etching of the sleeping author entitled *The Dream of Reason Produces Monsters,* should be taken literally (the title is not 'the *sleep* of reason'), these are not old ghosts returning, but new ones engendered by the dream of reason. According to mythology, monsters derive from the vengeance of the earth. Whoever mentally inspects the *oikos* (in the sense of ecology) will be overwhelmed by the catastrophic force of the side effects, and the belated consequences of the first Enlightenment. It is a force characterized by its invisibility. Why should we not, therefore, regard the current and coming catastrophes as monsters? That which cannot be integrated by human perception invariably takes on a ghostly quality. Here as well, a new sensibility has emerged. One need only compare the following passage from one of Kafka's final letters to Milena:

One can think about a distant person and one can grasp a close person, but all else is beyond human understanding. But writing letters means baring one's self to the ghosts, a moment for which they are greedily waiting. Written kisses do not reach their destination, but are drunk by ghosts along the way. It is this rich nourishment that enables them to multiply so unbelievably. Mankind senses this and fights against it; it was in order to neutralize this ghostliness among people as far as possible, and to achieve the natural transport and the peace of souls, that mankind invented the train, the car, the airplane; but nothing helps any more, these are obviously inventions created in falling, the opposing side is so much calmer and stronger, after the mail it invented the telegraph, the telephone, radio telegraphy. The ghosts will not starve, but we will be destroyed.[4]

The Second Boundary: The Standstill of Things

It is impossible to identify objects visually without bringing them to a standstill. The acquisition of the world in the searching grid of visual perception means mortification. Images are the corpses of things. The unrestricted realm of the imagination is the power of death. The only barrier that comes into question is the language that people can hear in common.

The eye, to the extent that it hears and harks back to the subject *qua* hunter, wants this standstill so that it can hit objects with greater accuracy. Power has always worked with techniques of immobilization and objectification. Ultimate perfection here would be the fully finished world in which nothing moves anymore, in which everything has been transformed either into ice or death – the earth as cemetery, or as the final depository after the last act of consumption. Things are implicitly in motion. They resist the pressure toward unequivocality. Whoever wishes to perceive them in their essence must let them go.

Their appearance and disappearance take place only out of the reach of the will to power. Beauty can only be understood as an ongoing state of fragility between chaos and order, one that occurs only on its own command. This is, and remains, an affront. The forces of immobilization try instead to fix objects in place, to prevent their disappearance or reappearance. Thus the fortunate accident of appearance is mistaken for the eternally valid abstraction. The logical consequence is the desire to cast away one's senses for ever. Hegel's dictum – that one can participate in modern life only with the loss of one's senses – clearly anticipates this state of affairs. Through the will to power the gaze is separated from the eye and placed in the mechanisms of image production, mechanisms that ultimately also do away with man, whether he be an engineer (inventor) or a hunter (observer). But once again, things will not turn out as planned. Whoever prefers pictures of bodies to bodies themselves will end up in the icy wastes of a senseless and asensual world. In the end, such a person drives out life together with death.

That images (instead of things) have once again begun to move is a twofold deception – both of the eyes and of the sense of community. Film and its technology cannot go beyond this fundamental construction. Images that move are proffered to the viewer under the pretence of the real, in the process isolating him from every other viewer. The salvation of the external world (as Kracauer, for example, hoped from the modern image machines) has not taken place. Instead, the development of the media has recently been showing more and more clearly its origins in spiritualism, the sought-for power over the world of the deceased, the summoning up of spirits by means of the media. The *sensus communis* is not a visual act but a linguistic passion, a way of listening to others in which the listener hears himself. But he who sees does not see himself, not even when a mirror is to hand. Seeing transfers the immobility of objects to the person who is doing the seeing. Today, seeing mortifies the viewer. Images, as the agents of a deathly power, create the place where seeing must be done. The cave of the movie theatre has, in the meantime, been reduced to the sarcophagal size of the computer work-station.

The Third Boundary: The Annihilation of Phenomena

It is, moreover, impossible to place an object under the monitoring gaze without ultimately annihilating it. What is described, on the one hand, as abstraction, as 'looking away from the given', means, on the other, the destruction of the common world. The eye is the most catastrophic of the senses. The gaze destroys phenomena.

The third boundary thus lies in the gaze of the 'evil eye'. There is no such thing as a good gaze, unless, perhaps, one counts that of the mother looking at her child. All other gazes install themselves in positions of control, and this even includes that loving gaze back at the wife who is lost to Hades. It was for this reason that Eurydice, the archetype of all phenomena, had to stay behind, for the second time as well. According to Jacques Lacan, this twice-lost lover is the most graphic example of the necessary 'missing the mark' of the other in the realm of the visual. The eye's desire is to control and to destroy, even that which it 'loves'. Whatever enters the field of view is lost, for the gaze itself (and not, simply, its incorrect use) is a weapon. One speaks here of the 'target', of the aim made accurate by concentration. This is the principle according to which the occupation of space by highly equipped systems functions down to the smallest detail. All past events are virtually already dead thanks to such an 'evil eye'. The smell of a corpse wafts from every image. The site of the visual is a zone of death. In a survey undertaken several years ago, a simple question was asked: Would you want to be present at the moment the world ends, if you were allowed to remain invulnerable while watching? Over ninety per cent of those asked said 'yes'. Virtually no one wanted to miss seeing the picture of the end. The questioners were shocked by the result, but made no attempt to understand it.

That images mortify the reality they depict was still heatedly discussed in the era in which photography was invented. The idea is virtually forgotten today amid the busy routine of image-making, and one could carry on regardless were there not so many weapons with eyes scrutinizing every square metre of the planet – all with the power to destroy, either intentionally or by accident. The virtual end of the phenomenal world has, however, an even more drastic impact in another respect. The expansion of the realm of the visual by means of technology has led to the assertion (which has, in the process, become almost unassailable) that there are actually no phenomena at all, and that none has ever existed. That a game of appearances and disappearances should be rhetorically neutralized amid a pictorial universe of ubiquitous sameness is, however, an irony of fate. The authenticity of the world – visible and common to all human beings – has indeed been lost for good, thanks to its overexposure. And seeing can no longer keep up either. As with all the other things that pressurize us today, this fate cannot be escaped.

The Fourth Boundary: The Fragmented Image

It is ultimately impossible to reproduce images to infinitude without destroying the yearning for a *single* image. The excessive outpouring of images invariably spoils the source of their fascination. The trauma of being in the world is thus stripped of its phantasmagorical protection. Perception in all its nakedness is once again confronted with the terror of reality.

To translate the experienced fragmentation of reality into the unity of the imaginary is (again, according to Jacques Lacan) to take the step from trauma to phantasma that occurs during the so-called 'mirror stage' as a provisional solution in the first year of extra-uterine life: The jubilatory reception of his mirror image by an entity that is still submerged in motor powerlessness... will henceforth represent in an exemplary situation the symbolic matrix in which the ego leaves behind its traces in an original form.... The total form of the body, by means of which the subject anticipates the maturation of its power in a kind of mirage, is given to it only as a shape, in an outside... For the *imagines*... the mirror image appears as the threshold of the visible world....[5]
The mirror stage is a drama whose inner tension extends from insufficiency to anticipation and devises the phantasms for the subject fixed on the loose delusion of spatial identification – phantasms which, starting from a fragmented form of the body, end in an image that we could describe in its entirety as 'orthopaedic', and in an armour that is taken up from a veracious identity whose rigid structures will determine the entire mental development of the subject.[6]

If the image (instead of the real body) is now reproduced and fragmented, the orthopaedic quality of the whole, and the compulsiveness of identity, come powerfully to light. The world is magical only to the extent that there is *one* image. If this image occurs in the plural, it is soon subjected to a process of banalization that is ultimately sustained by the empty spaces between the images. The unity of seer and face is the source of magic and, later, of the impregnability of dreaming people. There is an illumination from beyond that can be called maternal, because for every child the face of the mother was there first – in an otherwise merciless world. Anyone who is so securely 'in the picture' cannot be vanquished. But all division and doubling contribute to the erosion of desire. The image machines have set this process of demystification into relentless motion. What looks like endless expansion is merely the erasure of the trace of desire. For this reason, people will lose their desire to see, through the technical refinement of the gaze. The credibility of technical images is already virtually nil. They no longer refer to anything, and thus lose their place. The question – 'Where are the pictures – inside or outside?' – no longer finds a clear answer.

The abandonment of pictorial taboos forces us to participate, against our will, in the attempt to devalue the power of the visual images not through bans, but rather through exaggerated release, inward metastases. A new high point of involuntarily revealing expression is being reached, for example, by the new cyberspace technology, for which even the peep-show booth is not small enough. It would be hard to imagine anything more obscene than this 'imaging device', which functions like the visor of a motorcycle helmet. From without, however, it becomes understandable only as a reified act of blinding. How terrifying must modernity's *horror vacui* have become, for such remedies to so eagerly be seized upon! The fragmented image makes all mirrors blind, as, for example, Roland Barthes observed in his remarks on photography, made in response to the question of the maternal voice behind the mirror,[7] and which here leads to the assumption that there must be an inner connection between the adoration of the mother and the adoration of pictures, *punctum*.

At the other end of the list of worries stands the problem of the 'heavy users', those who already seem to themselves to be containers, even coffins of pictures. Just as there are sarcophagi, i.e., 'meat-eaters', now the time may have come for *iconophagi*. This possibility is also alluded to in, surprisingly, another small text by Leonardo da Vinci, who once again anticipates, although it is projected farther into the future, the fourfold impossibility of a definitive limit of seeing. It is a kind of riddle, probably read aloud by Leonardo himself five hundred years ago at the court of Milan. The answer (as in the earlier riddle of the Sphinx) was: 'man'. The riddle has an apocalyptic tone that should be heard in conjunction with Leonardo's praise of the eyes. Most surprising of all is his conclusion. It could apply to iconophagy:

We will see creatures on the earth that will constantly fight each other with great losses and often even deaths on both sides. They will know no limit in their evil. With their bare limbs they will chop down the trees in the gigantic forests of the world, and once they are sated they will, for the satisfaction of their lusts, spread death and suffering, hardship, fear and horror among all living beings.

In their extreme arrogance, however, they will want to go to heaven, but the weight of their limbs will hold them down. There will be nothing left on the earth, under the earth, or in the water that will not be persecuted, sought out, or destroyed by them, nor will there be anything that they will not drag from one country to another. Their body, however, will serve all living bodies that they have killed as grave and passageway.[8]

Translated from the German by Christian Caryl

1 Ulrich Sonnemann: *Tunnelstiche: Reden, Aufzeichnungen und Essays* (Frankfurt am Main, 1987). – Dietmar Kamper: *Hieroglyphen der Zeit: Texte vom Fremdwerden der Welt* (Munich, 1988).
2 Dietmar Kamper: 'Eine Menschheit, die im Bilde ist', *Wolkenkratzer Art Journal* (Frankfurt am Main), 4 (1989).
3 Leonardo da Vinci: *Philosophische Tagebücher* (Hamburg, 1958), p. 87.
4 Franz Kafka: *Briefe an Milena* (Frankfurt am Main, 1966), p. 199.
5 Jacques Lacan: *Schriften* (Olten, 1973), I, p. 64.
6 Ibid., p. 67.
7 Roland Barthes: *Die helle Kammer: Bemerkungen zur Philosophie* (Frankfurt am Main, 1985), p. 84 ff.
8 Leonardo da Vinci: *op. cit.*, p. 125.

Paul Virilio

Perspectives of Real Time

Supprimer l'éloignement tue.
René Char

In addition to atmospheric, hydrospheric and other well-known forms of pollution, there is an unnoticed kind of spatial pollution present, which I suggest we call Dromospheric – from *dromos:* speed. For contamination not only affects the elements and the flora and fauna of the natural world, it also affects the time-space of our planet. Since the geophysical milieu has been progressively reduced to nothing by the various available means of instantaneous communication and transportation, it has undergone an unsettling loss in its 'depth of field', which, in turn, has harmed man's relationship with his environment: the optic depth of landscape has rapidly diminished, with resulting confusion between the apparent horizon – on which each scene stands out – and the deep horizon of our collective unconscious. What is now becoming apparent is the last horizon of visibility, the trans-apparent horizon, a product of the optical amplification (generated by electro-optics and acoustics) of man's natural milieu.

There is, in fact, a hidden dimension to the communication revolution which affects duration, the lived time of our societies. And it is here, I think, that ecology discovers its own limits, its theoretical narrowness, since it denies itself access to systems of temporality associated with different eco-systems, particularly those which originate in the industrial and post-industrial technosphere. Science of the finite world and the human environment seems voluntarily to deprive itself of its relation to psychological time. Just as 'universal' science was denounced by Edmund Husserl,[1] ecology does not really examine the man-machine dialogue, the fine correlation between different orders of perception and the collective practices of communication and telecommunication. In short, ecology fails to register the impact of machine-time on the environment strongly enough, leaving this task to ergonomics and economics; indeed, to the merely 'political'.

Time and again, there has been this same disastrous failure to understand the relativist character of human activity in the context of industrial modernity. It is here that Dromology steps in. In effect, unless one envisages ecology as the public administration of the profits and losses of substances – the stocks making up the human milieu – this discipline can no longer develop independently of the temporal economy of 'interactive' activities and their rapid mutations. If, as Peguy insists, 'There is no history, only public duration', the speed and rhythm of the world should give rise not only to a 'true sociology' (as this poet has suggested) but, further, to an authentic 'public dromology'. Let us not forget that, in effect, the truth about phenomena is always limited by the suddenness of their appearance.

Let us now return to the probable reasons for 'public rhythm' having been overlooked. On our limited planet – which is becoming just that: one big earth – the absence of any collective resentment towards dromospheric pollution has resulted in the denial of the 'being of travel'. Despite various recent studies and debates concerning internment, and the carceral deprivations affecting this or that society denied its freedom of movement – for example, totalitarian or penal systems, blocades, states of siege – it seems we are still incapable of grasping seriously the question of trajectory, except in mechanical, ballistic or astronomical terms. Objectivity and subjectivity, certainly; but never *trajectivity*.

Despite the continued presence of a major anthropological question – that of nomadism and the 'sedentary' life – which emphasizes that the birth of the City is a major political formation in history – there is no understanding of the vectorial character of the transhumant species that we, in fact, are – or, indeed, its choreography. It seems there is no place between the objective and the subjective for the 'trajective' – the movement from here to there, from one place to the other – without which we will never attain a thorough understanding of the various ways of perceiving the worlds that have succeeded one another over the ages. They are systems of the visibility of appearances linked to the history of the techniques or modes of travel, of long distance communication, of the nature of the speed of transportation and transmission, bringing out a mutation in the 'depth of field'[2] and, therefore, in the optical range of the human environment. They are not simply evolutionary patterns of migration and settlement in different regions of the globe.

We are, therefore, faced today with the problem of the residual volume of the world's expanse, given the present overkill of our means of communication and telecommunication: on the one hand there is the extreme speed of electromagnetic waves, and on the other a limitation, a drastic reduction in the geophysical expanse of the 'big earth', brought about by subsonic, supersonic and, soon, hypersonic transport. As Zhao Fusan, a physicist, recently explained: 'contemporary travellers judge the world to be less and less exotic; they would be wrong, however, to believe that it has become uniform.' It is, indeed, the end of the 'external' world. The entire world has suddenly become *endotic,* and an end that implies the forgetting of spatial exteriority as well as temporal exteriority (now-future) in favour (and to the sole benefit) of the 'present' instant – that real instant of instantaneous telecommunication. How long will we have to wait for legally enforced speed limits? – which, of course, would have to be imposed not because of traffic accidents, but because of the risk of running out of time-space and the consequent threat of inertia (parking accidents, one might say).

'For what is a man profited, if he shall gain the whole world, and lose his own soul?' Let us not forget that to gain implies to arrive at, as much as it means to conquer or possess. For man to lose his own soul – *anima* – what is that but the very being of movement? Historically, we are confronted with some kind of split in the knowledge or experience of 'being in the world': on the one hand there is the nomad, the original for whom trajectory dominates (the movement of being), and on the other the sedentary, for whom subject and object take over, and the movement towards immovable possessions – the inertia that characterizes the sedentary and urban 'civi-lian', as against the nomad 'warrior'. This movement towards immovability, which today is growing as a result of the technologies of telecommunication and long-distance telepresence, will soon reach a state of absolute sedentariness, in which control of the environment in real time will win over the management of real territorial space.

This absolute and terminal sedentarization is the result of the dawn of the third and final horizon, indirect invisibility – the trans-apparent horizon, the product of telecommunications. A window now opens on the hitherto unimaginable possibility of a 'civilization of oblivion' coming about, a society of *live coverage* without future or past (because it is without expanse), without experience of the duration of space or time – a society intensely 'present', both here and there; in other words, a society that is telepresent world-wide. This also means the loss of the travel narrative, of course, and therefore of the possibility of any interpretation increased two-fold by a sudden loss of memory – or, rather, it means the paradoxical rise of an 'immediate memory', linked to the omnipotence of the image – *an image in real time,* which would no longer provide concrete (explicit) but, instead, discrete (implicit) information, floodlighting the reality of facts.

Thus, beyond the line of that apparent horizon – the first horizon of the world's landscape – the third, *squared-up,* horizon that is the screen scrambles the memory of the second horizon – that deep horizon of our memory of place and, thus, our orientation in and to the world. This results in a confusion of proximity and distance, of inside and outside, which gravely affects our sensibilities.

Lost Dimensions – The Halt of Time

If the topical City was formerly constituted around the gate and the port, the teletopical Meta-City now reconstitutes itself around the 'window' and the teleport – i.e., the screen and the timeslot. No more delay, *no more relief.* Volume is no longer the reality of things: it hides itself in the flatness of shapes. Already, 'life-size' is no longer the measure of the real; the real hides itself in the shrunken images on the screen. Like a person who apologizes for being fat, reality seems to be apologizing for having contours and relief.

If the interval becomes thin – 'infra-thin' – while abruptly becoming interfaced, then things – visible objects – become thin as well, and lose their weight and density.

According to the electromagnetic Law of Proximity, objects in the distance prevail over those that are near, and figures without bulk over those at hand. The leafy tree seen during a momentary pause is no longer the reference-tree of the vegetable kingdom: it marches through the static of stroboscopic perception.

'Those who believe I paint too fast only look too fast at me', wrote Van Gogh. Already, classical photography amounts to no more than freezing an image. With the decline in the volume and expanse of landscapes, reality is becoming sequential; cinematic procession has overtaken the stability and resistance of materials.

It has often been stated that vertigo is caused by the sight of vanishing vertical lines. Is then Italian Renaissance perspective of real space an early form of vertigo, issuing from the 'apparent' horizon? That is to say, a horizontal vertigo provoked by the freezing of time at the vanishing point? Giulio Carlo Argan, in his important text of 1947, wrote that 'The principle of intersection was therefore applied to time before it was to space – unless this new conception of space could quite simply be the result of the sudden stop in time?'[3]

Might not the famous perspectival relief of the Quattrocento be no more than vertigo provoked by the stop in time, in the (real) 'instant' of the vanishing point? Would not the inertia of this punctum at the vanishing point therefore be at the origin of this perspective of real space? (A perspective soon to be dismissed – 'Relief is the very soul of painting' wrote Leonardo da Vinci.) We recall the debate between Auguste Rodin and Paul Gsell about the truthfulness of the photographic shot: the sculptor declared, 'No, it is the artist who is true and photography that lies: because in reality time does not stand still.'[4]

The time with which we are dealing here is that of chronology – time that does not stop, that flows perpetually. And it is linear time to which we are accustomed. What was novel in the techniques of photosensitivity – then unnoticed by Rodin – was the introduction of a new

definition of photographic time – no longer the passage of time, but time exposing itself, or 'surfacing'. From that moment on, time as exhibition took precedence over the classical time of succession. The time of the sudden snapshot is, therefore, Timelight from the start. The exposure time of the photographic plate is nothing but the exposure of time itself, the space-time of photosensitive materials exposed to the light of speed – that is to say, to the frequency of the photon wave. Thus, what Rodin failed to notice is that only the surface of the shot stops the time of the representation of movement. With instant photograms – which laid the ground for the invention of the cinematographic sequence – time no longer stops. The strip, the recorded film-reel and, later, the video-casette in real time of permanent tele-surveillance all illustrate that unheard of innovation – a continuous light-time, in other words, the first major (scientific) discovery since the use of fire – that of an indirect light replacing the direct light of the sun or electricity, just as electricity had replaced daylight.

The Intense Present

Currently, the screen of television broadcasts *in real time* is no longer a *monochromatic* filter, which, as photographers know, only allows a single colour of the spectrum to penetrate, but a *monochronic* filter, which only gives us a glimpse of the present – the *intensive* present, a product of the speed limit of electromagnetic waves, which are no longer written in the chronological time of past/present/future, but in chronoscopic time – under-exposed/exposed/over-exposed. The perspective of real time in the trans-apparent horizon of video only exists, then, through the *inertia* of the present instant, where the perspective of real space of the 'apparent' horizon of the Quattrocento merely survived as a syncope, a stop-in-time, a vertigo at the heart of the body, about which Merleau-Ponty said: 'The body itself is in the world as the heart is in the organism: it continually keeps the visible spectacle alive, it animates it, nourishes it, and with it, makes up a system.'[5] 'Stop-in-time' in the intersection of vanishing lines in perspective geometry; stop-in-time in the snapshot; and then stop-in-time in the real instant via live television –

it certainly seems that the relief of the world (or, more exactly, its high-definition), is only the result of an imperfectible fixation of the present. A picnoleptic fixity, an infinitesimal absence of duration, without which the spectacle of the visible would simply not occur.

Just as the light from distant stars is refracted by an imposing mass, creating the illusion of 'gravitational optics', our perception of relief may be a kind of *fall-on-sight,* comparable to that of bodies in the Law of Universal Gravity. If such is the case, the perspective of real space in the Quattrocento would have been the first scientific intimation of it. In fact, from that time on optics becomes cinematic, and Galileo was later to prove this, against all opinion. With Renaissance perspectivists, we 'fell' into the volume of the visible spectacle in a gravific fashion. Quite literally, the world *opens up* in front of us... Later, much later, physiologists were to discover that the faster we move (in a car, for instance) the further ahead the eye focuses. Therefore, to the famous 'vertigo of vanishing lines' is added this projection of the focalization of the gaze. To illustrate this sudden amplification of vision that results from acceleration, there is the story of the parachutist who specializes in free-fall:

The fall-in-sight consists of evaluating visually, at any moment of the fall, your distance in relation to the ground. The evaluation of the height and the choice of the exact moment where you have to trigger the parachute results from a *dynamic visual impression.* When you fly at 1800 feet, you don't have the same visual impression at all as when you cover the same distance in a vertical fall at high speed. When you are at 6000 feet, you don't see the ground getting closer. On the other hand, when you're up to about 2400–1800 feet, you begin to see it 'coming'. The feeling quickly becomes terrifying, since the ground rushes towards you. The apparent diameter of the objects increases faster and faster and you suddenly have the sensation of seeing them not just getting closer, but suddenly opening up, *as if the ground were splitting.*[6]

This testimony is invaluable, because it illustrates in a truly gravific fashion the vertigo of perspective, its apparent weight. With this fall-in-sight, perspective geometry appears as that which it has never ceased to be: an acceleration of perception, where the very speed of

the free-fall reveals the fractal character of vision, resulting from the ocular adaptation or adjustment made at high speed. In this experience, from a certain distance and at a certain time, the ground does not get closer, it *opens up,* it splits – suddenly shifting from a 'full dimension' without vanishing lines to a 'fractionary' dimension with a window onto the visible spectacle.

Even if it appears humanly impossible to take this fall-in-sight to its conclusion, it is obvious, nevertheless, that vision there is strictly bound by gravity. The *accelerated* perspective is not so much that of the real space – whether vertical or horizontal – of Italian geometrists; it is, above all, that of the real time of falling bodies. The horizon of visibility of the 'fall-er' before his final impact depends first and foremost on the rapidity of his ocular adaptation, focus and imperceptible interruption of time, which depends on the very mass of his body. The being of the trajectory defines the perception of the subject through the mass of the object. The falling body suddenly becomes the body of the fall.

The Cinematic Optics

If isolation distorts perspective, here the isolation is that of the instant of any acceleration in the earth's gravity – 'perspective is not so much that of space but that of the time remaining, this falling time that depends closely on gravity. All geometric dimensions abruptly intermesh: first, the earth seems to Come Close, and then it seems to Open Up. The surface comes first, and then the vanishing lines of volume, before crashing on the point of impact; as for the line, it is *man,* the being of trajectory in a fall made free of all resistance.[7] (A dangerous exercise this, testing the dynamic visual impression – i.e., cinematic optics.)

Today, strangely enough, a growing number of adepts share this attraction to the void and its extreme sensations – rubber-band jumpers, cloud-surfers, base-jumpers, and so forth – as if the accelerated perspective was already prevalent over the more passive one of the perspectivists: suicidal experimentation with the inertia of a body carried by its mass, without help from anything but the air to lean on, in the relative wind of a dizzying displacement which has no goal other than to experiment with the weight of its own body.

On earth, the speed of liberation is seven miles per second. Below this, all speeds are conditioned by earthly attraction (gravity), including that of our vision of things. Centrifugal and centripetal force on the one hand; resistance to progression on the other. Any movement of physical displacement, whether horizontal or vertical, thus depends upon the force of gravity on the surface of the globe.

How can we not but try to evaluate the interaction between this gravity and our perception of the world's landscape? If, according to the Law of Universal Gravity, light is deflected by its proximity to a large mass, would not this very attraction (whose speed, let us recall, is equal to that of electromagnetic waves) influence appearances of the world, this visible spectacle of which Merleau-Ponty has spoken?

How are we to imagine, in effect, such an atmospheric spatial perspective, after losing the references 'high' and 'low'? – the same, this time, as the gap between 'near' and 'far' – without the resistance to forward motion. Astronauts have already experienced this disorder of the senses and the disorientation caused by real weightlessness; today, to recognize the state of things is to try and reinterpret the geometrical perspective of the Italian Renaissance. If, at the vanishing point, the visible spectacle opens up from the Quattrocento onwards, it is due to the force of terrestrial attraction, and not solely to the effects of convergence – the squinting metrics of tangible appearances of which the Italian artists were so fond. The organization of the new, apparent, horizon already depends upon time – upon that stop-in-time at the vanishing point – magisterially analysed by Argan. The present reorganization of appearances, and the emergence of the last, trans-apparent, horizon of visibility, constituted by the transparency of appearances transmitted instantaneously over long distance, can only be accomplished by surpassing the constraints of gravitational force. Contrary to the perspective of real geometrical space, the perspective of real time is no longer controlled by terrestrial weight; the trans-apparent horizon of the screen of 'live TV' escapes gravity by taking stock of the speed of light itself. If, like the images transmitted live, the screen possesses optic and geometrical properties that liken it to a window or the frame of a painting, then the constitution of

its videoscopic information depends, above all, on an unlimited acceleration of the force of gravity at 187,500 km per second.

The 'stop-in-time' in the vanishing-point of the Quattrocento gives way to a seamless video-frame (note the quest for a high-definition image); the only STOP, being a picnoleptic absence of the present instant, a stop which is also imperceptible to the TV viewer, who is spared the hallucination of an endless sequence. You have to live with it, commented Einstein – 'there is no fixed point in space', only an inertia of the real instant shaping the living present. A psychological duration, without which no perception of the world, nor any terrestrial landscape, would exist.

Expansion and Contraction

But let us return, in the guise of a conclusion, to the origin of the latest form of pollution, Dromospheric pollution. If the hegemonic influence of technical culture spreads and imposes itself absolutely upon on our planet, and brings with it an apparent territorial expansion, there is yet a hidden side to this development. Indeed, as the playwright Samuel Beckett remarked, 'Art tends not towards expansion but contraction.'

The very development of vehicles and different vectors of progression brings with it an imperceptible telluric contraction of the world and our immediate environment. The imperceptible 'stop-in-time' at the vanishing point of perspective is thus supplanted by a stop-in-the-world – in other words, an imperceptible retention of its extension and regional diversity. If the vertigo of real space was caused by the sight (the fall-in-sight) of the vanishing lines – a perspective accelerated by the anticipation of a fall into the void, for today's ultrafast 'voyeur-voyager', especially the TV viewer, the vertigo of real time is occasioned by inertia, an on-the-spot contraction of the spectator-passenger's body. The speed of the new electro-optic and acoustic milieu becomes the last void (the void of the quick) – a void that no longer depends upon intervals between places and things, and therefore the very extension of the world, but upon the interface of an instantaneous transmission of distant images, a geographical and geometrical holding pattern in which all volume and relief disappears.

It is the crisis, or more exactly, the accident of optical density, of the visual spectacle and landscape. As Théodore Monod wrote, 'There is nothing as overwhelming as seeing in advance, from the place one leaves, the place where one will reach that same evening or the following day.'

Loss of sight, or rather 'loss of earth' is a new kind of fall which is also a form of distance-pollution, in this 'art of voyage' practised by the nomads: a particular form of vertigo caused by the depth of field within the spectacle of the world's apparent horizon. Just like the contemporary metropolis dweller, this on-the-spot contraction has by now not only reached the zone of displacement and productive activity, as it once did the urban *bourgeoisie;* it reaches first and foremost the able body, over-equipped with interactive protheses – a body whose model has become the invalid, who is equipped to control his environment without moving.

Dromospheric pollution is, therefore, the form of pollution that attacks the alertness of the subject and the mobility of the object by atrophying travel to the point of rendering it useless. This major handicap results at once in the loss of a locomotive body by the TV viewer or passenger, and in a loss of that firm ground – the adventurous terrain of how it is to exist as a being in the world.

Translated from the French by Chris Kraus and Yvonne Shafir

1 Edmund Husserl, *La Terre ne se meut pas* (Paris, 1969).
2 Paul Virilio, *Lost Dimensions* (New York, 1991).
3 Gr. C. Argan and R. Wittkower, *Perspective et histoire au Quattrocento* (1990).
4 *L'Art* – Auguste Rodin's dialogues with P. Gsell (Paris, 1911).
5 Maurice Merleau-Ponty, *Phenomenologie de la perception* (Paris, 1945).
6 *L'Attrait du vide* (Paris, 1967).
7 Parachutists specializing in the free-fall often carry a small bag of talc or fireworks, in order to show this line of fall to spectators on the ground just before opening their parachutes.

THE ARTISTS IN THE EXHIBITION

JOHN M ARMLEDER   JON KESSLER
RICHARD ARTSCHWAGER   IMI KNOEBEL
MIROSŁAW BAŁKA   JEFF KOONS
FRIDA BARANEK   JANNIS KOUNELLIS
GEORG BASELITZ   ATTILA KOVÁCS
ROSS BLECKNER   GUILLERMO KUITCA
JONATHAN BOROFSKY   GEORGE LAPPAS
JEAN-MARC BUSTAMANTE   OTIS LAUBERT
JAMES LEE BYARS   GERHARD MERZ
PEDRO CABRITA REIS   OLAF METZEL
UMBERTO CAVENAGO   YASUMASA MORIMURA
CLEGG & GUTTMANN   REINHARD MUCHA
RENÉ DANIËLS   JUAN MUÑOZ
IAN DAVENPORT   BRUCE NAUMAN
JIŘI GEORG DOKOUPIL   CADY NOLAND
MARIA EICHHORN   MARCEL ODENBACH
JAN FABRE   ALBERT OEHLEN
SERGIO FERMARIELLO   PHILIPPE PERRIN
IAN HAMILTON FINLAY   DMITRI PRIGOV
PETER FISCHLI   DAVID WEISS   RICHARD PRINCE
GÜNTHER FÖRG   GERHARD RICHTER
KATHARINA FRITSCH   THOMAS RUFF
GILBERT & GEORGE   EDWARD RUSCHA
ROBERT GOBER   JULIÃO SARMENTO
ULRICH GÖRLICH   JULIAN SCHNABEL
RAINER GÖRSS   CINDY SHERMAN
FEDERICO GUZMÁN   MIKE AND DOUG STARN
PETER HALLEY   HAIM STEINBACH
FRITZ HEISTERKAMP   ROSEMARIE TROCKEL
GEORG HEROLD   BILL VIOLA
GARY HILL   JEFF WALL
JENNY HOLZER   FRANZ WEST
CRISTINA IGLESIAS   RACHEL WHITEREAD
MASSIMO KAUFMANN   BILL WOODROW
MIKE KELLEY   CHRISTOPHER WOOL
KAZUO KENMOCHI   VADIM ZAKHAROV

Captions in italics
refer to works not included
in the exhibition.

Untitled (FS 246), 1990, 270 x 200 x 110 cm

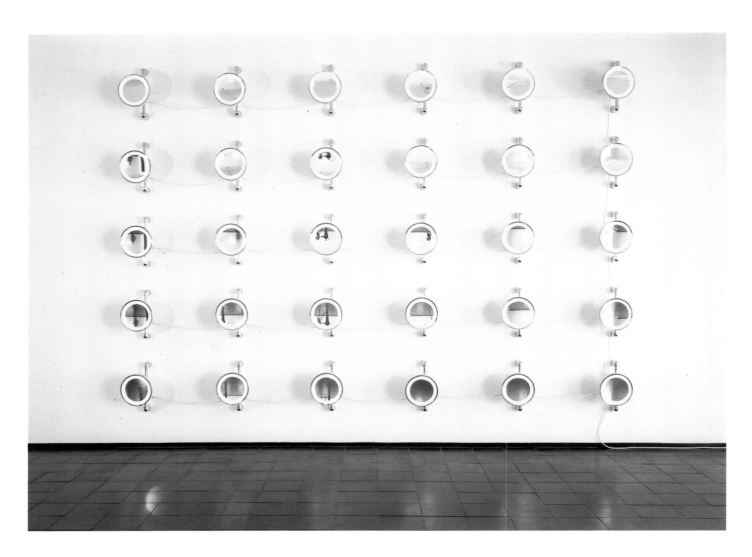

Untitled (FS 241), 1990, variable dimensions

Untitled (FS 196), 1988, acrylic on canvas, four metal stools, 91,5 x 244,5 x 59,5 cm

High Backed Chair, 1988, 164 x 78 x 104 cm

Door, 1990, 245x171x51 cm

Double Sitting, 1988, 192,5 x 173 cm

The Shadow, 1988, 179,5 x 153 cm

Oasis, 1989, c. 300 x 400 cm

Five Part Installation, 1990, variable dimensions

Untitled, 1990, iron wire, flexibles, plates, 300x300x300 cm

Bolo, 1990, iron wire, white marble, 100 x 440 x 480 cm

'45', 1989, 20 parts, 200 x 162 cm each, installation: Kunsthaus Zürich

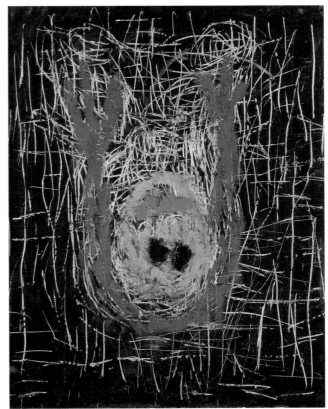

'45', 4. IX. 89 – 12. IX. 89

'45', 2. VI. 89

'45', 9. IX. 89

'45', 20. VII. 89 – 7. VIII. 89

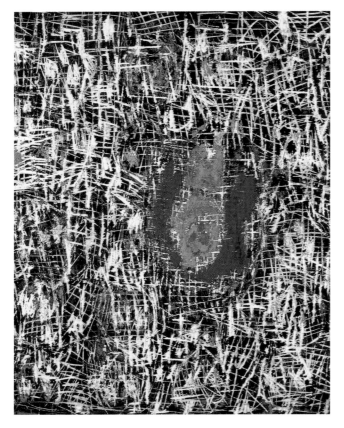

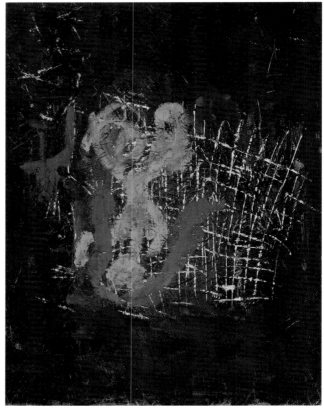

'45', 21. VII. 89 – 1. IX. 89   '45', 23. VII. 89 – 15. IX. 89

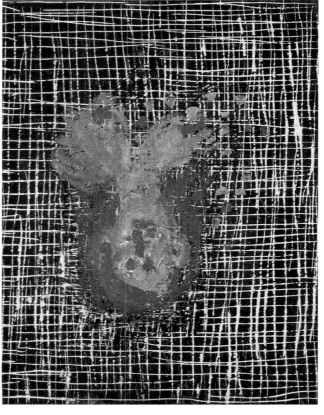

'45', 21. VII. 89 – 7. VIII. 89   '45', 18. VII. 89 – 27. VII. 89

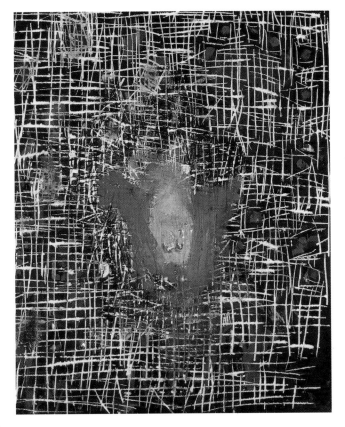

'45', VI. 89 – 20. VIII. 89

'45', 6. VIII. 89 – 8. VIII. 89

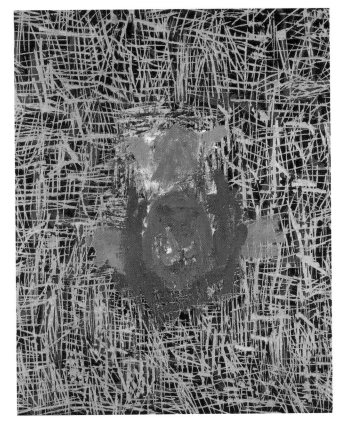

'45', 24. VIII. 89 – 3. IX. 89

'45', 11. VIII. 89 – 13. VIII. 89

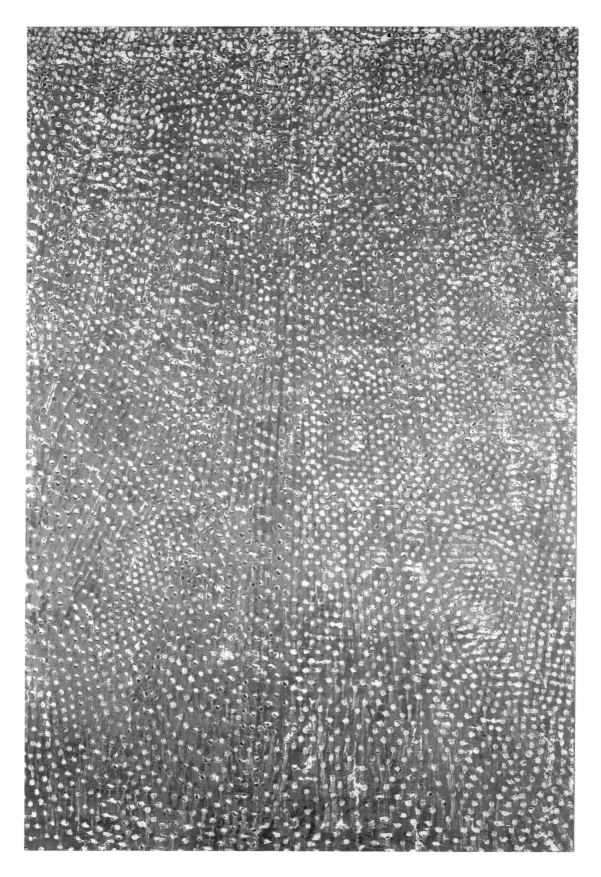

Cascade, 1990/91, 274 x 182 cm

Gold Count No Count, 1989, 274 x 183 cm

Dome, 1990/91, 243 x 243 cm

Ballerina Clown, 1989, mixed media, 915 x 518 x 270 cm

Ballerina Clown (studio photograph), 1989

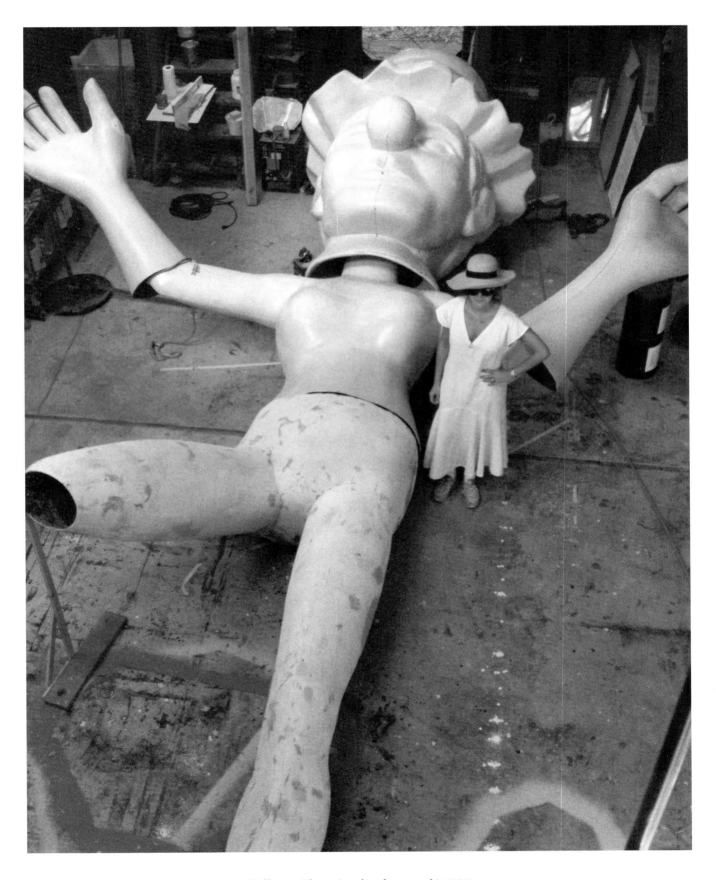

Ballerina Clown (studio photograph), 1989

Drawing for 'Ballerina Clown', 1988, pencil, ink, collage on paper, 39,4 x 25,4 cm

Bac à sable II/Box with Sand II, 1990, 28 x 231,5 x 182,5 cm

Lumière/Light, 1990, silkscreen on Plexiglas, 180×160 cm

Lumière/Light, 1990, silkscreen on Plexiglas, 180x160 cm

JAMES LEE BYARS →

THE MING-T'ANG WAS A MAGIC BUILDING SYMBOLIZING AND GIVING POWER OVER THE UNIVERSE. ANCIENT MONARCHS WERE SUPPOSED ALWAYS TO HAVE HAD ONE, AND THE CONFUCIAN CLASSICS CONTAIN MANY INDICATIONS AS TO HOW A MING-T'ANG ('HALL OF LIGHT') SHOULD BE BUILT, BUT THE DIFFERENT PASSAGES ARE HOPELESSLY AT VARIANCE. THE SUI DYNASTY, WHICH PRECEDED THE T'ANG, HAD NOT ATTEMPTED TO PUT UP A MING-T'ANG. BUT IN 630, SOON AFTER THE T'ANG DYNASTY CAME INTO POWER, IT WAS DECIDED THAT A MING-T'ANG OUGHT TO BE BUILT. THE PROPOSAL HUNG FIRE FOR HALF-A-CENTURY. THE REAL DIFFICULTY WAS NOT SO MUCH THE VARIANCE OF THE TEXTS AS THE FACT THAT THEY AGREE IN DESCRIBING A MODEST THATCHED BUILDING, JUST HIGH ENOUGH TO STAND UP IN, WHEREAS WHAT THE AUTHORITIES REALLY HAD IN MIND WAS A GIGANTIC MONUMENT, SYMBOLIZING THE MIGHT OF THE REIGNING DYNASTY. AT LAST, IN 687, SOON AFTER THE DOWAGER EMPRESS WU HOU DEPOSED HER SON AND BECAME RULER OF CHINA, ALL PRETENCE OF FOLLOWING ANCIENT PRECEDENTS WAS ABANDONED AND A COLOSSAL BUILDING OVER 300 FEET HIGH WAS PUT UP AT THE EASTERN CAPITAL, LO-YANG. IT WAS IN THREE TIERS. THE LOWEST WAS COLOURED GREEN, RED, WHITE AND BLACK, TO SYMBOLIZE THE FOUR SEASONS. THE MIDDLE TIER SYMBOLIZED THE TWELVE DOUBLE-HOURS AND HAD A ROUND ROOF IN THE FORM OF A GIGANTIC DISH SUPPORTED BY NINE DRAGONS.   ARTHUR WALEY

MANY MANY THINGS
THEY CALL TO MIND
CHERRY BLOSSOMS
BASHO

UNDER CHERRY BLOSSOMS
NONE ARE
STRANGERS
ISSA

AT PEOPLE'S VOICES
THE CHERRY BLOSSOMS
HAVE BLUSHED
ISSA

STILLNESS
THE SOUND OF CHERRY BLOSSOMS
FALLING DOWN
CHORA

WHAT A STRANGE THING
TO BE ALIVE
BENEATH THE
CHERRY BLOSSOMS
ISSA

CHERRY BLOSSOMS
CHERRY BLOSSOMS
IT WAS SUNG OF
THIS OLD TREE
ISSA

SIMPLY TRUST
DO NOT ALSO THE CHERRY
BLOSSOMS FLUTTER DOWN
JUST LIKE THAT
ISSA

THE SPRING NIGHT
IT HAS COME TO AN END
WITH DAWN ON THE
CHERRY BLOSSOMS
BASHO

THE CAPITAL

GOLDEN TOWER

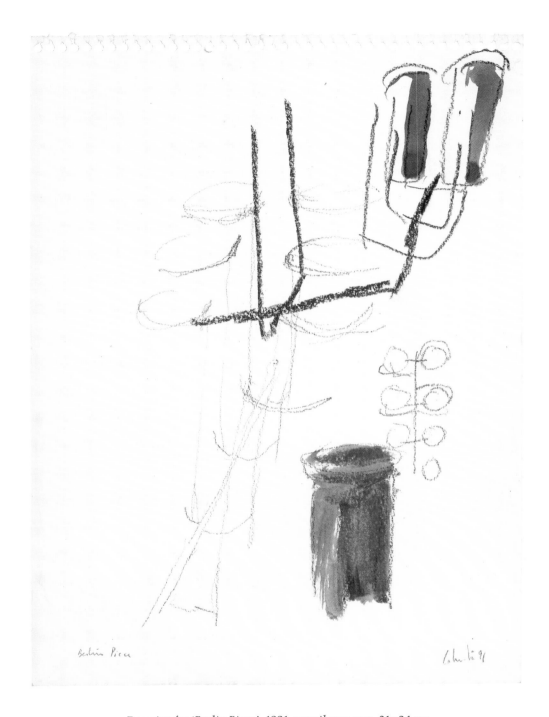

Drawing for 'Berlin Piece', 1991, pencil on paper, 31x24 cm

← JAMES LEE BYARS

Berlin Piece, 1991, 240 x 360 x 190 cm

Telescopico/Telescopic, 1990, galvanized sheet metal, 850 x 49 x 27 cm

A Sostegno dell'Arte/In Support of Art, 1990, galvanized sheet metal, 300x70x61 cm each

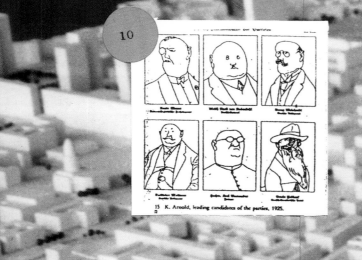

15 K. Arnold, leading candidates of the parties, 1925.

"Berliner,
wir arbeiten für:
wirtschaftlichen
Aufschwung,
soziale Gerech-
tigkeit, mehr
Sicherheit, für
die Hauptstadt
Berlin." *Eberhard Diepgen*

CDU

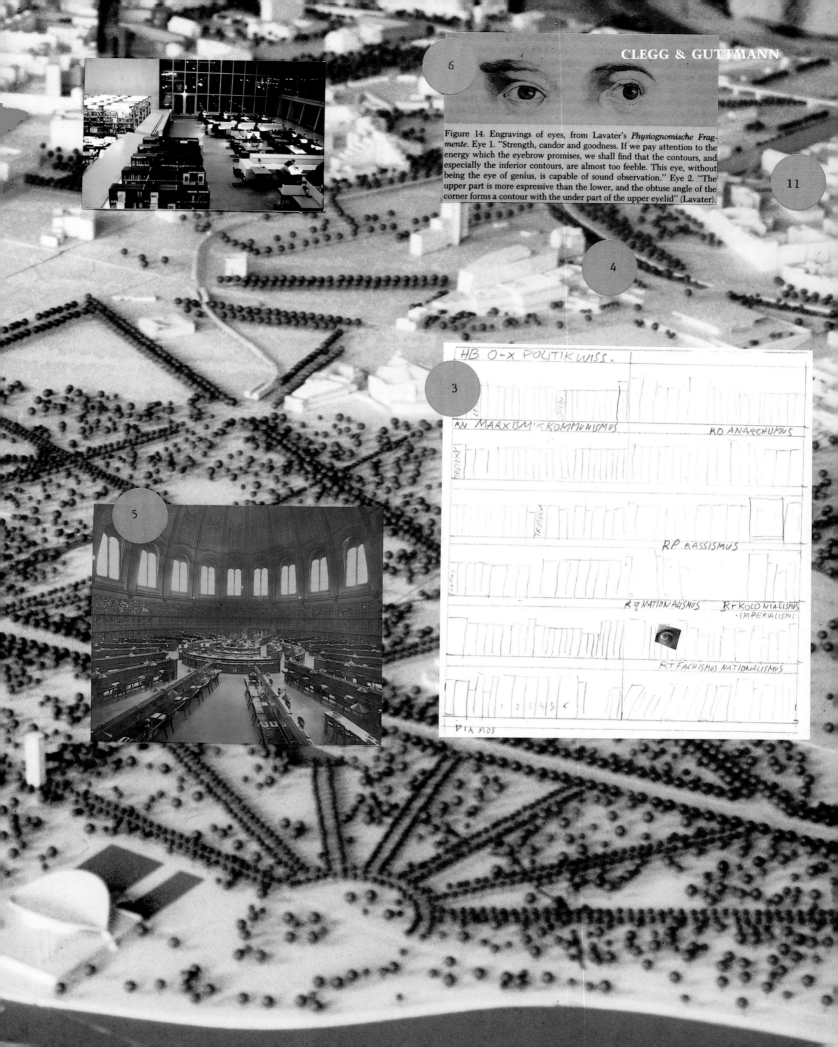

CLEGG & GUTTMANN

6

Figure 14. Engravings of eyes, from Lavater's *Physiognomische Fragmente.* Eye 1. "Strength, candor and goodness. If we pay attention to the energy which the eyebrow promises, we shall find that the contours, and especially the inferior contours, are almost too feeble. This eye, without being the eye of genius, is capable of sound observation." Eye 2. "The upper part is more expressive than the lower, and the obtuse angle of the corner forms a contour with the under part of the upper eyelid" (Lavater).

11

4

3

HB O-X POLITIK WISS.

RN MARXISM'R KOMMUNISMUS   RO ANARCHISMUS

TROTZKY

TROTZKY

RP RASSISMUS

R9 NATIONALISMUS   RT KOLONIALISMUS · IMPERIALISMUS

RT FACHISMUS NATIONALISMUS

1 2 3 4 5 C

DIA MOS

5

NOTES
1. The site of a poster for the 1990 local election in Berlin. The eyes and the mouth were displaced. (See note 2.)
2. The new site of the eyes -- a 1986 photograph of the face and bust of a high ranking businessman by C&G. The mouth was taken from an election poster of another German politician. (See note 7.)
3. A drawing of the contents of a shelf in the political science section in the Staadsbibliothek in Berlin (est. 1962) in its present location. (See note 4.) The eye which is pasted on the books classifed under the heading of Nazionalizmus belong to a German politician. (See note 2.) It seems that the heading conveys a characteristic of his political agenda.
4. The location of the Staadtsbibliothek in Berlin.
5. The reading room of the former Koeniglichebibliothek of East Berlin (est. 1701). The library contained some of the books which are now housed in the Staadsbibliothek. (See notes 3 and 4.)
6. A reproduction taken from Lavater's Physiognomische Fragmente describing the characteristics of a pair of eyes which are somewhat similar to those of the local political candidate whose eyes were displaced from the political poster. (See note 1.) Lavater's theories were influenced artists who worked in Berlin in the twenties, especially on those who produced political caricatures. (See note 10.)
7. A photograph of a second election poster in Berlin 1990. (See notes 2 and 3.)
8. The site intended for the "Physiognomical-Political Library". A project prepared by C&G for the group show Metropolis. Prior to this group show the exhibition space - which was designed by Martin Gropius - was dedicated to a show which revolved around Bismarck (1815-1898). (See note 3.)
9. The catalogue of Metropolis. (See note 8.)
10. A reproduction of Arnold's physiognomical political caricatures from the twenties. (See note 8.)
11. The location of the film studios where "Metropolis" was made. (See note 8.)
12. The Expressionists artists and film directors who worked in Berlin in the twenties (see notes 10 and 11) were fascinated by the story of Victor Frankenstein, a character from a novel by the same name by Mary Shelley (1816), who put together a human monster.

Terugkeer van de performance/Return Performance, 1987, 190x130 cm

Monk and Ministry, 1987, 102 x 180 cm

Palladium, 1986, 110x170 cm

Plattegronden/Plans, 1986, 141x190 cm

Untitled, 1991, 274 x 549 cm

Untitled, 1991, 230 x 457 cm

Badende VII/Bathers VII, 1991, 290 x 300 cm

Badende V/Bathers V, 1991, 240 x 250 cm

Badende IV/Bathers IV, 1991, 240×250 cm

Löwe im leeren Raum/Lion in Empty Space, 1990

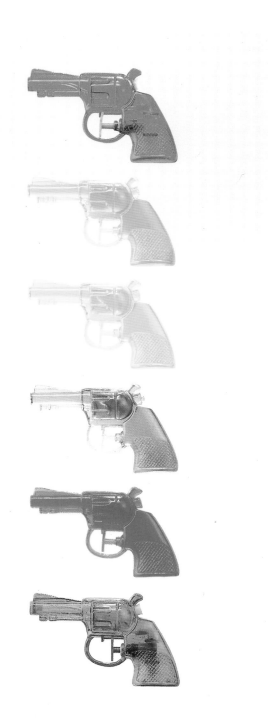

Vier Polyesterrevolver, zwei Wasserspritzrevolver/Four Polyester Pistols, Two Water Pistols, 1988

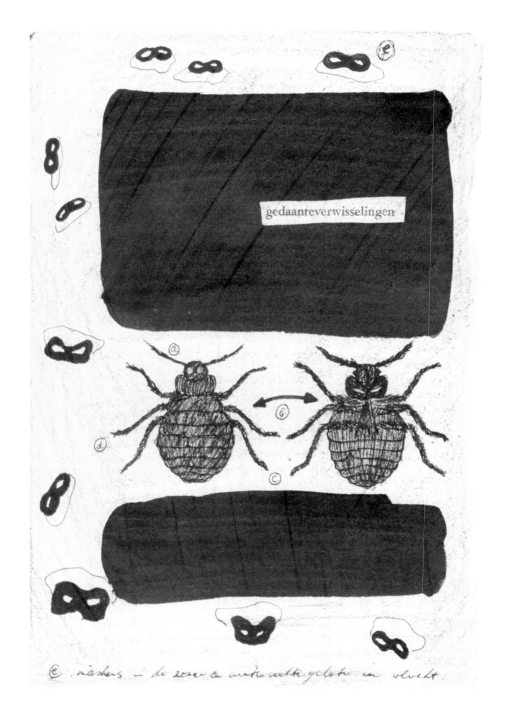

Metamorphose/Metamorphosis, 1979, indian ink and pencil on paper, 13,6x19,9 cm

Knipschaarhuis I, 1989, ballpoint on wood, 250x166x137 cm each

Tivoli near Malines, 1990, ballpoint on castle

Untitled, 1990, 170x178 cm

Untitled, 1990, 170x178 cm

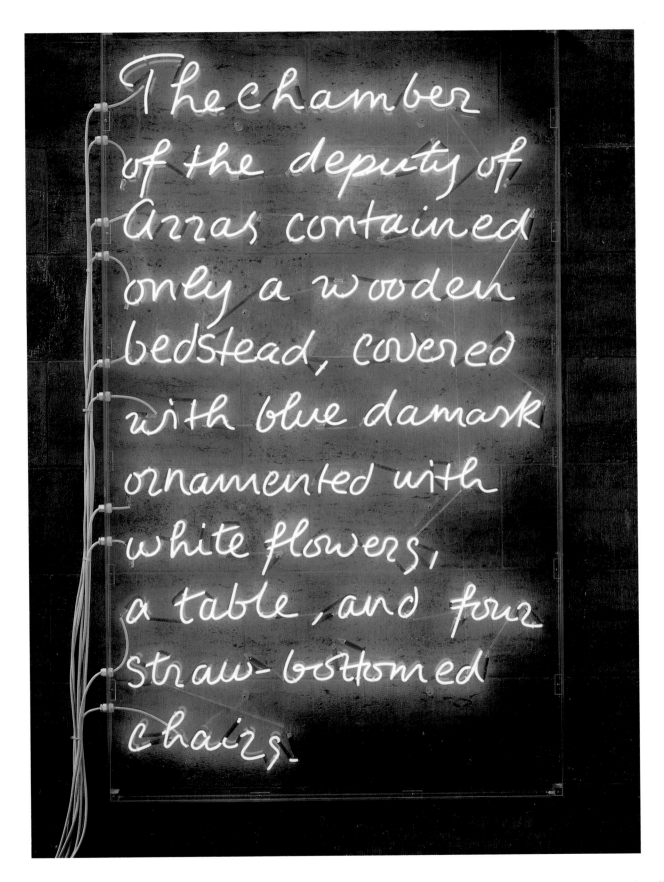

Matisse chez Duplay/Matisse at Duplay's, 1989, neon, 210x122x7 cm

Design drawing for 'Cythera', 1990 (detail) →

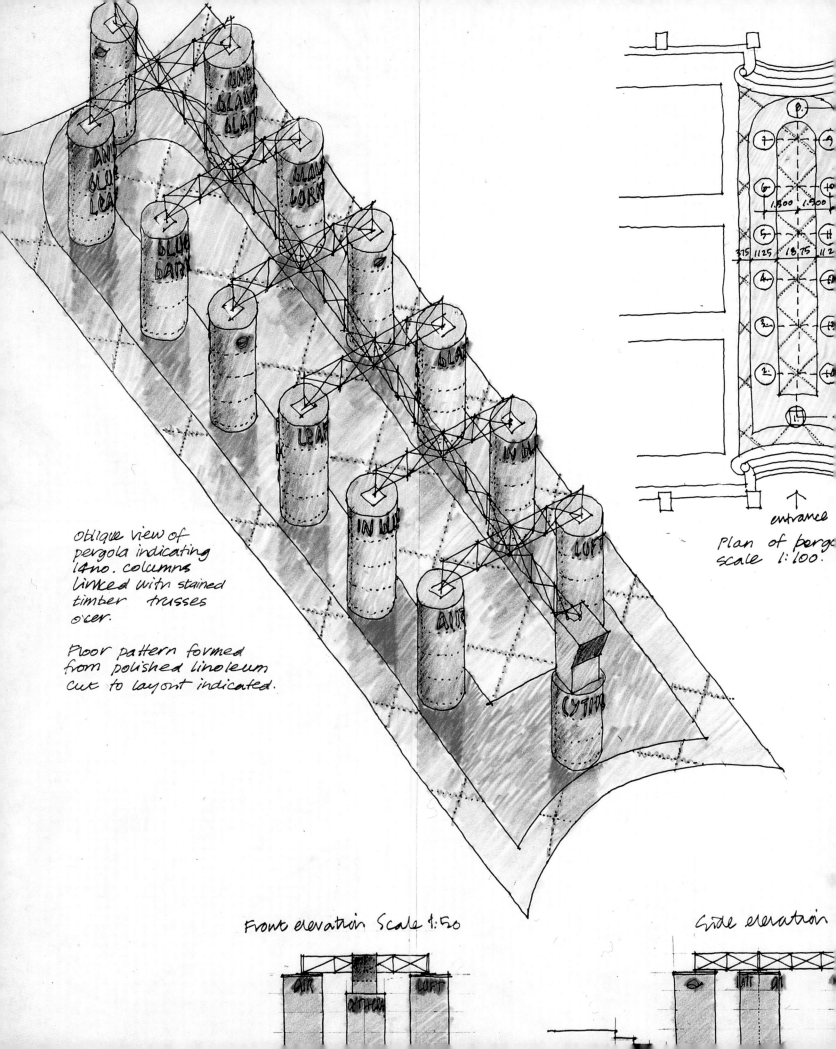

Oblique view of
pergola indicating
14no. columns
linked with stained
timber trusses
o'er.

Floor pattern formed
from polished linoleum
cut to layout indicated.

Plan of pergola
scale 1:100.

entrance

Front elevation Scale 1:50

Side elevation

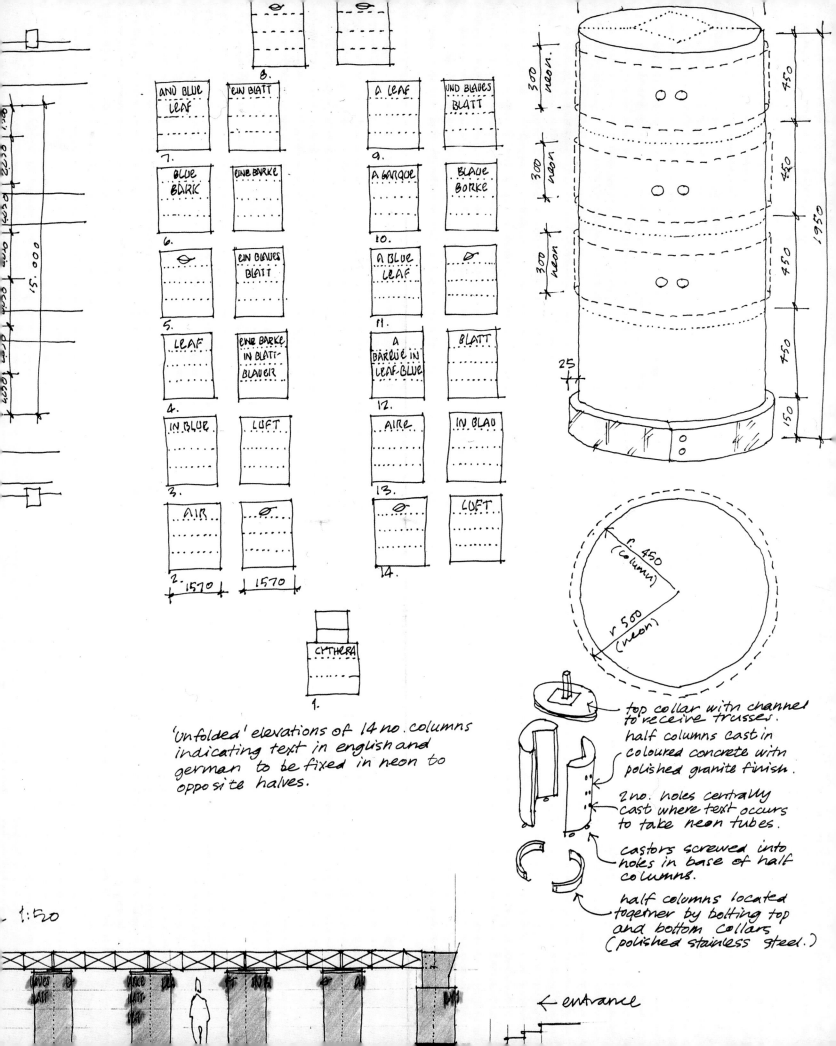

'Unfolded' elevations of 14 no. columns indicating text in english and german to be fixed in neon to opposite halves.

1:50

top collar with channel to receive trusses.

half columns cast in coloured concrete with polished granite finish.

2 no. holes centrally cast where text occurs to take neon tubes.

castors screwed into holes in base of half columns.

half columns located together by bolting top and bottom collars (polished stainless steel.)

← entrance

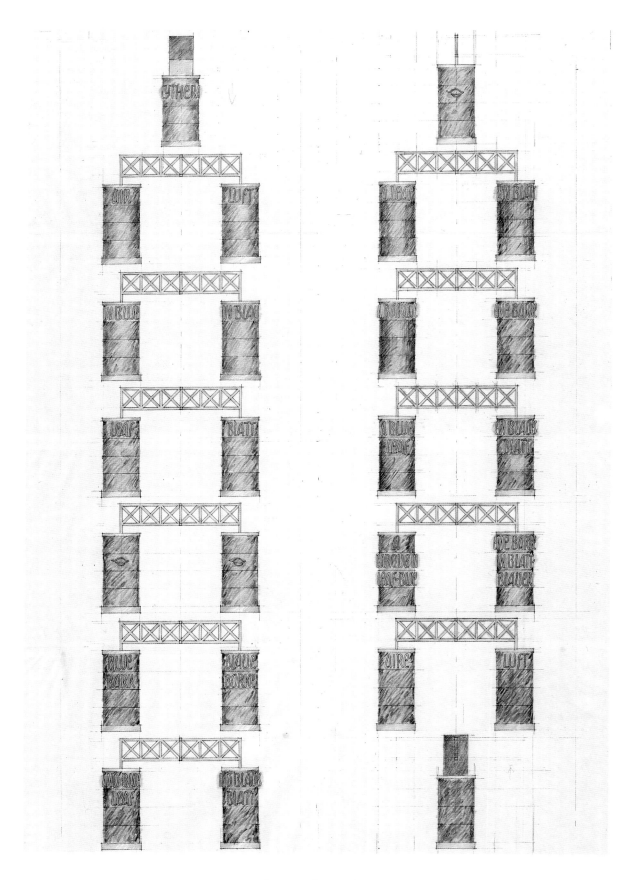

Design drawings for 'Cythera', 1990

Untitled, 1990, 44 x 66 cm

Untitled, 1990, 44 x 66 cm

Untitled, 1990, 44 x 66 cm

Untitled, 1990, 300 x 300 cm

Untitled, 1990, 300 x 300 cm

Villa Malaparte, 1990, 270×180 cm

Villa Malaparte, 1990, 270x180 cm

Weißes Bild/White Painting, 1990, tempera on canvas, wood, metal foil, lacquer, 140x100x8,5 cm

Schwarzes Bild/Black Painting, 1990, tempera on canvas, wood, metal foil, lacquer, 140x100x8,5 cm

Gelbes Bild/Yellow Painting, 1990, tempera on canvas, wood, metal foil, lacquer, 140x100x8,5 cm

Militant, Class War, Gateway, 1986, installation: Hayward Gallery, London, 1987

Militant, 1986, 363 x 758 cm

Class War, 1986, 363 x 1010 cm

Gateway, 1986, 363 x 758 cm

Untitled (Buttocks), 1990, 48 x 37,5 x 19 cm

Untitled (Big Torso), 1990, 60 x 44,5 x 28,5 cm

Untitled (Leg), 1990, wood, wax, cotton, leather, 28,6 x 20,3 x 81 cm

Untitled, 1990, installation with silver bromide emulsion, Westfälischer Kunstverein, Münster

Scultura bianca e nero / Black and White Sculpture , 1989, installation with silver bromide emulsion, Padiglione d'Arte Contemporanea, Milan

Design drawing for 'Hygroskopie, Nord Südtor'/'Hygroscopicity, North South Gate', 1991

Paraphysik (Paraphysics) (studio photograph), 1991, mixed media

← Las Fronteras Espirales/ Spiral Limits (detail), 1990

Raiz Circular/Circular Root, 1990, vinyl

The River's Edge, 1990, 229 x 495 cm

Total Recall, 1990, 216 x 246 cm

Schießstand/Shooting-gallery, 1989, mixed media, c. 170×350×95 cm

Museumskunst/Museum Art, 1991, mixed media, 176 x 360 x 72 cm

Vorsorgliche Handlungen/Preventive Steps, 1990, mixed media, variable dimensions

Mountain of Cocaine – Prototype I, 1990, mixed media, diameter: 90 cm, height: 198 cm

Untitled, 1990, bricks on black fur, 260 x 210 cm

And sat down beside her, 1990, video installation (detail)

Inasmuch As it is Always Already Taking Place, 1990, video installation

Installation: Times Square, New York, 1982

Installation: Piccadilly Circus, London, 1988/89

Installation: 'Railway Cars', 1987. project in Hamburg

Untitled, 1990, fibre-cement, 236 x 164 x 204 cm

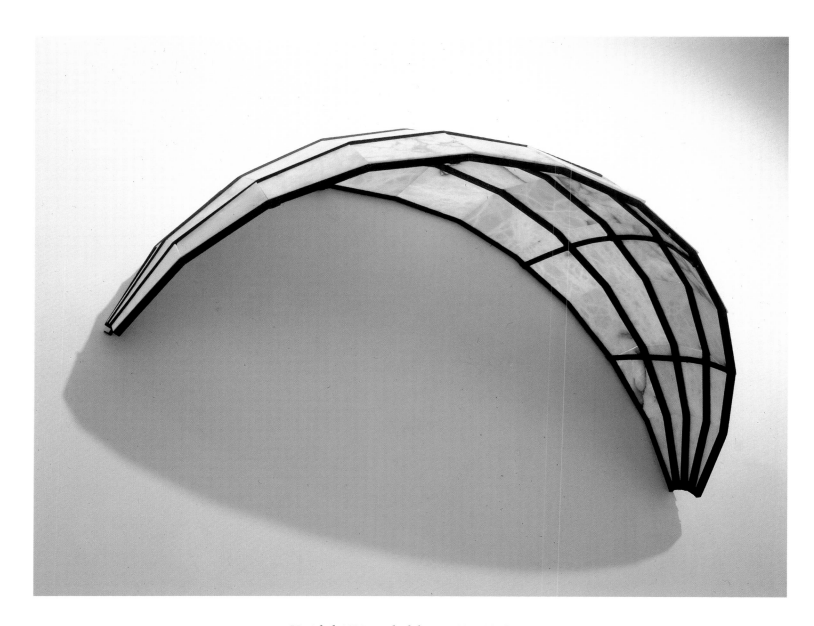

Untitled, 1989, steel, alabaster, 90 x 200 x 85 cm

Ubi consistam/Where Am I to Stand, 1990, silicone on gauze, lamps, 300 x 300 x 300 cm

Untitled, 1991, ink on colour photocopy, 29,7x21 cm

Untitled (painted by Wolfgang Zocha), 1990/91, 47,5 x 40 cm

Pogo the Clown (painted by John Wayne Gacy), 1988
oil on canvas, 46 x 36 cm

Untitled (painted by William Bonin), 1985
pastel on paper, 40,6 x 35 cm

Pay for Your Pleasure, 1988, 42 painted banners, installation: Museum of Contemporary Art, Los Angeles

Untitled, 1986, wood, coal, coal tar, creosote, overpainted photographs (installation photograph)

Untitled, 1989, wood, coal tar, creosote, 2200x120x120 cm

Birdrunner, 1990, 145 x 292 x 32 cm

Taiwan, 1987, variable dimensions

American Landscape, 1989, 122x171x76 cm

Keilrahmen/Stretcher, 1968/1989, 30x30 cm

Untitled, 1990, gloss paint on hardboard, 210x150 cm

Untitled, 1990, gloss paint on hardboard, 210x150 cm

Stacked, 1988, 155 x 135 x 79 cm

Popples, 1988, 74 x 58,5 x 30,5 cm

Vase of Flowers, 1988, mirrors, 184x135x2,5 cm

Untitled, 1990, terracotta, sea water, blood, steel plate, burlap sacks, coal, iron, variable dimensions

Untitled, 1990, steel containers, coal, 250x198x40 cm, installation: Bordeaux

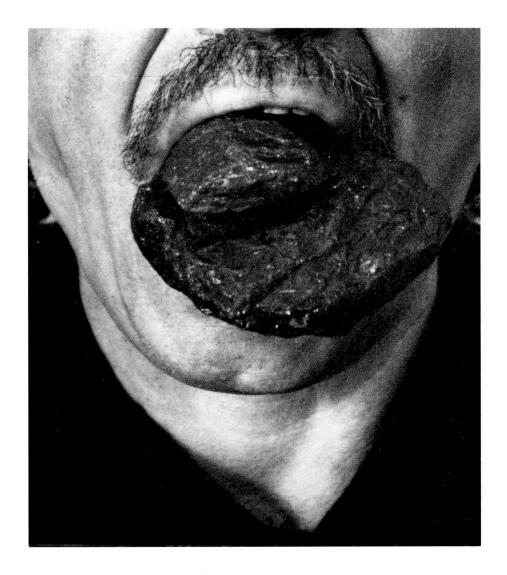

Porta murata/Walled-in Door, 1990, carbon, mouth of the artist

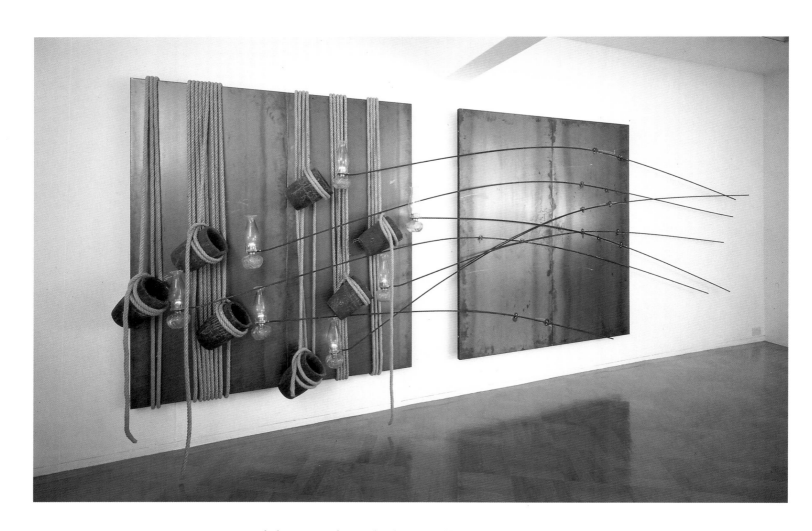

Untitled, 1990, steel, rope, buckets, paraffin lamps, 200 x 565 x 37 cm

A A A…A A, 1987, 100×200 cm

Collapse, 1987, 200×100 cm

Corona de Espinas/Crown of Thorns, 1990, 200 x 150 cm

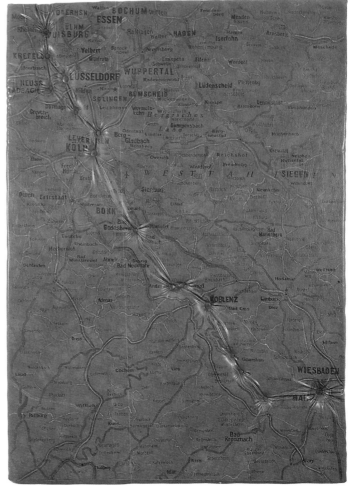

The River, 1989, 198 x 134 x 10 cm

Untitled Roads, 1990, 198 x 198 cm

In Seurat's Asnières (detail), 1990/91, 400 x 450 x 500 cm

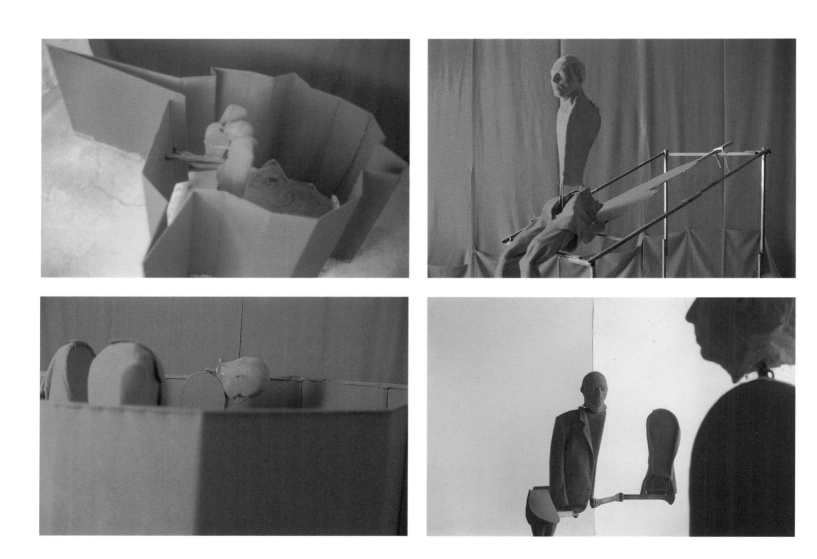

In Seurat's Asnières (details), 1990/91, 400 x 450 x 500 cm

The Outsider, 1989, variable dimensions

From the cycle 'The Albums', 1989,
Various fragments of refuse of a paint and varnishing workshop
mounted on panel, 100x70 cm

De Ordine Geometrico, 1990, installation: De Appel Foundation, Amsterdam

Den Menschen der Zukunft/For People of the Future, 1990, installation: Kunstverein Hannover

Costruire, 1989, installation: Kunsthalle Zürich

13. 4. 1981, 1987, steel, chromium, concrete, 1150 x 900 x 700 cm,
installation: Kurfürstendamm/Joachimstaler Straße, Berlin

Laborprobe/Laboratory Test, 1990, glass, aluminium, c. 400 x 500 x 400 cm,
installation: Westfälisches Landesmuseum für Kunst und Kulturgeschichte, Münster

112:104, 1991, design montage for METROPOLIS *project*

Playing with Gods II: Twilight, 1991, 360 x 250 cm

Playing with Gods III: At Night, 1991, 360 x 250 cm

Playing with Gods IV: Dawn, 1991, 360 x 250 cm

Hirschsprung, 1986, photograph

Oberwinden, 1986, photograph

Herborn (Dillkr.), 1982, photograph

Wissen (Sieg), 1986, photograph

Enanos/Dwarfs, 1989, papier mâché, 108 x 88 x 44 cm

Dos Centinelas/Two Guards, 1989, iron, 240x144x280 cm

Model for Animal Pyramid II, 1989, photo collage, 235 x 160 cm

Animal Pyramid, 1989, 366 x 213 x 244 cm

Model for Animal Pyramid I, 1989, photo collage, 206 x 163 cm

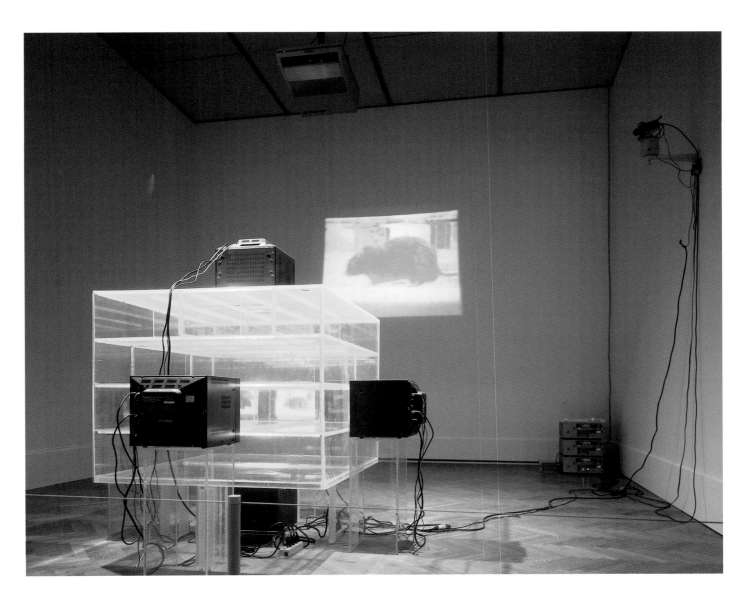

Rats and Bats (Learned Helplessness in Rats), 1988, video installation

Title Not Available, 1989, silkscreen on aluminium, 183x122 cm

The Big Shift, 1989, pipe, flags, cords, insect sprayer, 437x145x13 cm,
installation: American Fine Arts, New York

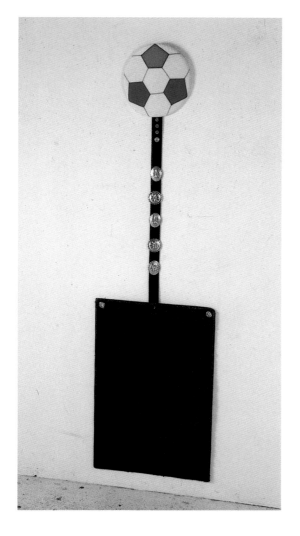

Pedestal, 1985, 47 x 71 x 7,5 cm

Blank for Serial, 1989, metal poles, red pillows, 381x381 cm,
installation: American Fine Arts, New York

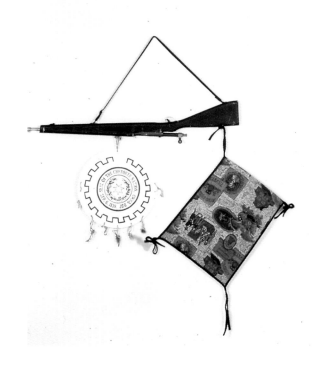

Early Americans, 1984,
107 x 40,5 x 10 cm

Wenn die Wand an den Tisch rückt/If the Wall Shifts Towards the Table, 1990, video (2 detail photographs)

Wenn die Wand an den Tisch rückt/If the Wall Shifts Towards the Table, 1990, video (detail photograph)

Fn 20, 1990, oil on canvas, 214x275 cm

Fn 4, 1990, 214 x 275 cm

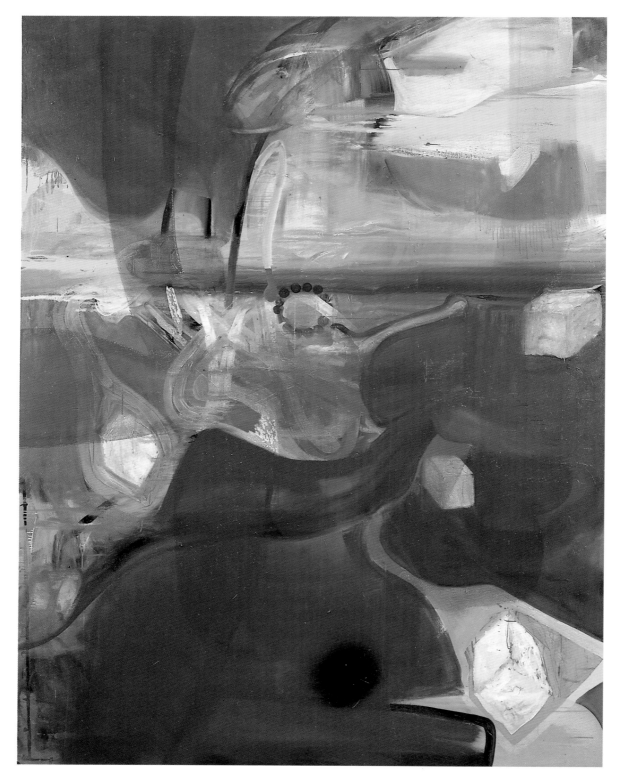

Fn 15, 1990, 275 x 214 cm

Photomontage for METROPOLIS, 1990

Photocollage for METROPOLIS, 1990

100 Possibilities for Installations (Russia), 1990, ink drawing, 21 x 29,7 cm

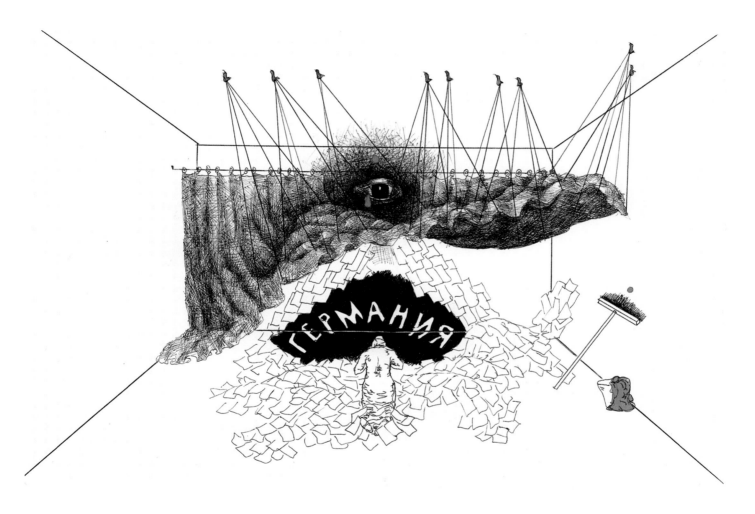

100 Possibilities for Installations (Germany), 1990, ink drawing, 21x29,7 cm

Do you know what it means to come home at night to a woman who'll give you a little love, a little affection, a little tenderness? It means you're in the wrong house, that's what it means.

Good Revolution, 1991, 457x227 cm

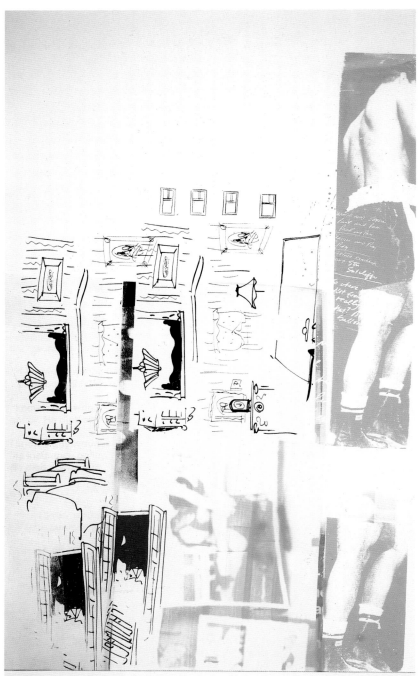

A man was on safari with his native guide when they came
upon a beautiful blond bathing naked in the stream. "My
god, who's that?" the man asked.
"Daughter of missionary, bwana," came the reply.
"I haven't seen a white woman in so long," the man sighed,
"that I'd give anything to eat her."
So the guide raised his rifle to his shoulder and shot her.

Why Did the Nazi Cross the Road?, 1991, 457 x 227 cm

GOOD NEWS AND BAD NEWS: A man walked into a doctor's office to get a check-up. After the examination the doctor says to the man, I've got good news and I've got bad news. The bad news is you're going to die in a year and there's nothing you can do about it. The good news is I'm having an affair with my secretary.

Sampling the Chocolate, 1991, 457x227 cm

I'll Fuck Anything that Moves, 1991, 457x227 cm

Wald (4)/Forest (4), 1990, 340 x 260 cm

Wald (2)/Forest (2), 1990, 340 × 260 cm

Wald (3)/Forest (3), 1990, 340 x 260 cm

Wald (1)/Forest (1), 1990, 340 x 260 cm

Stern 19h 04m/−70° / Star 19h 04m/−70°, 1990, 260×188 cm

Portrait (Andrea Knobloch), 1990, 210x165 cm

Portrait (Oliver Cieslik), 1990, 210x165 cm

Five past Eleven, 1989, 150 x 370 cm

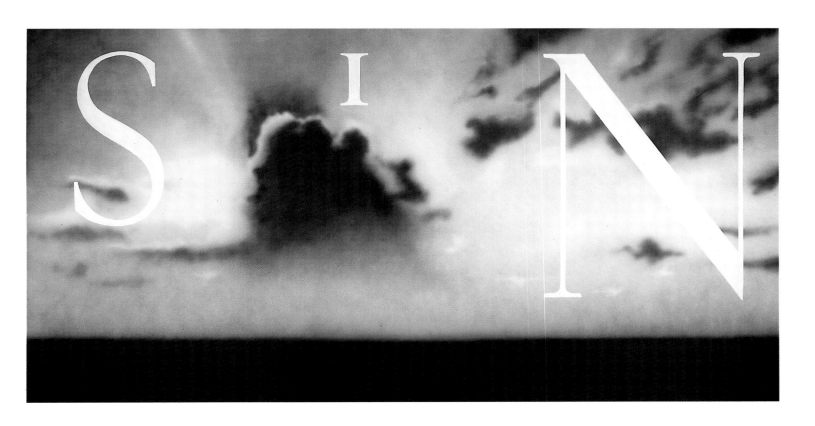

Sin, 1991, 178 x 350 cm

Industrial Strength Sleep, 1989, 150 x 370 cm

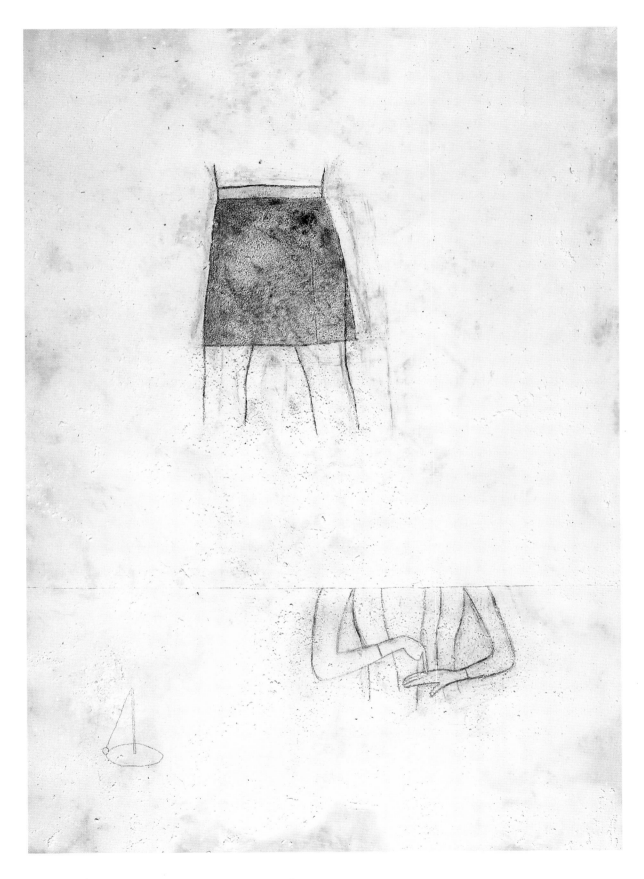

Metropolis, 1991, 285 x 205 cm

Dias de Escuro e de Luz – II (Jarro)/Days of Darkness and Light – II (Goblet), 1990, 190 x 341 cm

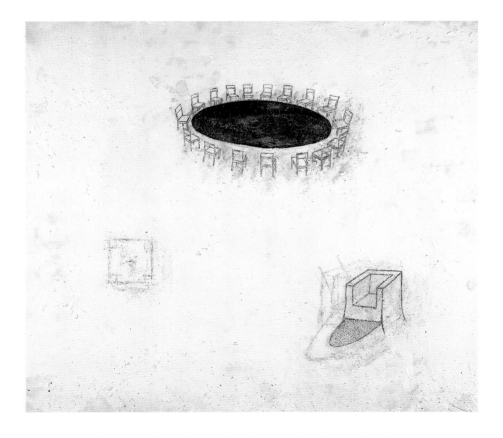

Dias de Escuro e de Luz – VII (Mesa)/Days of Darkness and Light – VII (Table), 1990, 190 x 220 cm

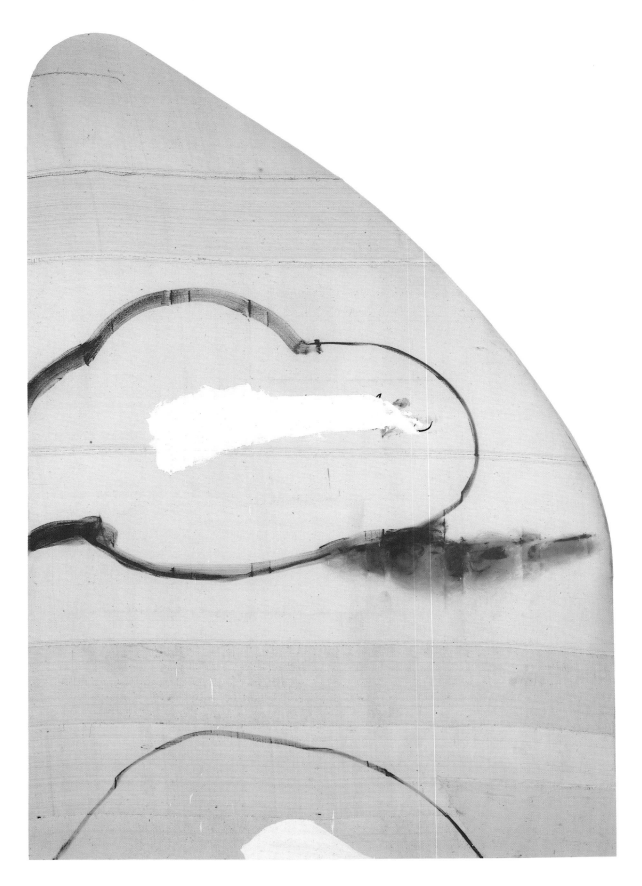

Jane Birkin # 1, 1990, 409 x 287 cm

Jane Birkin # 3 (Vito), 1990, 326 x 630 cm

Ozymandias, 1990, 396 x 549 cm

Untitled, 1991, 228 x 125 cm

Untitled, 1991, 228x125 cm

Untitled, 1991, 228 x 125 cm

Film Sphere with Pipe Clamps, studio photograph 1991

Montage for 'Film Sphere with Pipe Clamps', 1990

Blue Medusa, 1990, installation, 426 x 335 x 76 cm

Untitled (elephant foot stools), 1988, 102 x 325 x 59 cm (part 1)

Untitled (elephant skull), 1988, 225 x 109 x 105,5 (part 2)

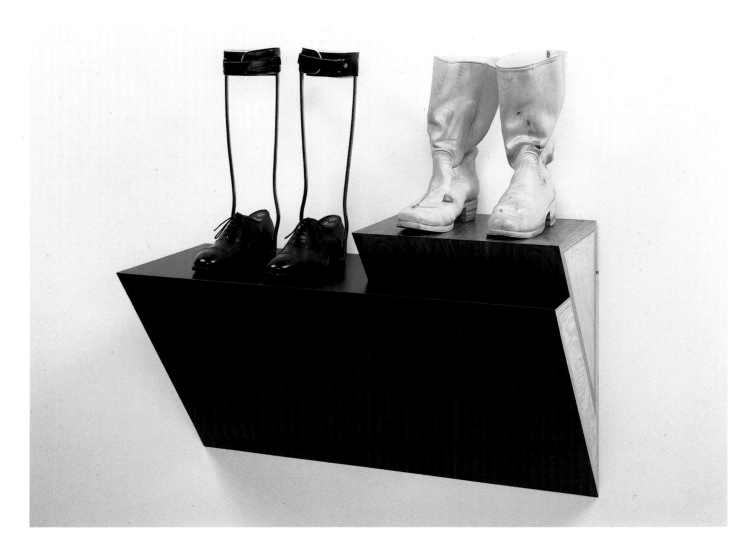

Untitled (shoes with braces, wooden boots), 1987, 58 x 91,5 x 40,5 cm

Daddy's Striptease Room, 1990, wood, cardboard box, paint, 50x70x50 cm

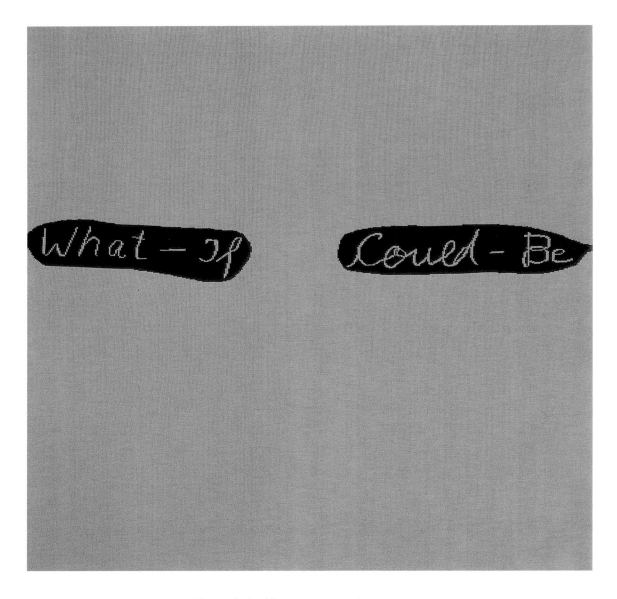

What – If Could – Be, 1990, wool, 150 x 155 cm

Untitled, 1988, wood, stockings, rice, 100 x 40 x 40 cm

The Theater of Memory, 1985, video installation

The City of Man, 1989, video/sound installation

Outburst, 1989, 229×312 cm

The Pine on the Corner, 1990, 119 x 149 cm

The Ventriloquist at a Birthday Party in October 1947, 1990, 229 x 352,4 cm

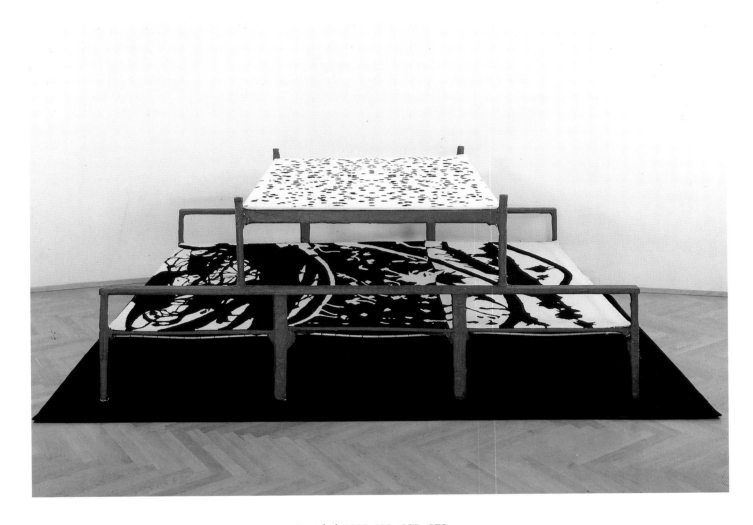

Untitled, 1990, 105 x 205 x 270 cm
'Esse est percipi'
Berkeley
Please use the beds for the act of reclining or sitting, as the case may be, after first removing your shoes.

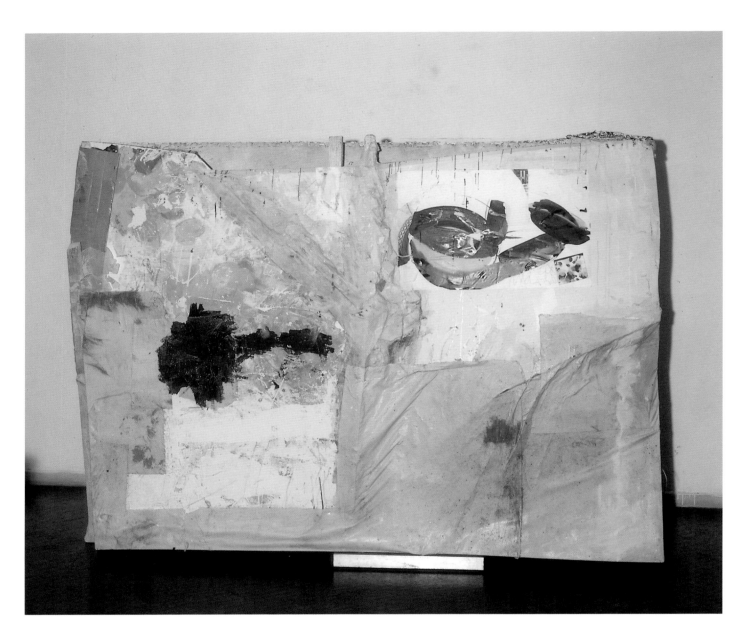

Otto sieht jetzt einen roten Würfel auf dem Tisch/Now Otto Sees a Red Cube on the Table, 1990, 166 x 52 x 220 cm

Liege/Couch, 1989, 66x73x174 cm

False Door, 1990, 214,6 x 40,6 x 152,4 cm, rear view

False Door, 1990, 214,6 x 40,6 x 152,4 cm, front view

Rut, 1990, 250 x 400 x 400 cm, studio photograph

Rut, 1990, 250 x 400 x 400 cm, studio photograph

In case of, 1988–1990, 84 x 70 x 51 cm

Why?, 1990, 274 x 183 cm

Untitled, 1990, 274 x 183 cm

Untitled, 1990, 274x183 cm

Local Commentary on Butterflies, 1990, 220x150 cm

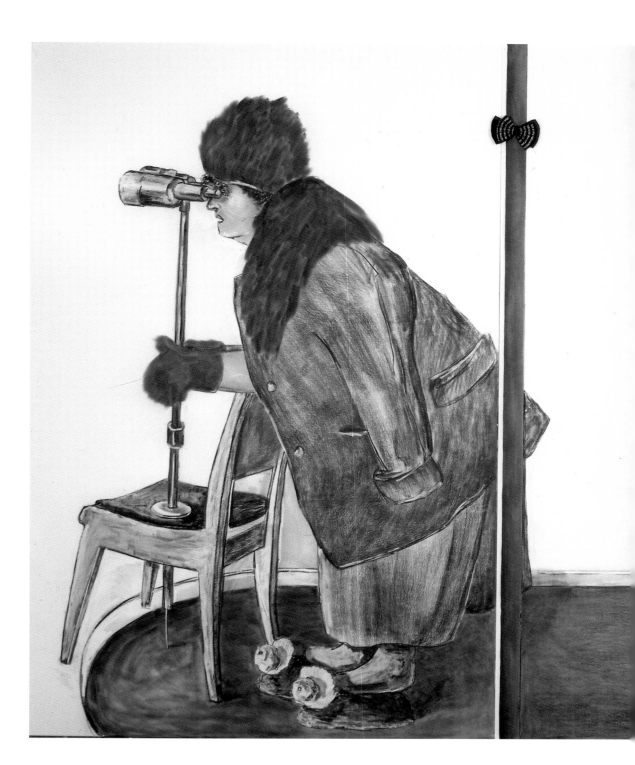

Local Commentary on Butterflies, 1990, 220 x 150 cm

BIOGRAPHIES AND NOTES ON THE ARTISTS

JOHN M ARMLEDER

Born Geneva, 1948. Studied at Ecole des Beaux-Arts, Geneva. Founder member of Groupe Ecart, 1969, organizing collaborative exhibitions, books and actions. Exhibitions at Galerie Ecart, Geneva, 1973–80. Co-founder of International Institutions Register, 1976. Set up Leathern Wing Scribble Press, 1977. Co-Founder of Laboratorio artists' cooperative, Milan, and founder member of Associated Art Publishers, 1977. One-man show at Kunstmuseum, Basle, 1980. Exhibitions at Galerie nächst St. Stephan, Vienna; Galerie Susanna Kulli, St. Gallen; John Gibson Gallery, New York; Galerie Tanit, Munich and Cologne; Anselm Dreher, Berlin; Daniel Buchholz, Cologne; and elsewhere. Swiss Pavilion at Venice Biennale, 1986. Took part in 'documenta 8', 1987. Lives in Geneva and New York.

Armleder's art draws on the resources of a wide range of avant-garde styles and movements, from Suprematism and Constructivism to the art of the 1960s and 1970s. In this context, his dot pictures and installations may be seen as a personal confrontation with Modernist positions, which he sardonically deflates or deconstructs with an infallible sense of 'good taste'. His *Furniture Sculptures* juxtapose and oppose furniture, objects and painting in such a way that every image or object has its place within a specific sphere, style, or context. The contacts between these various levels set up the thematic and visual tensions that define Armleder's work. 'Unlike Rauschenberg in the *Combine Paintings*, Armleder is not concerned with the gradations between the painting, the reproduction and the real object. The *Furniture Sculptures*, as he calls

them, intervene in painting by treating the picture no longer as an autonomous object but as a commodity, and by allowing commodities to be read as a possible extension of painting.' (Dieter Schwarz)

Reference Sources for List of Exhibitions and Bibliography

'John M Armleder', Kunstmuseum Winterthur, 1987 (later shown in Paris, Düsseldorf, Berlin) – 'John M Armleder. Furniture Sculpture 1980–1990', Musée Rath, Geneva 1990

Writings by the Artist (Selection)

'Oh! My Hat! D'après Ray Johnson pour Patrick Lux Lucchini', in: 'Patrick Lucchini' (catalogue), Galerie Gaëtan, Carouge 1974 – 'Escrits et entretiens' (with Helmut Federle and Olivier Mosset), Musée de Grenoble, Maison de la Culture et de la Communication, Saint-Etienne, 1987 – 'Les artistes sont trop vite papes en leur village', in: *La Suisse est-elle trop petite pour la création?*, Geneva 1989 – 'L'art est toujours public', in: *Art public, Actes du Colloque de l'AICA*, Geneva 1990

Catalogue and Monographs (Selection)

'891 und weitere Stücke', Kunstmuseum Basle, 1980 – 'Arbeiten auf Papier 1961–1983', Kunstmuseum Solothurn, 1983 – Städtische Galerie Regensburg (with Olivier Mosset), 1986 – 'La Biennale di Venezia', Venice 1986 – Musée de Peinture et de Sculpture, Grenoble 1987 – Daniel Buchholz and Galerie Tanit, *John M Armleder*, 2 vols, Cologne 1990

Catalogues of Collective Exhibitions (Selection)

'John Armleder/Martin Disler/Helmut Federle', Centre d'Art Contemporain, Geneva 1981 – 'Schweizer Kunst '70–'80', Kunstmuseum Lucerne, 1981 – 'Zeichen Fluten Signale. Neukonstruktiv und parallel', Galerie nächst St. Stephan, Vienna 1984 – 'Prospect 86', Frankfurt a.M. 1986 – 'documenta 8', Kassel 1987 – '"Stiller Nachmittag". Aspekte Junger Schweizer Kunst', Kunsthaus Zurich, 1987 – 'Offenes Ende. Junge Schweizer Kunst', Institut für moderne Kunst Nuremberg, 1987 – 'Furniture as Art', Museum Boymans-van Beuningen, Rotterdam 1988 – 'Farbe Bekennen', Museum für Gegenwartskunst, Basle 1988 – 'Cultural Geometry', Athens 1988 – 'Schlaf der Vernunft', Kassel 1988 – 'Escultura y dibujo, en diálogo. Cuatro artistas de Suiza', Círculo de Bellas Artes, Madrid 1988 – 'Psychological Abstraction', Athens 1989 – 'D & S Ausstellung', Hamburg 1989 – 'Wie-

ner Diwan. Sigmund Freud heute', Museum des 20. Jahrhunderts, Vienna, (Ritter Verlag) Klagenfurt 1989 – 'Seven Europeans', John Gibson Gallery, New York 1990

Other Literature (Selection)

Harry Zellweger: 'John M Armleder', *Das Kunstwerk*, No. 4/5, 1986 – Gabriele Boller: 'John M Armleder', *Kunst-Bulletin*, No. 3, 1987 – Dieter Schwarz: 'John Armleder, Olivier Mosset, Niele Toroni', *Noema Art Magazine*, No. 12–13, 1987 – Christoph Blase: 'John M Armleder. Der elegante Zigeuner', *Pan*, No. 6, 1988 – Daniel Soutif: 'Found and Lost. On the Object in Art', *Artforum*, October 1989 – Renate Wolff: 'Lebens-Künstler', *Zeitmagazin*, No. 43, 1990

RICHARD ARTSCHWAGER

Born Washington, 1923. Studied biology and cellular biology at Cornell University, Ithaca, New York. 1941–48 (with interruptions for war service in Europe). Served apprenticeship as a cabinetmaker and attended Amédée Ozenfant School, New York, for two years. Ran a furniture workshop in New York, 1953–60. Full-time professional artist since 1960. One-man shows at Leo Castelli Gallery, New York, from 1965. Exhibitions at Galerie Ricke, Co-

logne; Daniel Weinberg Gallery, San Francisco; Mary Boone Gallery, New York; Galerie Ghislaine Hussenot, Paris; and elsewhere. Took part in 'documenta 4', 1968, 'documenta 5', 1972, 'documenta 7', 1982, 'documenta 8', 1987. Kokoschka-Preis, Vienna, 1987. Lives in New York.

Artschwager's work is constantly being assigned to the most varied artistic tendencies, including pop, minimal, and conceptual art. He is now regarded as a pioneer in the artistic territory that lies between sculpture and everyday objects. Denatured pieces of furniture are central to his art. These pieces, specially made by Artschwager, are reduced to basics and often modified to the point of loss of function; they then become sculpture. The use of the 'tacky' material of Formica, in which any desired timber or woodgrain can be imitated, serves to underscore their artificiality. This ambiguous relation between form and material is frequently exploited by Artschwager to make his own wry, witty or erotic comments; it also appears in his paintings. These are frequently painted on Celotex from photographic originals, initially in black and white but later in colour. The banality of the subjects, and the contrast between the exact transcription of the motif and its simultaneous dissolution as a result of the resistance of the material, make these paintings into (often expensively framed) 'objects' of perception. The same goes for the *Blp*, an elongated oval shape derived from military radar systems, which has appeared in Artschwager's work since 1967, not only in his paintings but also in public as a kind of personal trademark. In a number of his works Artschwager has attempted to link sculpture with painting, or to create illusions of space through a trompe-l'œil effect. In recent years, he has started to paint the woodgrain effect of his sculptural 'models for thought' by hand. 'The common denominator of his various activities is the undermining of all expectations, whether categorical, perceptual or cognitive – a subversion that leads to an altered self-perception in the tradition of Classic Modernism... [Artschwager] is a master of lyrical irony and witty inspiration. Both protect his art from relapsing into a past historical context.' (Edward F. Fry)

Reference Sources for List of Exhibitions and Bibliography
'Artschwager, Richard', The Whitney Museum of American Art, New York 1988 (later shown in San Francisco, Los Angeles,

Madrid, Paris, Düsseldorf) – 'Richard Artschwager. Gemälde, Skulpturen, Zeichnungen, Multiples 1962–1989', Galerie Neuendorf, Frankfurt a. M. 1990

Writings by the Artist (Selection)
'The Hydraulic Door Check', *Arts Magazine*, No. 42, 1967 – 'Basket Table Door Window Mirror Rug' (with Catherine Kord), New York 1976

Catalogues and Monographs (Selection)
Museum of Contemporary Art (with Alan Shields), Chicago 1973 – 'Zu Gast in Hamburg', Kunstverein in Hamburg, 1978 – 'Richard Artschwager's Theme(s)', Albright-Knox Art Gallery, Buffalo 1979 – Kunsthalle Basle, 1985 – 'Recent Works', Daniel Weinberg Gallery, Los Angeles 1988

Catalogues of Collective Exhibitions (Selection)
'The New Art', Davison Arts Center, Wesleyan University, Middletown, Connecticut 1964 – 'Primary Structures', Jewish Museum, New York 1966 – 'documenta 4', Kassel 1968 – 'Kunst der sechziger Jahre. Sammlung Ludwig', Wallraf-Richartz-Museum, Cologne 1969 – 'When Attitudes Become Form', Kunsthalle Bern, 1969 – 'Pop Art Redefined', Hayward Gallery, London 1969 – 'Sonsbeek 71', Arnheim 1971 – 'documenta 5', Kassel 1972 – 'Ekstrem Realisme', Louisiana Museum, Humlebaek 1973 – '200 Years of American Sculpture', Whitney Museum of American Art, New York 1976 – 'La Biennale di Venezia', Venice 1976 – 'Improbable Furniture', Institute of Contemporary Art of the University of Pennsylvania, Philadelphia 1977 – 'A View of a Decade', Museum of Contemporary Art, Chicago 1977 – 'American Paintings of the 1970s', Albright-Knox Art Gallery, Buffalo 1978 – 'La Biennale di Venezia', Venice 1980 – 'Reliefs', Westfälisches Landesmuseum für Kunst und Kulturgeschichte, Münster 1981 – 'Westkunst', Cologne 1981 – 'documenta 7', Kassel 1982 – 'Furniture, Furnishing. Subject and Object', Rhode Island School of Design, Providence 1983 – 'Alibis', Centre Georges Pompidou, Paris 1984 – 'Content. A Contemporary Focus', Hirshhorn Museum and Sculpture Garden, Smithsonian Institution, Washington 1984 – 'An American Renaissance. Paintings and Sculpture since 1940', Museum of Art, Fort Lauderdale, Florida 1986 – 'Skulptur Projekte in Münster', (DuMont) Cologne 1987 – 'documenta 8', Kassel 1987 – 'Cultural Geometry', Athens 1988 – 'Richard Artschwager. His Peers and Persuasion (1963–1988)', Daniel Weinberg Gallery,

Los Angeles 1988 – 'Bilderstreit', Cologne 1989 – 'Prospect 89', Frankfurt a. M. 1989 – 'Life-Size', Jerusalem 1990

Other Literature (Selection)
Elizabeth C. Baker: 'Artschwager's Mental Furniture', *Art News*, No. 9, 1968 – Gregory Battcock (ed.): *Minimal Art. A Critical Anthology*, New York 1968 – Carter Ratcliff: 'New York Letter', *Art International*, No. 6, 1972 – Bernhard Kerber: 'Richard Artschwager', *Kunstforum International*, Vol. 10, 1974 – Roberta Smith: 'The Artschwager Enigma', *Art in America*, No. 10, 1979 – Coosje van Bruggen: 'Richard Artschwager', *Artforum*, No. 1, 1983 – Ronald Jones: 'Arroganz und Interpretation', *Wolkenkratzer Art Journal*, No. 4, 1988 – Hein-Norbert Jocks: 'Richard Artschwager', *Kunstforum International*, Vol. 104, 1989 – Katharina Hegewisch: 'Richard Artschwager. Blp – Das Gleiche – sich selbst – das Verschiedene und der wechselnde Kontext', *Künstler. Kritisches Lexikon der Gegenwartskunst*, issue 5, Munich 1989 – 'Collaboration Richard Artschwager,' *Parkett*, No. 23, 1990

MIROSŁAW BAŁKA

Born Warsaw, 1958. Studied at Academy of Art, Warsaw, 1980–85. First one-man show there, 1984. Exhibitions at Pokaz Galeria Warsaw; Galeria Labirynt, Lublin; Galeria PO, Zielona Góra; Galeria Dziekanka, Warsaw; Galerie Claes Nordenhake, Stockholm; and elsewhere. From 1986, exhibi-

tions with the Neue Bieriemienost (N.B.) Group. Took part in 'Possible Worlds' exhibition, London, and Venice Biennale (Aperto), 1990. Lives in Otwock.

Bałka's sculptures are made from found, used materials. For him, the history of the material is more important than the history of art; so his sculptural works often relate to everyday objects and exploit their narrative content. At the same time, through a reduction to simple forms, they refer to the process of abstraction that makes them into objects of contemplation. On the border between function and non-function, the sculptures in Bałka's exhibitions set up a dramatized dialogue. Laden with memories, they stimulate the viewer's poetic, associative capacity. Bałka: 'There is a kind of nostalgia you have in your blood. For me there is no border between my life and my art, so it is difficult to say where life finishes and the art begins.'

Reference Sources for List of Exhibitions and Bibliography
'Mirosław Bałka. Good God', Galeria Dziekanka, Warsaw 1990 – 'Possible Worlds. Sculpture from Europe', Institute of Contemporary Arts, Serpentine Gallery, London, 1990

Catalogue
'Precepta patris mei servivi semper', Pokaz Galeria, Warsaw 1986

Catalogues of Collective Exhibitions (Selection)
'Co Slychac' (What's New), Zaklady Norblin (Norblin Factory), Warsaw 1987 – 'B.K.K.', Haag Centrum voor Aktuele Kunst, The Hague 1988 – 'Polish Realities', Third Eye Centre, Glasgow 1988 – 'Middle Europe', Artists Space, New York 1989 – 'Dialog', Kunstmuseum Düsseldorf, 1989 – 'La Biennale di Venezia', Venice 1990

Other Literature (Selection)
Anda Rottenberg: 'Draught. Is Contemporary Art Decadent? Situation Poland', *Nike*, No. 16, 1987 – Joanna Kiliszek: 'Mirosław Bałka at Dziekanka Gallery', *Flash Art*, May/June 1990 – J. St. Wojciechowski: 'Mirosław Bałka', *Flash Art*, No. 130, 1990 – Irma Schlagheck: 'Polen. Aufbruch aus dem Untergrund', *Art*, January 1991

FRIDA BARANEK

Born Rio de Janeiro, 1961. Studied architecture at Universidade Santa Ursula, Rio de Janeiro, 1978–83; sculpture at Escola de Artes Visuaís and at Museu de Arte Moderna, Rio de Janeiro, 1982–84; and sculpture at Parsons School of Design, New York, 1984–85. First one-woman show at Petite Galerie, Rio de Janeiro, 1985. Exhibitions at Galeria Sergio Milliet, Funarte, Rio de Janeiro; Gabinete de Arte Raquel Arnaud, São Paulo. Took part in Venice Biennale (Aperto), 1990. Lives in São Paulo.

The sculpture of Frida Baranek is marked by extremes of tension. Filigree 'iron clouds' impinge on compact, closed forms. The work plays on the contrast between open, intricate, near-chaotic structures and the articulated grids imposed by an ordering impulse. Iron wires, stones and distorted metal plates are combined into three-dimensional objects. Poetic relationships between heaviness and lightness are generated by the encounter between the language of the material and the formal intervention of the artist. Stasis is set against instability. Self-contained though it is, the sculpture has implications of mobility.

Reference Source for List of Exhibitions and Bibliography
'Frida Baranek', Gabinete de Arte Raquel Arnaud, São Paulo 1990

Catalogue
Galeria Sergio Milliet, Funarte, Rio de Janeiro 1988

Catalogues of Collective Exhibitions (Selection)
'Jaú e Arte. Um Compromisso', Jaú s/a construtora e incorporadora, São Paulo, n.d. (1989) – 'Bienal de São Paulo', 1989 – 'La Biennale di Venezia', Venice 1990 – 'Frida Baranek, Ivens Machado, Milton Machado, Daniel Senise, Angelo Venosa', Sala 1, Rome 1990

Other Literature (Selection)
Sônia Salzstein Goldberg: 'Frida Baranek', *Revizta Galeria*, No. 20, 1990 – Edward Leffingwell: 'Tropical Bazaar', *Art in America*, June 1990

GEORG BASELITZ

Born Deutschbaselitz, Saxony, 1938. Studied painting at Hochschule für bildende und angewandte Kunst, East Berlin, 1956–57; moved to the West and studied at Hochschule für bildende Künste, West Berlin, 1957–64. First exhibition, with Eugen Schönebeck, in a derelict house in Berlin. First one-man exhibition at Galerie Werner & Katz, Berlin; one-man exhibitions since 1964 at Galerie Werner, Berlin (later Cologne and New York). Exhibitions at Galerie Friedrich & Dahlem, Munich; Galerie Heiner Friedrich, Munich and Cologne; Anthony d'Offay Gallery, London; Galerie Springer, Berlin; Mary Boone/Michael Werner Gallery, New York; Galerie Fred Jahn, Munich; and elsewhere. Villa Romana scholarship, Florence, 1965. Took part in 'documenta 5', 1972; 'documenta 7', 1982. Professor at Staatliche Akademie der Bildenden Künste, Karlsruhe, 1977–83. Showed first sculptures in German Pavilion at Venice Biennale, 1980. Professor at Hochschule der Künste, Berlin, 1983–88. Awarded title of Chevalier de l'Ordre des Arts et des Lettres, Paris, 1989. Lives at Derneburg, near Hildesheim, Lower Saxony.

In content and in form, Baselitz's world of imagery is characterized by fractures, dislocations and contradictions. Since the outset of his career his work has always had a representational content; and yet what interests him is not the thing represented – the anecdote – but painting itself. Parts of the body, portraits, landscapes and animals are simply pretexts for physical, gestural

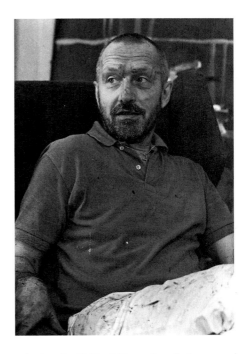

painting. In 1965–66 he painted pictures of male figures in isolation, including *Der neue Typ (The New Type)*. In 1966 he began to cut up, fragment, and rearrange the objects represented; this dismemberment heralded the inversion of the motif, which began in 1969. The object is painted upside-down in order to concentrate the viewer's attention on painting as painting. 'What happens in Baselitz's pictures is neither more nor less than what is visible in the pictures themselves. They are absolutely self-identical. His pictures are emancipated both from the context of the specific thinking that requires the picture to work as a picture and from the context of representation. Nor has his work anything to do with automatism: it is governed by the structural network of the elements of the inverted object. The picture is thus a genuinely autonomous, controlled object of sensory perception that has nothing to do with anything but itself.' (Theo Kneubühler) Since 1980, in addition to paintings, drawings, woodcuts and other prints, Baselitz has made wooden sculptures, which are rough-hewn and often painted.

Reference Source for List of Exhibitions and Bibliography
'Georg Baselitz', Kunsthaus Zurich, Städtische Kunsthalle Düsseldorf, 1990

Books and Writings by the Artist
1. *Pandämonium*, Manifesto with Eugen Schönebeck, Berlin 1961 – 2. *Pandämonium*, Manifesto with Eugen Schönebeck, Berlin 1962 – *Warum das Bild 'Die großen Freunde' ein gutes Bild ist!*, Berlin 1966 – *Zeichnungen zum Straßenbild*, Cologne 1982 – *Sächsische Motive*, Berlin 1985

Catalogues Raisonnés
Radierungen 1963–1974 / Holzschnitte 1966–1967, catalogue of prints, Städtisches Museum Leverkusen, Schloß Morsbroich, 1974 – *32 Linolschnitte aus den Jahren 1976–1979*, catalogue of large linocuts, Josef-Haubrich-Kunsthalle, Cologne 1979 – Fred Jahn: *Baselitz, peintre – graveur*, Vol. 1, catalogue of prints 1963–1974, Bern and Berlin 1983 – *Skulpturen und Zeichnungen 1979–1987*, catalogue of sculptures and of drawings for sculpture, Kestner-Gesellschaft, Hanover, 1987 – Fred Jahn: *Baselitz, peintre – graveur*, Vol. 2, catalogue of prints 1974–1982, Bern and Berlin 1987

Catalogues and Monographs (Selection)
Galerie Werner & Katz, Berlin 1963 – 'Zeichnungen', Kunstmuseum Basle, 1970 – 'Malerei, Handzeichnungen, Druckgraphik', Kunsthalle Bern, 1976 – 'La Biennale di Venezia', Venice 1980 – 'Georg Baselitz, Gerhard Richter', Städtische Kunsthalle Düsseldorf, 1981 – 'Das Straßenbild', Stedelijk Museum, Amsterdam 1981 – Kunstverein Braunschweig, 1981 – 'Holzplastik', Galerie Michael Werner, Cologne 1983 – 'Paintings 1960–83', Whitechapel Art Gallery, London 1983 – 'Zeichnungen 1958–1983', Kunstmuseum Basle, Stedelijk Van Abbemuseum, Eindhoven, 1984 – 'Skulpturen und Zeichnungen 1979–1987', Kestner-Gesellschaft, Hanover, 1987 – 'Dipinti 1965–1987', Palazzo Vecchio, Florence, Hamburger Kunsthalle, (Electa) Milan 1988 – Andreas Franzke: *Georg Baselitz*, Munich 1988 – 'Das Motiv. Bilder und Zeichnungen 1987–1988', Kunsthalle Bremen, 1988 – 'Holzschnitt 1966–1989', Kunsthalle Bielefeld, (Edition Cantz) Stuttgart 1989 – 'Bilder aus Berliner Privatbesitz', Staatliche Museen zu Berlin, Nationalgalerie, 1990

Catalogues of Collective Exhibitions (Selection)
'Figurationen', Württembergischer Kunstverein, Stuttgart 1967 – 'documenta 5', Kassel 1972 – 'Bienal de São Paulo', 1975 – 'documenta 6', Kassel 1977 – 'Der gekrümmte Horizont', Akademie der Künste, Berlin 1980 – 'A New Spirit in Painting', London 1981 – 'Westkunst', Cologne 1981 – 'documenta 7', Kassel 1982 – 'Zeitgeist', Berlin 1982 – 'Expressions', Saint Louis Art Museum, 1983 – 'Origen i Visió', Centre Cultural de la Caixa de Pensions, Barcelona 1984 – 'Skulptur im 20. Jahrhundert', Merian-Park, Basle 1984 – 'von hier aus', Düsseldorf, (DuMont) Cologne 1984 – 'La Grande Parade', Stedelijk Museum, Amsterdam 1984 – 'German Art in the 20th Century', Royal Academy of Arts, London, Staatsgalerie Stuttgart, (Prestel) Munich 1985 – 'Carnegie International', Museum of Art, Carnegie Institute, Pittsburgh 1985 – '1961 Berlinart 1987', The Museum of Modern Art, New York, (Prestel) Munich 1987 – 'Der unverbrauchte Blick', Berlin 1987 – 'Carnegie International', Carnegie Museum of Art, Pittsburgh 1988 – 'Refigured Painting. The German Image 1960–88', Toledo 1988, (Guggenheim Foundation) New York, (Prestel) Munich 1989 – 'Museum der Avantgarde. Die Sammlung Sonnabend New York', Berlin, (Electa) Milan 1989 – 'Open Mind', Ghent 1989 – 'Bilderstreit', Cologne 1989 – 'Einleuchten', Hamburg 1989

Other Literature (Selection)
Arwed D. Gorella: 'Der Fall Baselitz und das Gespräch', *Tendenzen*, No. 30, 1964 – Johannes Gachnang: 'Das Bild als Ereignis der Malerei', *Kunst-Nachrichten*, No. 1, 1976 – Wolfgang Max Faust/Gerd de Vries: *Hunger nach Bildern. Deutsche Malerei der Gegenwart*, Cologne 1982 – Andreas Franzke: *Skulpturen und Objekte von Malern des 20. Jahrhunderts*, Cologne 1982 – Mario Diacono: *Verso una nuova iconografia*, Reggio Emilia 1984 – Dieter Koepplin: 'Baselitz und Munch', *Kunst-Bulletin*, No. 7/8, 1985 – Johannes Gachnang: *Reisebilder. Berichte zur zeitgenössischen Kunst*, Vienna 1985 – Rudi Fuchs: 'Baselitz, peinture', *Artstudio*, No. 2, 1986 – 'Collaboration Georg Baselitz,' *Parkett*, No. 11, 1986 – Klaus Honnef: 'Kunst der Gegenwart', Cologne 1988 – Georg Baselitz: 'Galerie Baselitz, 17 Bilder nebst einem Selbstgespräch', *Du*, No. 7, 1989

ROSS BLECKNER

Born New York, 1949. Studied at New York University until 1971; California Institute of the Arts, Valencia, until 1973. First one-man show at Cunningham Ward Gallery, New York, 1975; one-man shows since 1979 at Mary Boone Gallery, New York. Exhibitions at Waddington Galleries, London; Galerie Max Hetzler, Cologne; Akira Ikeda Gallery, Tokyo; and elsewhere. Took part in 'Bi Nationale', Boston and Düsseldorf, 1988. Lives in New York.

Bleckner's painting is done in cycles, defined by technique and theme. He first made a reputation with his stripe paintings, works that have only the most tenuous connection with op art. They mark a confrontation with painting, in which strict geometry undergoes a metamorphosis into 'landscape'. Imprecise flecks of colour, or added ornamental elements, cause the stripes to start to flicker atmospherically. In Bleckner's many-faceted œuvre – which embraces paintings of the 'architecture of the sky' and of interiors, light phenomena and ornaments – he makes free use of art-historical quotations, visions and basic architectural patterns. The hallmark of his painting is an intense concern with light/dark contrasts; these often range as far as hallucinatory lightning flashes. Bleckner's paintings are built up layer by layer and treated with fire, wax, varnish and other materials. The result is a characteristic and unmistakable transparent skin, which imparts an 'inner glow' to the motifs. Ross Bleckner: 'The most interesting art is, in a way, the most despondent art... I've always been more interested in failed imagery and repressed imagery than in big popular imagery. I like a painting to possess a sense of theatre, a play between mood and confrontation. I want a constant expansion and contraction of sets of images. That way I can deal with the idea of disillusionment and collapse.'

Reference Source for List of Exhibitions and Bibliography
'Ross Bleckner', Kunsthalle Zurich, 1990 (later shown at Kölnischer Kunstverein, Cologne, Moderna Museet, Stockholm)

Catalogues and Monographs (Selection)
Mary Boone/Michael Werner Gallery, New York 1983 – Waddington Galleries, London 1988 – San Francisco Museum of Modern Art, 1988 – Mario Diacono Gallery, Boston 1989 – Milwaukee Art Museum, 1989 – Galería Soledad Lorenzo, Madrid 1990

Catalogues of Collective Exhibitions (Selection)
'Endgame. Reference and Simulation in Recent Painting and Sculpture', Institute of Contemporary Art, Boston 1986 – 'Biennial Exhibition', Whitney Museum of American Art, New York 1987 – 'Post-Abstract Abstraction', Aldrich Museum of Contemporary Art, Ridgefield, Connecticut 1987 – 'The Image of Abstraction', Museum of Contemporary Art, Los Angeles 1988 – 'The BiNational. American Art of the Late 80's', Boston, (DuMont) Cologne 1988 – 'NY Art Now. The Saatchi Collection', London 1988 – 'Carnegie International', Carnegie Museum of Art, Pittsburgh 1988 – 'Prospect 89', Frankfurt a.M. 1989 – 'Wiener Diwan. Sigmund Freud heute', Museum des 20. Jahrhunderts, Vienna, (Ritter Verlag) Klagenfurt 1989 – 'Weitersehen', Krefeld 1990

Other Literature (Selection)
Peter Halley: 'Ross Bleckner. Painting at the End of History', *Arts Magazine,* May 1982 – Robert Pincus-Witten: 'Defenestrations. Robert Longo and Ross Bleckner', *Arts Magazine,* November 1982 – Donald Kuspit: 'Ross Bleckner', *Artforum,* April 1984 – Dan Cameron: 'On Ross Bleckner's "Atmosphere" Paintings', *Arts Magazine,* February 1987 – Gianfranco Mantegna: 'The Ellipse of Reality. Ross Bleckner', *Tema Celeste,* May 1987 – John Zinsser: 'Ross Bleckner' (Interview), *Journal of Contemporary Art,* March 1988 – Stephen Ellis: 'Spleen and Ideal', *Parkett,* No. 20, 1989 – Lawrence Chua: 'Ross Bleckner', *Flash Art,* November 1989 – Norbert Messler: '"The Sky is Thin as Paper Here". Zu den Licht- und Nachtbildern von Ross Bleckner', *Noema Art Magazin,* No. 28, 1990

JONATHAN BOROFSKY

Born Boston, Massachusetts, 1942. Studied at Carnegie Mellon University, Pittsburgh, and Ecole de Fontainebleau, 1964; Yale School of Art and Architecture, New Haven, 1966. Taught at School of Visual Arts, New York, 1969–77; California Institute of the Arts, Los Angeles, 1977–80. First one-man show at Artists Space, New York, 1973; one-man shows since 1975 at Paula Cooper Gallery, New York. Exhibitions at Protetch McIntosh Gallery, Washington;

Galerie Rudolf Zwirner, Cologne; and elsewhere. Showed in 'documenta 7' and at Berlin 'Zeitgeist' exhibition, both 1982. Lives in Venice, California.

In the early 1970s Borofsky became known for works consisting of numbers written on sheets of paper, which he began in 1969 with the number 1. He exhibited his 'number work' as a stack of papers at his first one-man show in 1973. Numbers thereafter continued to appear in his sketches, self-portraits, and dream notations. These almost daily notes formed the basis of the installations that he began to build in 1975, combining wall-drawings, paintings, objects, sculptures, etc., under the heading 'All Is One' – so that every exhibition space becomes a *Gesamtkunstwerk,* a total work of art. Specific figures – running, flying, hammering beings, perforated silhouettes, skeletons, fishes, or a man in a hat – often run like leitmotifs through these installations, which frequently also exploit light and shadow effects. Borofsky first presented his *Ballerina-Clown* to the public in an installation in 1983. This is a three-dimensional version of the 1981 drawing *Entertainer (Self-Portraits as a Clown).* Since 1989 a version of this clown, over 10 metres (33 feet) high, has stood on a public building in Venice, California. In an interview, Borofsky said of it: 'I think it's a work of the imagination, and I think it's also conceptual. There's some thought going on here when I tell you that it's a reconciliation of opposites, a symbol of two different kinds of beings – male, female; two different kinds of performers. I've got some thoughts going on here as well about the symbol having some meaning. It's quite brash in its visualness, and it jumps right out at you. It's not something you have seen before. I know it's challenging to a lot of people.'

Reference Sources for List of Exhibitions and Bibliography
'Jonathan Borofsky', Philadelphia Museum of Art, The Whitney Museum of American Art, New York, 1984 (later shown in: Berkeley, Minneapolis, Washington) – 'Jonathan Borofsky', Tokyo Metropolitan Art Museum, The Museum of Modern Art, Shiga, 1987

Films
I dreamed a dog was walking a tightrope at 2,671,472, Videotape, 1980 – *Man in Space. Videotape 2*, 1982/83 – *Prisoners*, Videotape, 1985

Catalogues and Monographs (Selection)
'Dreams', Institute of Contemporary Arts, London, Kunsthalle Basle, 1981 – 'Zeichnungen' 1960–83, Kunstmuseum Basle, 1983 – Moderna Museet, Stockholm 1984

Catalogues of Collective Exhibitions (Selection)
'557,087', Seattle Art Museum, 1969 – '955,000', Vancouver Art Gallery, 1970 – '1979 Biennial Exhibition', Whitney Museum of American Art, New York 1979 – 'Drawing Distinctions. American Drawings of the Seventies', Louisiana Museum of Modern Art, Humlebaek 1981 – 'Westkunst-heute', Cologne 1981 – 'documenta 7', Kassel 1982 – 'Zeitgeist', Berlin 1982 – 'New York Now', Kestner-Gesellschaft, Hanover, 1982 – 'Bilder der Angst und der Bedrohung', Kunsthaus Zurich, 1983 – 'American Art since 1970', La Jolla Museum of Contemporary Art, La Jolla, California 1984 – 'Prospect 86', Frankfurt a.M. 1986 – '1961 Berlinart 1987', The Museum of Modern Art, New York, (Prestel) Munich 1987 – 'L'Epoque, la mode, la morale, la passion', Paris 1987 – 'The Biennale of Sydney', 1990

Other Literature (Selection)
Lucy Lippard: 'Jonathan Borofsky at 2,096,974', *Artforum*, November 1974 – Joan Simon: 'Jonathan Borofsky' (Interview), *Art in America*, November 1981 – Annelie Pohlen: 'Jonathan Borofsky. Zeichnungen', *Kunstforum International*, Vol. 66, 1983 – Richard Armstrong: 'Jonathan Borofsky', *Artforum*, February 1984 – Henriette Väth-Hinz: 'Jonathan Borofsky' (Interview), *Wolkenkratzer Art Journal*, No. 7, 1985 – Jane Hart: 'Substantive Spirit. Jonathan Borofsky's Projections', *Cover*, May 1990

JEAN-MARC BUSTAMANTE

Born Toulouse, 1952. First one-man show at Galerie Baudoin Lebon, Paris, 1982. Worked and exhibited in collaboration with Bernard Bazile as 'Bazilebustamante', 1983–87. One-man shows at Galerie Ghislaine Hussenot, Paris, since 1988. Exhibitions at Galerie Joost Declercq, Ghent; Galerie Paul Andriesse, Amsterdam; and elsewhere. Took part in 'documenta 8', 1987. Lives in Paris.

After a number of performances and works incorporating video and photography, and after the end of his collaboration with the artist Bernard Bazile, Bustamante began to concentrate on the sculptural qualities of everyday things. Under the title of *Interiors*, he has exhibited 'furniture-objects' including beds, tables and a baby's cradle. These objects are denatured, like models. They still recall their original function; but in the art context – and as art – the deliberate rejection of function, together with their spatial isolation, endows them with an intangible presence, that makes them into autonomous sculptures. Bustamante has pursued this concern with presence and memory in a number of cupboard-like sculptures, in image-laden shelving, and in colourful box-like objects made to evoke *Landscapes*. Large photographic blow-ups of unpeopled landscapes, flowers and interiors stand out from the wall and act as a counterpoint both to the sculptures and to the rooms where they appear. These 'stand-out' reproductions introduce quotations from reality into spaces in which they create a state of contemplative tranquillity.

Reference Source for List of Exhibitions
'Bustamante', Kunsthalle Bern, 1989

Catalogues (Selection)
Museum Haus Lange, Krefeld 1990 – 'Paysages, intérieurs', ARC Musée d'Art Moderne de la Ville de Paris, 1990

Catalogues of Collective Exhibitions (Selection)
With Bernard Bazile: 'Alles und noch viel mehr. Das poetische ABC', Kunsthalle Bern, Kunstmuseum Bern, 1985 – 'La Biennale di Venezia', Venice 1986 – 'The Biennale of Sydney', 1986 – 'Sonsbeek 86', Arnheim 1986 – 'A Distanced View', New Museum of Contemporary Art, New York 1986 – 'Die Große Oper oder die Sehnsucht nach dem Erhabenen', Bonner Kunstverein, Bonn 1987 – 'L'Epoque, la mode, la morale, la passion', Paris 1987
'documenta 8', Kassel 1987 – 'Possible Worlds. Sculpture from Europe, Institute of Contemporary Arts', Serpentine Gallery, London 1990 – 'Weitersehen', Krefeld 1990

Other Literature (Selection)
Jérôme Sans: 'Jean-Marc Bustamante', *Flash Art* (Italian edition), Summer 1988 – Paul Andriesse: 'Photographs by Jean-Marc Bustamante', *Kunst & Museumsjournaal*, No. 2, 1990 – Jean-François Chevrier: 'Jean-Marc Bustamante. Le lieu de l'Art' (Interview), *Galeries Magazine*, February/March 1990

JAMES LEE BYARS

Born Detroit, 1932. First of seven extended visits to Japan, 1957. First group action in 1960, also the stone sculpture *Tantric Figure* for the Whitney Museum, New York. Exhibition 'Ten Philosophical Sentences' at Jisha University, Kyoto, and one-man show at Marion Willard Gallery, New York, 1961. Founded World Question Center in 1969. One-man shows at Wide White Space, Antwerp, 1969 and 1973, and from 1971 onward at Galerie Michael Werner, Cologne. Exhibitions at Galerie René Block, Berlin; Galerie des Beaux-Arts, Brussels; Mary Boone Gallery, New York; and elsewhere. Took part in 'documenta 5', 1972, 'documenta 6', 1977, 'documenta 7', 1982. DAAD scholarship in Berlin, 1974. Action *The Holy Ghost*, in Piazza San Marco, for 1975 Venice Biennale. Lives in New York and Venice.

Byars may be described as a philosophical artist; his work is a pursuit of perfection. Even in his earliest performances he began to celebrate 'beauty', and to make it available through inexpensive materials – cloth or paper. The physical presence, the immaculateness and the colours of his materials combine in his work with minimal gestures, spoken or written language, and references to the East Asian aesthetic of simplicity. The artist himself appears before the public in fantastic garments or headgear, and sometimes blindfolded. This visibility on his part is meant to remain an unsolved riddle and at the same time an aesthetic 'revelation'; for what most interests Byars is questions. In all his meticulously assembled books, and in his statements in exhibition catalogues, he never vouchsafes an answer. The same attitude also defines this artist's objects and spatial creations. Minimalized basic forms, such as circles, crescents, spheres or rectangular blocks, each made in a range of sizes and materials – porphyry, marble, sandstone, paper – are silently arranged in the space. The colours gold, red and black have a special part to play in this: they operate to place the individual objects in a state of perfection and immateriality, and to define the environment. The *Golden Tower*, 333 metres high, which was presented in model form at Galerie Springer, Berlin, in 1974, remains a utopian dream. For the exhibition 'GegenwartEwigkeit', in 1990, Byars erected a 20-metre *Golden Tower with Changing Tops* in the courtyard of the Martin-Gropius-Bau. 'Beauty comes to light at the point where the possibilities of the real

coincide with the necessities of the ideal. To detect that point, over and over again, is the art of James Lee Byars; he has tamed beauty.' (Stephan Schmidt-Wulffen)

Reference Source for List of Exhibitions and Bibliography
James Elliott: *The Perfect Thought. Works by James Lee Byars*, University Art Museum, University of California, Berkeley 1990

Catalogues and Monographs (Selection)
'100.000 Minutes or 1/2 an Autobiography or the First Paper of Philosophy', Wide White Space, Antwerp 1969 – 'TH FI TO IN PH', Städtisches Museum Mönchengladbach, 1977 – Kunsthalle Bern, 1978 – 'Sechs Arbeiten', Galerie Michael Werner, Cologne 1981 – Westfälischer Kunstverein, Münster 1982 – Stedelijk Van Abbemuseum, Eindhoven 1983 – 'The Philosophical Palace / Palast der Philosophie', Städtische Kunsthalle Düsseldorf, 1986 – 'Beauty Goes Avantgarde', Galerie Michael Werner, Cologne 1987 – 'The Palace of Good Luck', Castello di Rivoli, Museo d'Arte Contemporanea, Turin 1989 – 'The Monument to Cleopatra', Galleria Cleto Polcina Artemoderna, Rome 1989

Catalogues of Collective Exhibitions (Selection)
'Prospect 69', Städtische Kunsthalle Düsseldorf, 1969 – 'Bilder, Objekte, Filme, Konzepte', Städtische Galerie im Lenbachhaus, Munich 1973 – 'documenta 6', Kassel 1977 – 'La Biennale di Venezia', Venice 1980 – 'Westkunst', Cologne 1981 – 'documenta 7', Kassel 1982 – 'Zeitgeist', Berlin 1982 – 'to the happy few. Bücher, Bilder, Objekte aus der Sammlung Speck', Museum Haus Lange, Museum Haus Esters, Krefeld 1983 – 'Skulptur im 20. Jahrhundert', Merian-Park, Basle 1984 – 'Ouverture', Castello di Rivoli, Turin 1984 – 'Spuren, Skulpturen und Monumente ihrer präzisen Reise', Kunsthaus Zurich, 1986 – 'La Biennale di Venezia', Venice 1986 – 'Beuys zu Ehren', Städtische Galerie im Lenbachhaus, Munich 1986 – 'Europa / Amerika. Die Geschichte einer künstlerischen Faszination seit 1940', Museum Ludwig, Cologne 1986 – 'SkulpturSein', Städtische Kunsthalle Düsseldorf, 1986 – 'Der unverbrauchte Blick', Berlin 1987 – 'Die Gleichzeitigkeit des Anderen', Kunstmuseum Bern, 1987 – 'documenta 8', Kassel 1987 – 'Übrigens sterben immer die Anderen. Marcel Duchamp und die Avantgarde seit 1950', Museum Ludwig, Cologne 1988 – 'Zeitlos', Berlin, (Prestel) Munich 1988 – 'Bilderstreit', Cologne 1989 – 'Wiener Diwan. Sigmund Freud heute', Museum des 20. Jahrhunderts, Vienna, (Ritter Verlag) Klagenfurt 1989 – 'Open Mind', Ghent 1989 – 'GegenwartEwigkeit', Martin-Gropius-Bau, Berlin 1990 – 'The Biennale of Sydney', 1990

Other Literature (Selection)
Harald Szeemann: 'James Lee Byars', *Chroniques de l'Art Vivant*, No. 40, 1973 – Reiner Speck: 'James Lee Byars', *Der Löwe*, No. 7, 1976 – Thomas Deecke: 'James Lee Byars. Aktionen und Ereignisse der Perfektion', *Kunstmagazin*, No. 1, 1979 – Thomas McEvilley: 'James Lee Byars and the Atmosphere of Question', *Artforum*, Summer 1981 – Remo Guidieri: 'Al di là della barriera. James Lee Byars', *Tema Celeste*, No. 9, 1986 – Stephan Schmidt-Wulffen: 'Schlafende Krokodile belauschen. Mit James Lee Byars auf Besuch im "Palast der Philosophie"', *Kunstforum International*, Vol. 87, 1987 – Wim van Mulders: 'This is the Ghost of James Lee Byars Calling', *Artefactum*, February/March 1988 – Donald Kuspit: 'James Lee Byars', *Artforum*, Summer 1989

PEDRO CABRITA REIS

Born Lisbon, 1956. One-man shows since 1986 at Galeria Cómicos, Lisbon. Exhibitions at Galeria Roma e Pavia, Porto; Bess Cutler Gallery, New York; Galería Juana de Aizpuru, Madrid; Galerie Joost Declercq, Ghent; Barbara Farber Gallery, Amsterdam; and elsewhere. Took part in the exhibition 'Ponton. Temse', Temse, Belgium, 1990. Lives in Lisbon.

With simple materials – panels, laths, plaster moulds – and with everyday props and lengths of tubing, Cabrita Reis makes sculptural arrangements that create associational spaces defined by the titles of his works, such as *La casa del silencio blanco (The House of White Silence)*. Outdoor and indoor installations combine architectural situations with a synthetic language of forms. Reality and artificiality, complexity and simplicity, an aesthetic of materials and an aesthetic of allusive quotation, are maintained in a tense equilibrium. The installations become spaces for experience. 'These rooms are, of course, inner spaces where we talk to ourselves and where we gather with our shadows. Their thresholds are both those we cross and those we discover within ourselves.' (Kevin Power)

Reference Source for List of Exhibitions
'Cabrita Reis, Rui Sanches. Arte Portugues Contemporaneo I', Fundación Luis Cernuda, Sala de Exposiciones, Seville 1990

Catalogues and Monographs (Selection)
'Cabeças, Árvores e Casas', Galeria Roma e Pavia, Porto 1988 – 'Melancolia', Bess Cut-

ler Gallery, New York 1989 – 'Alexandria', Convento de S. Francisco, Beja, Portugal 1990 – Contemporary Art Foundation, Amsterdam 1990

Catalogues of Collective Exhibitions (Selection)
'Le XXème au Portugal', Centre Albert Borschette, Brussels 1986 – 'Lusitanies. Aspects de l'Art Contemporain Portugais', Centre Culturel de l'Albigeois, Albi 1987 – 'Cabrita Reis, Gerardo Burmester, Nancy Dwyer, Stephan Huber', Galeria Pedro Oliveira / Roma e Pavia, Porto 1990 – 'Ponton. Temse', Museum van Hedendaagse Kunst, Ghent 1990 – 'Carnet de voyages – 1', Fondation Cartier pour l'Art Contemporain, Jouy-en-Josas 1990

UMBERTO CAVENAGO

Born Milan, 1959. First one-man show at Galleria Franz Paludetto, Turin, 1988. Exhibitions at Studio Marconi 17, Milan; Galleria Pinta, Genoa; Galerie Jean-Christophe Aguas, Bordeaux; and elsewhere. Took part in Venice Biennale (Aperto), 1990. Lives in Milan.

Cavenago's large metal constructions quote from everyday, mobile objects: lorries, bicycles, cranes, rail trucks. Drastically simplified, pared down almost to basic three-dimensional forms, they are transformed into sculptural objects. Monumental wheels underpin compact superstructures that sometimes look like great columns. The effect is one of motion in

stillness. Most of the works in which the artist operates with this paradox are conceived in terms of a specific space, in which they appear to support the ceiling. In their capacity as autonomous sculptures, such installations possess a simultaneous narrative element: the myth and the naivety of the machine.

Reference Source for List of Exhibitions
'Umberto Cavenago. Sala d'Attesa', Galleria Franz Paludetto, Turin 1988

Catalogues of Collective Exhibitions (Selection)
'Eleonora', Palazzo Ducale, Mantua 1987 – 'Il Cielo e Dintorni. Da Zero all'Infinito', Castello di Volpaia, Radda in Chianti 1988 – 'Palestra', Castello di Rivara, Rivara Canavese/Turin 1988 – 'Davvero. Ragioni Pratiche nell'Arte', L'Osservatorio, Milan 1988 – 'Examples. New Italian Art', Riverside Studios, London 1989 – 'Punti di Vista', Studio Marconi, Milan 1989 – 'La Biennale di Venezia', Venice 1990 – 'Arte e Comice', Palazzo Moroni, Bergamo 1990

Other Literature (Selection)
Anthony Iannacci: 'Umberto Cavenago', *Artforum*, No. 8, 1989 – Angela Vettese: 'Umberto Cavenago' (Interview), *Flash Art* (Italian edition), No. 156, 1990

CLEGG & GUTTMANN

Michael Clegg and Martin Guttmann were born in 1957. They have been working jointly since 1980. First joint show at Annina Nosei Gallery, New York, 1981. Exhibitions at Jay Gorney Modern Art, New York; Galerie Ghislaine Hussenot, Paris; Achim Kubinski, Stuttgart; and elsewhere. Took part in 'Prospect 86', Frankfurt am Main, 1986. They live in New York.

Clegg & Guttmann have made their reputation with carefully staged portraits of individuals, couples and groups. Initially, the sitters were mainly men, who assumed the attitudes of corporate executives, men of power and wealth, with symbolic and often artificial photographic backgrounds. Like seventeenth-century Dutch portrait painters, Clegg &Guttmann produce 'images of dominance'. They take on the role of the artist who works to a commission and involves the sitter, or else they arrange actors in groups. Clegg & Guttmann: 'We work as a team; our idea of making art presupposes an elaborate self-reflexive pro-

cess of production. – We use photographic language without thereby assuming the 'Photographic Moment', 'Reality Framed', etc. – We want to free our work from the standardized mode of photographic presentation as well as our own specific history. – Our reader is a person who can use the work, complete it, live through the work.' As well as portraits, Clegg & Guttmann photograph still lifes and – since 1986 – landscapes with art historical connections. The subjects of their most recent photographs have been library catalogues.

Reference Source for List of Exhibitions and Bibliography
'Clegg & Guttmann. Corporate Landscapes', Kunstverein Bremerhaven, Museum Schloß Hardenberg, Velbert, 1989

Catalogues and Monographs (Selection)
Galerie Löhrl am Abteiberg, Mönchengladbach 1985 – Achim Kubinski, Stuttgart 1987 – 'Collected Portraits', Württembergischer Kunstverein, Stuttgart, (Giancarlo Politi Editore) Milan 1988 – 'Portraits de groupes de 1980 à 1989', CAPC Musée d'Art Contemporain de Bordeaux, 1989

Catalogues of Collective Exhibitions (Selection)
'Infotainment', Texas Gallery, Houston, (J. Berg Press) New York 1985 – 'Prospect 86', Frankfurt a. M. 1986 – 'Biennial Exhibition', Whitney Museum of American Art,

New York 1987 – 'Fake', New Museum of Contemporary Art, New York 1987 – 'Contemporary Photographic Portraiture', Musée Saint-Pierre, Lyon 1988 – 'Locations', Galerie im Taxispalais, Innsbruck 1988 – 'Artificial Nature', Deste Foundation for Contemporary Art, House of Cyprus, Athens 1990 – 'Le désenchantement du monde', Villa Arson, Centre National d'Art Contemporain, Nice 1990

Other Literature (Selection)
Klaus Honnef: 'Clegg & Guttmann', Kunstforum International, Vol. 84, 1986 – Verena Auffermann: 'Das Leben wird inszeniert', Westermanns Monatshefte, November 1986 – Jerry Saltz: Beyond Boundaries, New York 1986 – David Robbins: 'Clegg & Guttmann' (Interview), Wolkenkratzer Art Journal, No. 2, 1987 – Klaus Ottmann: 'Clegg & Guttmann', Flash Art, No. 139, 1988 – Sylvie Couderc: 'Distance et Possession. Les Photographies de Jeff Wall et de Clegg & Guttmann', Artefactum, No. 25, 1988 – David Robbins: The Camera Believes Everything, Stuttgart 1988 – Nancy Spector: 'Breaking the Codes', Contemporanea, No. 6, 1989 – Urs Stahel: 'Clegg & Guttmann', Kunstforum International, Vol. 107, 1990

RENÉ DANIËLS

Born Eindhoven, 1950. One-man shows since 1978 at Galerie Helen van der Meij, later Galerie Paul Andriesse, Amsterdam. Exhibitions at Metro Pictures, New York; Produzentengalerie, Hamburg; Galerie Joost Declercq, Ghent; Galerie Rudolf Zwirner, Cologne; and elsewhere. Took part in 'documenta 7' and in 'Zeitgeist' exhibition, Berlin, 1982. Lives in Amsterdam.

Daniëls' painting is a distanced and many-layered confrontation with art, with the exhibition industry, and with the art trade. After a succession of paintings that reacted – often in witty and startling ways – to various aspects of artistic and literary modernism, he embarked in the mid 1980s on a series of perspective views of interiors containing 'pictures'. Title, conception and pictorial structure shift from one work to the next, as the work is constantly carried forward by a process of omission, addition, colour-change and metamorphosis. Eventually, the spatial perspective is transformed into an agglomeration of free-floating forms reminiscent of bow ties. Daniëls

pursues the exhibition theme in pictures in which scraps of text proliferate topographically. His attitude is one of sly humour, bringing fun into the seeming seriousness of the art trade by drawing on ambiguities of language and image. 'René Daniëls' work as a whole is structured as follows: one work is linked to another through obvious signs of likeness and avoids fitting into a pattern through obvious signs of unlikeness. The starting-point for the next picture is another element of unlikeness, and so on. Each new work thus takes René Daniëls one step further in the expansion of his œuvre, for which there is no predetermined plan, no strategy, and which has, in fact, the structure of a labyrinth.' (Ulrich Loock)

Reference Source for List of Exhibitions and Bibliography
'René Daniëls. Lentebloesem', Maison de la Culture et de la Communication, Saint-Etienne, Museum Boymans-van Beuningen, Rotterdam, (Galerie Paul Andriesse) Amsterdam 1990

Catalogues and Monographs (Selection)
Stedelijk Van Abbemuseum, Eindhoven 1978 – 'Schilderijen en tekeningen 1976–1986', Stedelijk Van Abbemuseum, Eindhoven 1986 – 'Kades-Kaden', Kunsthalle Bern, 1987

Catalogues of Collective Exhibitions (Selection)
'Westkunst-heute', Cologne 1981 – 'documenta 7', Kassel 1982 – ''60 '80 attitudes /

concepts / images', Stedelijk Museum, Amsterdam 1982 – 'Zeitgeist', Berlin 1982 – 'Steirischer Herbst 88', Grazer Kunstverein, Graz 1988 – 'Bilderstreit', Cologne 1989 – 'Weitersehen', Krefeld 1990

Other Literature (Selection)

Paul Groot: 'René Daniëls', *Flash Art*, No. 104, 1981 – Alied Ottevanger: 'Meanwhile … een tentoonstelling van René Daniëls in New York', *Metropolis M*, No. 2, 1984 – Jeanne Silverthorne: 'Rene Daniëls', *Artforum*, March 1985 – Els Hoek: 'René Daniëls 1978–1986 Onvoltooid verleden tijd', *Metropolis M*, No. 2, 1986 – Renate Puvogel: 'René Daniëls', *Das Kunstwerk*, June 1987 – Paolo Bianchi / Christoph Doswald: 'René Daniëls. Kades-Kaden', *Kunstforum International*, Vol. 91, 1987 – Alain Cueff: 'René Daniëls. The Space of Transitive Images', *Parkett*, Nr. 15, 1988 – Arno Vriends: 'René Daniëls', *Artefactum*, No. 33, 1990

IAN DAVENPORT

Born Sidcup, Kent, 1966. Studied at Northwich College of Art and Design, 1984–85; Goldsmith's College, London, 1985–88. One-man show at Waddington Galleries, London, 1990. Took part in 'British Art Show 1990' (travelling exhibition). Lives in London.

In Davenport's large paintings, the process of painting becomes its own theme. Monochrome vertical brushstrokes, mostly black or grey, are applied in large flat areas. The qualities of the application of the paint – the way it runs down the surface, the rhythm of the painting process – give the

paintings their individual structure. In a number of works, the use of controlled chance extends to the introduction of electric fans to direct the paint as it flows across the surface of the painting. A dialectical tension arises between the painted ground and its overpainting. Expression allies itself with the anonymity of self-generating runs of paint.

Reference Source for List of Exhibitions and Bibliography

'Ian Davenport', Waddington Galleries, London 1990

Catalogues of Collective Exhibitions (Selection)

'Th British Art Show 1990', McLellan Galleries, Glasgow, (South Bank Centre) London 1990 – 'Carnet de voyages-1', Fondation Cartier pour l'Art Contemporain, Jouy-en-Josas 1990

Other Literature (Selection)

Michael Archer: 'Ian Davenport, Gary Hume, Michael Landy. Karsten Schubert Gallery', *Artforum*, No. 6, 1989 – Liam Gillick: 'Ian Davenport', *Artscribe*, March/April 1990 – Enrique Juncosa: 'Ian Davenport', *Lápiz*, No. 72, 1990 – Inter Alia (Dave Beech / Mark Hutchinson): 'Ian Davenport. Waddingtons', *Artscribe*, January/February 1991

JIŘI GEORG DOKOUPIL

Born Krnov, Czechoslovakia, 1954. Studied in Cologne, Frankfurt am Main and New York, 1976–78. After a number of collective exhibitions with the Mülheimer Freiheit group, one-man shows since 1987 at Galerie Paul Maenz, Cologne. Exhibitions at Chantal Crousel, Paris; Leo Castelli Gallery, Sonnabend Gallery and Robert Miller Gallery, New York; Galería Juana de Aizpuru, Madrid and Seville; and elsewhere. Took part in 'documenta 7', 1982. Guest lecturer at Staatliche Kunstakademie, Düsseldorf, 1983–84, and Círculo de Bellas Artes, Madrid, 1989. Lives in Tenerife, Madrid and New York.

Around 1980, together with Peter Bömmels, Walter Dahn, Hans Georg Adamski, Gerhard Naschberger and Gerard Kever, Dokoupil was a member of the Mülheimer Freiheit group, a studio collective that generated a positive torrent of pictures in a vein of stylistic pluralism, irony, anarchy, and enjoyment of the commonplace. Even since the dissolution of the group, this

basic attitude has continued to prevail in Dokoupil's work as a whole. Clusters of works are held together by recurrent motifs, techniques or concepts: taboo-breaking, stylistic shifts, a blend of banalities with kitsch and stock symbols, or the plundering of art history. In 1983, working in conjunction with Walter Dahn, Dokoupil painted *Duschbilder (Shower Pictures)* and *Afrikabilder (Africa Pictures)*; in 1984 *Schnuller-Bilder (Baby's Dummy/Pacifier Pictures)*; and in 1984–85 *Kinder-Bilder (Children's Pictures)*. There followed, in 1985, *Sprachbilder (Language Pictures)*, sculptures made up of brand names, and landscape pictures; in 1986 a *New York-Serie (New York Series)*, in

1987 *Jesus-Bilder (Jesus Pictures)* and *Sternzeichen-Bilder (Star Sign Pictures)*; in 1989 *Rußbilder (Soot Pictures)* based on photographs; in 1990 *Muttermilch-Bilder (Breastmilk Pictures)* and *Frucht-Bilder (Fruit Pictures)*. 'A nostalgic obsession and a wasteland of consciousness, of banality and helplessness, find reflection in the extraordinary paintings of Dokoupil; in them, the perennial oscillation between irreconcilable possibilities and between opposing standpoints is made manifest.' (Armin Zweite)

Reference Source for List of Exhibitions and Bibliography

'Jiři Georg Dokoupil', Fundación Caja de Pensiones, Madrid 1989

Catalogues and Monographs (Selection)

'Neue Kölner Schule', Galerie Paul Maenz, Cologne 1982 – 'Die Duschbilder. Ricki 1982/1983' (works in collaboration with Walter Dahn), Produzentengalerie Hamburg, (Paul Maenz) Cologne 1983 – 'Die Afrika-Bilder' (works in collaboration with Walter Dahn), Groninger Museum, 1984 – 'Arbeiten aus 1981–84', Museum Folkwang, Essen, (Walther König) Cologne 1984 – 'Corporations & Products. The Sculptures / Die Skulpturen', Galerie Paul Maenz, Cologne 1985 – 'Bienal de São Paulo', 1985 – Ernst A. Busche / Paul Maenz (ed.): *Jiři Georg Dokoupil*, Cologne 1987 – Galerie Paul Maenz, Cologne, and Galería Leyendecker, Santa Cruz de Tenerife, 1987 – Robert Miller Gallery, New York 1989 – 'Zodiac', (Edition Bischofberger) Zurich 1989

In conjunction with a number of different galleries, Dokoupil has published seven volumes of his 'Drawings' to date.

Catalogues of Collective Exhibitions (Selection)

'Bildwechsel. Neue Malerei aus Deutschland', Akademie der Künste, Berlin 1981 – 'Nieuwe Duitse Kunst. I. Mülheimer Freiheit', Groninger Museum, 1981 – 'Die heimliche Wahrheit. Mülheimer Freiheit', Kunstverein Freiburg, 1981 – 'Die Seefahrt und der Tod. Mülheimer Freiheit', Kunsthalle Wilhelmshaven, 1981 – 'documenta 7', Kassel 1982 – 'La Biennale di Venezia', Venice 1982 – 'Zeitgeist', Berlin 1982 – 'ROSC. A Poetry of Vision', Dublin 1984 – 'von hier aus', Düsseldorf, (DuMont) Cologne 1984 – 'Origen i Visió', Centre Cultural de la Caixa de Pensions, Barcelona 1984 – '1945–1985. Kunst in der Bundesrepublik Deutschland', Nationalgalerie, Berlin 1985 – 'Wild Visionary Spectral. New German Art', Art Gallery of South Australia, Adelaide 1986 – 'The Biennale of Sydney', 1986 – 'Prospect 86', Frankfurt a.M. 1986 – 'Beuys zu Ehren', Städtische Galerie im Lenbachhaus, Munich 1986 – 'Sonsbeek 86', Arnheim 1986 – 'The Postmodern Explained to Children', Bonnefantenmuseum, Maastricht 1988 – 'Refigured Painting. The German Image 1960–88', Toledo 1988, (Guggenheim Foundation) New York, (Prestel) Munich 1989 – 'Museum der Avantgarde. Die Sammlung Sonnabend New York', Berlin, (Electa) Milan 1989 – 'Open Mind', Ghent 1989 – 'Einleuchten', Hamburg 1989 – 'Blau. Farbe der Ferne', Kunstverein Heidelberg, 1990 – 'Art & Publicité', Centre Georges Pompidou, Paris 1990

Other Literature (Selection)

Wolfgang Max Faust / Gerd de Vries: *Hunger nach Bildern. Deutsche Malerei der Gegenwart*, Cologne 1982 – Rainer Crone: 'Jiři Georg Dokoupil. The Imprisoned Brain', *Artforum*, March 1983 – Wilfried W. Dickhoff: 'Das letzte Abenteuer der Menschheit' (Interview), *Wolkenkratzer Art Journal*, No. 7, 1983 – Axel Hecht: 'Jiři Georg Dokoupil' (Interview), *Art*, August 1984 – Walter Grasskamp: 'Der vergeßliche Engel', Munich 1986 – Stephan Schmidt-Wulffen: *Spielregeln. Tendenzen der Gegenwartskunst*, Cologne 1987 – Stefan Szczesny (ed.): *Maler über Malerei. Einblicke-Ausblicke*, Cologne 1989

MARIA EICHHORN

Born Bamberg, 1962. Studied at Hochschule der Künste, Berlin, 1984–90. First one-woman show at Galerie Paranorm, Berlin, 1987. Exhibitions at Wewerka & Weiss Galerie, Berlin. Took part in exhibition 'L'ordine delle cose', Rome, 1991. Lives in Berlin.

Objects, language and spatial scenarios combine in Maria Eichhorn's work into a whole that is presented under the motto – also the title of one of her exhibitions – that 'The Visible Contains the Visible, the Visible Contains the Invisible' ('Das Sichtbare Beinhaltet Das Sichtbare, Das Sichtbare Beinhaltet Das Unsichtbare'). Her concern is with the language of objects: the discourse that they set in train between themselves, the space and the viewer. The exhibition context is brought into the work to frame its meaning. The work addresses the relationship between producer and recipient. The objects, often directly extracted from everyday life – or also 'identical' simulations – refer to their own sensory presence and simultaneously relate to something immaterial. Eichhorn's gallery presentations of objects, and the works in which she

incorporates objects taken from a billiard hall or from a private flat, define her relation to the social space in which the work situates itself.

Reference Source for List of Exhibitions and Bibliography

'Maria Eichhorn. D.S.B.D.S', Ausstellung 'So oder So', Künstlerhaus Bethanien, Berlin 1990

Publications by the Artist (Selection)

'Projekt "Entnutzte Treppe"', in: *Von der Imagination zum Objekt*, edited by HdK Berlin, 1987 – *34 Abbildungen und 35 Anmerkungen*, Berlin 1990 – *Präsentation von sechs Texten*, in: *A.N.Y.P.*, No. 3, 1991

Catalogue

'Arbeiten 1986/87', Galerie Paranorm, Berlin 1987

Catalogues of Collective Exhibitions (Selection)

'Klasse Hödicke', HdK Berlin, 1986 – 'Play Off', Quergalerie, HdK Berlin, 1988 – 'Supervision', Galerie Vincenz Sala, Berlin 1989 – 'Berlin März 1990', Kunstverein Braunschweig, 1990 – '1, 2, 3', Wewerka & Weiss Galerie, Berlin 1991 – 'L'ordine delle cose', Palazzo delle Esposizione, Rome 1991

Other Literature (Selection)

Marius Babias: 'Künstlergruppe Atelier III', *Kunstforum International*, Vol. 95, 1988 – Thomas Wulffen: 'Supervision', *Kunstforum International*, Vol. 102, 1989 – Thomas Wulffen: 'Berlin Art Now', *Flash Art*, No. 151, 1990 – Marius Babias: 'Im Zentrum der Peripherie', *Bildende Kunst*, No. 3, 1991

JAN FABRE

Born Antwerp, 1958. Studied at Royal Academy of Fine Arts and Institute for Arts and Crafts, Antwerp. First one-man show at Jordaenshuis, Antwerp, 1978. Exhibitions at Deweer Art Gallery, Otegem; Galerie De Selby, Amsterdam; Jack Tilton Gallery, New York; Galerie Ronny van de Velde, Antwerp; and elsewhere. Took part in Venice Biennale, 1984. Theatre, ballet and opera productions in Antwerp, Brussels, Venice, Berlin, Frankfurt am Main, Vienna, and elsewhere from 1980 onwards. *The Dance Sections* performed at 'documenta 8', 1987. Lives in Antwerp.

Fabre sees himself as an artist who synthesizes all the arts. In his stage plays, which combine body language, rhetoric and spatial situations into poetic, enigmatic, hermetic 'time images', he operates as author, actor, director, set designer and lighting designer, all in one. Similarly, in his work as an opera and ballet director, as a film-maker and as a writer, Fabre creates images that largely elude linguistic or rational interpretation. The method used in his drawings, in particular, depends on the interaction between direct bodily experience and the autonomy of the work of art. The colour blue stands at the core of his work: cloths, china owls, furniture, bathtubs and – in installations and stage works – whole rooms are coloured blue. In the drawings he uses a ballpoint pen to build up rhythmically structured, 'hallucinatory' planes that evoke a sense of immateriality. Additionally, Fabre has used Rorschach test blots and has commemorated the entomologist Jean-Henri Fabre (1823–1915) with drawings of animals intended to reconcile scientific knowledge with 'absence of language'. – 'The Blue Hour still exists, but only for the insomniac like Fabre – his drawings come out of the strange wakefulness that comes with insomnia, a wakefulness in which one is susceptible to hallucinations – who in artistically embodying it, gives it a new lease on inner life.' (Donald Kuspit)

Reference Source for List of Exhibitions, Theatrical Productions and Films
'Jan Fabre. Hé wat een plezierige zottigheid!', Galerie Ronny Van de Velde, Antwerp 1988 – 'Jan Fabre. Das Geräusch', Kunsthalle Basle 1990

Books by the Artist
Fabre's Book of Insects, Ghent 1990 – *16 Filmloupes,* Ghent 1991

Catalogues and Monographs (Selection)
'Vrienden', Provinciaal Museum, Hasselt 1984 – 'Tekeningen', Museum van Hedendaagse Kunst, Ghent 1985 – 'Modellen 1977–1985', Deweer Art Gallery, Otegem 1988 – 'Tekeningen, Objecten & Modellen', Provinciaal Museum voor Moderne Kunst, Ostend 1989 – 'Insecten en Ruimte', Museum Overholland, Amsterdam 1989 – Jack Tilton Gallery, New York 1989

Catalogues of Collective Exhibitions (Selection)
'La Biennale di Venezia', Venice 1984 – 'Uit het oude Europa. From the Europe of Old', Stedelijk Museum, Amsterdam 1987 – 'Signaturen', Museum van Hedendaagse Kunst, Ghent 1988 – 'Open Mind', Ghent 1989 – 'Artisti (della Fiandra). Artists (from Flanders)', Palazzo Sagredo, Venice, (Museum van Hedendaagse Kunst) Ghent 1990

Other Literature (Selection)
Felix Schnieder-Henninger: 'Die Stunde Blau. Prometheus Landschaft', *Wolkenkratzer Art Journal,* No. 5, 1988

SERGIO FERMARIELLO

Born Naples, 1961. First one-man show at Galleria Protirion, Split, 1989. Exhibitions at Galleria Lucio Amelio, Naples; Galleria Il Capricorno, Venice; Galerie Albrecht, Munich. Took part in 'Giovani artisti Saatchi & Saatchi' exhibition, Milan, 1989. Lives in Naples.

Fermariello's work embraces two diametrically opposed attitudes to painting. On one hand there are large hyperrealist paintings, done from magazine photographs and recalling the Hollywood 'film noir' aesthetic of the 1940s. On the other hand there is Fermariello's exploration of the process of painting itself, in which he puts down on canvas seemingly endless, pattern-like sequences of tiny signs that are somewhere between figure and script: 'Expanding toward infinity the duration of a work's cre-ation and subtracting from it any emotive valency, but at the same time revealing, through impalpable variations, a controlled lyricism, Fermariello reveals an affective but non-heroic vision of pictorial activity.' (Gregorio Magnani) – In recent works these signs have taken on an apparent motion, shifting like puzzle pictures as the viewer moves.

Catalogue
'Sergio Fermariello', Lucio Amelio, Naples 1989

Catalogues of Collective Exhibitions (Selection)
'Giovani artisti Saatchi & Saatchi', Milan 1989 – 'Magico primario una revisione', Galleria d'Arte Moderna, Comune di Cento, 1991

Other Literature (Selection)
Gregorio Magnani: 'The Scene of Absence. A New Generation of Italian Artists', *Arts Magazine,* April 1989 – Riccardo Notte: 'Fermariello l'immagine e il segno', *Mass Media,* No. 1, 1990 – Mauro Panzera: 'Vittoria Chierici, Sergio Fermariello, Carlo Ferraris, Paola Pezzi', *Tema Celeste,* No. 26, 1990 – Gabriele Perretta: 'Segnali da Napoli', *Flash Art* (Italian edition), October / November 1990

IAN HAMILTON FINLAY

Born Nassau, Bahamas, 1925. Childhood in Scotland, three and a half years' military service, then worked as a shepherd. In the 1950s wrote short stories; lived in Edinburgh 1959–64 and became involved in the international Concrete Poetry movement. Founded Wild Hawthorn Press in 1961. 'Standing Poems' from 1963; first book poems and three-dimensional texts from 1964. In 1966 Finlay moved to Stonypath, in the Scottish Lowlands, and there began work on the garden that became famous, from 1978 on, under the name of Little Sparta. In 1977, outbreak of the 'Little Spartan War' between Little Sparta and the Strathclyde Regional Council and Scottish Arts Council, from which Little Sparta emerged victorious in 1984. Exhibitions at Graeme Murray Gallery, Edinburgh; Victoria Miro Gallery, London; Galerie Jule Kewenig, Frechen/Bachem; Galleria Stampa, Basle; and elsewhere. From 1976, open-air installations in Stuttgart, Otterlo, Vienna, Eindhoven, Basle, and elsewhere. Honorary doctorate from University of Aberdeen, 1986; participated in 'documenta 8' in 1987. Lives at Dunsyre, Scotland.

Ever since Finlay's pioneer achievements in Concrete Poetry, language has been the point of departure for all his work. Increasingly, the words have liberated themselves from the page and from the book to take over the Little Sparta garden, in company with symbols and such basic forms as ship, house, and pedestal. Finlay's central themes, too, appeared early on. Linked leitmotifs – such as war and arcadia, avant-garde and neo-classicism, Third Reich and Greece, and the literature, philosophy, and art of the eighteenth and nineteenth century – blend to form a personal aesthetic. The making of the works is mostly done by Finlay's artist and craftsman friends. In the 1980s he added a new preoccupation with the French Revolution, which reached its climax – so far at least – in the line of guillotines at 'documenta 8'. Some of Finlay's museum installations and works for public spaces use Third Reich symbols; as a result, his concern with beauty and war, aesthetics and politics, and his dream of 'neo-classicism' as a 'rearmament programme for the arts', have lately given rise to some controversy.

Reference Sources for List of Exhibitions and Bibliography
'Ian Hamilton Finlay', Kunsthalle Basle, 1990 – 'Swallows Little Matelots', ACTA Galleria, Milan 1990

Books by the Artist
Since the 1960s Finlay has published a vast mass of his own books, volumes of poetry, postcards, poster poems and other printed items, both at his Wild Hawthorn Press and elsewhere. For select bibliographies see, inter alia, the 1990 Kunsthalle Basle catalogue and *Ian Hamilton Finlay & The Wild Hawthorn Press. A Catalogue Raisonné 1958–1990*, (Graeme Murray), Edinburgh 1990

Catalogues and Monographs (Selection)
Richard Demarco Gallery, Edinburgh 1969 – Scottish National Gallery of Modern Art, Edinburgh 1972 – Southampton Art Gallery, 1976 – 'Homage to Watteau', Graeme Murray Gallery, Edinburgh 1976 – 'Selected Ponds', Reno, Nevada 1976 – 'Collaborations', Kettle's Yard, Cambridge 1977 – Serpentine Gallery, London 1977 – 'Nature Over Again After Poussin', Collins Exhibition Hall, Glasgow 1980 – 'Coincidence in the Work of Ian Hamilton Finlay', Graeme Murray Gallery, Edinburgh 1980 – Stephen Bann: *A Description of Stonypath*, Stonypath Garden 1981 – 'Liberty, Terror and Virtue', Southampton Art Gallery, 1984 – Yves Abrioux: *Ian Hamilton Finlay. A Visual Primer*, Edinburgh 1985 – 'Inter Artes et Naturam', ARC Musée d'Art Moderne de la Ville de Paris, 1987 – 'Poursuites Révolutionnaires', Fondation Cartier, Jouy-en-Josas 1987 – Daniel Boudinetin: *Un paysage ou 9 vues du jardin de Ian Hamilton Finlay*, Fondation Cartier, Jouy-en-Josas 1987 – Victoria Miro Gallery, London 1987 – 'Exhibition on Two Themes', Galerie Jule Kewenig, Frechen / Bachem 1988 – 'Propositions', Musée d'Art Contemporain, Dunkirk 1988

Catalogues of Collective Exhibitions (Selection)
'Skulptur im 20. Jahrhundert', Merian-Park, Basle 1984 – 'Promenades', Parc Lullin, Geneva 1985 – 'Skulptur Projekte in Münster', (DuMont) Cologne 1987 – 'documenta 8', Kassel 1987 – 'buchstäblich wörtlich', Kölnischer Kunstverein, (SMPK Nationalgalerie) Berlin 1987 – 'Art in the Garden', Garden Festival, Glasgow 1988 – 'Pyramiden', Galerie Jule Kewenig, Frechen/Bachem 1989 – 'Prospekt 89', Frankfurt a.M. 1989

Other Literature (Selection)
Stephen Bann: 'Finlay's Little Sparta', *Creative Camera*, January 1983 – Lucius Burckhardt: 'Der bedeutungsvolle Garten des Ian Hamilton Finlay', *Anthos*, No. 4, 1984 – Claude Gintz: 'Neoclassical Rearmament', *Art in America*, February 1987 – Bernard Marcadé: 'Ian Hamilton Finlay or A Spoilsport in Dialectical Speculation', *Parkett*, No. 14, 1987 – Lucius Burckhardt: 'Ian Hamilton Finlays analytische Kriege', *Kunst-Bulletin*, No. 5, 1989 – Johannes Meinhardt: 'Ian Hamilton Finlay. Der Schrecken des Schönen', *Wolkenkratzer Art Journal*, No. 5, 1989 – Ina Conzen-Meairs: 'Ian Hamilton Finlay. Ästhetische Aufrüstung', *Künstler. Kritisches Lexikon der Gegenwartskunst*, issue 12, Munich 1990

PETER FISCHLI   DAVID WEISS

Peter Fischli, born Zurich 1952. Studied at Accademia di Belle Arti, Urbino, 1975–76; Accademia di Belle Arti, Bologna, 1976–77. Lives in Zurich.
David Weiss, born Zurich 1946. Studied at Kunstgewerbeschule Zurich, 1963–64; Kunstgewerbeschule Basle, sculpture class, 1964–66. Lives in Zurich.
First joint show at Galerie Stähli, Zurich, 1981. Exhibitions at Monika Sprüth Galerie, Cologne; Sonnabend Gallery, New York; Galerie Ghislaine Hussenot, Paris; and elsewhere. Took part in 'documenta 8', 1987.

Fischli/Weiss have been working together for ten years now, and they still constantly surprise, with new researches conducted in accordance with the motto: 'Whither the galaxy? Is there another bus coming?' They work in series, exploring the banality of everyday life and deriving a distinctive comic effect from the encounter between this and the 'sublimity' of art. Their approach is almost scientific, eschewing personal style in favour of objective vision. Fischli/Weiss let things do the work for them – as in their film *Der Lauf der Dinge (Things Take Their Course)*, enthusiastically received at 'documenta 8' – or else they involve them in daring combinations and balancing acts, as in *Stiller Nachmittag (Still Afternoon)*. The medium varies according to the subject under investigation. Sculptures, drawings, photographs and films are not there as techniques for their own sake but to serve the needs of the matter in hand. In *Plötzlich diese Übersicht (Suddenly This Overview)*, 180 miniature scenes and stories in terracotta represent the endeavour to impose an order on ordinary life and its memories. Their recent sculptures are moulded rubber replicas of commonplace items from our culture, from basins to pouffes. A most recent photographic series concerns the chic world of air travel. 'The strangely autonomous, essential qualitiy that overtakes even the most ordinary and lifeless objects (a car tyre, for instance), when they come under the influence of Fischli/Weiss, is the fruit of an artistic mentality in unstable equilibrium, oscillating between animistic seriousness, thorough-going scepticism and artistic frivolity.' (Patrick Frey)

Reference Source for List of Exhibitions and Bibliography
'Le désenchantement du monde', Villa Arson, Centre National d'Art Contemporain, Nice 1990

Books by the Artists
Ordnung und Reinlichkeit, Zurich 1981 – *Plötzlich diese Übersicht*, Zurich 1982

Films
Der geringste Widerstand, 1981 – *Der rechte Weg*, 1983 – *Der Lauf der Dinge*, 1987

Catalogues and Monographs (Selection)
'Stiller Nachmittag', 2 vols, Kunsthalle Basle, 1985 – 'Photographs', 20th São Paulo International Biennial, (Swiss Federal Office of Culture, Edition Patrick Frey) Zurich 1989 – 'Airports', Edition Patrick Frey und IVAM Instituto Valenciano de Arte Moderno, 1990 – Patrick Frey (ed.): *Das Geheimnis der Arbeit. Texte zum Werk von Peter Fischli & David Weiss*, Kunstverein, Munich, and Kunstverein für die Rheinlande und Westfalen, Düsseldorf, 1990

Catalogues of Collective Exhibitions (Selection)
'Saus und Braus', Städtische Galerie zum Strauhof, Zurich 1980 – 'Skulptur im 20. Jahrhundert', Merian-Park, Basle 1984 – 'Alles und noch viel mehr. Das poetische ABC', Kunsthalle Bern, Kunstmuseum Bern, 1985 –'Sonsbeek 86', Arnheim 1986 – 'Skulptur Projekte in Münster', (DuMont) Cologne 1987 – 'documenta 8', Kassel 1987 – 'Carnegie International', Carnegie Museum of Art, Pittsburgh 1988 – 'Museum der Avantgarde. Die Sammlung Sonnabend New York', Berlin, (Electa) Milan 1989 – 'Psychological Abstraction', Athens 1989 – 'The Biennale of Sydney', 1990

Other Literature (Selection)
'Collaboration Peter Fischli / David Weiss', *Parkett*, No. 17, 1988 – Further essays and critical comment on Fischli/Weiss in *Das Geheimnis der Arbeit*, 1990 (see above)

GÜNTHER FÖRG

Born Füssen, Bavaria, 1952. Studied at Akademie der Bildenden Künste, Munich, 1973–79. First one-man show there in 1974; one-man show at Rüdiger Schöttle, Munich, 1980. Exhibitions at Galerie Max Hetzler, Cologne; Galerie Grässlin-Ehrhardt, Frankfurt a.M.; Galerie Crousel-Robelin Bama, Paris; Galerie van Krimpen, Amsterdam; Luhring Augustine Gallery, New York; and elsewhere. Participated in 'von hier aus', Düsseldorf, 1984. Lives at Areuse, Switzerland.

Förg works in series, which differ among themselves both thematically and technically, but which are made in parallel and can be combined with each other. He uses photography, painting and sculpture as the media of a reflection on art and/or architecture and space. His large-scale photographs represent confrontations with the architectural aesthetic of the Bauhaus, say, or of Fascism. These photographs frequently contain no human figures. Framed and glazed with reflecting glass, they are installed in a space that also includes large-format, blurred portraits, or else framed mirrors on painted monochrome screens. The viewer thus becomes part of an aesthetic programme that refers to, say, the Bauhaus, or Constructivism, or Jean-Luc Godard, or Blinky Palermo. Large monochrome mural paintings (often in stairwells), and pictures in lead, set colours against other colours and materials in structured contrasts. Sculptures and reliefs in lead direct the eye to the material quality of the surface. 'Everything that Förg does is filled with his own life, even though his art is objective in its tendency. He makes art about art. His work is neither film, painting, sculpture nor photography; it is always film about film, painting about painting, photography about photography, sculpture about sculpture. And yet, at the same time, these are works about love, such as are seldom seen in Germany. It is all so light and dance-like that it is hard to understand for anyone who believes in art as unedited emotion.' (Paul Groot)

Reference Source for List of Exhibitions and Bibliography
'Günther Förg', Museum Fridericianum, Kassel, (Edition Cantz) Stuttgart 1990 (later shown at Museum van Hedendaagse Kunst, Ghent, Museum der bildenden Künste, Leipzig, Kunsthalle Tübingen, Kunstraum, Munich)

Catalogues and Monographs (Selection)
Galerie Max Hetzler, Stuttgart 1983 – Kunstraum, Munich, 1984 – Kunsthalle Bern, 1986 – Westfälischer Kunstverein, Münster 1986 – Museum Haus Lange, Krefeld 1987 – *Verzeichnis der Arbeiten seit 1973*, (Verlag Christoph Dürr) Munich 1987 – Haags Gemeentemuseum, The Hague 1988 – Newport Harbor Art Museum, Newport Beach, California 1989 – 'Gesamte Editionen / The Complete Editions 1974–1988', Museum Boymans-van Beuningen, Rotterdam, (Edition Cantz) Stuttgart 1989 – *Stations of the Cross*, (Edition Julie Sylvester) New York 1990

Catalogues of Collective Exhibitions (Selection)
'KunstLandschaft BundesRepublik', (Klett-Cotta) Stuttgart 1984 – 'von hier aus', Düsseldorf, (DuMont) Cologne 1984 – 'Günther Förg, Georg Herold, Hubert Kiecol, Meuser, Reinhard Mucha', Galerie Peter Pakesch, Vienna 1985 – 'Tiefe Blicke', Hessisches Landesmuseum Darmstadt, (DuMont) Cologne 1985 – 'Chambres d'amis', Ghent 1986 – 'Prospect 86', Frankfurt a.M. 1986 – 'Wechselströme', Bonner Kunstverein, Bonn, (Wienand) Cologne 1987 – 'blow-up. Zeitgeschichte', Württembergischer Kunstverein, Stuttgart 1987 – 'Broken Neon', Forum Stadtpark, Steirischer Herbst, Graz 1987 – 'Schlaf der Vernunft', Kassel 1988 – 'Arbeit in Geschichte – Geschichte in Arbeit', Kunsthaus und Kunstverein in Hamburg, 1988 – 'Prospect Photographie', Frankfurter Kunstverein, 1989 – 'Bilderstreit', Cologne 1989 – 'Objet/Objectif', Galerie Daniel Templon, Paris 1989 – 'Psychological Abstraction', Athens 1989 – 'Un' altra obiettività / Another objectivity', Centre National des Arts Plastiques, Paris, Museo d'Arte Contemporanea Luigi Pecci, Prato, (Idea Books) Milan 1989 – 'Einleuchten', Hamburg 1989 – 'Ponton. Temse', Museum van Hedendaagse Kunst, Ghent 1990

Other Literature (Selection)
Christoph Blase: 'Günther Förg / Jeff Wall', *Artis*, October 1985 – Paul Groot: 'Günther Förg. Im leeren Zentrum der Treppenhäuser', *Wolkenkratzer Art Journal*, No. 8, 1985 – Martin Hentschel: 'Günther Förg' (Interview), *Nike*, No. 8, 1985 – Stephan Schmidt-Wulffen: *Spielregeln. Tendenzen der Gegenwartskunst*, Cologne 1987 – Klaus Honnef: *Kunst der Gegenwart*, Cologne 1988 – Stephan Schmidt-Wulffen: 'Günther Förg' (Interview), *Flash Art*, No. 144, 1989 – 'Collaborations Günther Förg / Philip Taaffe', *Parkett*, No. 26, 1990

KATHARINA FRITSCH

Born Essen, 1956. Studied at Staatliche Kunstakademie, Düsseldorf, from 1977; master student under Fritz Schwegler, 1981. First show at Galerie Rüdiger Schöttle, Munich, 1984 (jointly with Thomas Ruff). Exhibitions at Galerie Johnen & Schöttle, Cologne; and elsewhere. Took part in the exhibition 'A Distanced View', New Museum of Contemporary Art, New York, 1986. Lives in Düsseldorf.

At first sight, Katharina Fritsch's object tableaux look like arrangements of saleable goods, devotional items or museum pieces. And yet these are not readymades. Objects are reproduced – often with a change of scale – and altered by monochrome painting or formal reduction. In specially made showcases, and on table and pedestal constructions, they relate symmetrically to each other in an order governed by shape, size or colour. The objects themselves are varied and frequently banal: toys, jewelry, vases or boxes. With economy and precision, Fritsch seeks to objectify the memories of situations and things. She pursues this aim further in her large spatial installations. A green elephant, a 'dinner party' of 32 identical men, a bookcase full of identical books, a yellow kitsch Madonna, a room full of candlesticks, create exemplary situations of their own. 'When individual things are singled out, this is not done in order to promote them to the status of an unchallenged idol in a doubt-free space. It is done in order to sharpen concentration, to grasp as clearly as possible what is given here and now. In the process, the viewer's feelings and thoughts will inevitably cross over to other images and memories of his or her own. And so these works become the prototypes of a precise vision of objects that carries the mind onward: crystallization points for the viewer's own experience. (Julian Heynen)

Reference Source for List of Exhibitions and Bibliography
'Katharina Fritsch. 1979–1989', Westfälischer Kunstverein, Münster, Portikus, Frankfurt a.M., (Verlag Walther König) Cologne 1989

Writings by the Artist
Werbeblatt 1, Düsseldorf 1981 – 'Friedhöfe', *Kunstforum International*, Vol. 65, 1983

Records by the Artist
Regen, 1987 – *Unken*, 1988

Catalogues and Monographs (Selection)
'Elefant', Kaiser Wilhelm Museum, Krefeld 1987 – Kunsthalle Basle, Institute of Contemporary Arts, London, 1988

Catalogues of Collective Exhibitions (Selection)
'von hier aus', Düsseldorf, (DuMont) Cologne 1984 – 'Von Raum zu Raum', Kunstverein in Hamburg, 1986 – 'Sonsbeek 86', Arnheim 1986 – 'A Distanced View', New Museum of Contemporary Art, New York 1986 – 'Anderer Leute Kunst', Museum Haus Lange, Krefeld 1987 – 'Skulptur Projekte in Münster', (DuMont) Cologne 1987 – 'BiNationale. Deutsche Kunst der späten 80er Jahre', Düsseldorf, (DuMont) Cologne 1988 – 'Carnegie International', Carnegie Museum of Art, Pittsburgh 1988 – 'Cultural Geometry', Athens 1988 – 'Culture and Commentary. An Eighties Perspective', Washington 1990 – 'New York. A New Generation', San Francisco Museum of Modern Art, 1990 – 'Objectives. The New Sculpture', Newport Beach, California 1990 – 'Weitersehen', Krefeld 1990

Other Literature (Selection)
Renate Puvogel: 'Katharina Fritsch. Elefant', *Kunstforum International*, Vol. 89, 1987 – Christoph Blase: 'On Katharina Fritsch', *Artscribe*, No. 68, 1988 – Hans Rudolf Reust: 'Rosemarie Trockel. Katharina Fritsch', *Artscribe*, No. 73, 1989 – 'Collaborations Katharina Fritsch/James Turrell,' *Parkett*, No. 25, 1990

GILBERT & GEORGE

Gilbert, born in the Dolomites, Italy, 1943. Attended Wolkenstein and Hallein art schools and Akademie der Bildenden Künste, Munich. George, born Devon, England, 1942. Studied at Dartington Adult Education Centre, Devon, Dartington Hall College of Art and Oxford School of Art.

Gilbert & George met at St Martin's School of Art, London, in 1967 and have worked jointly ever since. First joint exhibition, 'Three Works – Three Works', Frank's Sandwich Bar, London, 1968; first *Living Sculpture* presentation at St Martin's School of Art, London, 1969. Exhibitions at Nigel Greenwood Gallery, London; Anthony d'Offay Gallery, London; Sonnabend Gallery, New York; Galerie Ascan Crone, Hamburg; and elsewhere. Took part in 'documenta 5', 1972; 'documenta 6', 1977; 'documenta 7', 1982. They live in London.

Their first appearance as *Living Sculpture* in 1969 established Gilbert & George's trade-mark: their ordinary lounge suits. They declared themselves to be sculpture and their life to be a work of art: 'To be with art is all we ask.' As a *Singing Sculpture* they appeared in museums and galleries, at pop concerts and in night clubs. With hands and faces metallic bronze-painted, and carrying gloves and a stick, they mimed like automata for up to eight hours on end to the popular song *Underneath the Arches.* Information on their fairly unsensational life was supplied through charcoal drawings, paintings (triptychs), films and books. They also sent out postcards bearing statements on art. In 1971 they made their first 'photo pieces', arrangements of photographic prints on the wall. The themes of these works were alcoholic excess, grief,

decline and melancholy. From 1974 onwards, the grouping of the photographs was tightened by the introduction of a grid of black frames, and some of the photographs were tinted. Since 1980, still using the grid, they have produced monumental, strongly coloured photo pieces with an effect reminiscent of stained-glass windows. Religion, sexuality, city life, England, work, youth and – constantly – Gilbert & George form the subjects of these works.

Reference Source for List of Exhibitions and Bibliography
Wolf Jahn: *The Art of Gilbert & George,* London 1989 (German edition: Munich 1989)

Books by the Artists (Selection)
The Pencil on Paper Descriptive Works, London 1970 – *Art Notes and Thoughts,* London 1970 – *To Be with Art Is All We Ask,* London 1970 – *A Guide to the Singing Sculpture,* London 1970 – *A Day in the Life of George and Gilbert,* London 1971 – *Dark Shadow,* London 1976

Films (Selection)
The Nature of Our Looking, 1970 – *Gordon's Makes Us Drunk,* 1972 – *In the Bush,* 1972 – *The Portrait of the Artists as Young Men,* 1972 – *The World of Gilbert & George,* 1981

Catalogues and Monographs (Selection)
'The Paintings', Whitechapel Art Gallery, London 1971 – 'The Grand Old Duke of York', Kunstmuseum Lucerne, 1972 – Galerie im Taxispalais, Innsbruck 1977 – 'Photo-Pieces 1971–1980', Stedelijk Van Abbemuseum, Eindhoven 1980 – Baltimore Museum of Art, 1984 – 'Death Hope Life Fear', Castello di Rivoli, Turin 1985 – 'The Charcoal on Paper Sculptures 1970–1974', CAPC Musée d'Art Contemporain de Bordeaux, 1986 – 'The Paintings 1971', Fruitmarket Gallery, Edinburgh 1986 – 'The Complete Pictures 1971–1985', CAPC Musée d'Art Contemporain de Bordeaux, 1986 – 'Worlds and Windows by Gilbert and George', Anthony d'Offay Gallery, London, Robert Miller Gallery, New York, 1990

Catalogues of Collective Exhibitions (Selection)
'Konzeption Conception', Städtisches Museum Leverkusen, Schloß Morsbroich, 1969 – 'Information', The Museum of Modern Art, New York 1970 – 'documenta 5', Kassel 1972 – '"Konzept"-Kunst', Kunstmuseum Basle, 1972 – 'Kunst aus Fotografie', Kunstverein, Hanover, 1973 –

'Medium Fotografie', Städtisches Museum Leverkusen, Schloß Morsbroich, 1973 – 'Europe in the 70's', The Art Institute of Chicago, 1977 – 'documenta 6', Kassel 1977 – 'La Biennale di Venezia', Venice 1978 – 'Wahrnehmungen, Aufzeichnungen, Mitteilungen', Museum Haus Lange, Krefeld 1979 – 'Westkunst', Cologne 1981 – 'documenta 7', Kassel 1982 – 'Zeitgeist', Berlin 1982 – 'The Biennale of Sydney', 1984 – 'Dialog', Moderna Museet, Stockholm 1984 – 'Carnegie International', Museum of Art, Carnegie Institute, Pittsburgh 1985 – 'L'Epoque, la mode, la morale, la passion', Paris 1987 – 'British Art in the 20th Century', Royal Academy of Arts, London, Staatsgalerie Stuttgart, (Prestel) Munich 1987 – 'Current Affairs', Museum of Modern Art, Oxford 1987 – 'Uit het oude Europa. From the Europe of Old', Stedelijk Museum, Amsterdam 1987 – 'Museum der Avantgarde. Die Sammlung Sonnabend New York', Berlin, (Electa) Milan 1989 – 'Prospect 89', Frankfurt a.M. 1989 – 'Bilderstreit', Cologne 1989 – 'Life-Size', Jerusalem 1990

Other Literature (Selection)
Germano Celant: 'Gilbert & George', *Domus,* No. 508, 1972 – Jean-Christophe Ammann: 'Gilbert & George', *Das Kunstwerk,* No. 1, 1973 – Tomaso Trini: 'Gilbert & George', *Data,* No. 12, 1974 – Gislind Nabakowski: 'Gilbert & George', *Kunstforum International,* Vol. 43, 1981 – Giovan Battista Salerno: 'Gilbert, George, Samuel Beckett', *Flash Art,* No. 125, 1985 – Gary Watson: 'An Interview with Gilbert & George', *Artscribe,* August/September 1987 – 'Collaboration Gilbert & George,' *Parkett,* No. 14, 1987

ROBERT GOBER

Born Wallingford, Connecticut, 1954. Studied at Tyler School of Art, Rome, 1973–74; Bachelor of Arts, Middlebury College, Vermont, 1976. One-man shows since 1984 at Paula Cooper Gallery, New York. Exhibitions at Galerie Jean Bernier, Athens; Galerie Max Hetzler, Cologne; Daniel Weinberg Gallery, Los Angeles; and elsewhere. Took part in 'BiNational', Boston and Düsseldorf, 1988. Lives in New York.

Since 1984 Gober has been working with everyday objects, such as urinals, beds, playpens, doors, and garments, in the tradition of Marcel Duchamp. These objects are not presented as readymades, however: they are denatured by hand-crafted modifications. Gober installs his objects in a specific space, in juxtaposition with other objects or with wallpaper patterns of his own design, thus creating spatial situations that amount to a poetic, erotic, ironic critique of everyday life. 'A bed is an art object and is a bed; a bed is not a bed, because it is an art object, but then again it is still a bed… In Robert Gober's work a bed is both an art object and a shared bed, and then again it isn't. For his objects are subject to an ambiguity that marks a deliberate refusal to state a meaning. And so the bed, the sink, the urinal, and the chairs have something elusive, inexplicable, mysterious about them.' (Noemi Smolik)

Reference Source for List of Exhibitions and Bibliography
'Robert Gober', Museum Boymans-van Beuningen, Rotterdam, Kunsthalle Bern, 1990

Catalogues and Monographs (Selection)
Galerie Jean Bernier, Athens 1987 – Tyler Gallery, Tyler School of Art, Elkins Park, Pennsylvania 1988 – Institute of Chicago, 1988

Catalogues of Collective Exhibitions (Selection)
'Scapes', University Art Museum, Santa Barbara, California 1985 – 'New Sculpture. Robert Gober, Jeff Koons, Haim Steinbach', The Renaissance Society at the University of Chicago, 1986 – 'Art and Its Double', Madrid 1987 – 'Avant-Garde in the Eighties', Los Angeles County Museum of Art, 1987 – 'NY Art Now. The Saatchi Collection', London 1988 – 'Richard Artschwager. His Peers and Persuasion (1963–1988)', Daniel Weinberg Gallery, Los Angeles 1988 – 'A Project. Robert Gober and Christopher Wool', 303 Gallery, New York 1988 – 'Cultural Geometry', Athens 1988 – 'La Biennale di Venezia', Venice 1988 – 'Furniture as Art', Museum Boymans-van Beuningen, Rotterdam 1988 – 'The BiNational. American Art of the Late 80's', Boston, (DuMont) Cologne 1988 – 'Utopia Post Utopia', Institute of Contemporary Art, Boston 1988 – 'Horn of Plenty', Stedelijk Museum, Amsterdam 1989 – 'Prospect 89', Frankfurt a.M. 1989 – 'Gober, Halley, Kessler, Wool. Four Artists from New York', Kunstverein Munich 1989 – 'Einleuchten', Hamburg 1989 – 'Psychological Abstraction', Athens 1989 – 'Culture and Commentary. An Eighties Perspective', Washington 1990 – 'Objectives. The New Sculpture', Newport Beach, California 1990 – 'Life-Size', Jerusalem 1990 – 'The Biennale of Sydney', 1990

Other Literature (Selection)
Meyer Raphael Rubinstein/Daniel Weiner: 'Robert Gober', *Flash Art*, January/February 1988 – Maureen P. Sherlock: 'Arcadian Elegy. The Art of Robert Gober', *Arts Magazine*, September 1989 – Craig Gholson: 'Robert Gober', *Bomb*, Autumn 1989 – Lisa Liebman: 'The Case of Robert Gober', *Parkett*, No. 21, 1989 – Matthew Weinstein: 'The House of Fiction', *Artforum*, February 1990 – Gary Indiana: 'Success. Robert Gober', *Interview*, May 1990 – Noemi Smolik: 'Robert Gober', *Kunstforum International*, Vol. 109, 1990 – Renate Puvogel: 'Robert Gober', *Kunstforum International*, Vol. 111, 1991

ULRICH GÖRLICH

Born Alfeld, Bavaria, 1952. First one-man exhibition at Galerie des Kreuzberger Künstlerkreises, Berlin, 1976. Director of Werkstatt für Photographie, Kreuzberg, Berlin, 1978–1982. Studied at California Institute of the Arts, Valencia, 1982–83. From 1983, extension of photographic work and installation using silver bromide emulsion. From 1987 onward photographic installations at Galerie Fahnemann, Berlin. Various scholarships and prizes, including Otto Steinert-Preis awarded by Deutsche Gesellschaft für Photographie, 1987. Took part in 'documenta 8', 1987. Lives in Berlin.

Görlich on his own work: 'In the technique that I use, the photographic emulsion is applied to the wall and exposed and developed there. The pictures appear directly on the wall, with no apparent material base.' Görlich is thus able to present the photographic image in a spatial context without any intervening support. The space and the photograph interrelate directly and serve to interpret each other. This enables his photographs to transpose exterior space into interior space, to mask or reveal architectural features and to indicate political and social realities.

Reference Source for List of Exhibitions and Bibliography
'Ulrich Görlich', Westfälischer Kunstverein, Münster 1990

Catalogues
Galerie Fahnemann, Berlin 1987 – Kunstraum, Munich, 1988

Catalogues of Collective Exhibitions (Selection)
'documenta 8', Kassel 1987 – 'Per gli anni novanta. Nove artisti a Berlino', Padiglione d'Arte Contemporanea, Milan 1989 – 'D & S Ausstellung', Hamburg 1989 – 'Aus der Hauptstadt', Bonner Kunstverein, Bonn 1990

Other Literature (Selection)
Beatrice Bismarck: 'Ulrich Görlich', *Noema Art Magazine*, No. 11, 1987 – Thomas Wulffen: 'Ulrich Görlich. Fotoarbeiten', *Kunstforum International*, Vol. 88, 1987 – Gottfried Jäger: 'Bildgebende Fotografie', Cologne 1988 – Heinz Schütz: 'Ulrich Görlich', *Kunstforum International*, Vol. 94, 1988 – Karl Heinz Schmidt: 'Ulrich Görlich', *Artis*, No. 10, 1989

RAINER GÖRSS

Born Neustrelitz, 1960. Studied at Hochschule für bildende und angewandte Kunst, East Berlin, and Hochschule für Bildende Künste, Dresden, 1982–89. First one-man show at Galerie Treptow, Berlin; also appeared in performance of *langsam nässen* at Hochschule für Bildende Künste, Dresden, 1985. Exhibitions at Galerie 85, Berlin; Galerie Eigen + Art, Leipzig; Galerie Art Acker, Berlin; and elsewhere. Lives in Berlin.

In 1987–89, together with Micha Brendel, Else Gabriel and Via Lewandowsky, Görß belonged to the group Autoperforationsartisten, whose occasionally bloody performances in Berlin, Dresden and Leipzig incorporated experimental combinations of theatrical scenes, rituals, emotive actions, self-directed experiments, and verbal acrobatics. This juxtaposition and interweaving of heterogeneous elements reappears in Görß' own installations, sculptures and paintings. In his *Midgard* project (Kunstakademie, Dresden, 1989), for example, Görß combined woodcarvings, painted wooden panels, rusty iron objects, an insectarium and other elements into a complex spatial presentation. 'In a deliberately confusing welter of religious allusions, elementary signs and swirling conceptual manœuvres, Görß stirs history together with the present, links disparate discourses and remote ages in a single work, and gleans his way nomadically across "the spoilheap of history, no exit, no entry, and everything in motion".' (Christoph Tannert)

Books by the Artist
Entwerter Oder, 1984 – *Schaden*, 1985 – *U.S.W.*, 1986 – *Fotoanschlag*, 1988 – *Das Schwarz zieht die Bilder zusammen*, 1988 – *Frankfurter Altar*, 1990

Catalogue
'Rainer Görß. Midgard', Hochschule für Bildende Künste, Dresden, (Eigen + Art) Leipzig 1989

Catalogues of Collective Exhibitions (Selection)
'Moosrose', Galerie Fotogen, Dresden 1987 – 'Vom Ebben und Fluten', Leonhardi-Museum, Dresden 1988 – 'Permanente Kunstkonferenz', Galerie Weißer Elefant, Berlin 1989 – 'Zwischenspiele', Künstlerhaus Bethanien, (Neue Gesellschaft für bildende Kunst), Berlin 1989 – 'Autre allemagne hors les murs', La Villette, Paris 1920 – 'Europäische Werkstatt Ruhrgebiet', Kunsthalle Recklinghausen, 1990 – 'Die Kunst der Collage in der DDR', Kunstsammlung Cottbus, 1990

Other Literature (Selection)
G. H. Lybke: 'Midgard', *Bildende Kunst*, October 1989 – Christoph Tannert: 'Leben ist außer den staatlichen Sprachen. Produzenten- und Selbsthilfegalerien' and Durs Grünbein: 'Protestantische Rituale. Zur Arbeit der Autoperforationsartisten', in: Eckhart Gillen/Rainer Haarmann (eds) *Kunst in der DDR*, Cologne 1990

FEDERICO GUZMÁN

Born Seville, 1964. One-man shows at Galería La Máquina Española, Seville, from 1987. Exhibitions at Galerie Yvon Lambert, Paris; Galerie Anders Tornberg, Lund; Galerie Ascan Crone, Hamburg; Brooke Alexander Gallery, New York; and elsewhere. Took part in Venice Biennale (Aperto), 1988, and 'The Biennale of Sydney', 1990. Lives in New York.

Amorphous figurations form a focal point in Guzmán's work. In the pictures, tangled trails combine into cartographic abstractions and body outlines. The picture is continued into space by the use of wires and thin sheets of rubber cut into strips, which focus the viewer's attention on the borderline area between two and three dimensions. The picture continues in space. Punctuation marks, numbers and printed letters link typography with topography: an association specifically evoked in one of Guzmán's pictures. In some works he sets off strictly systematized, schematic silhouettes against wires that dangle, as if at random, out of the picture into the space of the room. Pictorial experience, for Guzmán, exists on a borderline.

Reference Source for List of Exhibitions
'Federico Guzmán', Brooke Alexander Gallery, New York 1990

Catalogues (Selection)
Galería La Máquina Española, Seville 1987 – Galerie Ascan Crone, Hamburg 1989

Catalogues of Collective Exhibitions (Selection)
'Andalucía, Puerta de Europa', Palacio de Exposiciones de Madrid, 1985 – 'Andalucía Pinturas', Europalia 85, Antwerp 1985 – '20. Certamen de Pintura. Fundación Luis Cernuda', Museo de Arte Contemporáneo, Seville 1986 – 'La Biennale di Venezia', Venice 1988 – 'The Biennale of Sydney', 1990

Other Literature (Selection)
Martijn van Nieuwenhuysen: 'Four Artists from Seville', *Flash Art*, February/March 1987 – Juan Vicente Aliaga: 'Spanish Art. A History of Disruption', *Artscribe*, March/April 1988 – Juan Vicente Aliaga: 'Conceptual Art in Spain. "Traditionalism Subtly Undermined"', *Art International*, Spring 1989 – Kirby Gookin: 'Federico Guzmán', *Artforum*, September 1990 – Bettina Semmer: 'One to One. Spanish Artist Federico Guzmán Harnesses the Power of Art Against Entropy', *Artscribe*, No. 82, 1990

PETER HALLEY

Born New York, 1953. Studied at Yale University, New Haven, to 1975 and University of New Orleans to 1978. First one-man show at Contemporary Art Center, New Orleans, 1978. Exhibitions at International With Monument, New York; Galerie Daniel Templon, Paris; Sonnabend Gallery, New York; Galleria Lia Rumma, Naples; Jablonka Galerie, Cologne; and elsewhere.

Took part in 'Europa/Amerika', Museum Ludwig, Cologne, 1986, and 'BiNationale', Boston and Düsseldorf, 1988. Lives in New York.

Halley explicitly relates to the American Abstract Expressionism of a Barnett Newman or a Mark Rothko. But in his case the work does not centre on a meditative experience of pictorial space: his brightly coloured, geometric paintings have a rather daunting, even aggressive, force. They concentrate on elements of metropolitan life, speed, intricacy, communication. There is no sign of a personal 'handwriting' in these works, which look rather like business logos. Cells with bars, chimneys and pure colour fields – some in dayglo colours – are connected by a linear system of tubes. Gradations of colour in individual pictorial elements suggest speed. The titles, and the artist's own essays, supply clues to the interpretation of the work, indicating a context of art historical reflections, sociopolitical issues and the aesthetics of urban life. Peter Halley: 'The idea of being both drawn to and alienated by the realities of the social and cultural condition that we are in is central to my sensibility. The complex thing about the state of culture that we're in, I think, is that the balance between positivity and negativity has become very tense. I've tried to make my work continue to be about a fluid range of affective reactions to our culture.'

Reference Source for List of Exhibitions
'Peter Halley', Museum Haus Esters, Krefeld 1989 (later shown at Maison de la Culture et de la Communication de Saint-Etienne)

Writings by the Artist
Peter Halley. Collected Essays 1981–1987, (Edition Galerie Bruno Bischofberger) Zurich 1988

Catalogue
Jablonka Galerie, Cologne 1988 (in collaboration with Sonnabend Gallery, New York)

Catalogues of Collective Exhibitions (Selection)
'Currents', Institute of Contemporary Art, Boston 1985 – 'Political Geometries. On the Meaning of Alienation', Hunter College, New York 1986 – 'Europa/Amerika', Museum Ludwig, Cologne 1986 – 'Endgame. Reference and Simulation in Recent Painting and Sculpture', Institute of Contemporary Art, Boston 1986 – 'Art and Its Double', Madrid 1987 – 'Biennial Exhibition', Whitney Museum of American Art, New York 1987 – 'Avant-Garde in the Eighties', Los Angeles County Museum of Art, 1987 – 'Post-Abstract Abstraction', Aldrich Museum of Contemporary Art, Ridgefield, Connecticut 1987 – 'Similia/Dissimilia', Städtische Kunsthalle Düsseldorf, 1987 – 'NY Art Now. The Saatchi Collection', London 1988 – 'Cultural Geometry', Athens 1988 – 'Museum der Avantgarde. Die Sammlung Sonnabend New York', Berlin, (Electa) Milan 1989 – 'La Couleur Seule', Musée Saint Pierre, Lyon 1988 – 'Hybrid Neutral. Modes of Abstraction and The Social', University of North Texas Gallery, 1988 – 'The BiNational. American Art of the Late 80's', Boston, (DuMont) Cologne 1988 – 'Carnegie International', Carnegie Museum of Art, Pittsburgh 1988 – 'Horn of Plenty', Stedelijk Museum, Amsterdam 1989 – 'Prospect 89', Frankfurt a.M. 1989 – '10 + 10. Contemporary Soviet and American Painters', Modern Art Museum of Fort Worth, (Abrams) New York, (Aurora) Leningrad, 1989 – 'Psychological Abstraction', Athens 1989 – 'Gober, Halley, Kessler, Wool. Four Artists from New York', Kunstverein, Munich 1989 – 'Weitersehen', Krefeld 1990

Other Literature (Selection)
Joshua Decter: 'Peter Halley', *Arts Magazine*, Summer 1986 – Fred Fehlau: 'Donald Judd and Peter Halley', *Flash Art*, Summer 1987 – Claudia Hart: 'Intuitive Sensitivity. An Interview with Peter Halley and Meyer Vaisman', *Artscribe*, November/December 1987 – Dan Cameron: 'In the Path of Peter Halley', *Arts Magazine*, December 1987 – Donald Kuspit: 'Peter Halley', *Artforum*, January 1988 – John Miller: 'Lecture Theatre. Peter Halley's Geometry and the Social', *Artscribe*, No. 74, 1989 – Giancarlo Politi: 'Peter Halley' (Interview), *Flash Art*, No. 150, 1990

FRITZ HEISTERKAMP

Born Borken, Westphalia, 1960. Studied philosophy, psychology, journalism and art history in Münster, 1979–81. Studied fine art at Werkhochschule, Cologne, 1981–1985; Hochschule der Künste, Berlin, from 1985. First one-man show at Galerie Urban Art, Berlin, 1986. Lives in Berlin.

Heisterkamp's objects postulate an elusive world situated somewhere between daily life and art. Often assembled from found

materials, they stress their own lack of function, even when – like *Vogelhaus (Aviary)* – they resemble everyday objects. They have undergone a finely calculated sea-change, with a deliberate touch of the grotesque that echoes the tradition of the readymade. 'The traditional Readymade suppresses its original practical usefulness; but in Heisterkamp's hands the art object – its organization not being intrinsic but mimetic, achieved by manipulating the real object or else by copying it in an inauthentic material – is stylized to express an autonomous and at the same time reflexive criterion of representation: it creates, maintains and emphasizes the functional context that is absent in practical terms.' (Marius Babias)

Reference Source for List of Exhibitions and Bibliography
'1, 2, 3', Wewerka & Weiss Galerie, Berlin 1991

Catalogues of Collective Exhibitions (Selection)
'Gentinetta, Gramming, Heisterkamp, Lorbeer, Lücke, Munk', Laden für Nichts, Berlin 1989 – 'Nord-Süd Gefälle', Künstlerwerkstatt Lothringerstraße 13, Munich 1989

Other Literature (Selection)
Marius Babias: 'Vom Hausmeister ernstgenommen', *Artis*, No. 4, 1990

GEORG HEROLD

Born Jena, 1947. Studied in Halle, 1969–73; at Akademie der bildenden Künste, Munich, 1974–76; Hochschule für Bildende Künste, Hamburg, 1977–82. Presented his first *Latte (Batten)* in Hamburg in 1977; then *Altes Gerippe – mieses Getitte (Old Bones – Measly Tits)*, with Albert Oehlen, at Künstlerhaus, Hamburg, 1979. From 1984, one-man exhibitions at Galerie Max Hetzler, Cologne. Exhibitions at Galerie Arno Kohnen, Düsseldorf; Galerie Susan Wyss, Zurich; Koury/Wingate Gallery, New York; Galería Juana de Aizpuru, Madrid and Seville; Galerie Gisela Capitain, Cologne; and elsewhere. Took part in 'Skulptur Projekte in Münster', Münster, 1987. Lives in Cologne.

Herold is an artist whose work attempts unexpected but precise statements on art, society and science. He first became well-known in 1977 through his sculptures, 'interpretations' of Lenin and of Dürer's *Hare*, made from roofing battens. Alongside pieces of this kind, with their confrontations between tradition and material, Herold also uses language as a medium, in works with oblique, wry, sarcastic or comic meaning. Material and language together become an assault on deterministic thought. Battens, pieces of refuse, drawings and photographs are directly inscribed, or else supplied with interpretative captions. 'Georg Herold likes stories that stand on the brink, stories that are skewed, absurd, off-beam. They permit him to deploy an idiosyncratic creativity that often has one foot firmly on the ground.' (Marianne Stockebrand) Besides battens, the unlikely materials favoured by Herold in his onslaught on good taste include underpants, bricks, carpets and – since 1989 – caviar: *Geld spielt keine Rolle (Money No Object)*.

Reference Source for List of Exhibitions and Bibliography
'Geld spielt keine Rolle', Kölnischer Kunstverein, Cologne 1990

Books by the Artist
Mode Nervo (with Albert Oehlen), Hamburg 1980 – *Facharbeiterficken* (with Werner Büttner and Albert Oehlen), Hamburg 1982

Catalogues and Monographs (Selection)
'Unschärferelation', Neue Gesellschaft für bildende Kunst, Berlin 1985 – Galerie Max Hetzler, Cologne 1985 – '1:1', Westfälischer Kunstverein, Münster 1986 – 'More Sculptures in Other Places. Arbeiten 82–88', Galerie Max Hetzler, Cologne 1988 – Kunsthalle Zurich, 1989 – San Francisco Museum of Modern Art, 1990 – 'Multiplied Objects and Prints', Galerie Gisela Capitain, Cologne 1990

Catalogues of Collective Exhibitions (Selection)
Über sieben Brücken mußt Du gehen, Galerie Max Hetzler, Stuttgart 1982 – 'Ich komme nicht zum Abendessen', Galerie Max Hetzler, Stuttgart 1984 – 'Günther Förg, Georg Herold, Hubert Kiecol, Meuser, Reinhard Mucha', Galerie Peter Pakesch, Vienna 1985 – 'What About Having Our Mother Back!', Institute of Contemporary Arts, London 1986 – 'Skulptur Projekte in Münster', (DuMont) Cologne 1987 – 'Similia / Dissimilia', Städtische Kunsthalle Düsseldorf, 1987 – 'Broken Neon', Forum Stadtpark, Steirischer Herbst, Graz 1987 – 'Made in Cologne', DuMont Kunsthalle, Cologne 1988 – 'BiNationale. Deutsche Kunst der späten 80er Jahre', Düsseldorf, (DuMont) Cologne 1988 – 'Bilderstreit', Cologne 1989 – 'Das Medium der Fotografie ist berechtigt, Denkanstöße zu geben', Collection F.C. Gundlach, Kunstverein in Hamburg, 1989 – 'Refigured Painting. The German Image 1960–88', Toledo 1988, (Guggenheim Foundation) New York, (Prestel) Munich 1989 – 'Objet / Objectif', Galerie Daniel Templon, Paris 1989 – 'Ponton. Temse', Museum van Hedendaagse Kunst, Ghent 1990

Other Literature (Selection)
Ernst Bierich: 'Der Latten Ohnsinn', *Tip. Berlin Magazin*, No. 14, 1985 – Barbara Catoir: 'Being an Artist is not a Goal' (Interview), *Artscribe*, No. 57, 1986 – Stephan Schmidt-Wulffen: *Spielregeln. Tendenzen der Gegenwartskunst*, Cologne 1987 – Friedemann Malsch: '"Nothing's Final – The Sculptural Principle – Flight into Mania". Thoughts on the Role of Form and Material in Georg Herold's Work', *Parkett*, No. 15, 1988 – Friedemann Malsch: 'Die Ziegelbilder', *Kunstforum International*, Vol. 100, 1989 – Kirby Gookin: 'A Phoenix Built from the Ashes', *Arts Magazine*, March 1990

GARY HILL

Born Santa Monica, California, 1951. Studied at Art Students' League, Woodstock, New York, 1969. First one-man show at Polaris Gallery, Woodstock, 1971. From 1974 onwards, artist in residence at various institutions; visiting professorships at Center for Media, State University of New York, Buffalo; Bard College, Annandale-on-Hudson, New York; and elsewhere. Took part in Venice Biennale, 1984, and 'documenta 8', 1987. Lives and teaches at Art Faculty, Cornish College of the Arts, Seattle, Washington.

Gary Hill, who began his career as a sculptor, has been working in video since the early 1970s. His thematic statements draw on all the technical resources of the camera, the recorder and the video image itself. Transforming the technology, he sets out to convey mental processes that explore aspects of perception. The principal theme in his work since the late 1970s has been 'image and language': the interweaving of visual and verbal experience. Hill's installations are spaces that cast the viewer as a participant in a developing situation. In a number of works Hill has used his own body as a medium of expression, showing himself both as 'Seer' and as 'Seen'. He defines the conceptual context by incorporating montages of quotations from Bateson, Blanchot, Lewis Carroll and the Gnostic philosophers. 'Hill's metaphorical use of video and his placing himself into situations where everything is liable to suddenly lose control, at times, seems excessive. But it is through this excess that he achieves a paradoxical mediation of immediacy, an infinitely reversible double, something both too close and too far away.' (Robert Mittenthal)

Reference Sources for List of Exhibitions, Videos and Video Installations and for Bibliography
'Gary Hill. And Sat Down Beside Her', Galerie des Archives, Paris 1990 – 'Energieen', Stedelijk Museum, Amsterdam 1990

Catalogues and Monographs (Selection)
'Cinq pièces avec vue', 2e Semaine Internationale de Vidéo, Centre Genevois de Gravure Contemporaine, Geneva 1987 – 'Disturbance (Among the Jars)', Musée d'Art Moderne, Villeneuve d'Ascq 1989 – 'Otherwordsandimages', Video Galleriet, Huset, Ny Carlsberg Glyptotek, Copenhagen 1990

Catalogue of Collective Exhitions (Selection)
'The Biennale of Sydney', 1982 – 'The Second Link. Viewpoints on Video in the Eighties', Walter Phillips Gallery, Banff Centre School of Fine Arts, Banff, Alberta 1983 – 'Biennial Exhibition', Whitney Museum of American Art, New York 1983 – 'La Biennale di Venezia', Venice 1984 – 'documenta 8', Kassel 1987 – 'The Arts for Television', Museum of Contemporary Art, Los Angeles, Stedelijk Museum, Amsterdam 1987 – 'L'Epoque, la mode, la morale, la passion', Paris 1987 – 'Expansion & Transformation', The 3rd Fukui International Video Biennale, Fukui, Japan 1989 – 'Passages de l'image', Centre Georges Pompidou, Paris 1990

Other Literature (Selection)
Lucinda Furlong: 'A Manner of Speaking' (Interview), *Afterimage*, No. 8, 1983 – Charles Hagen: 'Gary Hill. Primarily Speaking', *Artforum*, No. 6, 1984 – Jean-Paul Fargier: 'Z. Rybczinski et G. Hill. La ligne, le point, le pli', *Cahiers du Cinema*, No. 415, 1989 – Wulf Herzogenrath/Edith Decker: *Video-Skulptur retrospektiv und aktuell. 1963–1989*, Cologne 1989 – Jacinto Lageira: 'Gary Hill. L'Imageur du Desastre. The Imager of Disaster', *Galeries Magazine*, December 1990 / January 1991

JENNY HOLZER

Born Gallipolis, Ohio, 1950. Studied at Duke University, Ohio, 1968–70; University of Chicago, 1970; Ohio University, 1971; Rhode Island School of Design, Providence, 1975. Took part in Independent Study Program of Whitney Museum, New York, 1977, turning from abstract paintings and diagrammatic drawings to texts. One-woman shows at Institute for Art and Urban Resources, P. S. 1 and Franklin Furnace, New York, 1978. One-woman shows at Barbara Gladstone Gallery, New York, from 1982. Exhibitions at Onze Rue Clavel, Paris; Lisson Gallery, London; Galerie Crousel-Hussenot, Paris; Monika Sprüth Galerie, Cologne; and elsewhere. Took part in 'documenta 7', 1982, 'documenta 8', 1987, and Venice Biennale, 1990. Lives in New York.

Jenny Holzer's use of language is a consistent endeavour to subvert the use of sterotyped verbal messages in the media and in public generally. She started off in 1977 by publishing *Truisms* and 'common-sense' statements on posters, handbills and illuminated newscasters in urban space. Then she added texts on metal plates – attached to things like parking meters and telephone kiosks – and TV advertising spots. In 1982 she sent out her anonymous messages on the celebrated electronic billboards in Times Square in New York. In successive sequences (*Inflammatory Essays*, 1979–82; *Living*, 1980–82; *Survival*, 1983–85; *Under a Rock*, 1985–87; and *Laments*, 1987–89), her language installations, which range from simple phrases to whole short stories, have become ever more complex in both substance and aesthetic content. In gallery and museum exhibitions, she combines electronic newscasters, inscribed sarcophagi, benches, marble tablets and flooring panels into dramatic environments. An example is her one-woman show at the Solomon R. Guggenheim Museum in 1989, in which she made use of the architecture of the building by having a text running round the spiral ramp. In the U. S. Pavilion at the 1990 Venice Biennale, where she won the International Prize, she achieved a dramatic synthesis of all the visual and verbal media that she has used.

Reference Source for List of Exhibitions and Bibliography
'Jenny Holzer', Solomon R. Guggenheim Museum, (Abrams) New York 1989

Books by the Artist (Selection)
A Little Knowledge, New York 1979 – *Black Book*, New York 1980 – *Living* (with Peter Nadin), New York 1980 – *Hotel* (with Peter Nadin), New York 1980 – *Eating Through Living* (with Peter Nadin), New York 1981 – *Eating Friends* (with Peter Nadin), New York 1981 – *Truisms and Essays*, Halifax, Nova Scotia 1983 – *Laments*, New York 1989

Catalogues and Monographs (Selection)
Kunsthalle Basle, Le Nouveau Musée, Villeurbanne, 1984 – 'Personae' (with Cindy Sherman), Contemporary Arts Center, Cincinnati 1986 – 'Signs', Des Moines Art Center, Des Moines, Iowa 1986 – 'Signs', Institute of Contemporary Arts, London 1988 – 'Laments 1988–89', Dia Art Foundation, New York 1989 – 'The Venice Installation', United States Pavilion, La Biennale di Venezia, Venice (Buffalo Fine Arts Academy) Buffalo 1990

Catalogues of Collective Exhibitions (Selection)
'Westkunst-heute', Cologne 1981 – 'documenta 7', Kassel 1982 – 'Content. A Contemporary Focus 1974–1984', Hirshhorn Museum and Sculpture Garden, Smithsonian Institution, Washington 1984 – 'The Biennale of Sydney', 1984 – ' Ein anderes Klima. Aspekte der Schönheit in der zeitgenössischen Kunst', Städtische Kunsthalle Düsseldorf, 1984 – 'Kunst mit Eigen-Sinn', Museum des 20. Jahrhunderts, Vienna 1985 – 'Carnegie International', Museum of Art, Carnegie Institute, Pittsburgh 1985 – 'Prospect 86', Frankfurt a. M. 1986 – 'Sonsbeek 86', Arnheim 1986 – 'Art and Its Double', Madrid 1987 – 'L'Epoque, la mode, la morale, la passion', Paris 1987 – 'documenta 8', Kassel 1987 – 'Skulptur Projekte in Münster', (DuMont) Cologne 1987 – 'Cultural Geometry', Athens 1988 – 'In Other Words. Wort und Schrift in Bildern der konzeptuellen Kunst', Museum am Ostwall, Dortmund, (Edition Cantz) Stuttgart 1989 – 'A Forest of Signs. Art in the Crisis of Representation', Los Angeles 1989 – 'Image World. Art and Media Culture', Whitney Museum of American Art, New York 1989 – 'D & S Ausstellung', Hamburg 1989 – 'Energieën', Amsterdam 1990 – 'Culture and Commentary. An Eighties Perspective', Washington 1990 – 'Life-Size', Jerusalem 1990 – 'The Biennale of Sydney', 1990

Other Literature (Selection)
Hal Foster: 'Subversive Signs', *Art in America*, November 1982 – Carter Ratcliff: 'Jenny Holzer', *The Print Collector's Newsletter*, November/December 1982 – Jeanne Siegel: 'Jenny Holzer's Language Games' (Interview), *Arts Magazine*, December 1985 – Bruce Ferguson: 'Wordsmith' (Interview), *Art in America*, December 1986 – Jean-Pierre Bordaz: 'Jenny Holzer and the Spectacle of Communication', *Parkett*, No. 13, 1987 – John Howell: 'The Message is the Medium', *Artnews*, Summer 1988 – Steven Evans: 'Not all about death' (Interview), *Artscribe*, No. 76, 1989 – Jordan Mejias: 'Jenny Holzer', *Frankfurter Allgemeine Magazin*, No. 535, 1990 – Michael Auping: 'Jenny Holzer. The Venice Installation', *Noema Art Magazine*, No. 31, 1990 – Christiane Vielhaber: 'Jenny Holzer. "Man muß sich darüber im klaren sein, daß Betrachter Freiwillige sind"', *Künstler. Kritisches Lexikon der Gegenwartskunst*, issue 11, Munich 1990

CRISTINA IGLESIAS

Born San Sebastián, Spain, 1956. First one-woman show at Casa de Bocage, Setúbal, 1984. Exhibitions at Galería Cómicos, Lisbon; Galería Juana de Aizpuru, Madrid; Galería Marga Paz, Madrid; Galerie Ghislaine Hussenot, Paris; and elsewhere. Took part in Venice Biennale (Aperto), 1986. Lives at Torrelodones, near Madrid.

The sculptures of Cristina Iglesias are architectural in character. Materials such as concrete, iron, glass and alabaster panels are formed into spatial constructions. These are not free-standing but relate closely to the walls. They can neither be walked around nor entered. A number of the works quote from classical architectural forms. They combine different materials and seem either to prop up the wall or to grow out of it. Some more recent sculptures consist of compact, often interlocking sections of wall, the architecture of which – openings notwithstanding – looks closed and hermetic. In some cases these sculptures emit light from within through inserts of coloured glass or alabaster; these are spiritual spaces, somewhere between introversion and a contained openness, which keep their secret within themselves. 'The form which her sculptures take and the effects of the coloured glass evoke memories of similar things from the past. The suggestiveness which emanates from certain presences in her sculptures creates new presences: medievalism, the Romanesque crypt, the

Gothic stained-glass windows and their light effects... Her sculptures present the possibility of adding images with other contents to that which is observed. Mental images complete and alter what is seen. The mental space houses poetry.' (Bart Cassiman)

Reference Source for List of Exhibitions
'Cristina Iglesias', Stichting/Foundation De Appel, Amsterdam 1990

Catalogues and Monographs (Selection)
'Arqueologías', Casa de Bocage, Setúbal 1984 – Galería Cómicos, Lisbon 1986 – Kunstverein für die Rheinlande und Westfalen, Düsseldorf 1988

Catalogues of Collective Exhibitions (Selection)
'La Imagen del Animal', Caja de Ahorros, Madrid 1983 – 'La Biennale di Venezia', Venice 1986 – 'Cristina Iglesias, Juan Muñoz, Susana Solano', CAPC Musée d'Art Contemporain de Bordeaux, 1987 – 'Espagne 87. Dynamiques et Interrogations', ARC Musée d'Art Moderne de la Ville de Paris, 1987 – 'Spain. Art Today', Museum of Modern Art, Takanawa 1989 – 'The Biennale of Sydney', 1990

Other Literature (Selection)
Aurora García: 'Cristina Iglesias', *Artforum*, February 1988 – Uta Maria Reindl: 'Cristina Iglesias', *Kunstforum International*, Vol. 94, 1988 – Alexandre Melo: 'Cristina Iglesias', *Flash Art* (Spanish edition), No. 1, 1988 – Catherine Grout: 'Juan Muñoz, Cristina Iglesias. Sculpture', *Artstudio*, Autumn 1989

MASSIMO KAUFMANN

Born Milan, 1963. Studied philosophy at Milan University. One-man shows since 1987 at Studio Guenzani, Milan. Exhibitions at Studio Scalise, Naples; Galerie Faust, Geneva. Took part in exhibition 'Mailand Art Look' at Galerie Amer, Vienna, 1988. Lives in Milan.

Kaufmann's objects, installations or tableaux are visualizations of philosophical, historical and art-historical issues. In one series of works, the artist investigates the relationship between weight, form, figure and colour by, for instance, evoking a tension between calibrated weights in different colours, or by assigning weights to quotations from art history, or to images of the world, or to lengths of cloth. He links problems of substance and of meaning through an artistic process of confrontation and classification. The same happens in the construction of a map of the world made out of rulers, and in works combining signs, formulas, sketches and linguistic elements on cloths. Heaviness and lightness, measure, number and weight, are the defining factors of Kaufmann's work.

Reference Source for List of Exhibitions
Elena Pontiggia: *Delle misure, dei pesi con sei opere di Massimo Kaufmann*, (Edizioni El Bagatt) Bergamo 1989

Writings by the Artist
'Otras recensiones. Ding', *Flash Art* (Italian edition), No. 147, 1988/89 – 'Weltanschauung', *Juliet Art Magazine*, No. 39, 1989/90

Catalogues of Collective Exhibitions (Selection)
'Se i fisici producono dell'antimateria, sarà permesso agli artisti, già specialisti in angeli di dipingerla', Galleria Fac Simile, Milan 1986 – 'Carlo Guaita, Massimo Kaufmann, Marco Mazzucconi, Maurizzio Pellegrini', Galleria Lidia Carrieri, Rome 1988 – 'Mailand Art Look', Galerie Amer, Vienna 1988 – 'Il cielo e dintorni. Da zero all' infinito', Castello di Volpaia, Radda in Chianti 1988 – 'Davvero. Ragioni pratiche nell'arte', L'Osservatorio, Milan 1988 – 'Punti di vista', Studio Marconi, Milan 1989 – 'Carnet de Voyages-1', Fondation Cartier pour l'Art Contemporain, Jouy-en-Josas 1990

Other Literature (Selection)
Franco Mollica: 'Massimo Kaufmann. Studio Scalise', *Tema Celeste*, No. 27/28, 1990 – Angela Vettese: 'Intervista a Massimo Kaufmann', *Flash Art* (Italian edition), No. 160, 1991

MIKE KELLEY

Born Detroit, Michigan, 1954. Studied at University of Michigan, Ann Arbor, to 1976; California Institute of the Arts, Valencia, to 1978. First performance in Los

Angeles, 1978. First one-man show at Mizuno Gallery, Los Angeles, 1981. Exhibitions at Metro Pictures, New York; Rosamund Felsen Gallery, Los Angeles; Jablonka Galerie, Cologne; and elsewhere. Took part in Venice Biennale (Aperto) and 'BiNationale', Boston and Düsseldorf, 1988. Lives in Los Angeles.

Mainly based on quotations from and interpretations of contemporary mass culture, Kelley's work integrates the functioning of artistic, philosophical, psychological and ideological mechanisms. Texts, drawings, photographs and objects define specific thematic areas, some of which are then further elaborated in performance pieces. His work focuses on the collision between 'high' and 'low' culture and also between conceptual attitude and subjective interpretation – often with sardonic comments by the artist. Anything combines with anything. Kelley makes some startling connections, and he darts playfully from one element to another within his own predefined framework. In his installation *Pay for Your Pleasure,* for instance (1988), he sets 42 banners bearing portraits of and quotations from poets, philosophers, writers and other celebrities against one picture by a murderer. Further grotesque connections are drawn in a number of works based on erotic and sexual allusions. His use of caricatures, appliqué cloth dolls, word images and drawings combines 'serious' subject-matter with trite forms of presentation drawn from kitsch and everyday art. Mike Kelley: 'My interest in comic form, for instance, really comes from conceptualism. I had to decide what the simplest way of picturing something was – like the equivalent of writing. But I wanted to deal with how things were pictured, rather than how they were spoken.'

Reference Source for List of Exhibitions and Bibliography
'Mike Kelley', Jablonka Galerie, Cologne 1989

Writings by the Artist (Selection)
'The Parasite Lily', *High Performance,* No. 11/12, 1980 – 'The Monitor and the Merrimac', *High Performance,* No. 14, 1981 – 'Meditation on a Can of Vernors', *High Performance,* No. 17/18, 1982 – *Plato's Cave, Rothko's Chapel, Lincoln's Profile,* New York 1986 – 'Foul Perfection. Thoughts on Caricature', *Artforum,* January 1989

Catalogue
'Three Projects. Half A Man, From My Institution To Yours, Pay For Your Pleasure', The Renaissance Society at the University of Chicago, 1988

Catalogues of Collective Exhibitions (Selection)
'Sound', Los Angeles Institute of Contemporary Art, 1979 – 'Contemporary Drawings', University Art Museum, University of California, Santa Barbara 1981 – 'The First Show', Museum of Contemporary Art, Los Angeles 1983 – 'The Biennale of Sydney', 1984 – 'Biennial Exhibition', Whitney Museum of American Art, New York 1985 – 'Individuals. A Selected History of Contemporary Art. 1945–1986', Museum of Contemporary Art, Los Angeles 1986 – 'Avant-Garde in the Eighties', Los Angeles County Museum of Art, 1987 – 'Cal Arts. Skeptical Belief(s)', The Renaissance Society at the University of Chicago, 1987 – 'La Biennale di Venezia', Venice 1988 – 'Graz 1988', Grazer Kunstverein, Stadtmuseum Graz, 1988 – 'The BiNational. American Art of the Late 80's', Boston, (DuMont) Cologne 1988 – 'A Forest of Signs. Art in the Crisis of Representation', Los Angeles 1989 – 'Biennial Exhibition', Whitney Museum of American Art, New York 1989 – 'Prospect 89', Frankfurt a.M. 1989 – 'Le désenchantement du monde', Villa Arson, Centre National d'Art Contemporain, Nice 1990

Other Literature (Selection)
Howard Singermann: 'Mike Kelley', *Artforum,* December 1981 – Robert L. Pincus: 'Michael Kelley at Beyond Baroque and Rosamund Felsen', *Art in America,* September 1983 – Dan Cameron: 'Mike Kelley's Art of Violation', *Arts Magazine,* June 1986 – John Howell: 'Mike Kelley. Plato's Cave, Rothko's Chapel, Lincoln's Profile', *Artforum,* May 1987 – Holland Cotter: 'Eight Artists Interviewed', *Art in America,* May 1987 – Laurie Palmer: 'Mike Kelley. Renaissance Society', *Artforum,* September 1988 – Norbert Messler: 'Mike Kelley. Galerie Jablonka', *Artforum,* Summer 1989 – Jutta Koether: 'C-Culture and B- Culture', *Parkett,* No. 24, 1990

KAZUO KENMOCHI

Born Odawara, Kanagawa, Japan, 1951. First one-man show at Muramatsu Gallery, Tokyo, 1973. Exhibitions at Sato Gallery, Tokyo; Tokiwa Gallery, Tokyo; Galerie Maier-Hahn, Düsseldorf; Galerie Dioptre, Geneva; Independent Gallery, Tokyo; Interforme Atelier, Osaka; and elsewhere. Took part in 'Japanische Kunst der achtziger Jahre', Kunstverein, Frankfurt am Main. Lives in Tokyo.

Nearly all Kenmochi's sculptural works of the 1980s are gigantic in size. He uses tarred timbers to build tall, tapering columns, rampart-like spatial installations, shattered ships' hulls. The wood he uses is scrap, mostly from old buildings. Memories cling to the material. An element of earthly transience comes into play. The structure, and the surface treatment of the material, reinforce the atmosphere of decline and ruin. The works are haunted by a sense of them being the aftermath of devastation. This is true of many of Kenmochi's paintings, which he often juxtaposes with sculptural installations within the same space, and in which he uses overpainting to disrupt the reality of the photographic image. Here, reality becomes a precarious state.

Reference Source for List of Exhibitions
'Japanische Kunst der achtziger Jahre', Frankfurter Kunstverein, Frankfurt a.M., (Edition Stemmle) Schaffhausen 1990

JON KESSLER

Born Yonkers, New York, 1957. Studied at State University of New York, Purchase, to 1980; joined Independent Study Program, Whitney Museum, New York, 1981. First one-man show at Artists Space, New York, 1983. Exhibitions at Gallery Bellman, New York; Luhring Augustine & Hodes Gallery, New York; Galerie Max Hetzler, Cologne; Galerie Crousel-Robelin, Paris; Luhring Augustine Hetzler Gallery, Santa Monica; and elsewhere. Took part in São Paulo Biennale, 1985. Lives in New York and Paris.

Alongside 'object boxes' incorporating light projections and photographs, Kessler presents 'machines' that lead lives of their own, often as installations that fill a whole room. Kessler combines disparate materials and existing objects: stones, branches, hoses, everyday items. In a number of works, kitsch from China or Japan is quoted and mutated by being combined with high-tech machine design. Objects and light are used kinetically. The most recent sculptures incorporate architectural forms, transforming elements of modern metropolitan life into a play of light, motion, structure and imagination. 'These sculptures work like clocks that tell the collapse of time and erasure of cultural difference.' (David Joselit)

Reference Source for List of Exhibitions and Bibliography
'Le désenchantement du monde', Villa Arson, Centre National d'Art Contemporain, Nice 1990

Catalogues and Monographs (Selection)
Luhring, Augustine & Hodes Gallery, New York 1985 – Museum of Contemporary Art, Chicago 1986

Catalogues of Collective Exhibitions (Selection)
'An International Survey of Recent Painting and Sculpture', The Museum of Modern Art, New York 1984 – 'Biennial Exhibition', Whitney Museum of American Art, New York 1985 – 'Modern Machines. Recent Kinetic Sculpture', Whitney Museum at Philip Morris, New York 1985 – 'Bienal de São Paulo', 1985 – 'New Trends in Contemporary Sculpture. Ten Outstanding Sculptors of America and Japan', Contemporary Sculpture Center, Tokyo 1986 – 'Lumières, Perception-Projection', Centre International d'Art Contemporain de Montreal, 1986 – 'Endgame. Reference and Simulation in Recent Painting and Sculpture', Institute of Contemporary Art, Boston 1986 – 'NY Art Now. The Saatchi Collection', London 1988 – 'Horn of Plenty', Stedelijk Museum, Amsterdam 1989 – 'Gober, Halley, Kessler, Wool. Four Artists from New York', Kunstverein, Munich 1989 – 'Reorienting. Looking East', Third Eye Centre, Glasgow 1990 – 'Status of Sculpture', Espace Lyonnais d'Art Contemporain, Lyon 1990

Other Literature (Selection)
Richard Armstrong: 'Jon Kessler', *Artforum*, December 1983 – Michael Kohn: 'Jon Kessler', *Flash Art*, October 1984 – Joshua Decter: 'Jon Kessler', *Arts Magazine*, January 1986 – Jerry Saltz: *Beyond Boundaries*, New York 1987 – Renate Puvogel: 'Jon Kessler', *Kunstforum International*, Vol. 94, 1988 – Lynne Cooke: 'Anamnesis. The Work of Jon Kessler', *Artscribe*, May 1988 – Jeffrey Rian: 'Jon Kessler', *Galeries Magazine*, No. 30, 1989 – Daniela Goldmann: 'Jon Kessler. Conceptual Objects. The Transformation of the ready-made' (Interview), *Nike*, No. 30, 1989 – Susan Kandel: 'Jon Kessler at Luhring Augustine Hetzler', *Arts Magazine*, March 1990 – David Pagel: 'Jon Kessler', *Art Issues*, No. 10, 1990

IMI KNOEBEL

Born Dessau, 1940. Studied at Staatliche Kunstakademie, Düsseldorf, under Joseph Beuys, 1964–71. First joint show with Imi Giese at Charlottenborg, Copenhagen ('IMI + IMI'), 1968. Exhibitions at Galerie René Block, Berlin; Galerie Heiner Friedrich, Cologne and Munich; Achim Kubinski, Stuttgart; Galerie nächst St Stephan, Vienna; Galerie Erhard Klein, Bonn; Galerie Hans Strelow, Düsseldorf; and elsewhere. Took part in 'documenta 5', 1972, 'documenta 6', 1977, 'documenta 7', 1982, 'documenta 8', 1987. Lives in Düsseldorf.

Knoebel's conception of image and space is strongly influenced by his interest in Suprematism and Russian Constructivism. In 1968 he turned from a succession of *Line Pictures* to a quotation of Kazimir Malevich's *Black Cross*, which he modified by enlarging it to monumental dimensions and displacing it internally, as an object suspended freely in front of the wall. This approach to the materiality and spirituality of image, colour, surface and spatial position has turned Knoebel's exhibitions into places for reflection. The paintings combine two- and three-dimensional form; they mostly take the form of wooden boards in geometric shapes, either painted in monochrome or rough-surfaced, which are shown in isolation, or in large-scale arrangements, or stacked, or combined with other wooden objects or other materials. A constructional element is combined with the principle of randomness; order is juxtaposed with designed chaos. Prints and drawings, photographs and projections are further aspects of Knoebel's work. Knoebel deals with the theme of space in two variant forms. On the one hand he fills a space with a multiplicity of three-dimensional objects (as in *Space 19*, 1968), the precise arrangement of which oscillates between order and disorder. On the other hand he creates large, closed, cubic forms (*Heerstraße 16*, 1984), which duplicate the dimensions of Knoebel's studio kitchen. In exhibitions, Knoebel combines the aspects of his work in a variety of ways as units in an aesthetic discourse to which there can be no conclusion. 'The austerity of form evokes the infinite temptation of total boundlessness and the attendant sublime horror of self-dissolution. It evokes our vague longing for the true Ground of Being, for that inconceivable void in which we dream of taking refuge – and which, if we ever do encounter it, comes as a fall imagined in the spirit of Edgar Allan Poe: a fantastic journey into the beyond, the realm of uncertainty.' (Max Wechsler)

Reference Source for List of Exhibitions
'Imi Knoebel. Tentoonstellingsinstallaties. Ausstellungsinstallationen 1968–1988', Bonnefantenmuseum Maastrich, 1989

Catalogues and Monographs (Selection)
'Projektion 4/1–11,5/1–11', Stedelijk Museum, Amsterdam 1972 – Städtische Kunsthalle Düsseldorf, 1975 – Stedelijk Van Abbemuseum, Eindhoven 1982 – Kunstmuseum Winterthur, 1983 – Städtisches Museum Abteiberg, Mönchengladbach 1984 – 'Heerstraße 16', Wilhelm-Lehmbruck-Museum, Duisburg 1984 – Rijksmuseum Kröller-Müller, Otterlo 1985 – Staatliche Kunsthalle Baden-Baden, 1986 – Dia Art Foundation (with Joseph Beuys and Blinky Palermo), New York 1988 – 'Werken uit de verzameling Ingrid en Hugo Jung', Museum van Hedendaagse Kunst, Antwerp 1989 – 'L'Idea di Europa', Padiglione d'Arte Contemporanea di Milano, (De Luca Editori) Rome 1991

Catalogues of Collective Exhibitions (Selection)
'IMI Art etc.', Galerie René Block, Berlin 1968 – 'Strategy: Get Arts', Edinburgh International Festival, 1970 – 'Sonsbeek 71', Arnheim 1971 – 'Prospect 71. Projection', Städtische Kunsthalle Düsseldorf, 1971 – 'documenta 5', Kassel 1972 – '14x14', Staatliche Kunsthalle Baden-Baden, 1972 – 'Szene Rhein-Ruhr '72', Museum Folkwang, Essen 1972 – 'Medium Fotografie',

Städtisches Museum Leverkusen, Schloß Morsbroich, 1973 – 'Projekt '74', Wallraf-Richartz-Museum, Kunsthalle Köln, Kölnischer Kunstverein, Cologne 1974 – 'ProspectRetrospect', Städtische Kunsthalle Düsseldorf, (Verlag Walther König) Cologne 1976 – 'documenta 6', Kassel 1977 – 'Kunst in Europa na '68', Museum van Hedendaagse Kunst, Ghent 1980 – 'Pier + Ocean', Hayward Gallery, London 1980 – 'Art Allemagne Aujourd'hui', ARC Musée d'Art Moderne de la Ville de Paris, 1981 – 'documenta 7', Kassel 1982 – 'von hier aus', Düsseldorf, (DuMont) Cologne 1984 – '1945–1985. Kunst in der Bundesrepublik Deutschland', Nationalgalerie, Berlin 1985 – 'Die 60er Jahre. Kölns Weg zur Kunstmetropole', Kölnischer Kunstverein, Cologne 1986 – 'Beuys zu Ehren', Städtische Galerie im Lenbachhaus, Munich 1986 – 'Similia / Dissimilia', Städtische Kunsthalle Düsseldorf, 1987 – 'documenta 8', Kassel 1987 – 'Regenboog', Stedelijk Van Abbemuseum, Eindhoven 1987 – 'Brennpunkt Düsseldorf. Joseph Beuys – Die Akademie – Der allgemeine Aufbruch 1962–1987', Kunstmuseum Düsseldorf, 1987 – 'Rot Gelb Blau', Kunstmuseum St. Gallen, 1988 – 'Zeitlos', Berlin, (Prestel) Munich 1988 – 'BiNationale. Deutsche Kunst der späten 80er Jahre', Düsseldorf, (DuMont) Cologne 1988 – 'La razón revisada. Reason revised', Fundación Caja de Pensiones, Madrid 1988 – 'Prospect 89', Frankfurt a.M. 1989 – 'Bilderstreit', Cologne 1989 – 'Objet/Objectif', Galerie Daniel Templon, Paris 1989 – 'Pharmacon '90', Makuhari Messe, Tokyo 1990

Other Literature (Selection)
Gislind Nabakowski: 'W. Knoebel. Projektion x', *Flash Art*, No. 32/33/34, 1972 – Marlis Grüterich: 'Knoebel. Galerie Friedrich', *Kunstforum International*, Vol. 25, 1978 – Wolfgang Max Faust / Gerd de Vries: *Hunger nach Bildern*, Cologne 1982 – Karin Thomas: *Zweimal deutsche Kunst nach 1945*, Cologne 1985 – Johannes Stüttgen: 'Conversation avec Imi Knoebel', *Plus*, No. 1, 1985 – Bernhard Bürgi: 'Imi Knoebel', *Wolkenkratzer Art Journal*, No. 11, 1986 – Donald Kuspit: 'Imi Knoebel's Triangle', *Artforum*, January 1987 – Stephan Schmidt-Wulffen: *Spielregeln. Tendenzen der Gegenwartskunst*, Cologne 1987 – Johannes Meinhardt: 'Imi Knoebel. Topische Evidenz', *Kunstforum International*, Vol. 87, 1987 – Max Wechsler: 'Imi Knoebel. The Surveyal of Sensations', *Parkett*, No. 17, 1988 – Robert Starr: 'Beuys's Boys. Beuys, Knoebel, Palermo', *Art in America*, No. 3, 1988 – Karl Ruhrberg (ed.): *Zeit-*

zeichen. Stationen Bildender Kunst in Nordrhein-Westfalen, Cologne 1989 – Norbert Messler: 'Von Außen nach Innen nach Außen, denn', *Noema Art Magazine*, No. 29, 1990

JEFF KOONS

Born York, Pennsylvania, 1955. Studied at Maryland Institute, College of Art, Baltimore, 1972–75; School of the Art Institute of Chicago, 1975–76. First one-man show at The New Museum, New York, 1980. Exhibitions at International With Monument Gallery, New York; Daniel Weinberg Gallery, Los Angeles; Galerie Max Hetzler, Cologne; Sonnabend Gallery, New York; and elsewhere. Took part in 'Skulptur Projekte in Münster', Münster, 1987, and Venice Biennale (Aperto), 1990. Lives in New York.

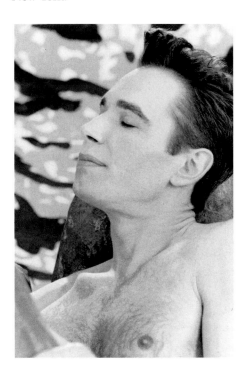

Jeff Koons's art is fuelled by irony, by the artist's capacity for self-presentation, and by a finely calculated manipulation of the strategies and mechanisms of the art market. Trite and kitschy items of everyday design and banal art are displayed in showcases. Koons takes toys, knick-knacks and rococo statuettes and has them cast in high-quality stainless steel, with all the glitter of luxury articles. He also makes sculptures of banal and erotic subjects in wood and porcelain, in stylized, blatantly artificial arrangements. Koons caused a stir at the 1990 Venice Biennale with a wooden sculpture, carved for him at Oberammergau, of a sex act with the Italian porno star and politician Cicciolina. *Made in Heaven* – the film of the sculpture – is due to reach the public in 1991. Koons: 'There's a certain sparseness and a certain emptiness about the work, an emptiness about the inside, which also creates an emptiness about the outside of the work. I believe that banality can bring salvation right now. Banality is one of the greatest tools that we have. It can seduce. It is a great seducer, because one automatically feels above it.'

Reference Sources for List of Exhibitions and Bibliography
'Jeff Koons', Museum of Contemporary Art, Chicago 1988 – 'Objectives. The New Sculpture', Newport Harbor Art Museum, Newport Beach, California 1990

Catalogues of Collective Exhibitions (Selection)
'Energie New York', Espace Lyonnais d'Art Contemporain, Lyon 1982 – 'A Fatal Attraction. Art and the Media', The Renaissance Society at the University of Chicago, 1982 – 'A Decade of New Art', Artists Space, New York 1984 – 'New Sculpture. Robert Gober, Jeff Koons, Haim Steinbach', The Renaissance Society at the University of Chicago, 1986 – 'Prospect 86', Frankfurt a.M. 1986 – 'Art and Its Double', Madrid 1987 – 'Skulptur Projekte in Münster', (DuMont) Cologne 1987 – 'NY Art Now. The Saatchi Collection', London 1988 – 'The BiNational. American Art of the Late 80's', Boston, (DuMont) Cologne 1988 – 'ReDefining the Object', University Art Galleries, Wright State University, Dayton, Ohio 1988 – 'Schlaf der Vernunft', Kassel 1988 – 'Cultural Geometry', Athens 1988 – 'Museum der Avantgarde. Die Sammlung Sonnabend New York', Berlin, (Electa) Milan 1989 – 'Psychological Abstraction', Athens 1989 – 'A Forest of Signs. Art in the Crisis of Representation', Los Angeles 1989 – 'Artificial Nature', Deste Foundation for Contemporary Art, House of Cyprus, Athens 1990 – 'Culture and Commentary. An Eighties Perspective', Washington 1990 – 'Jardins de Bagatelle', Galerie Tanit, Munich 1990 – 'Energieen', Amsterdam 1990 – 'La Biennale di Venezia', Venice 1990 – 'D&S Ausstellung', Hamburg 1990 – 'Life-Size', Jerusalem 1990 – 'The Biennale of Sydney', 1990 – 'Weitersehen', Krefeld 1990

Other Literature (Selection)
Giancarlo Politi: 'Luxury and Desire' (Interview), *Flash Art*, No. 132, 1987 – Roberta Smith: 'Rituals of Consumption', *Art in America*, No. 5, 1988 – 'Collaborations Jeff Koons / Martin Kippenberger,' *Parkett*, No. 19, 1989 – Stuart Morgan: 'Big Fun. Four Reactions to the New Jeff Koons', *Artscribe*, No. 75, 1989

JANNIS KOUNELLIS

Born Piraeus, 1936. Moved to Italy, 1956. First one-man show at Galleria La Tartaruga, Rome, 1960. Exhibitions at Galleria Gian Enzo Sperone, Turin and Rome; Galerie Folker Skulima, Berlin; Sonnabend Gallery, New York; Galleria Lucio Amelio, Naples; Galerie Konrad Fischer, Düsseldorf; Galleria Christian Stein, Turin and Milan; and elsewhere. First spatial installations at Galleria L'Attico, Rome, 1967. Took part in 'documenta 5', 1972, 'documenta 6', 1977, 'documenta 7', 1982. Lives in Rome.

Kounellis's work can be understood in terms of an encounter with language, myths and cultural history, and with political and aesthetic structures in space. In 1958–64 he produced pictures containing letters, numbers and flecks, which the artist used in the same way as a musical score. From 1967 on, Kounellis staged confrontations between the works of nature and artificial structures. In 1969, for instance, he exhibited eleven horses at a gallery in Rome. This significant step away from the canvas had its prehistory in works in which he had used parrots, other birds and plants, then fire, earth, coal and their residues. In the mid 1970s Kounellis started to fill in door and window openings with various materials such as stones, laths, plaster figures and fragments of pieces of furniture (most impressively at the Martin-Gropius-Bau in Berlin, for the 'Zeitgeist' exhibition of 1982). The aesthetic principle involved in the serial and cumulative presentation of these blocked openings recurs – strictly formalized – in Kounellis's wall pieces, which are poetic combinations of such materials as fire, gas, soot, steel, sackcloth, plaster debris and lead. Kounellis's 'politics of form', which also finds expression in theatrical scenes (on which he has collaborated since 1978 with Carlo Quartucci), may be described as the quest for the one image that unites lifeless and living material, tradition and progress, politics and the individual. Kounellis: 'We had decided to wait. Week after week we kept our promise; the result is our formal property…'

Reference Sources for List of Exhibitions and Bibliography
'Jannis Kounellis', Museo d'Arte Contemporanea, Castello di Rivoli, Turin, (Fabbri Editori) Milan 1988 – 'Via del Mare', Stedelijk Museum, Amsterdam 1990

Writings by the Artist
Kounellis's major texts are to be found in 'Odyssée Lagunaire. Ecrits et entretiens 1966–1989', Paris 1990

Catalogues and Monographs (Selection)
'L'Alfabeto di Kounellis', Galleria La Tartaruga, Rome 1961 – 'Il Giardino, I Giuochi', Galleria L'Attico, Rome 1967 – Kunstmuseum Lucerne, 1977 – Galleria Mario Diacono, Bologna 1978 – Museum Folkwang, Essen 1979 – Stedelijk Van Abbemuseum, Eindhoven 1981 – Städtische Galerie im Lenbachhaus, Munich 1985 – Museum of Contemporary Art, Chicago 1986 – Gloria Moure: *Kounellis*, Barcelona 1990

Catalogues of Collective Exhibitions (Selection)
'Schrift en Beeld', Stedelijk Museum, Amsterdam 1963 – 'When Attitudes Become Form', Kunsthalle Bern, 1969 – 'Arte Povera. 13 italienische Künstler', Kunstverein, Munich 1971 – 'documenta 5', Kassel 1972 – 'ProspectRetrospect, Städtische

Kunsthalle Düsseldorf, (Walther König) Cologne 1976 – 'documenta 6', Kassel 1977 – 'Westkunst', Cologne 1981 – 'A New Spirit in Painting', London 1981 – ''60 '80 attitudes / concepts / images', Stedelijk Museum, Amsterdam 1982 – 'documenta 7', Kassel 1982 – 'Zeitgeist', Berlin 1982 – 'Skulptur im 20. Jahrhundert', Merian-Park, Basle 1984 – 'Rosenfest. Fragment XXX', daadgalerie, Berlin 1984 – 'Carnegie International', Museum of Art, Carnegie Institute, Pittsburgh 1985 – 'Wien Fluß', Wiener Festwochen, Vienna 1986 – 'Terrae Motus 2', Villa Campolieto, Herculaneum, (Fondazione Amelio Istituto per l'Arte Contemporanea), Naples 1986 – 'Chambres d'amis', Ghent 1986 – 'Beuys zu Ehren', Städtische Galerie im Lenbachhaus, Munich 1986 – 'Positionen heutiger Kunst', Nationalgalerie, Berlin 1988 – 'La Biennale di Venezia', Venice 1988 – 'Carnegie International', Carnegie Museum of Art, Pittsburgh 1988 – 'Museum der Avantgarde. Die Sammlung Sonnabend New York', Berlin, (Electa) Milan 1989 – 'Bilderstreit', Cologne 1989 – 'Italian Art in the 20th Century', Royal Academy of Arts, London, Staatsgalerie Stuttgart, (Prestel) Munich 1989 – 'Die Endlichkeit der Freiheit', Berlin 1990

Other Literature (Selection)
Germano Celant: *Arte Povera*, Milan, London 1969 – Frank Popper: *Art-Action and Participation*, New York 1975 – Germano Celant: *Senza titolo 1974*, Rome 1976 – Achille Bonito Oliva: *Europe / America. The Different Avant-gardes*, Milano 1976 – Mario Diacono: *Verso una nuova iconografia*, Reggio Emilia 1984 – 'Collaboration Jannis Kounellis', *Parkett*, No. 6, 1985 – Germano Celant: *Arte Povera Arte Povera*, Milan 1985 – *Ein Gespräch / Una Discussione: Joseph Beuys, Jannis Kounellis, Anselm Kiefer, Enzo Cucchi*, Zurich 1986 – Alan Jones: 'Kounellis Unbound', *Arts Magazine*, No. 7, 1990

ATTILA KOVÁCS

Born Pécs, 1951. Studied architecture at Technical University, Budapest, 1969–74; Institute of Architectural Design, Pécs, 1974–78. Production designer for MaFilm since 1979. First one-man show at Bercsényi Klub, Budapest, 1974. Exhibitions at Pécsi Galéria, Pécs; Tatgalerie, Vienna; and elsewhere. Lives in Budapest.

Kovács has found a wide scope for the application of his pictorial and spatial ideas. He has created impressive exterior and interior sets for films directed by Pál Sándor, András Jeles, Gábor Szábó and István Szábó, incorporating quotations from the history of architecture, film and the other visual arts and subjecting them to a sculptural metamorphosis. His exhibition and stage designs, especially those for Richard Wagner's *Ring* (Turin, 1986–88), feature archaic forms, 'anti-design', technological myths and a strong feeling for material. Since 1986 he has made some extraordinary *Vampire Furniture*, as well as a number of sculptures and pictures in iron. The sculptures are quasi-abstract variations on themes from industrial architecture; the pictures depict industrial landscapes incorporating nude heroes or vampires in the style of a transmogrified Socialist Realism. 'Attila Kovács has substituted modern achievements for the classic objects of destruction. Industrial production itself is dying, and only ghosts and monsters can lend it a semblance of life.' (Lázló Beke)

Reference Source for List of Exhibitions and Bibliography
'Kovács Attila. Necropolis', Pécsi Galéria, Pécs 1987

Catalogues of Collective Exhibitions (Selection)
'La Biennale de Paris', 1982 – 'Nouvelle Biennale de Paris', 1985 – 'Töne und Gegentöne', Messepalast, Vienna 1985 – 'Bachman, Kovács, Rajk, Szalai', Dorottya utcai Galéria, Budapest 1986 – 'L'Art Contemporain Hongrois', Espace Lyonnais d'Art Contemporain, Lyon 1987 – 'Triumph', Charlottenborg, Copenhagen, Mücsarnok, Budapest, 1990

Other Literature (Selection)
Anni di Ferro: 'Movie Architecture', *Domus*, No. 644, 1983 – Juliana Balint: 'E solo un Film. Just a Movie', *Abitare*, December 1985 – Loránd Hegyi: *Ways from the Avantgarde*, Pécs 1989 – Loránd Hegyi: 'New Images of Identity', *Flash Art*, No. 145, 1989

GUILLERMO KUITCA

Born Buenos Aires, 1961. First one-man show at Galería Lirolay, Buenos Aires, 1974. Exhibitions at Julia Lublin Galería Del Retiro, Buenos Aires; Annina Nosei Gallery, New York; Galerie Barbara Farber, Amsterdam; Gian Enzo Sperone, Rome;

and elsewhere. Took part in São Paulo Biennale, 1985 and 1989. Lives in Buenos Aires.

In Kuitca's paintings, certain motifs constantly return, with variations, as the basis of an aesthetic transposition of experience. In Wuppertal in 1980 the artist saw Pina Busch's Dance Theatre, which inspired him to paint theatrical spaces and situations with an emotionally charged narrative content. He often works with visual quotations. One important leitmotif in his paintings is the Odessa Steps scene from Eisenstein's film *Battleship Potemkin*. At the end of the 1980s he turned to painting houses and maps. House interiors and plans provide variations on his theme of individual isolation; maps are critically reinterpreted to form a new image of the world. Kuitca's paintings are subtle, poetic meditations on melancholy, grief and desperation. 'With a certain poignancy, the paintings of Kuitca evoke a sense that the modern world is a diminished place.' (Charles Merewether)

Reference Sources for List of Exhibitions and Bibliography
'Guillermo David Kuitca. Obras, 1982–1988', (Julia Lublin Ediciones), Buenos Aires 1989 – 'Guillermo Kuitca', Gian Enzo Sperone, Rome 1990

Catalogues and Monographs (Selection)
Galerie Barbara Farber, Amsterdam 1990 – Witte de With, Centre for Contemporary Art, Rotterdam 1990

Catalogues of Collective Exhibitions (Selection)
'Bienal de São Paulo', 1985 – 'Art of the Fantastic. Latin-America. 1920–1987', Indianapolis Museum of Art, 1987 – 'U-ABC', Stedelijk Museum, Amsterdam 1989 – 'Bienal de São Paulo', 1989

Other Literature (Selection)
Achille Bonito Oliva: 'International Trans-Avantgarde', Milan 1983 – Pierre Restany: 'Buenos Aires 1985. Un momento esistenziale', *Domus*, No. 661, 1985 – Jorge Glusberg: 'Art in Argentina', Milan 1986 – Paola Morsiani: 'Guillermo Kuitca', *Juliet Art Magazine*, No. 48, 1990 – Robert Feintuch: 'Guillermo Kuitca at Annina Nosei', *Art in America*, No. 9, 1990 – Martijn van Nieuwenhuyzen: 'Guillermo Kuitca. Julio Galan', *Flash Art*, No. 154, 1990

GEORGE LAPPAS

Born Cairo, 1950. Studied psychology at Reed College, Portland, Oregon, 1969–73; architecture at Architectural Association School, London, 1975; sculpture at High School of Fine Arts, Athens, 1976–81. One-man shows at Zoumboulakis Galleries, Athens, from 1981. Exhibitions at Jean Bernier, Athens. Took part in Venice Biennale, 1988 (Aperto) and 1990. Professor at High School of Fine Arts, Athens, from 1989. Lives in Athens.

On the floor of a room Lappas spreads out a mass of tiny metal sculptures, a proliferation of metal cube outlines. These are combined with figures of animals and abstract constructions of poles to create a theatrical scene that the viewer can walk through. There is an unmistakable element of play in all this. The artist as *Homo ludens* combines conceptual considerations with narrative elements. The installations revolve around the theme of Chance and Necessity. The world of art, as a stage, turns out to be the space of an unfettered imagination. 'In George Lappas's work the viewer is invited to participate. Each installation has elements which can be moved, presenting new possibilities, new conclusions. The works are never self-contained, their meanings are not fixed.' (Tessa Jackson)

Reference Source for List of Exhibitions and Bibliography
'An Installation by George Lappas. Dice Works', Tramway, Glasgow 1990

Catalogues and Monographs (Selection)
'Abacus', Zoumboulakis Galleries, Athens

1983 – Athena Schinas: 'Space Perception in the Sculptur of George Lappas', Zoumboulakis Galleries, Athens 1983 – 'Animal Sketches', Zoumboulakis Galleries, Athens 1986 – 'Mappemonde', Zoumboulakis Galleries, Athens 1987 – 'Grecia. XLIV Biennale di Venezia 1990', Ministero della Cultura, Athens 1990

Catalogues of Collective Exhibitions (Selection)
'Bienal de São Paulo', 1987 – 'La Biennale di Venezia', Venice 1988 – 'Psychological Abstraction', Athens 1989

Other Literature (Selection)
Christos Papoulias: 'George Lappas' (Interview), *Tefchos*, July/August 1990

OTIS LAUBERT

Born Valaská/Banská Bystrica, Czechoslovakia, 1946. Studied at Middle School of Arts and Crafts, Bratislava, 1961–65. First one-man show at Dom Kultury Orlová, 1981. Exhibitions at Galerie Mladých, Brno; Junior Club, Chmelnice, Prague; Galerie Knoll, Vienna. Lives in Bratislava.

Lambert sees himself as an artist, as a poet and as a collector. In his installations he hangs found objects such as chewing-gum

wrappers, visiting-cards, used envelopes and sundry discarded fragments at eye-height from thin threads in a white room. The viewer can move around among them. The things are made to speak through the immediacy of their presence. They tell of the lack of freedom to which their circumscribed everyday functions have condemned them. Banality is transmuted into poetry. 'The motive of Laubert's creative work is the reanimation of refuse: the systematic rooting-out of unusable, forgotten, discarded, used-up things whose function has apparently been exhausted.' (Jana Geržová)

Catalogues

Výstavni Siň Domu Kultury Orlová, Kulturhaus Orlová, 1981 – Nádvoří Galerie Mladých, Brno 1987

GERHARD MERZ

Born Mammendorf, Munich, 1947. Studied at Akademie der Bildenden Künste, Munich, 1969–73. First one-man show at Kunstraum, Munich, 1975. Exhibitions at Galerie Rüdiger Schöttle, Munich; Galerie Konrad Fischer, Düsseldorf; Galerie Schellmann & Klüser, Munich; Barbara Gladstone Gallery, New York; Galerie Tanit, Munich; Galerie Marika Malacorda, Geneva; Galerie nächst St Stephan, Vienna; and elsewhere. Took part in 'documenta 6', 1977, 'documenta 7', 1982, 'documenta 8', 1987. Lives in Munich.

In 1971 Merz turned from metal sculptures to large grid-pattern and monochrome paintings, presented in groups and in series. The concern with 'colour as colour' has remained a leitmotiv of the artist's entire output. His aesthetic is a philosophical one;

in a conceptual sense, it represents the attempt to 'perfect' the positions of Classic Modernism, and notably those of Constructivism and Suprematism (Merz: 'It's not about inventing, it's about perfecting'). In the late 1970s he combined planes of colour with rigidly typographical texts and words. In 1982 Merz began working with silkscreened photographs from the realms of art, ethnography, landscape etc., combined for exhibition purposes with monochrome paintings and murals. Sumptuous frames emphasize the picture plane. Since the mid-1980s Merz's exhibitions have been spatial creations – total works of art – in which he assembles all his artistic resources, including lettering, colour and sculpture, under thematic headings. In recent years Merz has extended these scenic installations to include architectural elements. 'There has long been more art than there are walls to hang it on. Merz responds to this with a measure of cultural ecology: he makes more walls. Against the proliferation of minor art to set off designer sofas, dentists' surgeries and government corridors, he sets the fundamental issue of the mental space of art. Venturi's statement "Less is Bore" stands on its head Mies van der Rohe's architectural principle "Less is More". Merz strikes back against the mindless inanities of the Postmodern and sets that Modernist principle back on its feet again, Merz proclaims a Reformation of the established art trade; he is an iconoclast who casts down piffling images, an itinerant preacher who inveighs against the trade in indulgences between Art and Capital.' (Beat Wyss)

Reference Source for List of Exhibitions and Bibliography

'Gerhard Merz. Salve', Staatliche Kunsthalle Baden-Baden, 1987

Catalogues and Monographs (Selection)

Kunstraum München, 1975 – 'Zuschauer. I love my time. Beton', Kunstraum, Munich 1982 – 'Mondo Cane', FIAC 83, Paris, (Galerie Tanit) Munich 1983 – Laszlo Glozer / Vittorio Magnago Lampugnani: *Gerhard Merz. Tivoli*, Cologne 1986 – 'Dove Sta Memoria', Kunstverein, Munich 1986 – 'MCMLXXXVIII', Le Consortium, Dijon 1988 – 'Mnemosyne or the Art of Memory', Art Gallery of Ontario, Toronto 1988 – 'Costruire', Kunsthalle Zürich, 1989 – 'De Ordine Geometrico', Stiftung De Appel, Amsterdam 1990 – 'Den Menschen der Zukunft', Kunstverein Hannover, 1990

Catalogues of Collective Exhibitions (Selection)

'documenta 6', Kassel 1977 – 'Westkunstheute', Cologne 1981 – 'Art Allemagne Aujourd'hui', ARC Musée d'Art Moderne de la Ville de Paris, 1981 – 'documenta 7', Kassel 1982 – 'von hier aus', Düsseldorf, (DuMont) Cologne 1984 – 'The European Iceberg', Art Gallery of Ontario, Toronto, (Mazzotta) Milan 1985 – '1945–1985. Kunst in der Bundesrepublik Deutschland', Nationalgalerie, Berlin 1985 – 'Chambres d'amis', Ghent 1986 – 'Implosion. Ett postmodern perspektiv', Moderna Museet, Stockholm 1987 – 'documenta 8', Kassel 1987 – 'L'Epoque, la mode, la morale, la passion', Paris 1987 – 'Mythos Italien. Wintermärchen Deutschland', Haus der Kunst, Staatsgalerie Moderner Kunst, Munich 1988 – 'BiNationale. Deutsche Kunst der späten 80er Jahre', Düsseldorf, (DuMont) Cologne 1988 – 'Cultural Geometry', Athens 1988 – 'The Biennale of Sydney,' 1988 – 'Prospect 89', Frankfurt a.M. 1989 – 'Blickpunkte I', Musée d'Art Contemporain, Montreal 1989 – 'Einleuchten', Hamburg 1989 – 'Kunst der 80er Jahre. Aus der Sammlung Marx', Art 21'90, Basle 1990

Other Literature (Selection)

Dieter Hall: 'Gerhard Merz', *Ink-Dokumentation 5*, Zurich 1980 – Bazon Brock: 'Von Paulus zum Saulus. Zur Arbeit Mondo Cane von Gerhard Merz', *Kunstforum International*, Vol. 67, 1983 – Christoph Blase: 'Gerhard Merz. Eleganz mit hartem Konzept', *Wolkenkratzer Art Journal*, No. 8, 1985 – Laszlo Glozer: 'Gerhard Merz. Tivoli', *Parkett*, No. 7, 1986 – Stephan Schmidt-Wulffen: 'Room as Medium', *Flash Art*, No. 31, 1986 – Sara Rogenhofer/Florian Rötzer: 'An einer Ästhetik der Macht bin ich nicht interessiert' (Interview), *Kunstforum International*, Vol. 92, 1987/88 – Thomas Dreher: 'Gerhard Merz. Werke der 80er Jahre', *Artefactum*, No. 25, 1988 – Beat Wyss: 'Gerhard Merz. Costruire', *Noema Art Magazine*, No. 27, 1989 – Giorgio Maragliano: 'Gerhard Merz' (Interview), *Flash Art*, No. 152, 1990

OLAF METZEL

Born Berlin, 1952. Studied at Free University and Hochschule der Künste, Berlin, 1971–77. Bursary from German Academic Exchange Service (DAAD) to live in Italy, 1977–78. First installation, *Skulptur Böckhstrasse 7, 3.OG (Sculpture Böckhstrasse 7, Third Floor)*, Berlin, 1981. Exhibitions at Galerie Fahnemann, Berlin; Galerie Rudolf Zwirner, Cologne; Produzentengalerie, Hamburg; and elsewhere. Working grant from Kulturkreis of Federation of German Industry (BDI), Cologne, and from Senator for Cultural Affairs, Berlin, 1983. P.S.1, New York; Kunstfonds, Bonn; visiting professor at Hochschule für Bildende Künste, Hamburg, 1986. Participated in 'documenta 8' and won Villa Massimo prize, Rome, and Kunstpreis Glockengasse, Cologne, 1987. Kurt Eisner-Preis, Munich, 1990. Since 1990, professor at Akademie der Bildenden Künste, Munich. Lives in Munich.

Metzel's installations deal with spaces and places, their individual, aesthetic, and political qualities. After his early brutally direct onslaughts on the walls of apartments and houses, in most of which he used cutting wheels and crowbars and adopted a language of political symbolism, as in *Türkenwohnung Abstand 12.000,– DM VB (Flat for Turks, Key-Money 12,000 DM o.n.o.)* of 1982, he turned to sculptures that set a political mark on public places, where they acted as temporary monuments. A challenging example was *13. 4. 1981*, his contribution to the 'Skulpturenboulevard' show in Berlin in 1987, which consisted of a vast pile of police crush barriers, heaped up

in a conspicuous position on the Kurfürstendamm. Newspaper photographs, political symbols and 'found objects' serve as the basic material for sculptures that are often preceded and accompanied by a series of drawings. Most recently, Metzel has been working with the themes of communication (through newspapers, for example) and of electronic and chemical technology. 'Olaf Metzel's closeness to aggression, destruction, and violence springs from anger: anger at the fact that the world is not perfect. He works to change it, by giving expression through art to the conflicts within reality, and thus by expanding the possibilities of art.' (Uwe M. Schneede)

Reference Source for List of Exhibitions and Bibliography
'Olaf Metzel. Zeichnungen 1985–1990', Kunstraum Munich, 1990 (later shown at Westfälisches Landesmuseum für Kunst und Kulturgeschichte, Münster, Institut für moderne Kunst, Nuremberg)

Catalogues and Monographs (Selection)
Kunstraum, Munich 1982 – daadgalerie, Berlin 1984 – 'Olympische Kunst / Fünfjahrplan', Künstlerhaus Bethanien, Berlin 1985 – 'Flaschen und Nummern', Galerie Fahnemann, Berlin 1985 – 'Der Fälscher ist der Held der elektronischen Kultur', Galerie Rudolf Zwirner, Cologne 1989 – Galerie Fahnemann, Berlin 1989 – Produzentengalerie Hamburg, 1990 – Kurt Eisner-Preis 1990, München 1990

Catalogues of Collective Exhibitions (Selection)
'Situation Berlin', Galerie d'Art Contemporain des Musées de Nice, 1981 – 'Künstler-Räume', Kunstverein in Hamburg, 1983 – 'The Biennale of Sydney', 1984 – 'von hier aus', Düsseldorf, (DuMont) Cologne 1984 – 'Magirus 117. Kunst in der Halle', Ulm 1985 – 'Dem Frieden eine Form geben – zugehend auf eine Biennale des Friedens', Kunstverein in Hamburg, 1985 – 'Jenisch-Park. Skulptur', Hamburg 1986 – 'Skulpturenboulevard', Berlin 1987 – '1961 Berlinart 1987', The Museum of Modern Art, New York, (Prestel) Munich 1987 – 'documenta 8', Kassel 1987 – 'Skulptur Projekte in Münster', (DuMont) Cologne 1987 – 'Arbeit in Geschichte – Geschichte in Arbeit', Kunsthaus und Kunstverein in Hamburg, 1988 – 'Per gli anni novanta. Nove artisti a Berlino', Padiglione d'Arte Contemporanea, Milan 1989 – 'In Between and Beyond. From Germany', The Power Plant, Toronto 1989 – 'The Biennale of Sydney', 1990

Other Literature (Selection)
René Block: 'Olaf Metzel', *Das Kunstwerk*, No. 4–5, 1985 – Ursula Frohne: 'Olaf Metzel', *Wolkenkratzer Art Journal*, No. 4, 1986 – Michael Schwarz: 'Olaf Metzel. Stammheim, 1984', *Kunst und Unterricht*, No. 105, 1986 – Jürgen Hohmeyer: 'Systemträger ätzen', *Der Spiegel*, No. 24, 1989 – Wolfgang Blobel: 'Der Computer als Kunstobjekt. Olaf Metzel und die ästhetische Demontage des Elektronikfrusts', *Kunst und Elektronik*, No. 2, 1989

YASUMASA MORIMURA

Born Osaka, 1951. Studied at Kyoto City University of Art, 1971–78. First one-man show at Gallery Haku, Osaka, 1986. Exhibitions at ON Gallery, Osaka; Gallery NW House, Tokyo; Mohly Gallery, Osaka; Sagacho Exhibit Space, Tokyo; Nicola Jacobs Gallery, London; and elsewhere. Took part in Venice Biennale (Aperto), 1988. Lives in Osaka.

Morimura's large colour photographs are highly subjective presentations of the masterpieces of Western civilization. Well-known and much-reproduced works by Duchamp, Ingres, Manet, Velázquez and Van Gogh are recreated in detail and parodistically alienated. At one and the same time, the artist is the star performer, the scenic arranger and the property man. The history of art is seen as refracted through androgyneity, allusive eroticism and freakish poses. In a meeting of Eastern and Western traditions and attitudes, quotations take on a life of their own. Morimura's works 'weave a labyrinthine network of sightlines connecting the origi-

nal work, Morimura's work as an imitation of that, and the eye of the beholder. This is Morimura's individual, ironic approach to art history; and at the same time it is surely a ferocious critique of the rather cockeyed way in which the Japanese look at Western art.' (Makoto Murata)

Reference Source for List of Exhibitions and Bibliography
'Yasumasa Morimura', Nicola Jacobs Gallery, London 1990

Catalogue
'Daughter of Art History', Sagacho Exhibit Space, Tokyo 1990

Catalogues of Collective Exhibitions (Selection)
'Photographic Aspect of Japanese Art Today', Tochigi Prefectural Museum of Fine Arts, Utsunomiya 1987 – 'La Biennale di Venezia', Venice 1988 – 'East Meets West. Japanese and Italian Art Today', Art L.A. '88, Los Angeles Convention Center, 1988 – 'Against Nature. Japanese Art in the Eighties', San Francisco Museum of Modern Art, 1989 – 'Reorienting. Looking East', Third Eye Centre, Glasgow 1990 – 'Culture and Commentary. An Eighties Perspective', Washington 1990 – 'Japanische Kunst der achtziger Jahre', Frankfurter Kunstverein, Frankfurt a.M., (Edition Stemmle) Schaffhausen 1990

Other Literature (Selection)
Shinji Kohmoto: '"A Secret Agreement", Coco, Kyoto', *Flash Art,* No. 140, 1988 – Janet Koplos: 'Yasumasa Morimura at NW House', *Art in America,* June 1989 – Azby Brown: 'Yasumasa Morimura', *Artforum,* May 1990 – Kate Bush: 'Yasumasa Morimura', *Artscribe,* January/February 1991

REINHARD MUCHA

Born Düsseldorf, 1950. First one-man show, '...sondern stattdessen einen Dreck wie mich' ('...but instead rubbish like me'), at Verwaltungs- und Wirtschaftsakademie Düsseldorf, 1977. Exhibitions at Galerie Max Hetzler, Stuttgart and Cologne; Galerie Bärbel Grässlin, Frankfurt; Galerie Konrad Fischer, Düsseldorf; Galleria Lia Rumma, Naples; and elsewhere. Took part in 'Skulptur Projekte in Münster', Münster, 1987, and Venice Biennale, 1990. Lives in Düsseldorf.

As well as his script works – written on the reverse of sheets of glass – Mucha's installations, in particular, are based on the artist's own individual memories: his experiences of city life and of childhood, his moods and his intellectual encounters. These find objective form in the artist's confrontations with objects, some from his private life, others taken from the inventory of a museum or other exhibition venue: office furnishings, glass showcases, ladders or screens. From these elements Mucha weaves a sober poetry that belongs to the sphere of *bricolage.* The titles of his works often refer to specific places, or to his own emotional or intellectual positions. Working in an art context, Mucha uses the context of art itself: he presents its presentation – as he did with particular cogency in his contribution to the 1990 Venice Biennale, *Deutschlandgerät (Germany Apparatus).* 'Perhaps this is the source of mystery behind Reinhard Mucha's sculptures and installations: a devotion to things that has to be knowledgeable because it is interested in the history of precise connections among things and between people and things, because it is interested in the history of dealing with them and getting used to them, and finally because it is interested in the connection with the fate through which things in their turn participate in what Mucha calls collective biography.' (Patrick Frey)

Reference Source for List of Exhibitions
'Bernd und Hilla Becher, Reinhard Mucha. Deutscher Pavillon', La Biennale di Venezia, Venice 1990

Catalogues and Monographs (Selection)
'Annemarie- und Will-Grohmann-Stipendium 1981', Staatliche Kunsthalle Baden-Baden, 1981 – 'Wartesaal', Galerie Max Hetzler, Stuttgart 1982 – 'Das Figur-Grund Problem in der Architektur des Barock (für dich allein bleibt nur das Grab)', Württembergischer Kunstverein, Stuttgart 1985 – 'Gladbeck', Centre Georges Pompidou, Paris 1986 – 'Kasse beim Fahrer', Kunsthalle Bern, and 'Nordausgang', Kunsthalle Basle, 1987

Catalogues of Collective Exhibitions (Selection)
'WPPT', Kunst- und Museumsverein, Wuppertal 1978 – 'Kunst wird Material', Nationalgalerie, Berlin 1982 – 'Konstruierte Orte', Kunsthalle Bern, 1983 – 'von hier aus', Düsseldorf, (DuMont) Cologne 1984 – 'Günther Förg, Georg Herold, Hubert Kiecol, Meuser, Reinhard Mucha,' Galerie Peter Pakesch, Vienna 1985 – 'The European Iceberg', Art Gallery of Ontario, Toronto, (Mazzotta) Milan 1985 – 'De Sculptura', Wiener Festwochen, Messepalast, Vienna 1986 – 'The Biennale of Sydney', 1986 – 'Sieben Skulpturen', Kölnischer Kunstverein, Cologne 1986 – 'Implosion. Ett postmodern perspektiv', Moderna Museet, Stockholm 1987 – 'Skulptur Projekte in Münster', (DuMont) Cologne 1987 – 'BiNationale. Deutsche Kunst der späten 80er Jahre', Düsseldorf, (DuMont) Cologne 1988 – 'Zeitlos', Berlin, (Prestel) Munich 1988 – 'Bilderstreit', Cologne 1989 – 'Einleuchten', Hamburg 1989 – 'Open Mind', Ghent 1989 – 'Culture and Commentary. An Eighties Perspective', Washington 1990 – 'Life-Size', Jerusalem 1990 – 'Weitersehen', Krefeld 1990

Other Literature (Selection)
Germano Celant: 'Stations on a Journey', *Artforum,* No. 24, 1985 – Walter Grasskamp: *Der vergeßliche Engel,* Munich 1986 – Pier Luigi Tazzi: 'Reinhard Mucha', *Wolkenkratzer Art Journal,* No. 5, 1986 – Stephan Schmidt-Wulffen: 'Rooms As Medium', *Flash Art,* No. 131, 1986/1987 – Pier Luigi Tazzi: 'Reinhard Mucha', *Artforum,* No. 25, 1987 – Patrick Frey: 'Reinhard Mucha. Connections', *Parkett,* No. 12, 1987 – Philip Monk: 'Reinhard Mucha. The Silence of Presentation', *Parachute,* No. 51, 1988 – Julian Heynen: 'Reinhard Mucha', *Das Kunstwerk,* No. 41, 1989 – Alexander Pühringer: 'Reinhard Mucha. Eine Annäherung', *Noema Art Magazine,* No. 31, 1990

JUAN MUÑOZ

Born Madrid, 1953. Studied at Central School of Art and Design, and Croydon School of Art and Technology, London, 1979; Pratt Institute, New York, 1982. First one-man show at Galería Fernando Vijande, Madrid, 1984. Exhibitions at Galería Cómicos, Lisbon; Galerie Joost Declercq, Ghent; Galería Marga Paz, Madrid; Galerie Konrad Fischer, Düsseldorf; Lisson Gallery, London; Marian Goodman Gallery, New York; and elsewhere. Took part in 'Chambres d'amis' exhibition, Ghent, and Venice Biennale (Aperto), 1986. Lives in Madrid.

Since the mid 1980s, Muñoz has been using architectural elements such as balcony railings, balusters and minarets, which he isolates in space or minimally modifies. He achieves this isolation by intervening in the exhibition space, and in particular by a specific modification of the floor surface, which serves as an intrinsic part of the installation, extending space and segregating the object. Muñoz subjects the human figure to similar treatment: sculptures of separate parts of the body are isolated and combined with pieces of furniture. He arranges dummies, dwarfs, soldiers, marionettes and dancers – in bronze or in wood – on the floor, on consoles, on plinths or on scaffolding. He relates each figure, its pose, material, accessories and size, in dramatic terms, to the place, to its decor, and to the other elements of the installation. One theme that Muñoz has incorporated in a variety of guises into his metaphorical, theatrical spaces since 1989 is that of the dragon. Juan Muñoz: 'I build metaphors in the guise of sculpture, be-cause I do not know any other way to explain to myself what it is that troubles me.'

Reference Source for List of Exhibitions and Bibliography
'Juan Muñoz', The Renaissance Society at the University of Chicago, 1990 (later shown at Centre d'Art Contemporain, Geneva)

Catalogues and Monographs (Selection)
'Ultimos Trabajos', Galería Fernando Vijande, Madrid 1984 – FRAC des Pays de La Loire (with Lili Dujourie), Abbaye de Fontevraud, 1987 – 'Sculpture de 1985 à 1987', Musée d'Art Contemporain de Bordeaux, 1987

Catalogues of Collective Exhibitions (Selection)
'La Imagen del Animal', Caja de Ahorros, Madrid 1983 – 'V. Salón de los 16', Muséo Español de Arte Contemporáneo, Madrid 1985 – 'La Biennale di Venezia', Venice 1986 – '1981–1986. Pintores y Escultores Españoles', Fundación Caja de Pensiones, Madrid 1986 – 'Chambres d'amis', Ghent 1986 – 'Steirischer Herbst '88', Grazer Kunstverein, Graz 1988 – 'Magiciens de la terre', Centre Georges Pompidou, Grande Halle de la Villette, Paris 1989 – 'Spain Art Today', Museum of Modern Art, Takanawa, 1989 – 'Bestiarium. Jardin-Théâtre', Entrepôt-Galerie du Confort Moderne, Poitiers 1989 – 'Psychological Abstraction', Athens 1989 – 'Le Spectaculaire', Centre d'Histoire de l'Art Contemporain, Rennes 1990 – 'Objectives. The New Sculpture', Newport Beach, California 1990 – 'The Biennale of Sydney', 1990 – 'Possible Worlds. Sculpture from Europe', Institute of Contemporary Arts, Serpentine Gallery, London 1990 – 'Weitersehen', Krefeld 1990

Other Literature (Selection)
Kevin Power: 'Juan Muñoz', *Artscribe*, Summer 1987 – José-Luis Brea: 'Juan Muñoz. The System of Objects', *Flash Art*, January / February 1988 – Alexandre Melo: 'Some Things that Cannot Be Said Any Other Way', *Artforum*, May 1989 – Luk Lambrecht: 'Juan Muñoz', *Flash Art*, November/December 1989 – Kim Bradley: 'Juan Muñoz at Galería Marga Paz', *Art in America*, February 1990 – James Roberts: 'Juan Muñoz', *Artefactum, No. 32, 1990*

BRUCE NAUMAN

Born Fort Wayne, Indiana, 1941. Studied mathematics and art history at University of Wisconsin, Madison, 1960–64, and art at University of California, Davis, 1964–66. First one-man show at Nicholas Wilder Gallery, Los Angeles, 1966. Exhibitions at Leo Castelli Gallery, New York; Galerie Konrad Fischer, Düsseldorf; Sonnabend Gallery, Paris and New York; Galleria Sperone, Turin; Yvon Lambert, Paris; Sperone Westwater Gallery, New York; and elsewhere. Took part in 'documenta 4', 1968, 'documenta 5', 1972, 'documenta 6', 1977, 'documenta 7', 1982. Max-Beckmann-Preis, Frankfurt am Main, 1990. Lives in Galisteo, New Mexico.

Nauman uses the most varied media, themes and techniques in his work. His drawings, sculptures, installations, videos, photography, performance art, theatre and neon work eludes any attempt at stylistic classification. The use of each artistic medium springs from a conceptual process that is often recorded in drawings. In the 1960s Nauman worked with his own body in a number of ways. In performances, videos and photographs, he gave an exemplary presentation of self-experiences and bodily actions; sculptures in the most varied materials, existed in relation to the artist's own body. At the beginning of the 1970s Nauman's works became more concerned with the definition of space. Sculptures based on models for imaginary tunnels formulated spatial situations. The viewer was increasingly drawn, into the work. Nauman's *Live-Taped Video Corridor* (1969–70) is an example of a work requiring direct involvement. At the same time, his work began to take on a political character. Lettering and figures outlined in neon spoke of war, violence and sexuality. Sculptures took torture as their theme (*South American Circle*, 1981). In his installations over the past few years, Nauman has devised alarming scenarios and visions. Fear and menace are evoked and become physical experiences. Carousel-like revolving installations put the viewer in the place of the pursuer and of the pursued. Animal bodies dangling in contorted postures, or deformed like cloned monstrosities; a disturbing demonstration of *Learned Helplessness in Rats* (1988); wax casts of human heads; and the video Installation *Clown Torture* (1987): all these assail the viewer and turn him into a thinking, feeling, suffering participant. Nauman, 1987: 'The true artist helps the world by revealing mystic truths.'

Reference Source for List of Exhibitions and Bibliography

Coosje van Bruggen: *Bruce Nauman*, (Rizzoli) New York 1988 – Jörg Zutter (ed.): 'Bruce Nauman. Skulpturen und Installationen. 1985–1990', Museum für Gegenwartskunst, Basle, (DuMont) Cologne 1990, (later shown at Städtische Galerie im Städelschen Kunstinstitut, Frankfurt a. M.)

Books and Writings by the Artist (Selection)

Pictures of Sculptures in a Room, Davis, (California) 1965–1966 – *Burning Small Fires*, San Francisco 1968 – *LAAir*, New York 1970 – *Floating Room*, New York 1973 – *Flayed Earth/Flayed Self (Skin/Sink)*, Los Angeles 1974 – *The Consummate Mask of Rock*, Buffalo 1975 – *Forced Perspective*, Düsseldorf 1975

Catalogues and Monographs (Selection)

Leo Castelli Gallery, New York 1968 – 'Work from 1965 to 1972', Los Angeles County Museum of Art, 1972 – '1/12 Scale Models for Underground Pieces', Albuquerque Museum, 1981 – '1972–1981', Rijksmuseum Kröller-Müller, Otterlo 1981 – 'Neons', Baltimore Museum of Art, 1982 – Museum Haus Esters, Krefeld 1983 – Whitechapel Art Gallery, London 1986 – 'Drawings / Zeichnungen 1965–1986', Museum für Gegenwartskunst, Basle 1986 – 'Prints 1970–89', Castelli Graphics, Lorence Monk Gallery, New York, Donald Young Gallery, Chicago, 1989

Catalogues of Collective Exhibitions (Selection)

'American Sculpture of the Sixties', Los Angeles County Museum of Art, 1967 – 'documenta 4', Kassel 1968 – 'Op Losse Schroeven. Situaties en Cryptostructuren', Stedelijk Museum, Amsterdam 1969 – 'When Attitudes Become Form', Kunsthalle Bern, 1969 – 'Konzeption Conception', Städtisches Museum Leverkusen, Schloß Morsbroich, 1969 – 'Tokyo Biennale '70. Between Man and Matter', Tokyo Metropolitan Art Gallery, 1970 – 'Conceptual Art, Arte Povera, Land Art', Galleria Civica d'Arte Moderna, Turin 1970 – 'Information', The Museum of Modern Art, New York 1970 – 'Sixth Guggenheim International Exhibition', Solomon R. Guggenheim Museum, New York 1971 – 'Sonsbeek 71', Arnheim 1971 – 'documenta 5', Kassel 1972 – 'Contemporanea', Parcheggio di Villa Borghese, Rome 1973 – 'Idea and Image in Recent Art', Art Institute of Chicago, 1974 – 'Spiralen und Progressionen', Kunstmuseum Luzern, 1975 – 'Drawing Now. 1955–1975', The Museum of Modern Art, New York 1976 – 'documenta 6', Kassel 1977 – 'Skulptur-Ausstellung in Münster', Westfälisches Landesmuseum für Kunst und Kulturgeschichte, Münster 1977 – 'La Biennale di Venezia', Venice 1978 – 'Werke aus der Sammlung Crex', Ink Halle für Internationale neue Kunst, Zurich 1978 – 'Pier + Ocean', Hayward Gallery, London 1980 – 'La Biennale di Venezia', Venice 1980 – 'Drawing Distinctions. American Drawings of the Seventies', Louisiana Museum, Humlebaek 1981 – 'Westkunst', Cologne 1981 – 'documenta 7', Kassel 1982 – 'Skulptur im 20. Jahrhundert', Merian-Park, Basle 1984 – 'Content. A Contemporary Focus. 1974–1984', Hirshhorn Museum and Sculpture Garden, Smithsonian Institution, Washington 1984 – 'Transformations in Sculpture', Solomon R. Guggenheim Museum, New York 1985 – 'Sonsbeek 86', Arnheim 1986 – 'Chambres d'amis', Ghent 1986 – 'Individuals. A Selected History of Contemporary Art. 1954–1986', Museum of Contemporary Art, Los Angeles 1986 – 'L'Epoque, la mode, la morale, la passion', Paris 1987 – 'Skulptur Projekte in Münster', (DuMont) Cologne 1987 – 'Schlaf der Vernunft', Kassel 1988 – 'Zeitlos', Berlin, (Prestel) Munich 1988 – 'Museum der Avantgarde. Die Sammlung Sonnabend New York', Berlin, (Electa) Milan 1989 – 'Bilderstreit', Cologne 1989 – 'Open Mind', Ghent 1989 – 'Einleuchten', Hamburg 1989 – 'Life-Size', Jerusalem 1990 – 'Energieen', Amsterdam 1990 – 'The Biennale of Sydney', 1990

Other Literature (Selection)

Fidel A. Danieli: 'The Art of Bruce Nauman', *Artforum*, No. 4, 1967 – Marcia Tucker: 'PheNAUMANology', *Artforum*, No. 4, 1970 – Willoughby Sharp: 'Bruce Nauman' (Interview), *Avalanche*, No. 2, 1971 – Robert Pincus-Witten: 'Bruce Nauman. Another Kind of Reasoning', *Artforum*, No. 6, 1972 – Jürgen Harten: 'T for Technics, B for Body', *Art and Artists*, November 1973 – Germano Celant: *Das Bild einer Geschichte 1956–1976. Die Sammlung Panza di Biumo*, Milan 1980 – Coosje van Bruggen: 'Bruce Nauman. Entrance, Entrapment, Exit', *Artforum*, No. 10, 1986 – 'Collaboration Bruce Nauman,' *Parkett*, No. 10, 1986 – Joan Simon: 'Breaking the Silence' (Interview), *Art in America*, No. 9, 1988 – Wulf Herzogenrath/Edith Decker (eds): *Video-Skulptur retrospektiv und aktuell. 1963–1989*, Cologne 1989 – Lois E. Nesbit: 'Lie Down, Roll Over. Bruce Nauman's Body-Conscious Art Reawakens New York', *Artscribe*, No. 82, 1990

CADY NOLAND

Born Washington, D. C., 1956. First one-woman show at White Columns, New York, 1988. Exhibitions at Wester Singel, Rotterdam; American Fine Arts Co., New York; Anthony Reynolds Gallery, London; Massimo de Carlo, Milan; Luhring Augustine Hetzler, Santa Monica; and elsewhere. Took part in the exhibition 'Einleuchten', Deichtorhallen, Hamburg, 1989, and Venice Biennale (Aperto), 1990. Lives in New York.

Cady Noland's assemblages and installations use the narrative potential of found everyday objects, and of press photographs, to make a political and social statement on the historic and contemporary condition of American culture. Consumer goods, American symbols (flags, hamburgers, beer, etc.), and items connected with sport and police work, are grouped on the floor or mounted on metal armatures. Alongside them stand perforated photographic silhouettes, often of cowboys. Metal plaques bear photographic enlargements recording the lives and deaths of political figures, including Lincoln, Kennedy and Patricia Hearst. Metal crush barriers and mobility aids are other symbolic elements that appear in her large, space-filling works. 'Her assemblages form an intricate webbed jewelry slung around the neck of American culture. Noland's installations exhibit a complex American identity spoken in the vernacular.' (Kirby Gookin)

Reference Sources for List of Exhibitions and Bibliography
'Status of Sculpture', Espace Lyonnais d'Art Contemporain, Lyon 1990 – 'Cady Noland / Félix Gonzáles-Torres. Objekte, Installationen, Wandarbeiten', Neue Gesellschaft für Bildende Kunst, Berlin 1990 (later shown at Museum Fridericianum, Kassel)

Catalogues of Collective Exhibitions (Selection)
'White Columns Update', White Columns, New York 1988 – 'Works, Concepts, Processes, Situations, Information', Galerie Hans Mayer, Düsseldorf 1988 – 'Filling in the Gap', Richard L. Feigen & Co., Chicago 1989 – 'A Climate of Site', Galerie Barbara Farber, Amsterdam 1989 – 'Einleuchten', Hamburg 1989 – 'La Biennale di Venezia', Venice 1990 – 'Jardins de Bagatelle', Galerie Tanit, Munich 1990 – 'Art Against Aids', American Foundation for Aids Research, New York 1990 – 'Cady Noland, Sam Samore, Karen Sylvester', Galerie Max Hetzler, Cologne 1990

Other Literature (Selection)
Robert Nickas: 'Entropy and the New Objects', *El Paseante,* October 1988 – Daniela Salvioni: 'Cady Noland. The Homespun Violence of the Hearth', *Flash Art,* October 1989 – Jan Avgikos: 'Degraded World', *Artscribe,* No. 78, 1989 – Lisa Liebmann: 'Cady Noland at American Fine Arts', *Art in America,* November 1989 – Jeanne Siegel: 'The American Trip. Cady Noland's Investigations', *Arts Magazine,* December 1989 – Klaus Ottmann: 'Cady Noland. La mort en action', *Art Press,* No. 148, 1990 – Dan Cameron: 'Changing Priorities in American Art', *Art International,* No. 10, 1990 – Michele Cone: 'Cady Noland' (Interview), *Journal of Contemporary Art,* No. 2, 1990

MARCEL ODENBACH

Born Cologne, 1953. Studied architecture, art history and semiotics at Technische Hochschule, Aachen (Dipl. Ing.), 1974–79. *Day Drawings,* 1975–79. First one-man show at Galerie Hinrichs, Lohmar, 1976. Exhibitions at Galerie Philomene Magers, Bonn; Stampa, Basle; Galerie Ascan Crone, Hamburg; and elsewhere. From 1976, video performances (to 1981) and video installations; from 1980, original collage drawings. Förderpreis Glockengasse, 1982. Karl-Schmidt-Rottluff-Stipendium Darmstadt, 1983. First Prize Locarno Film and Video Festival, 1984. Took part in 'documenta 8', 1987. Lives in Cologne.

Odenbach's work can be divided into three distinct but related areas. His large collage drawings are often based on architectural elements, into which photographic or literary quotations are inserted. The drawings and texts insert a personal view into the torrential flow of information, both in words and in images, that has become an inescapable part of present-day life. The drawings are autonomous, but parts of them can also be read as scores and sketches for the video works. In his videotapes Odenbach uses montage, repetition and cross-fading techniques, stock Hollywood sets, news items, and a classical music backing, to combine disparate visual worlds into a single discourse. The artist's own experiences and memories – transposed into media terms – are incorporated as themes. The same happens in Odenbach's video installations. Everyday objects, static in space, are set against actions on screen. In other installations, seats are

used to mock the typical posture of the TV voyeur. 'In Odenbach's video installations there is a suggestion of hazy story-lines, sliding around in time, presenting illusory realities. And yet these are no mere empty fictions: for they contain the imaginative material for counter-images entirely free of illusion.' (Zdenek Felix)

Reference Source for List of Exhibitions, Videos and Video Installations and for Bibliography
'Marcel Odenbach', Centro de Arte Reina Sofia, Madrid 1989 (wrongly dated 1988)

Catalogues and Monographs (Selection)
'Videoarbeiten', Museum Folkwang, Essen 1981 – Walter Phillips Gallery (with Michael Buthe), Banff, Alberta 1983 – 'Im Tangoschritt zum Aderlass' (with Klaus vom Bruch), Neue Gesellschaft für bildende Kunst, Berlin 1985 – 'As If Memories Could Deceive Me', Institute of Contemporary Art, Boston 1986 – Anthony Reynolds Gallery, London 1986 – 'Dans la vision périphérique du témoin', Centre Georges Pompidou, Paris 1987 – 'House & Garden', Galerie Ascan Crone, Hamburg 1987 – 'Stehen ist Nichtumfallen', Badischer Kunstverein, Karlsruhe 1988

Catalogues of Collective Exhibitions (Selection)
'Kölner Künstler persönlich vorgestellt', Kölnischer Kunstverein, Cologne 1979 – 'German Video and Performance', A Space, Toronto 1980 – 'Freunde – Amis…?', Rheinisches Landesmuseum, Bonn 1980 – 'Art Allemagne Aujourd'hui', ARC Musée d'Art Moderne de la Ville de Paris, 1981 – 'The Luminous Image', Stedelijk Museum, Amsterdam 1984 – 'von hier aus', Düsseldorf, (DuMont) Cologne 1984 – 'Alles und noch viel mehr. Das poetische ABC', Kunsthalle Bern, Kunstmuseum Bern, 1985 – 'Rheingold', Palazzo della Società Promotrice, Turin, (Wienand) Cologne 1985 – '1945–1985. Kunst in der Bundesrepublik Deutschland', Nationalgalerie, Berlin 1986 – 'Wechselströme', Bonner Kunstverein, Bonn, (Wienand) Cologne 1987 – 'documenta 8', Kassel 1987 – 'L'Epoque, la mode, la morale, la passion', Paris 1987 – 'La Biennale di Venezia', Venice 1988 – 'Sei Artisti Tedeschi', Castello di Rivara, Rivara / Turin 1989 – 'Passages de l'image', Centre Georges Pompidou, Paris 1990

Other Literature (Selection)
Jürgen Schweinebraden: 'Einführung zur Arbeit Marcel Odenbachs', *Kunstforum International,* Vol. 35, 1979 – Annelie Poh-

len: 'Marcel Odenbach. Video-Installationen', *Kunstforum International*, Vol. 49, 1982 – Wulf Herzogenrath (ed.): *Videokunst in Deutschland 1963–1982*, Stuttgart 1982 – Wolfgang Preikschat: 'American Brave New World und Deutsche Historizität. Video-Kunst von John Sanborn, Klaus vom Bruch und Marcel Odenbach', *Noema Art Magazine*, No. 7/8, 1986 – Paul Virilio: 'Où va la vidéo?', *Cahiers du Cinéma*, Autumn 1986 – Wulf Herzogenrath/ Edith Decker (eds): *Video-Skulptur retrospektiv und aktuell. 1963–1989*, Cologne 1989 – Michael Tarantino: 'Marcel Odenbach', *Artforum*, September 1990

ALBERT OEHLEN

Born Krefeld, 1954. Trained in book trade, 1970–73. With Werner Büttner, founded *Liga zur Bekämpfung des widersprüchlichen Verhaltens* (League Against Contradictory Behaviour) in 1976; first issue of *Dum Dum*, official organ of the League, 1977. Studied at Hochschule für Bildende Künste, Hamburg, 1977–81. With Werner Büttner, mural for Welt bookshop, Hamburg, 1978. With Georg Herold, exhibition 'Altes Geripp – mieses Getitte' (Old Bones – Measly Tits), at Künstlerhaus, Hamburg, 1979. Project *Samenbank für DDR-Flüchtlinge (Sperm Bank for East German Refugees)*, with Werner Büttner and Georg Herold, 1980. One-man shows at Galerie Max Hetzler, Stuttgart (later Cologne), from 1981. Exhibitions at Galerie Ascan

Crone, Hamburg; Sonnabend Gallery, New York; Galerie Six Friedrich, Munich; Galerie Grässlin-Ehrhardt, Frankfurt am Main; Galería Juana de Aizpuru, Madrid; Galerie Peter Pakesch, Vienna; and elsewhere. Took part in 'Mülheimer Freiheit und interessante Bilder aus Deutschland', Galerie Paul Maenz, Cologne, 1980, and 'BiNationale', Düsseldorf and Boston, 1988. Lives in Madrid.

Albert Oehlen's multimedia works are often done in collaboration with other artists: Werner Büttner, Georg Herold, Martin Kippenberger. His output includes musical and literary works, book projects, readings, photomontages, drawings, carpet designs and prints; but painting is its central focus. His concern is with the possibilities of paint (Oehlen: 'No looking back in anger; the picture's out in front'). He uses colour, technique and style in such a way as to undermine his overt motifs, with their often deliberately banal props and allusions. Mostly produced in series, these works are painting about painting. Abstraction and figuration are juxtaposed or interpenetrate. The ethos shifts between affirmation and aesthetic indifference. The picture – which often incorporates elements of language – becomes a half-ironic commentary on the 'situation' of art and the world. Albert Oehlen: 'I'm not trying to criticize, but to make something clear, to reduce a picture to what it really is, and what it must signify. The observer can be overfed with surrealism, with symbols, with meaning, and seduced into orgies of interpretation. People do it time and time again, and perhaps I do it too, because I can't prevent it. But I'm trying to make it clear that it isn't meant that way.'

Reference Sources for List of Exhibitions and Bibliography

'Albert Oehlen. Abräumung. Prokrustische Malerei 1982–84', Kunsthalle Zurich 1987 – 'Refigured Painting. The German Image 1960–88', The Toledo Museum of Art, Toledo, Ohio 1988, (Guggenheim Foundation) New York, (Prestel) Munich 1989 (later shown in: New York, Williamstown, Mass., Düsseldorf, Frankfurt a.M.)

Books by the Artist (Selection)

Mode Nervo (with Georg Herold), Hamburg 1980 – *Facharbeiterficken* (with Werner Büttner and Georg Herold), Hamburg 1982 – *Angst vor Nice (Ludwig's Law)* (with Werner Büttner), Hamburg 1985 – *Gedichte. Zweiter Teil* (with Martin Kippenberger), Berlin 1987

Catalogues and Monographs (Selection)

'Rechts blinken – links abbiegen' (with Werner Büttner), Neue Gesellschaft für bildende Kunst, Berlin 1982 – 'Das Geld', Galerie Max Hetzler, Cologne 1984 – 'Farbenlehre', Galerie Ascan Crone, Hamburg 1985 – 'Zeichnungen', Galerie Borgmann-Capitain, Cologne 1986 – 'Teppiche', Galerie Grässlin-Ehrhardt, Frankfurt a.M. 1987 – 'Gemälde', Galerie Max Hetzler, Cologne 1988 – 'Obras Recientes', Galería Juana de Aizpuru (with Martin Kippenberger), Madrid 1989 – 'Linolschnitte +', Forum Stadtpark, Graz, Galerie Gisela Capitain, Cologne 1989 – 'Realidad Abstracta' (with Markus Oehlen), Nave Sotoliva, Santander 1990

Catalogues of Collective Exhibitions (Selection)

'Bildwechsel. Neue Malerei aus Deutschland', Akademie der Künste, Berlin 1981 – 'Gegen-Bilder', Badischer Kunstverein, Karlsruhe 1981 – '12 Künstler aus Deutschland', Kunsthalle Basel, Museum Boymans-van Beuningen, Rotterdam, 1982 – 'Über sieben Brücken mußt Du gehen', Galerie Max Hetzler, Stuttgart 1982 – 'Wahrheit ist Arbeit', Museum Folkwang, Essen 1984 – 'Origen i Visió', Centre Cultural de la Caixa de Pensions, Barcelona 1984 – 'von hier aus', Düsseldorf, (DuMont) Cologne 1984 – 'What about having our mother back!', Institute of Contemporary Arts, London 1986 – 'Broken Neon', Steirischer Herbst, Forum Stadtpark, Graz 1987 – 'Arbeit in Geschichte. Geschichte in Arbeit', Kunsthaus und Kunstverein in Hamburg, 1988 – 'BiNationale. Deutsche Kunst der späten 80er Jahre', Düsseldorf, (DuMont) Cologne 1988 – 'Museum der Avantgarde. Die Sammlung Sonnabend New York', Berlin, (Electa) Milan 1989 – 'Georg Herold, Albert Oehlen, Christopher Wool', The Renaissance Society at the University of Chicago, 1989 – 'Bilderstreit', Cologne 1989 – 'Zeichnungen I', Grazer Kunstverein, Graz 1990

Other Literature (Selection)

Wolfgang Max Faust / Gerd de Vries: *Hunger nach Bildern. Deutsche Malerei der Gegenwart*, Cologne 1982 – Klaus Honnef: 'Albert Oehlen', *Kunstforum International*, Vol. 68, 1983 – Matthew Collings: 'Being Right' (Interview), *Artscribe*, September/October 1985 – Donald B. Kuspit: 'Albert Oehlen at Sonnabend', *Art in America*, September 1986 – Jutta Koether: 'Ground Control ... Albert Oehlen's Carpets', *Artscribe*, May 1987 – Stephan Schmidt-Wulffen: *Spielregeln. Tendenzen der Gegenwartskunst*, Cologne 1987 – Sophie Schwarz: 'Albert Oehlen. Killing Off Painting Yet Still Continuing', *Flash Art*, No. 141, 1988 – Klaus Honnef: *Kunst der Gegenwart*, Cologne 1988 – Martin Prinzhorn: 'Hinter dem Bild findet gar keine Schlacht statt. Zur postungegenständlichen Malerei Albert Oehlens', in: *Fama und Fortune Bulletin*, Galerie Peter Pakesch, Vienna, Winter 1990

PHILIPPE PERRIN

Born Grenoble, 1964. First one-man show at Centre Culturel Franco-Voltaïque, Ouagadougou, Upper Volta (Burkina Faso), 1983. Works with Air de Paris agency, Nice. Took part in Venice Biennale (Aperto), 1990. Lives in Nice.

Perrin situates his works at the point of intersection between everyday life and art. He presents himself in photographs in the pose of a gunslinger and describes himself as 'The Son of a Bitch'. Embracing the clichés of the mass media, he transposes the theme of violence – in sport and in daily life – to the realm of art. In an empty, stylized boxing-ring he sets a photograph of himself as a practitioner of savate (French boxing). The title of the work, *Hommage à Arthur Cravan*, cites the name of a celebrated Dadaist figure who made a reputation as a boxer. Perrin uses advertising and public

relations strategies as artistic devices to define the present-day art world. This is not so much a critique, or a debunking operation, as a process of assimilation. 'Perrin's art ... proposes *no* truths, nor does it rest on any analysis, either sociological or historical. It has the unique quality of not being long-winded. It puts forward no theories and no doctrines. It is therefore the very opposite of vulgarity.' (Eric Troncy)

Reference Source for List of Exhibitions
'Le Cinq. French Contemporary Art', Tramway, Glasgow 1990

Publications by the Artist
Philippe Perrin is Alive, 1988 – *Maintenant*, 1988 – *Jour de Haine*, 1990

Catalogue
'Hommage à Arthur Cravan', Orangerie, Grenoble 1987

Catalogues of Collective Exhibitions (Selection)
'French Kiss', Halle Sud, Geneva 1990 – 'La Biennale di Venezia', Venice 1990 – 'Courts-métrages immobiles', Prigioni, Venice 1990

Other Literature (Selection)
Stuart Morgan: 'Cold Comfort', *Artscribe*, Summer 1988 – Jean-Yves Jouannais: 'Philippe Perrin. Boxe, obscénité, mystification', *Art Press*, May 1990 – Liam Gillick: 'Philippe Perrin, Philippe Parreno, Pierre Joseph. Air de Paris', *Artscribe*, November/December 1990

DMITRI PRIGOV

Born Moscow, 1940. Studied sculpture at Stroganov Art Institute, Moscow, leaving in 1967. Numerous essays and other literary works since 1971. First one-man show at Struve Gallery, Chicago, 1989. Exhibitions at Galerie Krings-Ernst, Cologne; Interart, Berlin; and elsewhere. In Berlin as guest of artists programme of DAAD, German Academic Exchange Service, 1990. Lives in Moscow; currently resident in Berlin.

Prigov's work is powered by the interpenetration of literature and visual art. Alongside his literary and critical texts, public readings and lectures on contemporary Russian art, he produces pictures and installations that incorporate the language medium. Image and text create a visual-

verbal nexus that often incorporates current political allusions. This is exemplified by a number of works in which he has combined the word *Glasnost* with emblematic images. Politics, daily life and art interpenetrate. Prigov: 'My work has always developed in reaction to the cultural mainstream. When a lofty, ethereal tone was the order of the day, my vocabulary consisted exclusively of Soviet clichés... But my aim isn't opposition, it's dialogue. My works must be stylistically at variance with the general trend so as to accumulate a critical mass capable of withstanding the enormous might of the mainstream.'

Reference Source for List of Exhibitions
'Ich lebe – Ich sehe. Künstler der 80er Jahre in Moskau', Kunstmuseum Bern, 1988

Literary Publications (Selection)
Russian:
in: *Ardis Catalog*, Ann Arbor 1982 – *Literaturnoje A-Ja*, Paris 1985 – *Ogonjok, Junost, Kowtscheg, Serkala Almanach*, Moscow 1989 – *Almanach Poesii*, No. 52, 1989
Russian-German
in: *Neue Russische Literatur*, Salzburg 1979/80 – Günter Hirt/Sascha Wonders (eds): *Kulturpalast. Neue Moskauer Poesie und Aktionskunst*, Wuppertal 1984
German:
in: *Durch*, No. 2, 1987 – *Schreibheft*, No. 29, 1987 – *Gruppa*, 1989 – *Schreibheft*, No. 35, 1990
Russian-English:
in: *Berkeley Fiction Review*, 1985/86

Catalogues of Collective Exhibitions (Selection)
'Is-Kunst-Wo', Karl-Hofer-Gesellschaft, Westbahnhof, Berlin 1988 – 'In de USSR en erbuiten', Stedelijk Museum, Amsterdam 1990

Other Literature (Selection)
Viktor Tupitsin: 'What could we say more about Prigov' (Russian, Interview), *Flash Art* (Russian edition), No. 1, 1989 – Viktor Misiano: 'Arts & Letters' (Interview), *Contemporanea*, No. 1, 1989

RICHARD PRINCE

Born Panama Canal Zone, 1949. First one-man show at Ellen Sragrow Gallery, New York, 1976. Exhibitions at Artists Space, New York; Metro Pictures, New York; International With Monument, New York; Jablonka Galerie, Cologne; Barbara Gladstone Gallery, New York; Jay Gorney Modern Art, New York; and elsewhere. Took part in Venice Biennale (Aperto) and 'BiNational', Boston and Düsseldorf, 1988. Lives in New York.

Prince works with an inexhaustible fund of reproduced images. He photographs advertising and magazine photos, manipulates shots of sunsets, or assembles sections of pictures into tableaux. This process of 're-photography' implies no criticism of the images he uses. What interests him is the fascination that emanates from them. He would like the viewer to believe in the pictures. The artist's prose texts are also about this 'second' reality. After a series of works using photographs of luxury articles, and another using photographs of persons in matching poses and with matching accessories, Prince turned in 1980 to the theme of Marlboro cowboys. In 1984 he produced the first of his *Gangs*, details cropped from American specialist magazines (showing truckers, surfers, bikers' clubs, etc.). At the end of the 1980s he introduced sculpturally formed monochrome images – quotations from the aesthetics of industrial design – as a foil and contrast to his continuing work with pre-existent visual material. In 1986 Prince started working with cartoons and verbal jokes, which he reproduces, redraws or writes out by hand. When asked how he got the idea, Prince answered: 'I live here. I live in New York. I live in America. I live in the world. I live in 1988. It comes from doing cartoons. It comes from wanting to put out a fact. There's nothing to interpret. There's nothing to appreciate. There's nothing to speculate about. I wanted to point to it and say what it was. It's a joke.'

Reference Source for List of Exhibitions and Bibliography
'Richard Prince. Spiritual America', IVAM, The Valencian Institute of Modern Art, (Aperture Books) New York 1989

Writings by the Artist (Selection)
'Eleven Conversations', *Tracks Magazine*, Autumn 1976 – *War Pictures*, New York 1980 – *Menthol Pictures*, Buffalo 1980 – *Why I Go to the Movies Alone*, New York 1983 – *Pamphlet*, Le Nouveau Musée, Villeurbanne 1983

Catalogues and Monographs (Selection)
Magasin – Centre National d'Art Contemporain de Grenoble, 1988 – Barbara Gladstone Gallery, New York 1988 – Jablonka Galerie, Cologne 1989 – 'Jokes, Gangs, Hoods', Jablonka Galerie, Galerie Gisela Capitain, Cologne 1990

Catalogues of Collective Exhibitions (Selection)
'Body Language', Hayden Gallery, Massachusetts Institute of Technology, Cambridge 1981 – 'Jenny Holzer, Barbara Kruger, Richard Prince', Knight Gallery, Spirit Square Arts Center, Charlotte, North Carolina 1984 – 'New York. Ailleurs et Autrement', ARC Musée d'Art Moderne de la Ville de Paris, 1984 – 'Biennial Exhibition', Whitney Museum of American Art, New York 1985 – 'Wien Fluß', Wiener Secession, Vienna 1986 – 'The Biennale of Sydney', 1986 – 'La Biennale di Venezia', Venice 1988 – 'The BiNational. American Art of the Late 80's', Boston, (DuMont) Cologne 1988 – 'Horn of Plenty', Stedelijk Museum, Amsterdam 1989 – 'Photography Now', Victoria and Albert Museum, London 1989 – 'Inside World', Kent Fine Art, New York 1989 – 'Prospect 89', Frankfurt a. M. 1989 – 'Bilderstreit', Cologne 1989 – 'The Photography of Invention', National Museum of American Art, Washington 1989 – 'Prospect Photographie', Frankfurter Kunstverein, 1989 – 'A Forest of Signs. Art in the Crisis of Representation', Los Angeles 1989 – 'Image World. Art and Media Culture', Whitney Museum of American Art, New York 1989 – 'D & S Ausstellung', Hamburg 1989 – 'Life-Size', Jerusalem 1990

Other Literature (Selection)
Kate Linker: 'On Richard Prince's Photographs', *Arts Magazine*, November 1982 – Brian Wallis: 'Mindless Pleasures. Richard Prince's Fictions', *Parkett*, No. 6, 1985 – Jeffrey Rian: 'Social Science Fiction' (Interview), *Art in America*, No. 3, 1987 – Isabelle Graw: 'Wiederaufbereitung', *Wolkenkratzer Art Journal*, No. 2, 1988 – Daniela Salvioni: 'Richard Prince. Jokes Epitomize the Social Unconscious', *Flash Art*, No. 141, 1988 – Stuart Morgan: 'Tell Me Everything' (Interview), *Artscribe*, No. 73, 1989 – Jerry Saltz: 'Sleight/Slight of Hand. Richard Prince's "What a Business"', 1988', *Arts Magazine*, No. 5, 1990

GERHARD RICHTER

Born Dresden, 1932. Studied at Hochschule für Bildende Künste, Dresden, 1951–56; after leaving the GDR, at Staatliche Kunstakademie, Düsseldorf, 1961–63. After his 'Demonstation für den Kapitalistischen Realismus' (with Konrad Lueg), at Möbelhaus Berges, Düsseldorf, 1963, first one-man show at Galerie Heiner Friedrich, Munich, 1964. Exhibitions at Galerie René Block, Berlin; Galerie Alfred Schmela, Düsseldorf; Galerie Konrad Fischer, Düsseldorf; Galleria Lucio Amelio, Naples; Galerie Rudolf Zwirner, Cologne; Sperone Westwater Gallery, New York; Marian Goodman Gallery, New York; Anthony d'Offay Gallery, London; and elsewhere. Professor at Staatliche Kunstakademie, Düsseldorf, from 1971. Has also taught in Hamburg; Halifax, Nova Scotia; and Frankfurt. Kunstpreis 'Junger Westen', 1967; Arnold-Bode-Preis, 1981; Oskar-Kokoschka-Preis, 1985; Kaiserring der Stadt Goslar, 1988. Member of Akademie der Künste,

Berlin, since 1975. Took part in 'documenta 5', 1972, 'documenta 6', 1977, 'documenta 7', 1982, 'documenta 8', 1987. Lives in Cologne.

Richter's pictures constantly reflect new aspects of painting. The individual groups of works are impossible to reduce to a common denominator, and they often evolve in parallel. In 1963, with Konrad Lueg, Richter founded 'Capitalist Realism', which also included among its adherents in the 1960s KP Bremer, Hödicke, Polke and others. Richter's painting is based on banal found photographs, or bits torn out of newspapers, mostly interpreted in low-definition black and white. However, his works are not mere enlargements or copies of photographs; they are paintings in their own right, statements about pictorial reality. Since 1968 Richter's works have become more colourful. The definition has been reduced to a blur. At the same time, he has done black and white paintings based on aerial photographs of cities; coloured, unpeopled landscapes; colour plates; and paintings on the theme of the colour grey. In 1972 Richter began to take his own photographs. In 1976 he began to paint highly coloured 'abstract paintings', often monumental enlargements of small, gestural oil sketches. In quantitative terms, these paintings now form the largest category of his output. In parallel with them, he has pursued his work with photography in paintings of clouds, of Vesuvius, of landscapes and of still lifes with candles, apples or death's-heads (*Vanitas* motifs). In 1988 he painted a series concerned with German terrorism (the RAF group), under the title *October 18, 1977*. Since 1972 Richter has exhibited his systematic collection of photographic source materials under the title of *Atlas*.

Reference Source for List of Exhibitions and Bibliography
Jürgen Harten (ed.): 'Gerhard Richter. Bilder/Paintings 1962–1985', Städtische Kunsthalle Düsseldorf, (DuMont) Cologne 1986 (later shown in Berlin, Bern, Vienna) – 'Gerhard Richter 1988/89', Museum Boymans-van Beuningen, Rotterdam 1989

Catalogues and Monographs (Selection)
Galerie René Block, Berlin 1964 – Museum Folkwang, Essen 1970 – Kunstverein für die Rheinlande und Westfalen, Düsseldorf 1971 – 'La Biennale di Venezia', Venice 1972 – Städtisches Museum Mönchengladbach, 1974 – Klaus Honnef: *Gerhard Richter*, Recklinghausen 1976 – Centre Georges Pompidou, Paris 1977 – '128 Details from a Picture (Halifax 1978)', Nova Scotia College of Art and Design, Halifax 1978 – 'Abstract Paintings', Stedelijk Van Abbemuseum, Eindhoven 1978 – 'Georg Baselitz, Gerhard Richter', Städtische Kunsthalle Düsseldorf, 1981 – Musée d'Art et d'Industrie, Saint Etienne 1984 – Ulrich Loock/Denys Zacharopoulos: *Gerhard Richter*, Munich 1985 – 'Werken op papier. 1983–1986', Museum Overholland, Amsterdam 1986 – Art Gallery of Ontario, Toronto 1988 – 'Atlas', Städtische Galerie im Lenbachhaus, Munich 1989 – '18. Oktober 1977', Museum Haus Esters, Krefeld, (Walther König) Cologne 1989

Catalogues of Collective Exhibitions (Selection)
'Neuer Realismus', Haus am Waldsee, Berlin, Kunstverein Braunschweig, 1967 – 'Kunst der sechziger Jahre. Sammlung Ludwig', Wallraf-Richartz-Museum, Cologne 1969 – 'Jetzt', Kunsthalle, Cologne 1970 – 'documenta 5', Kassel 1972 – 'Prospect 73', Städtische Kunsthalle Düsseldorf, 1973 – 'documenta 6', Kassel 1977 – 'Aspekte der 60er Jahre. Sammlung Reinhard Onnasch', Nationalgalerie, Berlin 1978 – 'The Biennale of Sydney', 1979 – 'A New Spirit in Painting', London 1981 – 'Westkunst', Cologne 1981 – 'documenta 7', Kassel 1982 – ''60'80 attitudes/concepts/images', Stedelijk Museum, Amsterdam 1982 – 'von hier aus', Düsseldorf, (DuMont) Cologne 1984 – 'Aufbrüche', Städtische Kunsthalle Düssel-dorf, 1984 – 'The European Iceberg', Art Gallery of Ontario, Toronto, (Mazzotta) Milan 1985 – 'Rheingold', Palazzo della Società Promotrice, Turin, (Wienand) Cologne 1985 – '1945–1985. Kunst in der Bundesrepublik Deutschland', Nationalgalerie, Berlin 1985 – 'German Art in the 20th Century', Royal Academy of Arts, London, Staatsgalerie Stuttgart, (Prestel) Munich 1985 – 'Wechselströme', Bonner Kunstverein, Bonn, (Wienand) Cologne 1987 – 'documenta 8', Kassel 1987 – 'Der unverbrauchte Blick', Berlin 1987 – 'Rot Gelb Blau', Kunstmuseum St. Gallen, 1988 – 'Refigured Painting: The German Image 1960–88', Toledo 1988, (Guggenheim Foundation) New York, (Prestel) Munich 1989 – 'Bilderstreit', Cologne 1989 – 'Life-Size', Jerusalem 1990

Other Literature (Selection)
Juliane Roh: *Deutsche Kunst der 60er Jahre*, Munich 1971 – René Block: *Graphik des Kapitalistischen Realismus*, Berlin 1971 – Heiner Stachelhaus: 'Doubts in the Face of Reality: The Paintings of Gerhard Richter', *Studio International*, No. 184, 1972 – Klaus Honnef: 'Problem Realismus. Die Medien des Gerhard Richter', *Kunstforum International*, Vol. 4/5, 1973 – Wolfgang Max Faust/Gerd de Vries: *Hunger nach Bildern*, Cologne 1982 – Werner Krüger/Wolfgang Pehnt: *Künstler im Gespräch* (Interview), Cologne 1984 – Coosje van Bruggen: 'Gerhard Richter. Painting as a Moral Act', *Artforum*, May 1985 – Ulrich Wilmes: 'Gerhard Richter. Das Scheinen der Wirklichkeit im Bild', *Künstler. Kritisches Lexikon der Gegenwartskunst*, issue 3, Munich 1988 – Jan Thorn-Prikker: 'Gerhard Richter. 18. October 1977' (with interview), *Parkett*, No. 19, 1989

THOMAS RUFF

Born Zell am Harmersbach, Black Forest, 1958. Studied at Staatliche Kunstakademie, Düsseldorf, under Bernd Becher. One-man shows at Galerie Rüdiger Schöttle, Munich, from 1981. Exhibitions at Galerie Konrad Fischer, Düsseldorf; Galerie Johnen & Schöttle, Cologne; Galerie Sonne, Berlin; Galerie Crousel-Robelin, Paris; 303 Gallery, New York; XPO Galerie, Hamburg; and elsewhere. Took part in Venice Biennale (Aperto), 1988. Lives in Düsseldorf.

Between 1981 and 1985 Ruff took a series of portrait photographs of Düsseldorf friends and acquaintances, some in front of coloured backgrounds. His aim in these photographs was to achieve as neutral, 'objective' and unpsychological an image of a person as possible. These small photographs formed the conceptual basis for the two-metre portraits that he painted from 1986 onwards. In front of a neutral background, the mostly youthful sitters face the viewer frontally. Details of physiognomy and dress present themselves with exaggerated precision; there are no shadows. As far as possible, interpretation is excluded. In 1986, Ruff began to take similarly neutral pictures of the functional architecture of houses and factories. Since 1989 the artist has also shown large-scale photographs of constellations, based on negatives from the *ESO/SRC Atlas of the Southern Sky*. In exhibitions, Ruff often combines portrait, architecture and star photographs in such a way as to make connections between them. 'Whatever the object of his camera may be – his own contemporaries, the most neutral forms of architecture or the remotest corners of space – the image defined by the camera shows human beings, or their work, or the trace of their work; even if the latter amounts to no more than the white streak of a passing satellite. Any distance, from arm's reach to infinity, can ultimately be referred to the perfect and timeless metaphor of flatness: the photograph.' (Els Barents)

Reference Source for List of Exhibitions
'Thomas Ruff. Portretten, Huizen, Sterren', Stedelijk Museum, Amsterdam 1989 (later shown at Centre National d'Art Contemporain – Magasin Grenoble, Kunsthalle Zurich)

Catalogues and Monographs (Selection)
Museum Schloß Hardenberg, Velbert, (Verlag Walther König) Cologne 1988 – May 36 Galerie, Lucerne 1988

Catalogues of Collective Exhibitions (Selection)
'Ausstellung B', Künstlerwerkstatt Lothringer Straße, Munich 1982 – 'Das Auge des Künstlers. Das Auge der Kamera', Pinacoteca Comunale, Ravenna 1985 – 'Reste des Authentischen', Museum Folkwang, Essen 1986 – 'Foto/Realismen', Villa Dessauer, Bamberg, (Kulturkreis im BDI and Kunstverein Munich) 1987 – 'La Biennale di Venezia', Venice 1988 – 'BiNationale. Deutsche Kunst der späten 80er Jahre', Düsseldorf, (DuMont) Cologne 1988 – 'Bilder. Elke Denda, Michael van Ofen, Thomas Ruff', Museum Haus Esters, Krefeld 1988 – '32 Portraits. Photography in Art', Kunstrai, Amsterdam 1989 – 'Tenir l'Image à Distance', Musée d'Art Contemporain, Montreal 1989 – 'Mit Fernrohr durch die Kunstgeschichte', Kunsthalle Basle, 1989 – 'Melencolia', Galerie Grita Insam, Vienna 1989 – 'Museumsskizze', Kunsthalle Nuremberg, 1989 – 'Dorothea von Stetten-Kunstpreis 1990', Kunstmuseum Bonn, 1990 – 'Hacia el paisaje', Centro Atlántico de Arte Moderno, Las Palmas de Gran Canaria 1990 – 'Weitersehen', Krefeld 1990

Other Literature (Selection)
Lucie Beyer: 'Thomas Ruff', *Flash Art*, No. 134, 1987 – Karlheinz Schmid: 'Kühl, karg und immer in Serie', *Art*, November 1987 – Eric Troncy: 'Thomas Ruff', *Art Press*, No. 124, 1988 – Meyer Raphael Rubinstein: 'Apollo in Düsseldorf. The Photographs of Thomas Ruff', *Arts Magazine*, October 1988 – Raija Fellner: 'Thomas Ruff, Porträts', *Artefactum*, No. 26, 1988 – Hanna Humeltenberg: 'The Magic of Reality in Thomas Ruff's Pictures'', *Parkett*, No. 19, 1989 – John Dornberg: 'Thomas Ruff', *Artnews*, April 1989 – Isabelle Graw: 'Aufnahmeleitung' (Interview), *Artis*, October 1989 – Gregorio Magnani: 'Ordering Procedures', *Arts Magazine*, March 1990

EDWARD RUSCHA

Born Omaha, Nebraska, 1937. Studied at Chouinard Art Institute, Los Angeles, 1956–60. First one-man show at Ferus Gallery, Los Angeles, 1963. Exhibitions at Rudolf Zwirner, Cologne; Leo Castelli Gallery, New York; Nigel Greenwood Gallery, London; Galerie Ricke, Cologne; James Corcoran Gallery, Santa Monica; Karsten Schubert Ltd, London; and elsewhere. Took part in 'documenta 5', 1972, 'documenta 6', 1977, 'documenta 7', 1982. Lives in Los Angeles.

Ruscha's pictures can be seen and read on a number of different levels. They are mostly dominated by letters, words and sentences, in which the linguistic content – in the form of opinions, moods, questions, slogans or conceptions – is related to the look of the lettering. Layout and typography are used either to concentrate the statement or else to introduce ambiguities. The context for language is supplied by painting, whether monochrome, colour plane, or illustration

of landscapes or objects. Language and image – and the image of language – interpenetrate. In their artificiality, Ruscha's paintings, drawings and prints relate to a Hollywood movie aesthetic, as exemplified in the typography of film titles and titling. 'Painting, in the paintings of Edward Ruscha, is without history, nor does it tell stories; and yet it is invaded by stories of all kinds, by extracts from the most diverse tales, by narrative archetypes without beginning or end, by quotations and slogans. They confront us there, as active elements within the painting, these displaced stories with their obstinately strange banality.' (Alain Cueff) In the 1970s Ruscha experimented with the use of organic substances, like foodstuffs and fat, instead of paint. Since the mid 1980s he has been making silhouette paintings, and paintings with texts partially whited out. Ruscha has been publishing books, mostly wordless sequences of photographs, since 1963.

Reference Source for List of Exhibitions and Bibliography
'Edward Ruscha', Musée National d'Art Moderne, Centre Georges Pompidou, Paris 1989 (later shown in Rotterdam, Barcelona, London, Los Angeles) – 'Ed Ruscha. New Paintings and Drawings', Karsten Schubert Ltd, London 1990

Books by the Artist (Selection)
Twentysix Gasoline Stations, 1963 – *Various Small Fires and Milk*, 1964 – *Every Building on the Sunset Strip*, 1966 – *Royal Road Test* (with Mason Williams, Patrick Blackwell), 1967 – *Nine Swimming Pools and a Broken Glass*, 1968 – *Babycakes*, New York 1970 – *Colored People*, 1972 – *Hard Light* (with Lawrence Weiner), Hollywood 1978

Films
Premium, 1970 – *Miracle*, 1975

Catalogues and Monographs (Selection)
'Books', Galerie Heiner Friedrich, Munich 1970 – Minneapolis Institute of Arts, 1972 – 'Prints and Publications 1962–74', Arts Council of Great Britain, 1975 – 'Paintings, Drawings and Other Work', Albright-Knox Art Gallery, Buffalo 1976 – Stedelijk Museum, Amsterdam 1976 – 'Graphic Works', Auckland City Art Gallery, Auckland, New Zealand 1978 – 'Guacamole Airlines and Other Drawings', New York 1980 – 'New Works', Arco Center for the Visual Art, Los Angeles 1981 – 'The Works', San Francisco Museum of Modern Art, (Hudson Press) New York 1982 – 'Octobre des Arts',

Musée Saint Pierre, Lyon 1985 – '4 x 6. Zeichnungen', Westfälischer Kunstverein, Münster 1986 – Institute of Contemporary Art, Nagoya, Japan 1988 – 'Words Without Thoughts Never to Heaven Go', Lannan Museum, Lake Worth, Florida 1988 – Touko Museum of Contemporary Art, Tokyo 1989 – 'Los Angeles Apartments', Whitney Museum of American Art, New York 1990

Catalogues of Collective Exhibitions (Selection)
'Word and Image', Solomon R. Guggenheim Museum, New York 1965 – 'La Biennale de Paris', 1967 – 'Konzeption Conception', Städtisches Museum Leverkusen, Schloß Morsbroich, 1969 – '557.087', Seattle Museum of Art, 1969 – 'Pop Art', Hayward Gallery, London 1969 – 'Information', The Museum of Modern Art, New York 1970 – 'Sonsbeek 71', Arnheim 1971 – 'documenta 5', Kassel 1972 – 'Painting and Sculpture in California. The Modern Era', San Francisco Museum of Modern Art, 1976 – 'Illusion and Reality', Australian National Gallery, Canberra 1977 – 'documenta 6', Kassel 1977 – 'Words', Whitney Museum of American Art, New York 1977 – 'American Paintings of the 1970's', Albright-Knox Art Gallery, Buffalo 1978 – 'Aspekte der 60er Jahre. Aus der Sammlung Reinhard Onnasch', Nationalgalerie, Berlin 1978 – 'Pier + Ocean', Hayward Gallery, London 1980 – 'No Title. The Collection of Sol LeWitt', Wesleyan University, Middletown, Connecticut 1981 – 'Westkunst', Cologne 1981 – 'Castelli and His Artists. Twenty Five Years', Aspen Center for the Visual Arts, Aspen, Colorado 1982 – 'documenta 7', Kassel 1982 – 'Gemini G.E.L. Art and Collaboration', National Gallery of Art, Washington, (Abbeville Press) New York 1984 – 'Individuals. A Selected History of Contemporary Art. 1945–1986', Los Angeles Museum of Contemporary Art, 1986 – 'Photography and Art. Interactions since 1946', Los Angeles County Museum of Art, 1987 – 'Lost and Found in California. Four Decades of Assemblage Art', Pence Gallery, Santa Monica 1988 – 'Prospect 89', Frankfurt a.M. 1989 – 'Sigmund Freud heute', Museum des 20. Jahrhunderts, Vienna, (Ritter Verlag) Klagenfurt 1989 – 'Artificial Nature', Deste Foundation for Contemporary Art, House of Cyprus, Athens 1990 – 'The Biennale of Sydney', 1990

Other Literature (Selection)
John Coplans: 'Concerning "Various Small Fires". Edward Ruscha Discusses His Perplexing Publications' (Interview), *Art-*

forum, No. 5, 1965 – David Bourdon: 'A Heap of Words About Ed Ruscha', *Art International*, No. 9, 1971 – Willoughby Sharp: '"…a Kind of a Huh?"' (Interview), *Avalanche*, No. 7, 1973 – Eleanor Antin: 'Reading Ruscha', *Art in America*, No. 6, 1973 – Peter Plagens: *The Sunshine Muse. Contemporary Art on the West Coast*, New York 1974 – Carrie Rickey: 'Ed Ruscha. Geographer', *Art in America*, No. 9, 1982 – Peter Schjeldahl: 'Edward Ruscha', *Arts and Architecture*, No. 3, 1982 – Fred Fehlau: 'Ed Ruscha' (Interview), *Flash Art*, No. 138, 1988 – 'Collaboration Edward Ruscha', *Parkett*, No. 18, 1988 – Renate Puvogel: 'Edward Ruscha', *Kunstforum International*, Vol. 108, 1990

JULIÃO SARMENTO

Born Lisbon, 1948. Studied painting at Escola Superior de Belas Artes, Lisbon. First one-man exhibition at Galeria Texto, Lourenço Marques (Maputo), Mozambique, 1974. Exhibitions at Galería Juana de Aizpuru, Seville; Pedro Oliveira, Porto; Bernd Klüser, Munich; Galeria Cómicos, Lisbon; Galería Marga Paz, Madrid; Xavier Hufkens, Brussels; and elsewhere. Took part in 'documenta 7', 1982, 'documenta 8', 1987. Lives in Sintra.

Construction and deconstruction are the two defining impulses of Sarmento's paintings. The pictorial space is an agglomeration of particles, each of which is an image:

figurative scenes, abstract signs, words and quotations from art history and media reality. The picture is a pictorial discourse; interpretation requires the collaboration of the viewer – whose response is provoked, in part, by the disparities between the component iconographic units, which play on cipher, caricature and factual allusion. 'Sarmento undertakes to cover every aspect of conscious and unconscious thought and feeling. His personal language of imagery is a reflection of the human capacity to think in images, and to connect emotions with images. The realm of sensory perception is assimilated through his expressive use of the material of paint. But Sarmento is also aware of the boundaries that continually stop one short.' (Bettina Pauly)

Reference Sources for List of Exhibitions
'Julião Sarmento. As velocidades da pele', Galeria Cómicos, Lisbon 1989 – 'Julião Sarmento. Gemälde und Arbeiten auf Papier', Städtische Galerie am Markt, Schwäbisch Hall 1990

Writings by the Artist (Selection)
'Über meine Arbeit im Allgemeinen', *Kunstforum International*, Vol. 33, 1979 – *Arta & Language*, 1982

Catalogues and Monographs (Selection)
Galeria Cómicos, Lisbon 1985 – Museo de Bellas Artes de Málaga, 1986 – 'Bilder und Zeichnungen 1986–1988', Galerie Bernd Klüser, Munich 1988

Catalogues of Collective Exhibitions (Selection)
'La Biennale de Paris', 1980 – 'La Biennale di Venezia', Venice 1980 – 'documenta 7', Kassel 1982 – 'Depois do Modernismo', Sociedade Nacional de Belas Artes, Lisbon 1983 – 'Kunst mit Photographie', Nationalgalerie, Berlin 1983 – 'La Imagen del Animal', Caja de Ahorros, Madrid 1983 – 'Terrae Motus I', Fondazione Amelio, Villa Campolieto, Herculaneum, (Electa) Naples 1984 – '11 European Painters', Europalia, National Gallery, Athens 1985 – 'Prospect 86', Frankfurt a.M. 1986 – 'documenta 8', Kassel 1987 – 'Lusitanies. Aspects de l'Art Contemporain Portugais', Centre Culturel de l'Albigeois, Albi 1987 – 'Farbe Bekennen', Museum für Gegenwartskunst, Basle 1988 – 'Última Frontera. 7 Artistes Portuguesos', Centre d'Arte Santa Mònica, Barcelona 1990

Other Literature (Selection)
Floris M. Neusüss: *Fotografie als Kunst. Kunst als Fotografie*, Cologne 1979 – João Pinharanda: 'Julião Sarmento', *Neue Kunst in Europa*, No. 5, 1984 – Kevin Power: 'Julião Sarmento at Cómicos', *Artscribe*, No. 56, 1986 – Marga Paz: 'Interview with Julião Sarmento', *Flash Art*, No. 131, 1986/1987 – Christoph Blase: 'Julião Sarmento', *Noema Art Magazine*, No. 11, 1987 – Gabi Czöppan: 'Julião Sarmento', *Kunstforum International*, Vol. 96, 1988 – Alexandre Melo: 'Julião Sarmento', *Artforum*, No. 8, 1989 – Maria Leonor Nazaré: 'Julião Sarmento', *Artefactum*, No. 30, 1989 – João Pinharanda: 'The Geometric Place of the Heart. Julião Sarmento', *Tema Celeste*, No. 22–23, 1989

JULIAN SCHNABEL

Born New York, 1951. Studied at University of Houston, Texas, 1969–73; Whitney Museum Independent Study Program, New York, 1973–74. First one-man show at Contemporary Arts Museum, Houston, 1976; first European one-man show at Galerie Dezember, Düsseldorf, 1978. Exhibitions at Mary Boone Gallery, New York; Galerie Bruno Bischofberger, Zurich; Anthony d'Offay Gallery, London; Leo Castelli Gallery, New York; The Pace Gallery, New York; Galerie Yvon Lambert, Paris; and elsewhere. Took part in Venice Biennale, 1980, and 'Zeitgeist' exhibition, Berlin, 1982. Lives in New York.

In his mostly large paintings, Schnabel works on a wide variety of supports, including plates, earth, maps of the world, velvet, liturgical vestments, and tarpaulins. The encounter between these extraordinary base materials and an expressive gestural style makes for works that challenge the viewer and evoke worlds of mystical, ecstatic, primitive or religious imagery. The inner worlds and memories embodied in the paintings manifest themselves in a formal language based on contrast and collisions between disparate elements. His output as a whole is deliberately diverse, both in content and in form. In 1983 he produced the first of his sculptures, which often perform a balancing act with materials from the most varied sources. In 1987–88 Schnabel was working on *Recognitions*, a series of paintings first exhibited in the former monastery of Cuartel del Carmen in Seville. Sculptures, written names of saints and mystics, religious symbols and articles of devotion are applied to military truck tarpaulins in such a way as to combine into

a labyrinth of meanings involving mysticism, ecclesiastical and military power, and the history of Europe. 'It is part of Julian Schnabel's strength that he confronts us with naked creative power: sometimes brutally, and sometimes subtly, subliminally and seductively. This immediacy leaves us defenceless; there are no criteria of comparison behind which we could take cover.' (Jean-Christophe Ammann)

Reference Sources for List of Exhibitions and Bibliography
'Julian Schnabel', Museo d'Arte Contemporanea, Prato 1989 – 'Julian Schnabel. Sculpture 1987–1990', The Pace Gallery, New York 1990

Catalogues and Monographs (Selection)
Kunsthalle Basel, 1981 – Stedelijk Museum, Amsterdam 1982 – Tate Gallery, London 1982 – 'Paintings 1975–1986', Whitechapel Art Gallery, London 1986 – 'Reconocimientos. The Recognitions Paintings', Cuartel del Carmen, Seville 1988 – 'Arbeiten auf Papier 1975–1988', Museum für Gegenwartskunst, Basle, (Prestel) Munich 1989 – 'Kabuki Paintings', Osaka National Museum of Modern Art, 1989 – 'Tableaux. Tati. Les plus bas prix', Yvon Lambert, Paris 1990

Catalogues of Collective Exhibitions (Selection)
'La Biennale di Venezia', Venice 1980 – 'A New Spirit in Painting', London 1981 – 'Westkunst-heute', Cologne 1981 – 'Issues. New Allegory', Institute of Contemporary

Art, Boston 1982 – '60 '80 'attitudes/concepts/images', Stedelijk Museum, Amsterdam 1982 – 'La Biennale di Venezia', Venice 1982 – 'Zeitgeist', Berlin 1982 – 'New York Now', Kestner-Gesellschaft Hannover, 1982 – 'New Figuration in America', Milwaukee Art Museum, 1982 – 'New Art', Tate Gallery, London 1983 – 'La Grande Parade', Stedelijk Museum, Amsterdam 1984 – 'Ouverture', Castello di Rivoli, Turin 1984 – 'Carnegie International', Museum of Art, Carnegie Institute, Pittsburgh 1985 – 'Beuys zu Ehren', Städtische Galerie im Lenbachhaus, Munich 1986 – 'Individuals. A Selected History of Contemporary Art. 1945–1986', Museum of Contemporary Art, Los Angeles 1986 – 'Prospect 86', Frankfurt a.M. 1986 – 'Der unverbrauchte Blick', Berlin 1987 – 'Post-Abstract Abstraction', The Aldrich Museum of Contemporary Art, Ridgefield, Connecticut 1987 – 'Standing Sculpture', Castello di Rivoli, Turin 1987 – 'Carnegie International', Carnegie Museum of Art, Pittsburgh 1988 – 'Bilderstreit', Cologne 1989 – 'Wiener Diwan. Sigmund Freud heute', Museum des 20. Jahrhunderts, Vienna, (Ritter Verlag) Klagenfurt 1989 – 'Culture and Commentary', Washington 1990 – 'GegenwartEwigkeit', Martin-Gropius-Bau, Berlin 1990 – 'The Biennale of Sydney', 1990

Other Literature (Selection)
Edit DeAk: 'Julian Schnabel', *Art-Rite*, May 1975 – Robert Pincus-Witten: 'Julian Schnabel. Blind Faith', *Arts Magazine*, No. 56, 1982 – Achille Bonito Oliva: *Avanguardia Transavanguardia*, Milan 1982 – Hilton Kramer: 'Julian Schnabel', in *Art of Our Time. The Saatchi Collection*, New York/London 1984 – Gerald Marzorati: 'Julian Schnabel. Plate it as it Lays', *Artnews*, No. 84, 1985 – Donald Kuspit: 'Julian Schnabel. Die Rückeroberung des Primitiven', *Wolkenkratzer Art Journal*, No. 10, 1985 – Matthew Collings: 'Modern Art. Julian Schnabel', *Artscribe*, No. 59, 1986 – Giancarlo Politi: 'Julian Schnabel', *Flash Art*, No. 130, 1986 – Catherine Millet: 'Julian Schnabel l'impatient' (Interview), *Art Press*, No. 110, 1987 – Brooks Adams: 'I Hate to Think. The New Paintings of Julian Schnabel', *Parkett*, No. 18, 1988 – Andrew Renton: 'Julian Schnabel. The Perpetual Task of Living up to a Name', *Flash Art*, No. 145, 1989

CINDY SHERMAN

Born Glen Ridge, New Jersey, 1954. Studied at State University College of Buffalo, New York, 1972–76. First one-woman show at Hallwalls, Buffalo, 1979. Exhibitions since 1980 at Galerie Chantal Crousel, Paris; Galerie Schellmann & Klüser, Munich; Rhona Hoffman Gallery, Chicago; Monika Sprüth Galerie, Cologne; La Máquina Española, Madrid; and elsewhere. Took part in 'documenta 7' and Venice Biennale, 1982. Guggenheim Fellowship, 1983. Skowhegan Medal for Photography, 1989. Lives in New York.

Cindy Sherman sets up photographs of herself in varying roles and identities. She is her own model, property stylist, lighting supervisor and (mostly) photographer, creating meticulous and perfect simulations of the body language and detail of mass-media images. In her first black and white photographs, taken in 1976–80 under the title of *Untitled Film Stills*, she appeared in a variety of roles, from frowzy housewife to sophisticated star, that look as if they were taken from films of the 1950s. In the photographic sequences that followed, which were taken in colour, Sherman worked her way through the whole range of contemporary female stereotypes. In the celebrated 1982 series *Ordinary People* she made use of light effects to create psychological portraits. Cindy Sherman: 'These are pictures of emotions personified, entirely of themselves with their own presence – not of me. The issue of the identity of the model is no more interesting than the possible symbolism of any other detail…

I'm trying to make other people recognize something of themselves rather than me.' After a series showing women and androgynous individuals in outré costumes and poses, she turned in 1985 to visions based on horror stories, fairytales and myths, followed in 1986 by images of atrocity and repulsion in which Sherman's body is often visible only in fragments. More recently, after a photographic sequence on the French Revolution, she has turned to simulations of Renaissance portraiture.

Reference Source for List of Exhibitions and Bibliography
'Künstlerinnen des 20. Jahrhunderts', Museum Wiesbaden, 1990

Catalogues and Monographs (Selection)
'Photographs', Contemporary Arts Museum, Houston 1980 – Stedelijk Museum, Amsterdam, (Schirmer/Mosel) Munich 1982 – Art Gallery, Fine Arts Center, State University of New York at Stony Brook, 1983 – Musée d'Art et d'Industrie, Saint Etienne 1983 – Peter Schjeldahl / I. Michael Danoff: *Cindy Sherman*, New York 1984 – 'Photographien', Westfälischer Kunstverein, Münster 1985 – 'Personae: Jenny Holzer/Cindy Sherman', Contemporary Arts Center, Cincinnati 1986 – Whitney Museum of American Art, New York, (Schirmer/Mosel) Munich 1987 (3rd, expanded edition)) – *Untitled Film Stills. Cindy Sherman*, Munich 1990

Catalogues of Collective Exhibitions (Selection)
'Four Artists', Artists Space, New York 1978 – 'Ils se disent peintres. Ils se disent photographes', ARC Musée d'Art Moderne de la Ville de Paris, 1980 – 'Autoportraits Photographiques', Centre Georges Pompidou, Paris 1981 – 'La Biennale di Venezia', Venice 1982 – 'documenta 7', Kassel 1982 – '20th Century Photographs from the Museum of Modern Art', Seibu Museum of Art, Tokyo 1982 – 'Back to the U.S.A.', Kunstmuseum Lucerne, 1983 – 'The Biennale of Sydney', 1984 – 'Alibis', Centre Georges Pompidou, Paris 1984 – 'Content. A Contemporary Focus 1974–1984', Hirshhorn Museum, Smithsonian Institution, Washington 1984 – 'Autoportrait à l'époque de la photographie', Musée Cantonal des Beaux-Arts, Lausanne 1985 – 'Prospect 86', Frankfurt a.M. 1986 – 'Individuals. A Selected History of Contemporary Art. 1945–1986', Museum of Contemporary Art, Los Angeles 1986 – 'Staging the Self. Self-Portrait Photography 1840's–1980's', National Portrait Gallery, London 1986 –

'Art and Its Double', Madrid 1987 – 'blow-up. Zeitgeschichte', Württembergischer Kunstverein, Stuttgart 1987 – 'Photography and Art', Los Angeles County Museum of Art, 1987 – 'Implosion. Ett postmodern perspektiv', Moderna Museet, Stockholm 1987 – 'L'Epoque, la mode, la morale, la passion', Paris 1987 – 'Photography Now', Victoria and Albert Museum, London 1989 – 'The Photography of Invention', National Museum of American Art, Washington 1989 – 'Bilderstreit', Cologne 1989 – 'A Forest of Signs. Art in the Crisis of Representation', Los Angeles 1989 – 'Culture and Commentary. An Eighties Perspective', Washington 1990 – 'Energieën', Amsterdam 1990 – 'Life-Size', Jerusalem 1990 – 'The Biennale of Sydney', 1990

Other Literature (Selection)
Klaus Honnef: 'Cindy Sherman', *Kunstforum International*, Vol. 60, 1983 – Andreas Kallfelz: 'Cindy Sherman. Ich mache keine Selbstportraits' (Interview), *Wolkenkratzer Art Journal*, No. 4, 1984 – 'Cindy Sherman', special issue, *Camera Austria*, No. 15/16, 1984 – Leo van Damme: 'Cindy Sherman. I Don't Want to Be a Performer' (Interview), *Artefactum*, No. 2, 1985 – Stephen W. Melville: 'The Time of Exposure. Allegorical Self-Portraiture in Cindy Sherman', *Arts Magazine*, No. 60, 1986 – Donald Kuspit: 'Inside Cindy', *Artscribe*, No. 65, 1987 – Ken Johnson: 'Cindy Sherman and the Anti-Self. An Interpretation of her Imagery', *Arts Magazine*, No. 62, 1987 – Germano Celant: *Unexpressionism. Art Beyond the Contemporary*, New York 1989 – Eleanor Heartney: 'Cindy Sherman. Metro Pictures', *Art News*, May 1990

MIKE and DOUG STARN

Born Absecon, New Jersey, 1961. Studied at School of the Museum of Fine Arts, Boston, 1980–85. Two-man shows at Stux Gallery, Boston and New York, 1985 onward. Exhibitions at Fred Hoffman Gallery, Santa Monica; Akira Ikeda Gallery, Tokyo; Leo Castelli, New York; and elsewhere. Took part in 'BiNational', Boston and Düsseldorf, 1988. They live in New York.

The Starn twins have been doing photography since their childhood. But they are not primarily interested in the illustrative aspect of the medium. Their works, many of which are on a large scale, are made in the darkroom by manipulating photographic paper, which they tear, crumple, and stick; the individual images are dissociated from their contexts and absorbed into all-encompassing tableaux. The traces of the working process are not wiped out; they form part of the concept. The artists also emphasize the frame, which is designed to fit each individual work. With the tools of montage, they quote and modify – among other things – works of classical fine art. Their work has recently become markedly relief-like and sculptural. Mike and Doug Starn: 'On some level our method of composition is very innocent – it's just a form of playing, making something a little more interesting to look at. By using several pieces of paper, an illusion of depth is established. You can focus on the sheets of paper and the tape and the method of construction, or you could just look at the image as an image. We like the spaces between these two different ways of looking. We make something sculptural out of something that's actually two-dimensional.'

Reference Source for List of Exhibitions and Bibliography
Andy Grundberg: *Mike and Doug Starn*, (Abrams) New York 1990 – 'Doug & Mike Starn', Stux Gallery, New York 1990

Catalogues of Collective Exhibitions (Selection)
'Whitney Biennial', Whitney Museum of American Art, New York 1987 – 'The BiNational. American Art of the Late 80's', Boston, (DuMont) Cologne 1988 – 'NY Art Now. The Saatchi Collection', London 1988 – 'Photography Now', Victoria and Albert Museum, London 1989 – 'The Photography of Invention. American Pictures of the 1980s', National Museum of American Art, Smithsonian Institution, Washington 1989 – 'Wiener Diwan. Sigmund Freud heute', Museum des 20. Jahrhunderts, Vienna, (Ritter Verlag) Klagenfurt 1989 – 'L'Invention d'un Art', Centre Georges Pompidou, Paris 1989 – 'All Quiet on the Western Front?', Espace Dieu, Paris 1990

Other Literature (Selection)
Joseph Masheck: 'Of One Mind. Photos by the Starn Twins of Boston', *Arts Magazine*, March 1986 – Jack Bankowsky: 'The Starn Twins', *Flash Art*, Summer 1987 – Ulrike Henn: 'The Starn Twins', *Art*, May 1988 – Robert Pincus-Witten: 'Being Twins. The Art of Doug and Mike Starn', *Arts Magazine*, October 1988 – Robert Mahoney: 'Doug and Mike Starn', *Arts Magazine*, January 1989 – Francine A. Koslow: 'New Life for Old Masters', *Contemporanea*, September 1989 – Klaus Ottmann: 'Mike & Doug Starn' (Interview), *Journal of Contemporary Art*, No. 1, 1990 – Paolo Bianchi: 'Mike & Doug Starn', *Kunstforum International*, Vol. 107, 1990

HAIM STEINBACH

Born Israel 1944, United States citizen since 1962. Studied at Pratt Institute, Brooklyn, 1962–68, and Yale University, New Haven, 1971–73. First one-man show at Panoras Gallery, New York, 1969. Exhibitions at Jay Gorney Modern Art, New York; Sonnabend Gallery, New York; Galleria Lia Rumma, Naples Yvon Lambert, Paris; and elsewhere. Since 1983 has also exhibited jointly with 'Group Material' (including 'documenta 8', 1987). Participated in the 'Schlaf der Vernunft' exhibition at the Museum Fridericianum, Kassel, 1988. Lives in New York.

Since the 1970s, Haim Steinbach has concerned himself with everyday objects and their presentation. Initially these were articles bought in junk stores and introduced as art objects into a museum or exhibition to tell their own individual stories and to encounter other things and other artworks. His work since 1984 reveals an aesthetic process whereby objects are increasingly minimalized and isolated. A group of identical objects is confronted with another group; each group occupies its own specially made wall plinth. These object groups begin to enter into – or to negate – reciprocal relationships, both between themselves and with the wall plinths. This kind of presentation has the effect of endowing the mass-produced articles of use, consumption, and luxury with some of the aura of meaning implied by the art context. The viewer is required to establish relationships between himself and the objects, between the objects themselves, and between the plinths. These triangular, meticulously crafted plinths may be seen as fields for the interplay of objects that range from pretentious kitsch by way of modernist design to packaging. Most recently, Steinbach has also been using cupboard-like objects as a form of presentation.

Reference Source for List of Exhibitions and Bibliography
'Objectives. The New Sculpture', Newport Harbor Art Museum, Newport Beach, California 1990

Catalogue
'Haim Steinbach. Oeuvres Récentes', CAPC Musée d'Art Contemporain de Bordeaux, 1988

Catalogues of Collective Exhibitions (Selection)
'New York Now', Phoenix Art Museum, 1979 – 'Infotainment', Texas Gallery, Houston, (J. Berg Press) New York 1985 – 'Arts & Leisure', The Kitchen, New York 1986 – 'Prospect 86', Frankfurt a.M. 1986 – 'Art and Its Double', Madrid 1987 – 'Reconstruct', John Gibson Gallery, New York 1987 – 'Les Courtiers du Désir', Centre Georges Pompidou, Paris 1987 – 'NY Art Now. The Saatchi Collection', London 1988 – 'Schlaf der Vernunft', Kassel 1988 – 'Cultural Geometry', Athens 1988 – 'ReDefining the Object', University Art Galleries, Wright State University, Dayton, Ohio 1988 – 'The BiNational. American Art of the Late 80's', Boston, (DuMont) Cologne 1988 – 'Innovations in Sculpture 1985–1988', Aldrich Museum of Contemporary Art, Ridgefield, Connecticut 1988 – 'Museum der Avantgarde. Die Sammlung Sonnabend New York', Berlin, (Electa) Milan 1989 – 'Repetition', Hirschl & Adler Modern, New York 1989 – 'D & S Ausstellung', Hamburg 1989 – 'A Forest of Signs. Art in the Crisis of Representation', Los Angeles 1989 – 'Jardins de Bagatelle', Galerie Tanit, Munich 1990 – 'Life-Size', Jerusalem 1990

Other Literature (Selection)
Robert Nickas: 'Shopping With Haim Steinbach' (Interview), *Flash Art*, April 1987 – Germano Celant: 'Haim Steinbach's Wild, Wild Wild West', *Artforum*, December 1987 – Holland Cotter: 'Haim Steinbach. Shelf Life', *Art in America*, May 1988 – Paul Taylor: 'Haim Steinbach. An Easygoing Aesthetic that Appeals to the Flaneur in Many of Us', *Flash Art*, May/June 1989

ROSEMARIE TROCKEL

Born Schwerte, near Dortmund, 1952. Studied painting at Werkkunstschule, Cologne, 1974–78. One-woman shows at Monika Sprüth Galerie, Cologne, since 1983. Exhibitions at Galerie Ascan Crone, Hamburg; Galerie Friedrich, Bern; Donald Young Gallery, Chicago; Galerie Michael Werner, Cologne; and elsewhere. Took part in 'BiNationale', Düsseldorf and Boston, 1988. Lives in Cologne.

Rosemarie Trockel's work is almost impossible to categorize, or to comprehend from any single viewpoint. It evades comprehensive interpretation because her

drawings, paintings, sculptures and objects reveal no single thematic or stylistic programme. Every one of her works is meant as a unique artistic act. Nevertheless, it is possible to discern a number of specific motifs that run through a succession of variations: death's-heads, monkey faces, and – over and over again – vases and other vessels. Another evident theme is that of museum presentation, as evidenced in the hanging of pictures or in the use of glass showcases and plinths. Trockel's artistic positions and visual reflections – image and language, the world of objects as transformed by a female vision, eroticism voyeurism – take shape in a portfolio of drawings, on which the artist is constantly working, and which frequently become the basis of larger works. She won fame for her knitted pictures, pullovers and other garments, which turn political symbols, trade-marks and emblems into (computeraided) patterns. 'Rosemarie Trockel confronts us with considerable problems of self-discovery. She denies us the global view, the possible extrapolation. She forces us to reconstruct the female semantic connections within ourselves, thus undermining our perceptions through a process in which we give ourselves away step by step.' (Jean-Christophe Ammann)

Reference Sources for List of Exhibitions and Bibliography
'Rosemarie Trockel', Kunsthalle Basle, Institute of Contemporary Arts, London,

1988 – 'Künstlerinnen des 20. Jahrhunderts', Museum Wiesbaden, 1990

Catalogues and Monographs (Selection)
'Plastiken 1982–83', Galerie Philomene Magers, Bonn, Monika Sprüth Galerie, Cologne, 1983 – 'Skulpturen und Bilder', Galerie Ascan Crone, Hamburg 1984 – 'Bilder – Skulpturen – Zeichnungen', Rheinisches Landesmuseum Bonn, 1985 – Monika Sprüth Galerie (with A. R. Penck), Galerie Michael Werner, Cologne 1990

Catalogues of Collective Exhibitions (Selection)
'Licht bricht sich in den oberen Fenstern', Im Klapperhof 33, Cologne 1982 – 'Bella Figura', Wilhelm-Lehmbruck-Museum, Duisburg 1984 – 'Kunst mit Eigen-Sinn', Museum des 20. Jahrhunderts, Vienna 1985 – 'Synonyme für Skulptur', trigon 85, Neue Galerie am Landesmuseum Joanneum, Graz 1985 – 'Sonsbeek 86', Arnheim 1986 – 'The Biennale of Sydney', 1986 – 'Wechselströme', Bonner Kunstverein, Bonn, (Wienand) Cologne 1987 – 'Jutta Koether, Bettina Semmer, Rosemarie Trockel', La Máquina Española, Seville 1987 – 'Similia/Dissimilia', Städtische Kunsthalle Düsseldorf, 1987 – 'Camouflage', Scottish Arts Council, Edinburgh 1988 – 'Cultural Geometry', Athens 1988 – 'Arbeit in Geschichte – Geschichte in Arbeit', Kunsthaus and Kunstverein in Hamburg, 1988 – 'Made in Cologne', DuMont Kunsthalle, Cologne 1988 – 'BiNationale. Deutsche Kunst der späten 80er Jahre', Düsseldorf, (DuMont) Cologne 1988 – 'Refigured Painting. The German Image 1960–88', Toledo 1988, (Guggenheim Foundation) New York, (Prestel) Munich 1989 – 'Das Verhältnis der Geschlechter', Bonner Kunstverein, Bonn 1989 – 'Prospect 89', Frankfurt a. M. 1989 – 'Bilderstreit', Cologne 1989 – 'Objet/Objectif', Galerie Daniel Templon, Paris 1989 – 'Psychological Abstraction', Athens 1989 – 'Einleuchten', Hamburg 1989 – 'Jardins de Bagatelle', Galerie Tanit, Munich 1990 – 'Life-Size', Jerusalem 1990 – 'A Vint Minuts de Paris', Galería Joan Prats, Barcelona 1990 – 'The Biennale of Sydney', 1990

Other Literature (Selection)
Lucie Beyer: 'Rosemarie Trockel', *Flash Art*, No. 119, 1984 – Annelie Pohlen: 'Rosemarie Trockel', *Kunstforum International*, Vol. 81, 1985 – Nona Nyffeler: 'Rosemarie Trockels Strickbilder', *Wolkenkratzer Art Journal*, No. 2, 1986 – Jutta Koether: 'The Resistant Art of Rosemarie Trockel', *Artscribe*, No. 62, 1987 – Doris von Drateln: 'Endlich ahnen, nicht nur wissen' (Interview), *Kunstforum International*, Vol. 93, 1988 – Stephan Schmidt-Wulffen: '"Ich kenne mich nicht aus" ... Rosemarie Trockel und die Philosophie', *Noema Art Magazine*, No. 22, 1989

BILL VIOLA

Born New York, 1951. Graduated from School of Visual and Performing Arts, Syracuse University, 1973. Studied and worked with David Tudor and belonged to the Rainforest music group, 1973–80. Technical director of video production at Art/Tapes/22 Video Studio, Florence, 1974–76. Artist in Residence at the experimental studio of the state-owned television station WNET, New York, 1976–80. Took part in 'documenta 6', 1977. Recipient of numerous fellowships and prizes for his videotapes. Lives in Long Beach, California.

Viola's videotapes and video installations focus on a confrontation with the phenomenon of time, its rhythm, its acceleration and deceleration. This takes place through technical manipulations, dislocations of size relationships, images in parallel, and the closed-circuit technique. In the video installations, issues of time appear in conjunction with spatial experiences designed to elicit from the viewer an active, direct, quasi-physical involvement in what goes on. In the installation *Reasons for*

Knocking at an Empty House (1982), for instance, the viewer sits wearing headphones and facing a monitor on which he sees the artist, who whispers something to him and appears to fall asleep; meanwhile a menacing figure looms from behind. Works in which Viola uses disparities of scale include *Room for St John of the Cross* (1983), in which a tiny monastic cell, with a small monitor, is contrasted with an overpowering projection of a mountain landscape. In one of his most recent video installations, *Passage* (1987), images are seen flickering at the far end of a narrow corridor. If the viewer enters the space, he finds himself right up against the projection, so that a 'normal' viewing of the sequence, a slow-motion film of a child's birthday, is never possible. Viola's leitmotif: 'The relation between image, space and body, and the way in which the time factor changes how it is perceived.' (Dieter Daniels)

Reference Source for List of Exhibitions, Videos and Video Installations and for Bibliography
'Expansion & Transformation: The 3rd Fukui International Video Biennale', Fukui 1989

Writings by the Artist (Selection)
'The European Scene and Other Observations', in: Ira Schneider / Beryl Korot (eds): *Video Art*, New York 1976 – 'The Porcupine and the Car', *Image Forum* (Tokyo), No. 3, 1981 – 'Sight Unseen. Enlightened Squirrels and Fatal Experiments', *Video 80*, No. 4, 1982 – 'Video As Art', *Video Systems*, No. 7, 1982 – 'Some Recommendations on Establishing Standards for the Exhibition and Distribution of Video Works', in: *The Media Arts in Transition*, Walker Art Center, Minneapolis 1983 – *I Do Not Know What It Is I Am Like*, Los Angeles 1986

Catalogues and Monographs (Selection)
ARC Musée d'Art Moderne de la Ville de Paris, 1983 – 'Summer 1985', Museum of Contemporary Art, Los Angeles 1985 – 'Installations and Videotapes', The Museum of Modern Art, New York 1987 – 'Survey of a Decade', Contemporary Arts Museum, Houston 1988 – 'The City of Man', Brockton Art Museum/Fuller Memorial, Brockton, Massachusetts 1989

Catalogues of Collective Exhibitions (Selection)
'Projekt '74', Wallraf-Richartz-Museum, Kunsthalle Köln, Kölnischer Kunstverein, Cologne 1974 – 'La Biennale de Paris', 1975

– 'Biennial Exhibition', Whitney Museum of American Art, New York 1975 – 'documenta 6', Kassel 1977 – ''60 '80 attitudes / concepts / images', Stedelijk Museum, Amsterdam 1982 – 'Currents', Institute of Contemporary Art, Boston 1985 – 'La Biennale di Venezia', Venice 1986 – 'Ritratti. Greenaway, Martinis, Pirri, Viola', Taormina Arte 1987 Festival, Rome 1987 – 'L'Epoque, la mode, la morale, la passion', Paris 1987 – 'The Arts for Television', Museum of Contemporary Art, Los Angeles, Stedelijk Museum, Amsterdam, 1987 – 'Carnegie International', Carnegie Museum of Art, Pittsburgh 1988 – 'Einleuchten', Hamburg 1989 – 'Passages de l'image', Centre Georges Pompidou, Paris – 'Life-Size', Jerusalem 1990

Other Literature (Selection)
John Minkowsky: 'Bill Viola's Video Vision', *Video 81*, Autumn 1981 – Bettina Gruber/Maria Vedder (eds.): *Kunst und Video*, Cologne 1983 – Dany Bloch: 'Les Vidéo-paysages de Bill Viola', *Art Press*, No. 80, 1984 – Eric de Moffarts: 'Bill Viola. La Vidéo et l'Image-temps', *Artefactum*, No. 11, 1985 – Raymond Bellour: 'An Interview with Bill Viola', *October*, No. 34, 1985 – Anne-Marie Duguet: 'Les Vidéos de Bill Viola. Une poétic de l'espace-temps', *Parachute*, No. 45, 1986/87 – Dieter Daniels: 'Bill Viola', *Kunstforum International*, Vol. 92, 1988 – Wulf Herzogenrath/Edith Decker (eds.): *Video-Skulptur retrospektiv und aktuell. 1963–1989*, Cologne 1989 – Michael Nash: 'Bill Viola' (Interview), *Journal of Contemporary Art*, No. 2, 1990

JEFF WALL

Born Vancouver, Canada, 1946. Studied art history in Vancouver, 1964–68. Worked in the field of conceptual art, 1969–71. Lived in London, 1970–73, where he studied at the Courtauld Institute of Art, University of London. Doctorate in art history, 1973. Taught in various places from 1974; professor at Centre for the Arts, Simon Fraser University, Vancouver, 1976; professor at University of British Columbia, Department of Fine Arts, Vancouver, 1987. First one-man show of photographic works at Nova Gallery, Vancouver, 1978. Exhibitions at David Bellman Gallery, Toronto; Galerie Rüdiger Schöttle, Munich; The Ydessa Gallery, Toronto; Galerie Johnen & Schöttle, Cologne; Marian Goodman Gallery, New York; and elsewhere. Participated in 'documenta 7', 1982, and 'documenta 8', 1987. Lives in Vancouver.

Jeff Wall's photo pieces show precisely calculated scenes of everyday life, portraits, landscapes, and interiors. Wall's use of light boxes with fluorescent light endows his large-format cibachrome transparencies with a penetrating strength and luminous intensity that is intended – unlike analogous forms in advertising – not to manipulate but to make possible a clear, critical observation of a staged reality at a specific moment. The pieces can be understood as allegories. The body language, actions and gestures of the people shown reflect common patterns of social behaviour. Moments of physical violence and destruction, scenes showing the life of the underclass or the attitudes of the bourgeoisie, apparently random panoramic views: all provide a precise insight into social realities. This is what makes Wall's meticulous aesthetic into a political statement. 'The otherness of Wall's luminescent image is the product of two contradictory movements – one projective, the other introjective. The world's images seem to emanate from the display case at the same time as they crash against the pane of glass.' (Arielle Pélenc)

Reference Source for List of Exhibitions and Bibliography
'Jeff Wall', Vancouver Art Gallery, 1990

Writings by the Artist (Selection)
Berlin Dada and the Notion of Context, Master's thesis, University of British Columbia, Vancouver 1970 – 'Dan Graham's Kammerspiel', in: *Dan Graham* (catalogue), The Art Gallery of Western Australia, Perth 1984 – 'La Mélancolie de la Rue. Idyll and Monochrome in the Work of Ian Wallace 1967–82', in: *Ian Wallace. Selected Works 1970–87* (catalogue), Vancouver Art Gallery, 1988 – 'Bezugspunkte im Werk von Stephan Balkenhol', in: *Stephan Balkenhol* (catalogue), Kunsthalle Basle, 1988

Catalogues and Monographs (Selection)
Art Gallery of Greater Victoria, Victoria, British Columbia 1979 – 'Selected Works', The Renaissance Society at the University of Chicago, 1983 – 'Transparencies', Institute of Contemporary Arts, London 1984 – 'Transparencies', Munich 1986, New York 1987 – 'Young Workers', Museum für Gegenwartskunst, Basle 1987 – Le Nouveau Musée, Villeurbanne 1988 – Westfälischer Kunstverein, Münster 1988 – Marian Goodman Gallery, New York 1989

Catalogues of Collective Exhibitions (Selection)
'557,087', Seattle Art Museum, 1969 – '955,000', Vancouver Art Gallery, 1970 – 'Westkunst-heute', Cologne 1981 – 'documenta 7', Kassel 1982 – 'Ein anderes Klima. Aspekte der Schönheit in der zeitgenössischen Kunst', Städtische Kunsthalle, Düsseldorf 1984 – 'Difference. On Representation and Sexuality', New Museum of Contemporary Art, New York 1984 – 'Günther Förg en Jeff Wall. Fotowerken', Stedelijk Museum, Amsterdam 1985 – 'Prospect 86', Frankfurt a. M. 1986 – 'blow up. Zeitgeschichte', Württembergischer Kunstverein, Stuttgart 1987 – 'documenta 8', Kassel 1987 – 'Utopia Post Utopia', Institute of Contemporary Art, Boston 1988 – 'Images Critiques. J. Wall, D. Adams, A. Jaar, L. Jammes', ARC Musée d'Art Moderne de la Ville de Paris, 1989 – 'Dan Graham, Jeff Wall. The Children's Pavilion', Galerie Roger Pailhas, Marseille 1989 – 'Les Magiciens de la Terre', Centre Georges Pompidou, La Grande Halle de la Villette, Paris 1989 – 'Un'altra obiettività / Another objectivity', Centre National des Arts Plastiques, Paris, Museo d'Arte Contemporanea Luigi Pecci, Prato, (Idea Books) Milan 1989 – 'Bestiarium. Jardin-Théâtre', Entrepôt-Galerie du Confort Moderne, Poitiers 1989 – 'Life-Size', Jerusalem 1990 – 'Culture and Commentary. An Eighties Perspective', Washington 1990 – 'Weitersehen', Krefeld 1990

Other Literature (Selection)
Donald B. Kuspit: 'Looking up at Jeff Wall's Modern "Appassionamento"', *Artforum*, No. 20, 1982 – Jörg Johnen / Rüdiger Schöttle: 'Jeff Wall', *Kunstforum International*, Vol. 65, 1983 – 'Collaborations Christian Boltanski / Jeff Wall,' *Parkett*, No. 22, 1989

FRANZ WEST

Born Vienna, 1947. Studied sculpture at Akademie der bildenden Künste, Vienna. First one-man show at Galerie Hamburger, Vienna, 1970. Exhibitions at Galerie nächst St. Stephan, Vienna; Galerie Peter Pakesch, Vienna; Galerie Christoph Dürr, Munich; Galerie Ghislaine Hussenot, Paris; Galleria Mario Peroni, Rome; Jänner Galerie, Vienna; and elsewhere. Took part in 'Westkunst heute', Cologne, 1981; 'Skulptur Projekte in Münster', 1987, and Venice Biennale, 1990. Lives in Vienna.

West's artistic ideas take shape in a wide variety of media, including video, film, music, photography, painting, books and sculpture; but it is as a sculptor that he is best known. His sculptures are not merely aesthetic objects, but ways to physical experience: the convex and concave parts of his *Paßstücke (Fitting Pieces)* are meant for direct body contact. Similarly, his sculptures since 1984, mostly made of papier mâché and sometimes based on found objects, demand the viewer's mental involvement: their enigmatic form, and the tactile quality of their 'skin', give rise to multifarious associations. The recent *Seats and Recliners* – works in iron and steel that are both sculpture and furniture at the same time – are materially stable but optically fragile. With a spartan kind of playfulness, the theme of sitting and lying down becomes open to direct bodily perception. These are 'direct associative transformations of traditional pieces of furniture, objects whose codified forms both appeal to fundamental modes of human behaviour and imply bodily responses, while at the same time – because they are isolated works of art – appearing to prohibit them'. (Hans Hollein)

Reference Source for List of Exhibitions
'Franz West. Austria – Biennale di Venezia 1990', Venice, (Ritter Verlag) Klagenfurt 1990

Catalogues and Monographs (Selection)
'Legitime Skulptur', Neue Galerie am Landesmuseum Joanneum, Graz 1986 – 'Ansicht', Wiener Secession, Vienna 1987 – Kunsthalle Bern, 1988 – 'Schöne Aussicht', Portikus, Frankfurt a.M. 1988 – Pier Luigi Tazzi: *Franz West. Fontana Romana*, Roma 1988 – Museum Haus Lange, Krefeld 1989 – 'Possibilities', Institute for Contemporary Art, P.S.1 Museum, Long Island City, New York 1989 – 'Nemo plus juris transferre potest quam ipse habet' (with Herbert Brandl), Galerie Grässlin-Ehrhardt, Frankfurt a.M. 1989

Catalogues of Collective Exhibitions (Selection)
'Westkunst-heute', Cologne 1981 – 'Neue Skulptur', Galerie nächst St. Stephan, Vienna 1982 – 'Weltpunkt Wien. Un regard sur Vienne: 1985', Pavillon Joséphine, Strasbourg, (Löcker Verlag) Vienna / Munich 1985 – 'Spuren, Skulpturen und Monumente ihrer präzisen Reise', Kunsthaus Zurich, 1985 – 'De Sculptura', Messepalast, Vienna 1986 – 'Sonsbeek 86', Arnheim 1986 – 'SkulpturSein', Städtische Kunsthalle Düsseldorf, 1986 – 'Skulptur Projekte in Münster', (DuMont) Cologne 1987 – 'Anderer Leute Kunst', Museum Haus Lange, Krefeld 1987 – 'Actuelle Kunst in Oostenrijk', Museum van Hedendaagse Kunst, Ghent 1987 – 'La Biennale di Venezia', Venice 1988 – 'Zeitlos', Berlin, (Prestel) Munich 1988 – 'Open Mind', Ghent 1989 – 'Wittgenstein. Das Spiel des Unsagbaren', Wiener Secession, Vienna 1989 – 'Einleuchten', Hamburg 1989 – 'Herbert Brandl, Ernst Caramelle, Franz West', ARC Musée d'Art Moderne de la Ville de Paris, 1990 – 'Casinò Fantasma', Institute for Contemporary Art, P.S.1 Museum, Long Island City, New York 1990 – 'Possible Worlds. Sculpture from Europe', Institute of Contemporary Arts, Serpentine Gallery, London, 1990 – 'Weitersehen', Krefeld 1990

Other Literature (Selection)
Franz West/Ferdinand Schmatz/Peter Pakesch: 'Aus einem Gespräch, Vienna, November 1985', *Domus*, No. 668, 1986 – Annelie Pohlen: 'Franz West', *Kunstforum International*, Vol. 85, 1986 – Peter Mahr: 'Franz West at Peter Pakesch', *Artscribe*, January/February 1987 – Helmut Draxler: 'Franz West. Plastiker der Psyche', *Kunst und Kirche*, No. 1, 1987 – Harald Szeemann: 'Franz West ou la baroque de l'ame et de l'esprit en fragments séchés', *Art Press*, No. 133, 1989 – Helmut Draxler: 'Franz West. The anti-body to anti-body', *Artforum*, March 1989 – Anton Gugg: 'Franz West', *Noema Art Magazine*, Nr. 31, 1990 – Brigitte Felderer / Herbert Lachmayer: 'Potentially inaccessible – factually accessible. On Franz West', *Parkett*, No. 24, 1990

RACHEL WHITEREAD

Born London, 1963. Studied at Brighton Polytechnic, 1982–85; Slade School of Art, London, 1985–87. First one-woman show at Carlile Gallery, London, 1988. Exhibitions at Chisenhale Gallery, London; Arnolfini Gallery, Bristol; Karsten Schubert Ltd, London; and elsewhere. Took part in 'Einleuchten' exhibition, Hamburg 1990. Lives in London.

The focal point of Whiteread's sculptural work is the relationship between object and space. She brings this within the scope of direct experience by filling the space adjacent to such objects as cupboards, tables or beds with plaster of paris and presenting the

result – after the removal of the objects – as a sculpture. There is an allusion here to the traditional sculptural process of 'lost wax' casting; except that in this case it is the objects themselves that are lost. They remain present only through the imprint that they make in the 'materialized space' around them. Absence becomes remembered presence: a device – laden, in this artist's work, with autobiographical elements – through which space and time are conjoined.

Reference Source for List of Exhibitions
'The British Art Show 1990', McLellan Galleries, Glasgow, (The South Bank Centre) London 1990

Catalogues of Collective Exhibitions (Selection)
'Concept 88 Reality 89', University of Essex Gallery, 1989 – 'Einleuchten', Hamburg 1989

Other Literature (Selection)
Kate Bush: 'British Art Show', *Artscribe*, No. 81, 1990 – Andrew Renton: 'Ghost', *Flash Art*, No. 154, 1990 – Liz Brooks: 'Rachel Whiteread', *Artscribe*, November/December 1990

BILL WOODROW

Born near Henley-on-Thames, Oxfordshire, 1948. Studied at Winchester School of Art, 1967–68, St Martin's School of Art, London, 1968–71, and Chelsea School of Art, London, 1971–72. First one-man show at Whitechapel Art Gallery, London, 1972, followed by a long gap. Next one-man show at Künstlerhaus, Hamburg, 1979. Exhibitions at Lisson Gallery, London; Barbara Gladstone Gallery, New York; Galerie Paul Maenz, Cologne; Galerie Fahnemann, Berlin; and elsewhere. Took part in 'documenta 8', 1987. Lives in London.

Woodrow's sculptures are complex structures in several parts, which proliferate into the surrounding space. Woodrow first takes found objects, such as car parts, refrigerators and household appliances, and forms them into new objects ranging from a burp gun to a guitar. An 'umbilical cord' links these separate, often painted components of the sculpture, which constitute the basic material of the new form; other everyday objects – garments, pieces of cloth and general junk – are added. By a process that can only be called decomposition, Wood-

row creates wry, poetic situations that exploit the narrative dimension of the objects that they include. 'Woodrow's sculptures define a precisely demarcated space, a zone in which they exist autonomously, by and for themselves. Within this space, objects and images lose their individuality and assume a general character. They exchange their specific historic meaning for an aesthetic, timeless setting.' (Lynne Cooke) In the late 1980s, Woodrow began to make steel sculptures made up of discrete elements that are apparently 'stitched together' in space to form landscapes, animals, trees and objects. Elements of language are added to expand the narrative aspect of these sculptures.

Reference Source for List of Exhibitions and Bibliography
'Bill Woodrow. Eye of the Needle. Sculptures 1987–1989', Musée des Beaux-Arts, Le Havre, Musée des Beaux-Arts, Calais, 1989

Catalogues and Monographs (Selection)
'Beaver, Bomb and Fossil', Museum of Modern Art, Oxford 1983 – 'Soupe du Jour', Musée de Toulon, 1984 – Kunsthalle Basle, 1985 – 'Natural Produce. An Armed Response', La Jolla Museum of Contemporary Art, La Jolla, California 1985 – 'Sculpture 1980–86', The Fruitmarket Gallery, Edinburgh 1986 – 'Positive Earth. Negative Earth', Kunstverein Munich 1987 – 'Point of Entry. New Sculptures', Imperial War

Museum, London 1989 – *Etchings*, (Margarete Roeder Editions) New York 1990

Catalogues of Collective Exhibitions (Selection)
'Englische Plastik heute', Kunstmuseum Lucerne, 1982 – 'Leçons des Choses', Kunsthalle Bern, 1982 – 'La Biennale di Venezia', Venice 1982 – 'Bienal de São Paulo', 1983 – 'Terrae Motus I', Fondazione Amelio, Villa Campolieto, Herculaneum (Electa) Naples 1984 – 'Space Invaders', MacKenzie Art Gallery, Regina, Saskatchewan 1985 – '7000 Eichen', Kunsthalle Tübingen, 1985 – 'A Quiet Revolution. British Sculpture since 1965', Museum of Contemporary Art, Chicago, San Francisco Museum of Modern Art, 1987 – 'documenta 8', Kassel 1987 – 'Current Affairs', Museum of Modern Art, Oxford 1987 – 'Een Keuze / A Choice', Kunstrai 87, Amsterdam 1987 – 'Affinities and Intuitions. The Gerald S. Elliott Collection of Contemporary Art', Art Institute of Chicago, 1990

Other Literature (Selction)
Mark Francis: 'Bill Woodrow. Material Truths', *Artforum*, January 1984 – Lynne Cooke: 'Bill Woodrow. The Ship of Fools', *Parkett*, No. 12, 1987 – Dan Cameron: 'De-Construction Sites. Recent Sculpture by Martin Kippenberger, Serge Spitzer, and Bill Woodrow', *Arts Magazine*, March 1988 – Mona Thomas: 'Bill Woodrow', *Beaux Arts*, No. 67, 1989 – John Roberts: 'Bill Woodrow', *Artscribe*, January 1990

CHRISTOPHER WOOL

Born Chicago, 1955, First one-man show at Cable Gallery, New York, 1984. Exhibitions at Luhring Augustine & Hodes Gallery, New York; Jean Bernier, Athens; Galerie Max Hetzler, Cologne; Daniel Weinberg Gallery, Los Angeles; Galleria Christian Stein, Turin; and elsewhere. Took part in 'BiNationale', Boston and Düsseldorf, 1988. Lives in New York.

Writing and ornament are the basis of Wool's painting. Letters and words, sometimes combined into legible structures of meaning or forcibly extracted from a larger context, present themselves on the surface of the painting in strictly organized form, as do the ornaments. The word paintings look stencilled; the ornament paintings look roller-stamped. These techniques lead to a qualitative redefinition of the content that is presented. The word paintings bear a reference to the aesthetic of lettering, and simultaneously to speech as a vehicle of meaning. By dint of repetition the empty ornamental forms become a rhythmic, painterly grid pattern. In both cases, painting transforms the pure sign – coloured or not – into an isolated verbal and visual abstraction. The result is a process of reflection on the possibilities and distinctions represented by image, painting, language and subject matter. 'These panels of lettering and ornament' open up... a space in which the picture is left in, or restored to, a state of pure potential. In between text and ornament, the idea of the painting emerges without being shown – because it is impossible to present. The idea is nonlocal, motionless and ahistorical. Christopher Wool thus establishes "the picture" as his theme by – literally and figuratively – not articulating it... His theme is the picture, not as a given but as a virtual reality.' (Christoph Schenker)

Reference Source for List of Exhibition and Bibliography
'Christopher Wool. New Work', San Francisco Museum of Modern Art, 1989

Books by the Artist (Selection)
Empire of the Goat, 1985 – *Black Book*, Thea Westreich Associates, New York, and Galerie Gisela Capitain, Cologne 1989

Catalogues and Monographs (Selection)
'A Project' (with Robert Gober), 303 Gallery, New York 1988 – Galerie Gisela Capitain, Cologne 1988 – 'Works on Paper', Luhring Augustine Gallery, New York 1990 – 'Cats in Bag Bags in River', Museum Boymans-van Beuningen, Rotterdam 1991

Catalogues of Collective Exhibition (Selection)
'Information as Ornament', Feature Gallery, Chicago 1988 – 'The BiNational. American Art of the Late 80's', Boston, (DuMont) Cologne 1988 – 'Abstraction in Question', John and Mable Ringling Museum of Art, Sarasota, Florida 1989 – 'Horn of Plenty', Stedelijk Museum, Amsterdam 1989 – 'Prospect 89', Frankfurt a.M. 1989 – 'Herold, Oehlen, Wool', The Renaissance Society at the University of Chicago, 1989 – 'Biennial Exhibition', Whitney Museum of American Art, New York 1989 – 'Gober, Halley, Kessler, Wool. Four Artists from New York', Kunstverein, Munich 1989 – 'New Work. A New Generation', San Francisco Museum of Modern Art, 1990

Other Literature (Selection)
Colin Westerbeck: 'Christopher Wool', *Artforum*, September 1986 – Jerry Saltz: 'This is the End. Christopher Wool's Apocalypse Now', *Arts Magazine*, September 1988 – Steven Evans: 'Robert Gober / Christopher Wool', *Artscribe*, November / December 1988 – Norbert Messler: 'Christopher Wool', *Artscribe*, March / April 1989 – Catherine Liu: 'Christopher Wool. At the Limits of Image Making and Meaning Production', *Flash Art*, March / April 1989 – Dan Cameron: 'Unfixed States. Notes on Christopher Wool's New Editions', *Print Collector's Newsletter*, March / April 1990 – Jutta Koether / Karen Marta: 'Am Anfang war das Wort' (Interview) *Noema Art Magazine*, No. 30, 1990 – Jenifer P. Borum: 'Christopher Wool at Luhring Augustine', *Artforum*, November 1990

VADIM ZAKHAROV

Born Dushanbe, Tadzhikistan, 1959. Studied education at Lenin Institute, Moscow, specializing in art and graphics, 1977–82. After a number of exhibitions in private homes, one-man show at Apt-Art, Moscow, 1983 and 1984. Exhibitions at Galerie Peter Pakesch, Vienna; Galerie Sophia Ungers, Cologne; and elsewhere. Took part in 'Ich lebe – ich sehe. Künstler der 80er Jahre in Moskau', Kunstmuseum Bern, 1988. Lives in Moscow.

Zakharov's work as an artist began in the early 1980s with own-body experiences and experiments on human perception. All his works, including pictures and sculptures, reflect processes. They are based on an aesthetic of extremes. Series of almost monochrome images coexist with works incorporating figurative, symbolic scenes that often come close to caricature. Textual inserts contain references to the artist's own life, or else they are 'situation commentaries'. Most recently, Zakharov has been concentrating on complex, self-referential systems of pictorial exploration that can sumultaneously be read as metaphors of the computer age. Of his series *Reproduction*, Zakharov says: 'This work expresses the principle of contagion. To me, the removal of the spoilt blue plate in the sixth picture is the sign that infection has entered the system.'

Reference Source for List of Exhibitions and Bibliography
'Vadim Zakharov', Kunstverein Freiburg, 1989

Catalogue
Galerie Peter Pakesch, Vienna 1989

Catalogues of Collective Exhibitions (Selection)
'Come Yesterday and You'll be First', Contemporary Russian Arts Center of America, Newark, New Jersey 1983 – 'Ich lebe – Ich sehe. Künstler der 80er Jahre in Moskau', Kunstmuseum Bern, 1988 – 'Sowjetkunst heute', Museum Ludwig, Cologne 1988 – 'Is-Kunst-wo', Karl-Hofer-Gesellschaft, Westbahnhof, Berlin 1988 – '10 + 10. 'Contemporary Soviet and American Painters', Modern Art Museum of Fort Worth, (Abrams) New York, (Aurora) Leningrad,

1989 – 'Müvészet helyett Müvészet. 7 Képzömüvész Moszkvából. Art instead of Art. 7 Artists from Moscow', Mücsarnok, Budapest 1989 – 'Momentaufnahme. Junge Kunst aus Moskau', Altes Stadtmuseum, Münster 1989 – 'Artisti russi contemporanei. Contemporary Russian Artists', Museo d'Arte Contemporanea Luigi Pecci, Prato 1990 – 'Between Spring and Summer', Institute of Contemporary Art, Boston, Tacoma Art Museum, Tacoma, Washington 1990 – 'Eduard Stejnberg, Vadim Zacharov, Joeri Al'bert', Stadsgalerij, Heerlen, Netherlands 1990 – 'Von der Revolution zur Perestroika', Kunstmuseum Lucerne, (Hatje) Stuttgart 1990 – 'In de USSR en erbuiten', Stedelijk Museum, Amsterdam 1990

Other Literature (Selection)
Eric A. Peschler: *Künstler in Moskau*, (Edition Stemmle) Schaffhausen 1988 – Jamey Gambrell: 'Perestroika Shock', *Art in America*, February 1989 – Noemi Smolik: 'Vadim Zakharov', *Artforum*, October 1989

The biographical and bibliographical section above, has been compiled with a view to practical usefulness. For each artist there is first a brief biographical outline, giving details of gallery connections and first exhibitions, then a brief account of his or her work. Then comes the title of a catalogue that serves as a reference source for further information. The sections that follow list material useful for a further exploration of the artist's work. So vast is the store of available information on the contemporary art scene that only a selection of these can be listed. We are grateful to those who have supplied us with information, not all of which we have been able to verify.

Michael Glasmeier, Wolfgang Max Faust, Gerti Fietzek

Translated from the German by David Britt

WORKS IN THE EXHIBITION

John M Armleder

1   *Untitled (FS 199)*
     1988
     Metallic blinds, vinyl couch
     263 x 244 x 66 cm
     Galerie 1900–2000, Paris

2   *Untitled (FS 241)*
     1990
     30 make-up mirrors
     Mirror: diameter 25,5 cm
     Mirror mount: 40 cm
     Distance: 60 cm
     Overall dimensions:
     393 x 277 x 18,5 cm
     Galerie Daniel Buchholz, Cologne

3   *Untitled (FS 246)*
     1990
     Furniture elements
     270 x 200 x 110 cm
     Galerie Tanit, Munich/Cologne

Richard Artschwager

4   *High Backed Chair*
     1988
     Painted wood and rubberized hair
     164 x 78 x 104 cm
     The Rivendell Collection

5   *The Shadow*
     1988
     Acrylic on celotex and wood
     179,5 x 153 cm
     Collection Emily Fisher Landau,
     New York

6   *Double Sitting*
     1988
     Acrylic on celotex
     192,5 x 173 cm
     Collection of Agnes Gund, New
     York, promised gift to The Museum
     of Modern Art

7   *Up and Out*
     1990
     Formica and wood
     239 x 166 x 114 cm
     The Oliver Hoffmann Collection

8   *Door*
     1990
     Formica on wood and chrome-plated
     brass
     245 x 171 x 51 cm
     The Kouri Collection

Mirosław Bałka

9   *Oasis*
     1989
     Lathes of wood, wheat, milk, cable
     Variable dimensions (c. 300 x 400 cm)
     Galerie Isabella Kacprzak, Cologne

10   *Five Part Installation*
     1990
     3 parts: wood in steel construction,
     30 x 20 x 4,5 cm each
     1 part: sponge, salt water, plate in
     steel construction,
     200 x 60 x 170 cm
     1 part: wood in steel construction,
     60 x 30 x 6,5 cm
     Galerie Nordenhake, Stockholm

Frida Baranek

11   *Untitled*
     1991
     Iron wire, flexibles, stone
     C. 300 x 300 x 200 cm
     Courtesy the artist

Georg Baselitz

12   *'45'*
     2. VI. 89 – 15. IX. 89
     1989
     Oil and tempera on glued plywood,
     planed
     20 parts
     200 x 162 cm each
     Kunsthaus Zürich

Ross Bleckner

13   *Gold Count No Count*
     1989
     Oil on canvas
     274 x 183 cm
     Collection Mickey/Larry Beyer,
     Cleveland, Ohio
     Courtesy Mary Boone Gallery,
     New York

14   *Architecture of the Sky*
     1990
     Oil on canvas
     269 x 233 cm
     Courtesy Mary Boone Gallery,
     New York

15   *Cascade*
     1990/91
     Oil on canvas
     274 x 182 cm
     Courtesy Mary Boone Gallery,
     New York

16   *Dome*
     1990/91
     Oil on canvas
     243 x 243 cm
     Lambert Art Collection, Geneva
     Courtesy Mary Boone Gallery,
     New York

Jonathan Borofsky

17   *Ballerina Clown*
     1982–1990
     Cast fibreglass, steel and aluminium
     interior structure with intricate
     motor cable system
     915 x 610 x 550 cm
     Courtesy Paula Cooper Gallery,
     New York

Jean-Marc Bustamante

18   *Bac à sable II /*
     Box with Sand II
     1990
     Concrete and painted steel
     28 x 231,5 x 182,5 cm
     Galleria Locus Solus, Genoa

19   *Lumière / Light*
     1990/91
     Silkscreen on Plexiglas
     142 x 187 cm
     Collection of the artist

20   *Lumière / Light*
     1990/91
     Silkscreen on Plexiglas
     142 x 187 cm
     Collection of the artist

21   *Lumière / Light*
     1990/91
     Silkscreen on Plexiglas
     187 x 142 cm
     Collection of the artist

22   *Lumière / Light*
     1990/91
     Silkscreen on Plexiglas
     187 x 142 cm
     Collection of the artist

James Lee Byars

23   *The Capital of the*
     Golden Tower
     1991
     High-grade steel, gold, wood
     Capital: diameter 250 cm
     Height: 125 cm
     Plinth: 40 x 400 x 400 cm
     Galerie Michael Werner, Cologne
     and New York

Pedro Cabrita Reis

24   *Berlin Piece*
     1991
     Plaster, copper
     240 x 360 x 190 cm
     Collection of the artist

Umberto Cavenago

25 *A Sostegno dell'Arte/*
In Support of Art
1991
Galvanized steel, wall paint
6 elements
600 x 90 x 80 cm each
Franz Paludetto, Turin

Clegg & Guttmann

26 *Political-Physiognomical Library*
1991
Cibachrome, Plexiglas, wooden
frame, filing box
18 parts: 184 x 84 cm each
9 parts: 75 x 98 cm each
Jay Gorney Modern Art, New York,
Galerie Christian Nagel, Cologne

René Daniëls

27 *Plattegronden/Plans*
1986
Oil on canvas
141 x 190 cm
Bonnefantenmuseum, Maastricht

28 *Palladium*
1986
Collage
Canvas, glass
110 x 170 cm
Private collection

29 *Terugkeer van de performance/*
Return Performance
1987
Oil on canvas
190 x 130 cm
Private collection, Amsterdam

30 *Monk and Ministry*
1987
Oil on canvas
102 x 180 cm
Jo + Marlies Eyck, Wijlre

Ian Davenport

31 *Untitled*
1991
Matt black and satin black
household paints on canvas
274 x 549 cm
Courtesy Waddington Galleries,
London

32 *Untitled*
1991
White gloss and varnish household
paints on canvas
230 x 457 cm
Courtesy Waddington Galleries,
London

Jiři Georg Dokoupil

33 *Badende IV/Bathers IV*
1991
Soot on canvas
240 x 250 cm
Reiner Opoku, Cologne,
Galerie Bischofberger, Zürich

34 *Badende V/Bathers V*
1991
Soot on canvas
240 x 250 cm
Reiner Opoku, Cologne,
Galerie Bischofberger, Zürich

35 *Badende VII/Bathers VII*
1991
Soot on canvas
290 x 300 cm
Reiner Opoku, Cologne,
Galerie Bischofberger, Zürich

36 *Badende VIII/Bathers VIII*
1991
Soot on canvas
300 x 290 cm
Reiner Opoku, Cologne,
Galerie Bischofberger, Zürich

Maria Eichhorn

37 *Wand ohne Bild/Wall without*
Painting
1991
Wall painting
541 x 660 x 20 cm
Wewerka & Weiss Galerie, Berlin

Jan Fabre

38 *Knipschaarhuis II*
1990
Ballpoint on wood
2 parts, 450 x 250 x 300 cm each
Collection of the artist

Sergio Fermariello

39 *Untitled*
1990
Acrylic on panel
180 x 250 cm
Private collection, Berlin

40 *Untitled*
1990
Mixed media on panel
170 x 178 cm
Collection Francesco Serao, Naples

41 *Untitled*
1990
Mixed media on panel
170 x 178 cm
Collection Bruno e Fortuna Condi,
Naples

Ian Hamilton Finlay

42 *Cythera*
1991
Artificial stone, high-grade steel,
linoleum, neon
C. 250 x 1500 x 600 cm
Galerie Jule Kewenig, Frechen/
Bachem

Peter Fischli   David Weiss

43 *Untitled*
1990
Photographic work
14 parts, 44 x 66 cm each
Monika Sprüth Galerie, Cologne

44 *Untitled*
1990
Sculpture
3 parts
20 x 50 cm each
Monika Sprüth Galerie, Cologne

Günther Förg

45 *Untitled (WVZ-Nr. 238/90)*
1990
Acrylic, sheet lead, wood
300 x 300 cm
Galerie Max Hetzler, Cologne

46 *Untitled (WVZ-Nr. 239/90)*
1990
Acrylic, sheet lead, wood
300 x 300 cm
Galerie Max Hetzler, Cologne

47 *Villa Malaparte (WVZ-Nr. 240/90)*
1990
Colour photograph, framed
270 x 180 cm
Galerie Max Hetzler, Cologne

48 *Villa Malaparte (WVZ-Nr. 241/90)*
1990
Colour photograph, framed
270 x 180 cm
Galerie Max Hetzler, Cologne

49 *Villa Malaparte (WVZ-Nr. 242/90)*
1990
Colour photograph, framed
270 x 180 cm
Galerie Max Hetzler, Cologne

50 *Villa Malaparte (WVZ-Nr. 245/90)*
1990
Colour photograph, framed
270 x 180 cm
Galerie Max Hetzler, Cologne

51 *Untitled*
1990
Acrylic, sheet lead, wood
300 x 300 cm
Collection Dr. Speck, Cologne

Katharina Fritsch

52 *Roter Raum mit Kamingeräusch/*
Red Room with Fireplace Crackle
1991
Wall paint, sound tape
Collection of the artist

Gilbert & George

Triptych

53 *Militant*
1986
Hand-dyed prints
363 x 758 cm
Private collection, London

54 *Class War*
1986
Hand-dyed prints
363 x 1010 cm
Private collection, London

55 *Gateway*
1986
Hand-dyed prints
363 x 758 cm
Private collection, London

Robert Gober

56 *Untitled (Buttocks)*
1990
Wax, wood, painted oil, human hair
48 x 37,5 x 19 cm
Colección Tubacex

57 *Untitled (Leg)*
1990
Wood, wax, leather, cotton, human
hair
31 x 15 x 51,5 cm
Courtesy Thomas Ammann, Zürich

58 *Untitled (Big Torso)*
1990
Wax, pigment, human hair
60 x 44,5 x 28,5 cm
Private collection, Madrid

Ulrich Görlich

59 *Siegesallee*
1991
Installation on photo emulsion
2 parts
340 x 500 cm each

Rainer Görß

60 *Hygroskopie, Nord Südtor/*
Hygroscopicity, North South Gate
1991
Steel, upholstered doors, sugar, water
C. 400 x 500 cm
Collection of the artist

Federico Guzmán

61 *Las Fronteras Espirales/*
Spiral Limits
1990
Rubber
Variable dimensions
Collection Antoine Candau,
Courtesy Galería La Máquina
Española, Madrid, and
Gallery Brooke Alexander,
New York

62 *Fe de Pobre 91/*
Faith of the Poor 91
1991
Bulk glue on silkscreen
60 x 47 cm
Galerie Yvon Lambert, Paris

63 *Dibujo de Sampletown/*
Drawing of Sampletown
1991
Conductive paint on canvas and wire
Variable dimensions
Courtesy Brooke Alexander, New
York, and La Máquina Española,
Madrid

64 *Retrato sin Bordes/*
Image without Margins
1991
Conductive paint on felt
195 x 135 cm
Courtesy Brooke Alexander, New
York, and La Máquina Española,
Madrid

65 *Raices Circulares/*
Circular Roots
1991
Rubber
Variable dimensions
Courtesy Brooke Alexander, New
York, and La Máquina Española,
Madrid

66 *Starpower*
1991
Oil monotype on paper on canvas
122 x 122 cm
Courtesy Brooke Alexander, New
York, and La Máquina Española,
Madrid

Peter Halley

67 *Total Recall*
1990
Day-Glo acrylic, acrylic, Roll-A-Tex
on canvas
216 x 246 cm
Courtesy Jablonka Galerie, Cologne

68 *The River's Edge*
1990
Day-Glo acrylic, acrylic, Roll-A-Tex
on canvas
229 x 495 cm
Mottahedan Collection
Courtesy Jablonka Galerie, Cologne,
and Sonnabend Gallery, New York

69 *The Western Sector*
1990
Day-Glo acrylic, acrylic, Roll-A-Tex
on canvas
249 x 241 x 10 cm
Collezione Achille e Ida Maramotti
Albinea, Reggio Emilia, Italy,
Courtesy Jablonka Galerie, Cologne

Fritz Heisterkamp

70 *Untitled*
1991
Plastics, metal
Variable dimensions
Collection Issinger, Berlin

Georg Herold

71 *Präventivmaßnahme/*
Preventive Step
1991
Wood, iron, plastic, textiles
Variable dimensions
Galerie Max Hetzler, Cologne

Gary Hill

72 *Inasmuch As it is Always Already*
Taking Place
1990
Video installation
Collection of the artist

Jenny Holzer

73 *Untitled*
1991
Selections from 'Truism', 'Survival'
and 'Living' series
LED outdoor sign
Variable dimensions
Courtesy the artist

Cristina Iglesias

74 *Untitled (Berlin I)*
1991
Steel, fibre-cement, glass
225 x 325 x 80 cm
Collection of the artist

75 *Untitled (Berlin II)*
1991
Steel, glass
200 x 100 x 90 cm
Collection of the artist

76 *Untitled (Berlin III)*
1991
Steel, alabaster
200 x 100 x 90 cm
Collection of the artist

Massimo Kaufmann

77 *Ding*
1991
Silicone on gauze and projection
screen
350 x 350 x 300 cm
180 x 180 cm
Studio Guenzani, Milan

Mike Kelley

78 *Pay for Your Pleasure*
1988
42 banners: oil on Tyvek,
245 x 120 cm each
Collection The Museum of Contemporary Art, Los Angeles: Gift of
Timothy P. and Suzette L. Flood
Painting by Wolfgang Zocha,
1990/91, oil on canvas, 47,5 x 40 cm

Kazuo Kenmochi

79 *Untitled*
1991
Wood, creosote, charcoal tar
2800 x 300 x 350 cm
Collection of the artist

Jon Kessler

80 *Taiwan*
1987
Mixed media with lights and motors
Variable dimensions
The Eli Broad Family Foundation,
Santa Monica, California

81 *American Landscape*
1989
Wood, steel, glass, mechanics, lights
122 x 171 x 76 cm
Milton Fine

82 *Birdrunner*
1990
Steel, photomural, Plexiglas, stuffed
bird, lights, motor
145 x 292 x 32 cm
Courtesy the artist and Luhring
Augustine Gallery, New York

Imi Knoebel

83 *Untitled*
1991
Hardboard
30 x 30 x 8,5 cm
Collection of the artist

84 *Untitled*
1991
Hardboard
336 x 112 x 8,5 cm
Collection of the artist

85 *Untitled*
1991
Lacquer, hardboard
260 x 300 x 8,5 cm
Collection of the artist

86 *Untitled*
1991
Lacquer, hardboard
240 x 450 x 8,5 cm
Collection of the artist

Jeff Koons

87 *Saint John the Baptist*
1988
Porcelain
143,5 x 76 x 62 cm
Collection of the artist

88 *Little Girl*
1988
Mirror
160 x 164 x 15 cm
Galerie Beaubourg, Marianne +
Pierre Nahon, Paris

89 *Stacked*
1988
Polychromed wood
155 x 135 x 79 cm
F. Roos Collection, Switzerland

90 *String of Puppies*
1988
Polychromed wood
107 x 157 x 94 cm
Collection of the artist

91 *Popples*
1988
Porcelain
74 x 58,5 x 30,5 cm
Gaby + Wilhelm Schürmann,
Aachen

Jannis Kounellis

92 *Untitled*
1991
Fragments of wood
Variable dimensions
Courtesy the artist

Attila Kovács

93 *Mould*
1987
Polished iron plate
100 x 200 cm
Collection of the artist

94 *Transylvanian Landscape
Memorial of Bela Lugosy*
1986
Polished iron sheet
100 x 200 cm
Musée d'Art Contemporain de Lyon

95 *AAA … AA*
1987
Polished iron sheet
100 x 200 cm
Musée d'Art Contemporain de Lyon

96 *Collapse*
1987
Polished iron plate
200 x 100 cm
Courtesy Stuart Levy Gallery,
New York

97 *Turn*
1987
Polished iron sheet
100 x 200 cm
Collection of the artist

Guillermo Kuitca

98 *The River*
1989
Mixed media on canvas
198 x 134 x 10 cm
Collection Francesco Pellizzi

99 *Corona de Espinas /
Crown of Thorns*
1990
Acrylic and oil on canvas
200 x 150 cm
Collection J. Lagerwey,
The Netherlands

100 *Untitled Roads*
1990
Mixed media on mattress
198 x 198 cm
Gian Enzo Sperone, Rome

101 *Untitled Roads*
1990
Mixed media on mattress
(Triptych)
198 x 437 cm
Gian Enzo Sperone, Rome

George Lappas

102 *In Seurat's Asnières*
1990/91
Iron, cloth, plaster, mixed media
400 x 450 x 500 cm
Collection of the artist

Otis Laubert

103 *The Outsider*
1989
Mixed media
Base: 620 x 550 cm
Height: c. 300 cm
Collection of the artist

Gerhard Merz

104 *Pavillon für eine Monochromie /*
Pavilion for a Monochrome
1991
Architectural model, pane of frosted
glass, 4 high-grade steel mounts,
plinth, iron casting
Model: 140 x 70 x 15 cm
Pane of glass: 300 x 300 x 1,5 cm
High-grade steel mounts:
12 x 12 x 12 cm each
Plinth: 140 x 50 x 70 cm
Iron casting: 100 x 100 x 8 cm
Collection of the artist

Olaf Metzel

105 *112 : 104*
1991
Wood, aluminium, steel pipe,
plastics
C. 400 x 850 x 550 cm
Collection of the artist

Yasumaso Morimura

106 *Playing with Gods I: Afternoon*
1991
Computer-manipulated photo,
Type C print; frame
360 x 250 cm
Collection of the artist

107 *Playing with Gods II: Twilight*
1991
Computer-manipulated photo,
Type C print; frame
360 x 250 cm
Collection of the artist

108 *Playing with Gods III: At Night*
1991
Computer-manipulated photo,
Type C print; frame
360 x 250 cm
Collection of the artist

109 *Playing with Gods IV: Dawn*
1991
Computer-manipulated photo,
Type C print; frame
360 x 250 cm
Collection of the artist

Reinhard Mucha

110 *Walsum*
1986
Wood, felt, glass, synthetic resin
varnish
130 x 200 x 54 cm
Private collection

111 *Kalkar*
1988
Wood, synthetic resin varnish, felt,
glass
70 x 200 x 32 cm
Private collection

112 *Liblar*
1989
Wood, aluminium, felt, glass,
synthetic resin varnish
111 x 223 x 27 cm
Collection Sanders, Amsterdam

113 *BBK-Edition*
1990
2 exhibition posters, framed, offset,
synthetic resin varnish, glass, wood
2 parts, 115,4 x 86,7 x 5 cm each
Private collection

114 *Norden*
1991
Wood, glass, felt
111,2 x 223 x 28,5 cm
Galerie Max Hetzler, Cologne

Juan Muñoz

115 *Threshold*
1991
Terracotta
Variable dimensions
Collection of the artist

Bruce Nauman

116 *Rats and Bats*
(Learned Helplessness in Rats)
1988
Video installation
Gerald S. Elliott, Chicago,
Illinois

117 *Proposal for Animal Pyramid*
1989
Photo collage
202 x 157 cm
Purchased with funds from the
Melva and Martin Bucksbaum
Director's Discretionary Fund for
Acquisition and Innovation.
Commission for the Sculpture Park,
Des Moines Art Center, Des Moines,
Iowa

118 *Animal Pyramid*
1989
Foam
366 x 213 x 244 cm
Private collection, Berlin

Cady Noland

119 *Early Americans*
1984
Model practice gun, round Indian
souvenir, flat cushion
107 x 40,5 x 10 cm
Collection Tony Shafrazi,
New York

120 *Pedestal*
1985
Mat, belt, flat cloth, soccer ball
47 x 71 x 7,5 cm
Courtesy American Fine Arts Co.,
New York

121 *Chicken in a Basket*
1989
Mixed media
C. 50 x 40 x 15 cm
Private collection
Courtesy Thea Westreich

122 *SLA Group Shot # 1*
1990
Silkscreen on aluminium (0,95 cm)
183 x 183 cm
Courtesy American Fine Arts Co.,
New York

123 *SLA Group Shot # 2*
1990
Silkscreen on aluminium
183 x 153 cm
Courtesy American Fine Arts Co.,
New York

124 *SLA Group Shot # 3*
1990
Silkscreen on aluminium
183 x 153 cm
Courtesy American Fine Arts Co.,
New York

125 *Patty Hearst Wooden Template*
1990
(artist's proof)
plywood (1,3 cm)
183 x 153 cm
Courtesy American Fine Arts Co.,
New York

126 *Enquirer Page Wooden Template*
1990
Plywood
183 x 153 cm
Courtesy American Fine Arts Co.,
New York

127 *Psychedelic 'Vet Head' with Metal Plate*
1990
Plywood, flag, scarves
153 x 153 cm
Courtesy American Fine Arts Co., New York

128 *Title Not Available*
1991
Metal gates
91,5 x 137 x 5 cm
Courtesy American Fine Arts Co., New York

129 *Title Not Available*
1991
6 gate pieces
Gates c. 200 x 135 x 5 cm each, 152 x 140 x 5 cm, 142 x 229 x 5 cm
Courtesy American Fine Arts Co., New York

130 *Title Not Available (two metal baskets)*
1991
Car parts, beer cans, car gunk (grease)
72 x 51 x 25,5 cm
39,5 x 33 x 28 cm
Courtesy the artist and American Fine Arts Co., New York

131 *Title Not Available*
1991
Metal walkers and other objects
variable dimensions
Courtesy the artist and American Fine Arts Co., New York

132 *Title Not Available*
1991
Metal baskets, objects
61 x 30,5 x 25,5 cm
Courtesy American Fine Arts Co., New York

Marcel Odenbach

133 *Wenn die Wand an den Tisch rückt / If the Wall Shifts Towards the Table*
1990
Video
Zentrum für Kunst und Medientechnologie Karlsruhe – Museum für Gegenwartskunst, Courtesy Ascan Crone, Hamburg

Albert Oehlen

134 *Fn 4*
1990
Oil on canvas
214 x 275 cm
Galerie Max Hetzler, Cologne

135 *Fn 15*
1990
Oil on canvas
275 x 214 cm
Galerie Max Hetzler, Cologne

136 *Fn 31*
1990
Oil on canvas
274 x 214 cm
Galerie Max Hetzler, Cologne

Philippe Perrin

137 *This Is a Love Song*
1991
Mixed media (installation, photo, video, painting, adhesive letters)
Air de Paris, Nice

Dmitri Prigov

138 *100 Possibilities for Installations (China)*
1991
Mixed media
Variable dimensions
Collection of the artist

Richard Prince

139 *I'll Fuck Anything that Moves*
1991
Acrylic and silkscreen paint on canvas
457 x 227 cm
Courtesy Barbara Gladstone Gallery, New York

140 *Good Revolution*
1991
Acrylic and silkscreen paint on canvas
457 x 227 cm
Courtesy Barbara Gladstone Gallery, New York

141 *Why Did the Nazi Cross the Road?*
1991
Acrylic and silkscreen paint on canvas
457 x 227 cm
Courtesy Barbara Gladstone Gallery, New York

142 *Sampling the Chocolate*
1991
Acrylic and silkscreen paint on canvas
457 x 227 cm
Courtesy Barbara Gladstone Gallery, New York

Gerhard Richter

143 *Wald (1) / Forest (1)*
1990
Oil on canvas
340 x 260 cm

144 *Wald (2) / Forest (2)*
1990
Oil on canvas
340 x 260 cm

145 *Wald (3) / Forest (3)*
1990
Oil on canvas
340 x 260 cm

146 *Wald (4) / Forest (4)*
1990
Oil on canvas
340 x 260 cm

Thomas Ruff

147 *Stern / Star 19h 04m / – 70°*
1990
Colour print
260 x 188 cm

148 *Portrait 1990 (Andrea Knobloch)*
1990
Colour print
210 x 165 cm

149 *Portrait 1990 (Anna Giese)*
1990
Colour print
210 x 165 cm

150 *Portrait 1990 (Oliver Cieslik)*
1990
Colour print
210 x 165 cm

Edward Ruscha

151 *Industrial Strength Sleep*
1989
Acrylic on canvas
150 x 370 cm
Leo Castelli Gallery, New York

152 *Five past Eleven*
1989
Acrylic on canvas
150 x 370 cm
Hirshhorn Museum and Sculpture Garden, Smithsonian Institution, Washington, D.C., Joseph H. Hirshhorn Purchase Fund, 1989

153 *Sin*
1991
Acrylic, oil on canvas
178 x 350 cm
Collection of the artist

Julião Sarmento

154 *Dias de Escuro e de Luz – II (Jarro)/*
Days of Darkness and Light – II
(Goblet)
1990
Mixed media on canvas
190 x 341 cm
Fundação de Serralves, Oporto

155 *Dias de Escuro e de Luz – VII*
(Mesa)/
Days of Darkness and Light – VII
(Table)
1990
Mixed media on canvas
190 x 220 cm
Galeria Pedro Oliveira, Oporto

156 *Metropolis*
1991
Mixed media on canvas
285 x 205 cm
Galerie Bernd Klüser, Munich

Julian Schnabel

157 *Jane Birkin # 1*
1990
Oil, gesso on sail material
409 x 287 cm
Courtesy the artist

158 *Jane Birkin # 3 (Vito)*
1990
Oil paint, gesso, resin on cotton
326 x 630 cm
Courtesy The Pace Gallery,
New York

159 *Ozymandias*
1990
Oil, gesso, resin and leather on white
tarpaulin
396 x 549 cm
Galerie Bruno Bischofberger, Zürich

Cindy Sherman

160 *Untitled (No. 234)*
1987–1991
Colour photograph
228 x 125 cm
The artist,
Metro Pictures, New York

161 *Untitled (No. 237)*
1987–1991
Colour photograph
228 x 125 cm
The artist,
Metro Pictures, New York

162 *Untitled (No. 239)*
1987–1991
Colour photograph
228 x 125 cm
The artist,
Metro Pictures, New York

163 *Untitled*
1987–1991
Colour photograph
228 x 125 cm
The artist,
Metro Pictures, New York

Mike and Doug Starn

164 *Film Sphere with Pipe Clamps*
1990/91
Toned ortho film, pipe clamps,
silicone, steel
Sphere: 458 cm
Courtesy Stux Gallery, New York,
and Leo Castelli Gallery, New York

Haim Steinbach

165 *Untitled*
(shoes with braces, wooden boots)
1987
Plastic laminated wood shelf with
objects
58 x 91,5 x 40,5 cm
Collection of the artist
Courtesy Jay Gorney Modern Art,
New York, and Sonnabend Gallery,
New York

166 *Untitled*
(elephant foot stools, elephant skull)
1988
Plastic laminated wood shelf with
objects
Black shelf:
102 x 325 x 59 cm
White shelf:
225 x 109 x 105,5 cm
Collection of the artist
Courtesy Jay Gorney Modern Art,
New York, and Sonnabend Gallery,
New York

Rosemarie Trockel

167 *Untitled (No. 1, 3 hot plates)/*
Ohne Titel (Nr. 1, 3 Herdplatten)
1991
Sheet steel with stove-enamel finish,
3 hot plates
200 x 80 x 80 x 10 cm
Corner construction
Monika Sprüth Galerie, Cologne

168 *Ohne Titel (Nr. 2, 2 Herdplatten)/*
Untitled (No. 2, 2 hot plates)
1991
Sheet steel with stove-enamel finish,
2 hot plates
200 x 70 x 10 cm
Monika Sprüth Galerie, Cologne

169 *Ohne Titel (Nr. 3, 4 Herdplatten)/*
Untitled (No. 3, 4 hot plates)
1991
Sheet steel with stove-enamel finish,
4 hot plates
200 x 100 x 10 cm
Galerie Ascan Crone, Hamburg,
Monika Sprüth Galerie, Cologne

170 *Ohne Titel (Nr. 4, 1 Herdplatte)/*
Untitled (No. 4, 1 hot plate)
1991
Sheet steel with stove-enamel finish,
1 hot plates
200 x 100 x 10 cm
Monika Sprüth Galerie, Cologne

171 *Ohne Titel (Nr. 5, 4 Herdplatten)/*
Untitled (No. 5, 4 hot plates)
1991
Sheet steel with stove-enamel finish,
4 hot plates
200 x 100 x 10 cm
Monika Sprüth Galerie, Cologne

Bill Viola

172 *The City of Man*
1989
Video/sound installation
The Rivendell Collection
Sound equipment provided with the
assistance of JBL Professional
Products, Los Angeles

Jeff Wall

173 *Outburst*
1989
Cibachrome transparency,
fluorescent light, display case
229 x 312 cm
Collection of The Vancouver Art
Gallery

174 *The Pine on the Corner*
1990
Cibachrome transparency,
fluorescent light, display case
Work: 135 x 165 cm
Image: 119 x 149 cm
Courtesy Galerie Johnen & Schöttle,
Cologne

175 *The Ventriloquist at a Birthday Party in October 1947*
1990
Cibachrome transparency, fluorescent light, display case
Light box: 249 x 372,4 x 25 cm
Image: 229 x 352,4 cm
Galleria Christian Stein, Milan

176 *The Crooked Path*
1991
Cibachrome transparency, fluorescent light, display case
Image: 119 x 149 cm
Courtesy Galleria Christian Stein, Milan

Franz West

177 *Liege / Couch*
1989
Multiple, edition of 20
66 x 73 x 174 cm
(In collaboration with Gilbert Bretterbauer and Hans Kuppelwieser)
Jänner Galerie, Vienna

178 *Otto sieht jetzt einen roten Würfel auf dem Tisch / Now Otto Sees a Red Cube on the Table*
1990
Hardboard, wood, metal bars, cardboard box, glue, iron, paper
166 x 52 x 220 cm
Galerie Peter Pakesch, Vienna

179 *Untitled*
1990
Wood, iron, paper, carpet
105 x 205 x 270 cm
Galerie Peter Pakesch, Vienna

Rachel Whiteread

180 *Valley*
1990
Plaster, glass
94 x 185 x 97 cm
Luhring Augustine Gallery, New York

181 *Cell*
1990
Plaster, polystyrene
123 x 124,5 x 52 cm
Courtesy Laure Genillard Gallery, London

182 *False Door*
1990
Plaster
214,6 x 40,6 x 152,4 cm
Karsten Schubert Ltd, London

183 *Untitled*
1991
Plaster
C. 30 x 188 x 137 cm
Karsten Schubert Ltd, London

Bill Woodrow

184 *In case of*
1988–1990
Glass, plastic, wax, coins, water
84 x 70 x 51 cm
Collection of the artist

185 *Rut*
1990
Bronze
250 x 400 x 400 cm
Collection of the artist

Christopher Wool

186 *Why? (W 22)*
1990
Enamel on aluminium
274 x 183 cm
Courtesy the artist and Luhring Augustine Gallery, New York

187 *Untitled (W 26 A-E)*
1990
5 panels: 2 parts *Run*, 3 parts *Dog*
274 x 183 cm each
Courtesy the artist and Luhring Augustine Gallery, New York

Vadim Zakharov

188 *Local Commentary on Butterflies*
1990
Graphite on canvas, lamp
5 parts
220 x 150 cm each
Galerie Sophia Ungers, Cologne

SELECTED BIBLIOGRAPHY

The art of the present day is a force-field, held in tension by a network of theoretical, art-historical and sociopolitical affinities. This is the subject of the Bibliography that follows. Alongside the catalogues of large collective exhibitions, cited in the Artists' Biographies in abbreviated form, it lists the books and catalogues that serve to define the conceptual context of the exhibition. It also lists major publications by the contributors to the METROPOLIS catalogue.

Ästhetik im Widerstreit, edited by Christine Pries and Wolfgang Welsch, Weinheim 1990

A Forest of Signs. Art in the Crisis of Representation, (cat.) The Museum of Contemporary Art, Los Angeles 1989

Aisthesis. Wahrnehmung heute oder Perspektiven einer anderen Ästhetik, edited by Karlheinz Barck et al, Leipzig 1990

Alibis, (cat.) Centre Georges Pompidou, Musée National d'Art Moderne, Paris 1984

Alles und noch viel mehr. Das poetische ABC. Die Katalog-Anthologie der 80er Jahre, edited by G. J. Lischka, Bern 1985

Alloway, Lawrence: *Network. Art and the Complex Present*, Ann Arbor, Michigan 1984

All Quiet on the Western Front?, (cat.) Espace Dieu, Paris 1990

A New Necessity. First Tyne International 1990, edited by Declan McGonagle, (cat.) Gateshead, Tyne & Wear 1990

A New Spirit in Painting, edited by Christos M. Joachimides, Norman Rosenthal, Nicholas Serota, (cat.) Royal Academy of Arts, London 1981

Arbeit in Geschichte. Geschichte in Arbeit, edited by Georg Bussmann, (cat.) Kunsthaus and Kunstverein in Hamburg, (Nishen) Berlin 1988

Ars Electronica, edited by Gottfried Hattinger, Peter Weibel and Morgan Russel, 2 vols (cat.), Linz 1990

Art and Its Double. A New York Perspective. El Arte y su Doble. Una perspectiva de Nueva York, edited by Dan Cameron, (cat.) Fundación Caja de Pensiones, Madrid 1987

Art and Technology, edited by René Berger and Lloyd Eby, New York 1986

Art Conceptuel, Formes Conceptuelles. Conceptual Art, Conceptual Forms, edited by Christian Schlatter, (cat.) Galerie 1900 △ 2000, Paris 1990

Art & Publicité 1890–1990, (cat.) Centre Georges Pompidou, Musée National d'Art Moderne, Paris 1990

Artificial Nature, edited by Jeffrey Deitch and Dan Friedman, (cat.) Deste Foundation for Contemporary Art, House of Cyprus, Athens 1990

Art of Our Time. The Saatchi Collection, 4 vols, London/New York 1984

Art Talk. The Early 80s, edited by Jean Siegel, New York 1990

Artware. Kunst and Elektronik, edited by David Galloway, Düsseldorf/Vienna/New York 1987

Aspre Pianure, Dolci Vette, edited by Miriam Cristaldi, (cat.) Museo di Sant'Agostino, Genoa, (Electa) Milan 1989

A vint minuts de Paris, (cat.) Galerie Joan Prats, Barcelona 1990

Baudrillard, Jean: *Amérique*, Paris 1986

Baudrillard, Jean: *Cool Memories. 1980–1985*, Paris 1987

Baudrillard, Jean: *Das Jahr 2000 findet nicht statt*, Berlin 1990

Baudrillard, Jean: *Laßt Euch nicht verführen*, Berlin 1983

Baudrillard, Jean: *Paradoxe Kommunikation*, Bern 1989

Beuys zu Ehren, edited by Armin Zweite, (cat.) Städtische Galerie im Lenbachhaus, Munich 1986

Bestiarium. Jardin-Théâtre, (cat.) Entrepôt-Galerie du Confort-Moderne, Poitiers 1989

Bilderstreit. Widerspruch, Einheit und Fragment in der Kunst seit 1960, edited by Siegfried Gohr and Johannes Gachnang, (cat.) Museum Ludwig in den Rheinhallen der Kölner Messe, Cologne 1989

Bildwelten, Denkbilder, edited by Hans Matthäus Bachmayer, Otto van de Loo and Florian Rötzer, Munich 1986

BiNationale. Deutsche Kunst der späten 80er Jahre, edited by Jürgen Harten and David A. Ross, (cat.) Städtische Kunsthalle, Kunstsammlung Nordrhein-Westfalen, Kunstverein für die Rheinlande und Westfalen, Düsseldorf, (DuMont) Cologne 1988 (see *The BiNational*)

Block, Ursula/Michael Glasmeier: *Broken Music. Artists' Recordworks*, edited by Berliner Künstlerprogramm des DAAD, gelbe Musik Berlin, 1989

blow up. Zeitgeschichte, (cat.) Württembergischer Kunstverein, Stuttgart 1987

Blumenberg, Hans: *Die Sorge geht über den Fluß*, Frankfurt am Main 1987

Blumenberg, Hans: *Höhlenausgänge*, Frankfurt am Main 1989

Bodenskulptur, (cat.) Kunsthalle Bremen, 1986

Böhringer, Hannes: *Begriffsfelder. Von der Philosophie zur Kunst*, Berlin 1985

Böhringer, Hannes: *Moneten. Von der Kunst zur Philosophie*, Berlin 1990

Bohrer, Karl Heinz: *Der romantische Brief. Die Entstehung ästhetischer Subjektivität*, Munich/Vienna 1987

Bohrer, Karl Heinz: *Nach der Natur. Über Politik und Ästhetik*, Munich 1988

Bonito Oliva, Achille: *Im Labyrinth der Kunst*, Berlin 1982

Bonito Oliva, Achille: *Dialoghi d'artista. Incontri con l'arte contemporanea 1970–1984*, Milan 1984

Bonito Oliva, Achille: *Transavantgarde International*, Milan 1982

Briggs, John/F. David Peat: *Turbulent Mirror. An Illustrated Guide to Chaos Theory and the Science of Wholeness*, New York 1989

Brock, Bazon: *Ästhetik gegen erzwungene Unmittelbarkeit. Die Gottsucherbande. Schriften 1978–1986*, Cologne 1986

Brock, Bazon: *Die Re-Dekade. Kunst und Kultur der 80er Jahre*, Munich 1990

Celant, Germano: *Arte Povera. Arte Povera. Storie e protagonisti*, Milan 1985

Celant, Germano: *Unexpressionism. Art beyond the Contemporary*, New York 1988

Chambres d'Amis, (cat.) Museum van Hedendaagse Kunst, Ghent 1986

Charles, Daniel: *Poetik der Gleichzeitigkeit*, Bern 1987

Charles, Daniel: *Zeitspielräume. Performance Musik Ästhetik*, Berlin 1989

Crowther, Paul: *Critical Aesthetics and Post-Modernism*, London 1989

Culture and Commentary. An Eighties Perspective, edited by Kathy Halbreich, (cat.) Hirshhorn Museum and Sculpture Garden, Smithsonian Institution, Washington D.C. 1990

Cultural Geometry, edited by Jeffrey Deitch, (cat.) Deste Foundation for Contemporary Art, House of Cyprus, Athens 1988

Daedalus. Die Erfindung der Gegenwart, edited by Gerhard Fischer et al, Basle/Frankfurt am Main 1990

Damisch, Hubert: *Auf die Gefahr hin, zu sehen*, Bern 1988

Das Erhabene. Zwischen Grenzerfahrung und Größenwahn, edited by Christine Pries, Weinheim 1989

Das konstruierte Bild. Fotografie – arrangiert und inszeniert, edited by Michael Köhler, (cat.) Kunstverein München, Munich (Edition Stemmle) Schaffhausen 1989

Dekonstruktion? Dekonstruktivismus? Aufbruch ins Chaos oder neues Bild der Welt?, edited by Gert Kähler, Braunschweig 1990

Der Schein des Schönen, edited by Dietmar Kamper and Christoph Wulf, Göttingen 1989

Der unverbrauchte Blick. Kunst unserer Zeit in Berliner Sicht, edited by Christos M. Joachimides, (cat.) Martin-Gropius-Bau, Berlin 1987

Der Verfall eines alten Raumes, (cat.) Werkbund-Archiv, Neue Gesellschaft für Bildende Kunst, Museumspädagogischer Dienst Berlin, 1988

Der verzeichnete Prometheus. Kunst, Design, Technik, Zeichen verändern die Wirklichkeit, edited by Hermann Sturm, (cat.) Museum Folkwang, Essen, Museum für Gestaltung, Basle, (Nishen) Berlin 1988

Die Endlichkeit der Freiheit. Berlin 1990. Ein Ausstellungsprojekt in Ost und West, edited by Wulf Herzogenrath, Joachim Sartorius and Christoph Tannert, Berlin 1990

Die erloschene Seele. Disziplin, Geschichte, Kunst, Mythos, edited by Dietmar Kamper and Christoph Wulf, Berlin 1988

Die Große Oper oder die Sehnsucht nach dem Erhabenen, (cat.) Bonner Kunstverein, Bonn, Frankfurter Kunstverein, Frankfurt am Main 1987

Die sich verselbständigenden Möbel. Objekte und Installationen von Künstlern, (cat.) Kunst- und Museumsverein im Von der Heydt-Museum, Wuppertal 1985

Die unvollendete Vernunft. Moderne versus Postmoderne, edited by Dietmar Kamper and Willem Reijen, Frankfurt am Main 1987

Die wiedergefundene Metropole. Neue Malerei in Berlin, edited by Christos M. Joachimides, (cat.) Palais des Beaux-Arts, Brussels, Kulturabteilung der Bayer AG Leverkusen, (Frölich & Kaufmann) Berlin 1984

Discourses. Conversations in Postmodern Art and Culture, edited by Russell Ferguson, Marcia Tucker et al, Cambridge 1990

Discussions in Contemporary Culture, edited by Hal Foster, Seattle 1987

'documenta 7', 2 vols (cat.), Kassel 1982

'documenta 8', 3 vols (cat.), Kassel 1987

Druyen, Thomas C.: *Die Wahrnehmung der Pluralität. Abschied vom Zeitgeist*, Achern 1990

D & S Ausstellung, edited by Frank Barth, Jürgen Schweinebraden, Karl Weber and Thomas Wulffen, (cat.) Kunstverein in Hamburg, 1989

Duve, Thierry de: *Au nom de l'art. Pour une archéologie de la modernité*, Paris 1989

Duve, Thierry de: *Cousus de fil d'or*, Villeurbanne 1990

Ebeling, Hans: *Ästhetik des Abschieds. Kritik der Moderne*, Freiburg/Munich 1989

Eco, Umberto: *Im Labyrinth der Vernunft. Texte über Kunst und Zeichen*, Leipzig 1990

Einleuchten. Will, Vorstel und Simul in HH, edited by Harald Szeemann, (cat.) Deichtorhallen Hamburg, 1989

El Jardín Salvaje, edited by Dan Cameron, (cat.) Fundación Caja de Pensiones, Sala de Exposiciones, Madrid 1991

Endgame. Reference and Simulation in Recent Painting and Sculpture, (cat.) Institute of Contemporary Art, Boston, (MIT Press) Cambridge 1986

Energieen, (cat.) Stedelijk Museum, Amsterdam 1990

Export, Valie: *Das Reale and sein Double: Der Körper*, Bern 1987

Faust, Wolfgang Max: *Bilder werden Worte. Zum Verhältnis von bildender Kunst und Literatur. Vom Kubismus bis zur Gegenwart*, Cologne 1987

Faust, Wolfgang Max/Gerd de Vries: *Hunger nach Bildern. Deutsche Malerei der Gegenwart*, Cologne 1982

Flusser, Vilém: *Angenommen*, Göttingen 1989

Flusser, Vilém: *Die Schrift*, Göttingen 1987

Flusser, Vilém: *Für eine Philosophie der Fotografie*, Göttingen 1983

Flusser, Vilém: *Ins Universum der technischen Bilder*, Göttingen 1985

Flusser, Vilém: *Krise der Linearität*, Bern 1988

Flusser, Vilém: *Nachgeschichten. Essays, Vorträge, Glossen*, Düsseldorf 1990

Frank, Peter: *Intermedia. Die Verschmelzung der Künste*, Bern 1987

Frank, Peter/Michael McKenzie: *New, Used & Improved*, New York 1987

Gachnang, Johannes: *Reisebilder. Berichte zur zeitgenössischen Kunst*, edited by Troels Andersen, Vienna 1985

GegenwartEwigkeit. Spuren des Transzendenten in der Kunst unserer Zeit, edited by Wieland Schmied, (cat.) Martin-Gropius-Bau, Berlin, (Edition Cantz) Stuttgart 1990

German Art in the 20th Century. Painting and Sculpture 1905–1985, edited by Christos M. Joachimides, Norman Rosenthal and Wieland Schmied, (cat.) Royal Academy of Arts, London, (Prestel) Munich 1985

Goodman, Nelson/Catherine Z. Elgin: *Reconceptions in Philosophy and Other Arts and Sciences*, Indianapolis 1988

Grasskamp, Walter: *Der vergeßliche Engel. Künstlerportraits für Fortgeschrittene*, Munich 1986

Grasskamp, Walter: *Die unbewältigte Moderne. Kunst und Öffentlichkeit*, Munich 1989

Groys, Boris: *Gesamtkunstwerk Stalin. Die gespaltene Kultur in der Sowjetunion*, Munich/Vienna 1988

Het Lumineuze Beeld. The Luminous Image, (cat.) Stedelijk Museum, Amsterdam 1984

High & Low. Modern Art and Popular Culture, edited by Kirk Varnedoe and Adam Gropnik, (cat.) The Museum of Modern Art, New York 1990

Hommage-Demontage, edited by Uli Bohnen, (cat.) Neue Galerie – Sammlung Ludwig, Aachen , (Wienand) Cologne 1988

Horn of Plenty. Sixteen Artists from NYC, (cat.) Stedelijk Museum, Amsterdam 1989

Im Netz der Systeme, edited by Ars Electronica, Berlin 1990

Implosion. Ett postmodern perspektiv, (cat.) Moderna Museet, Stockholm 1987

In Between and Beyond. From Germany, edited by Louise Dompierre, (cat.) The Power Plant, Toronto 1989

In de USSR en erbuiten. 28 Kunstenaars 1970–1990, (cat.) Stedelijk Museum, Amsterdam 1990, (cat.) Galerie Tanit, Munich 1990

Individuals. A Selected History of Contemporary Art. 1945–1986, edited by Howard Singerman, (cat.) The Museum of Contemporary Art, Los Angeles, (Abbeville Press) New York 1986

In Other Words. Wort und Schrift in Bildern, edited by Anna Meseure, (cat.) Museum am Ostwall, Dortmund, (Edition Cantz) Stuttgart 1989

Japanische Kunst der achtziger Jahre, edited by Fumio Nanjo and Peter Weiermair, (cat.) Frankfurter Kunstverein, Frankfurt am Main (Edition Stemmle) Schaffhausen 1990

Jardins de Bagatelle, (cat.) Galerie Tanit, Munich 1990

»Je est un Autre.« De Rimbaud, (cat.) Galeria Cómicos, Lisbon 1990

Jenisch-Park. Skulptur, (cat.) Kulturbehörde Hamburg – Kunst im öffentlichen Raum, Hamburg 1986

Jeudy, Henri Pierre: *Parodies de l'autodestruction*, Paris 1985

Kamper, Dietmar: *Das gefangene Einhorn. Texte aus der Zeit des Wartens*, Munich/Vienna 1983

Kamper, Dietmar: *Hieroglyphen der Zeit. Texte vom Fremdwerden der Welt*, Munich/Vienna 1988

Kamper, Dietmar: *Zur Soziologie der Imagination*, Munich/Vienna 1986

Kittler, Friedrich: *Grammophon, Film, Typewriter*, Berlin 1986

Kneubühler, Theo: *Malerei als Wirklichkeit*, Berlin 1985

Kneubühler, Theo: *Wegsehen*, Berlin 1986

Kofman, Sarah: *Mélancolie de l'art*, Paris 1985

Kramer, Hilton: *The Revenge of the Philistines*, New York 1985

Krauss, Rosalind E.: *Der Impuls zu sehen*, Bern 1988

Krauss, Rosalind E.: *The Originality of the Avant-Garde and Other Modernist Myths*, Cambridge, Massachusetts/London 1985

Kummer, Raimund/Hermann Pitz/Fritz Rahmann: *Büro Berlin. Ein Produktionsbegriff*, Künstlerhaus Bethanien, Berlin 1986

Kunst im öffentlichen Raum. Anstöße der 80er Jahre, edited by Volker Plagemann, Cologne 1989

Kunst in der DDR, edited by Eckhart Gillen and Rainer Haarmann, (Cologne) 1990

Kunstkombinat DDR. Eine Dokumentation 1945–1990, edited by Museumspädagogischen Dienst Berlin, 1988, 1990

KunstLandschaft BundesRepublik. Junge Kunst in deutschen Kunstvereinen. Geschichte, Regionen und Materialien, (cat.) Arbeitsgemeinschaft deutscher Kunstvereine, Stuttgart 1984

Kunst und Politik der Avantgarde, edited by Syndicat Anonym, Frankfurt am Main 1989

Kuspit, Donald: *The Critic is Artist. The Intentionality of Art*, Ann Arbor, Michigan 1984

La Biennale di Venezia, (cat.) Venice 1990

L'Art Conceptuel, une perspective, edited by Claude Gintz, (cat.) ARC Musée d'Art Moderne de la Ville de Paris, 1989

L'Art et le temps. Regards sur la quatrième dimension, (cat.) Société des Expositions du Palais des Beaux-Arts, Brussels 1984

Le Bot, Marc: *Images du corps*, Aix 1986

Le Bot, Marc: *L'Œil du peintre*, Paris 1984

Le désenchantement du monde, (cat.) Villa Arson, Centre National d'Art Contemporain, Nice 1990

L'Epoque, la mode, la morale, la passion. Aspects de l'art d'aujourd'hui 1977–1987, (cat.) Centre Georges Pompidou, Musée National d'Art Moderne, Paris 1987

Les Magiciens de la Terre, (cat.) Centre Georges Pompidou, La Grande Halle de la Villette, Paris 1989

L'espace et le temps aujourd'hui, edited by Emile Noël, Paris 1983

Liberté & Egalité. Freiheit und Gleichheit. Wiederholung und Abweichung in der neueren französischen Kunst, (cat.) Museum Folkwang, Essen, (DuMont) Cologne 1989

Life-Size. A Sense of the Real in Recent Art, edited by Suzanne Landau, (cat.) The Israel Museum, Jerusalem 1990

Lippard, Lucy R.: *Mixed Blessings. New Art in a Multicultural America*, New York 1990

Lippe, Rudolf zur: *Der schöne Schein. Existentielle Ästhetik*, Bern 1988

Lippe, Rudolf zur: *Sinnenbewußtsein. Grundlegung einer anthropologischen Ästhetik*, Reinbek near Hamburg 1987

Lischka, G. J.: *Die Schönheit der Schönheit. Superästhetik*, Bern 1986

Lischka, G. J.: *Kulturkunst. Die Medienfalle*, Bern 1987

Lischka, G. J.: *Über die Mediatisierung. Medien und Re-Medien*, Bern 1988

Lovejoy, Margot: *Postmodern Currents. Art and Artists in the Age of Electronic Media*, London 1989

Luhmann, Niklas: *Archimedes und wir*, Berlin 1987

Luhmann, Niklas: *Erkenntnis als Konstruktion*, Bern 1988

Lyotard, Jean-François: *Die Moderne redigieren*, Bern 1989

Lyotard, Jean-François: *La Condition postmoderne*, Paris 1979

Lyotard, Jean-François: *Le Postmoderne expliqué aux enfants*, Paris 1986

Lyotard, Jean-François: *L'Inhumain. Causeries sur le temps*, Paris 1988

Lyotard, Jean-François: *Peregrinations, Law, Form, Event*, New York 1988

Lyotard, Jean-François: *Philosophie und Malerei im Zeitalter ihres Experimentierens*, Berlin 1986

Maler über Malerei. Einblicke – Ausblicke. Künstlerschriften zur Malerei der Gegenwart, edited by Stefan Szczesny, Cologne 1989

Marquard, Odo: *Aesthetica und Anaesthetica. Philosophische Überlegungen*, Paderborn/Munich/Vienna/Zurich 1989

Marquard, Odo: *Krise der Erwartung. Stunde der Erfahrung. Zur ästhetischen Kompensation des modernen Erfahrungsverlustes*, Konstanz 1982

Mediendämmerung. Zur Archäologie der Medien, edited by Peter Klier and Jean-Luc Evard, Berlin 1989

Meier-Seethaler, Carola: *Ursprünge und Befreiungen. Eine dissidente Kulturtheorie*, Zurich 1988

Meine Zeit. Mein Raubtier. Eine Autonome Ausstellung, (cat.) Kunstpalast, Düsseldorf 1988

Moderne oder Postmoderne? Zur Signatur des gegenwärtigen Zeitalters, edited by Peter Koslowski, Robert Spaemann and Reinhard Löw, Weinheim 1986

Möbel als Kunstobjekt, edited by Kulturreferat der Landeshauptstadt München, (cat.) Künstlerwerkstatt Lothringer Straße 13, Munich 1988

Museum der Avantgarde. Die Sammlung Sonnabend New York, edited by Christos M. Joachimides, (cat.) Hamburger Bahnhof, Berlin, (Electa) Milan 1989

Mythos und Moderne. Begriff und Bild einer Rekonstruktion, edited by Karl Heinz Bohrer, Frankfurt am Main 1983

Nachschub. The Köln Show, edited by Isabelle Graw, (Katalog, Spex-Verlagsgesellschaft) Cologne 1990

Nairne, Sandy: *State of the Art. Ideas & Images in the 1980s*, London 1987

1961 Berlinart 1987, edited by Kynaston McShine, (cat.) The Museum of Modern Art, New York, (Prestel) Munich 1987

1984 – im toten Winkel, edited by Ulrich Bischoff, (cat.) Kunsthaus and Kunstverein in Hamburg, 1984

Noli me tangere, (cat.) Musée Cantonal des Beaux-Arts Sion, 1990

Nolte, Jost: *Kollaps der Moderne. Traktat über die letzten Bilder*, Hamburg 1989

NY Art Now. The Saatchi Collection, edited by Dan Cameron, London 1988

Objectives. The New Sculpture, edited by Paul Schimmel, (cat.) Newport Harbor Art Museum, Newport Beach, California 1990

Objet/Objectif, edited by Rainer Crone and David Moos, (cat.) Galerie Daniel Templon, Paris 1989

Open Mind (Gesloten Circuits), (cat.) Museum van Hedendaagse Kunst, Ghent, (Fabbri) Milan 1989

Origen i Visió, edited by Christos M. Joachimides, (cat.) Centre Cultural de la Caixa de Pensions, Barcelona 1984

Out There: Marginalization and Contemporary Culture, edited by Russell Ferguson, Martha Gever et al, Cambridge 1990

Paetzold, Heinz: *Profile der Ästhetik. Der Status von Kunst und Architektur in der Postmoderne*, Vienna 1990

Passages de l'image, (cat.) Centre Georges Pompidou, Musée National d'Art Moderne, Paris 1990

Per gli anni novanta. Nove artisti a Berlino, edited by Christos M. Joachimides, (cat.) Padiglione d'Arte Contemporanea, Milan 1989

Philosophen – Künstler, edited by Gerhard-Johann Lischka, Berlin 1986

Philosophie der neuen Technologie, edited by Ars Electronica, Berlin 1989

Pickshaus, Peter Moritz: *Kunstzerstörer. Fallstudien: Tatmotive und Psychogramme*, Reinbek near Hamburg 1988

Pincus-Witten, Robert: *Postminimalism into Maximalism. American Art 1966–1986*, Ann Arbor, Michigan 1987

Pollock and After. The Critical Debate, edited by Francis Frascina, London 1985

Ponton. Temse, (cat.) Temse, edited by Museum van Hedendaagse Kunst, Ghent 1990

Positionen heutiger Kunst, (cat.) Nationalgalerie, Staatliche Museen Preußischer Kulturbesitz, Berlin 1988

Possible Worlds. Sculpture from Europe, (cat.) Institute of Contemporary Arts, Serpentine Gallery, London, 1990

Postmoderne. Alltag, Allegorie und Avantgarde, edited by Christa and Peter Bürger, Frankfurt am Main 1987

Postmoderne und Dekonstruktion. Texte französischer Philosophen der Gegenwart, edited by Peter Engelmann, Stuttgart 1990

Postmodernism and Its Discontents. Theories, Practices, edited by Ann Kaplan, London 1990

Prospect 86, (cat.) Frankfurter Kunstverein, Frankfurt am Main 1986

Prospect 89, Schirn Kunsthalle, Frankfurter Kunstverein, Frankfurt am Main 1989

Prospect Photographie, (cat.) Frankfurter Kunstverein, Frankfurt am Main 1989

Psychological Abstraction, (cat.) Deste Foundation for Contemporary Art, House of Cyprus, Athens 1989

Qu'est-ce que la sculpture moderne?, edited by Margit Rowell, (cat.) Centre Georges Pompidou, Musée National d'Art Moderne, Paris 1986

Raumbilder. Cinco Escultores Alemanes en Madrid, (cat.) Ministerio de Cultura, Direccion General de Bellas Artes y Archivos, Centro Nacional de Exposiciones, Madrid 1987

Refigured Painting. The German Image 1960–88, edited by Thomas Krens, Michael Govan and Joseph Thompson, (cat.) The Toledo Museum of Art, Toledo, Ohio, 1988, (Guggenheim Foundation) New York, (Prestel) Munich, 1989

Ressource Kunst. Die Elemente neu gesehen, edited by Georg Jappe, Cologne 1989

Robins, Corinne: *The Pluralist Era. American Art 1968–1981*, New York 1984

Rosset, Clément: *Le philosophe et les sortilèges*, Paris 1985

Rosset, Clément: *Le réel. Traité de l'idiotie*, Paris 1977

Saltz, Jerry: *Beyond Boundaries. New York's New Art*, New York 1986

Schlaf der Vernunft, edited by Veit Loers, (cat.) Museum Fridericianum, Kassel 1988

Schmidt, Siegfried J.: *Kunst. Pluralismen, Revolten*, Bern 1987

Schmidt-Wulffen, Stephan: *Spielregeln. Tendenzen der Gegenwartskunst*, Cologne 1987

Seitter, Walter: *Der große Durchblick. Unternehmensanalysen*, Berlin 1983

Seitter, Walter: *Jacques Lacan und*, Berlin 1984

Similia/Dissimilia. Modes of Abstractions in Painting, Sculpture and Photography Today. Abstraktionen in Malerei, Skulptur und Photographie heute, edited by Rainer Crone, (cat.) Städtische Kunsthalle Düsseldorf, 1987

Skulptur Projekte in Münster, edited by Kasper König and Klaus Bußmann, (cat.) Westfälisches Landesmuseum für Kunst und Kulturgeschichte, Münster, (DuMont) Cologne 1987

SkulpturSein, edited by Harald Szeemann, (cat.) Städtische Kunsthalle Düsseldorf, 1986

Sloterdijk, Peter: *Kopernikanische Mobilmachung und ptolemäische Abrüstung*, Frankfurt am Main 1987

Sonsbeek 86, 2 vols (cat.), Arnheim 1986

Spazi '88. Spaces '88, (cat.) Museo d'Arte Contemporanea Luigi Pecci, Prato, (Electa) Milan 1988

Spuren, Skulpturen und Monumente ihrer präzisen Reise, (cat.) Kunsthaus Zürich, 1985

Status of Sculpture, (cat.) Espace Lyonnais d'Art Contemporain, Lyon 1990

Steiner, George: *Real Presences*, London 1989

Szeemann, Harald: *Individuelle Mythologien*, Berlin 1985

Technologisches Zeitalter oder Postmoderne?, edited by Walther Zimmerli, Munich 1988

10 + 10. Contemporary Soviet and American Painters, (cat.) Modern Art Museum of Fort Worth, (Abrams) New York, (Aurora) Leningrad, 1989

Terrae Motus, (cat.) Fondazione Amelio, Naples, Grand Palais, Paris, (Guida Editori) Naples 1987

The Arts for Television, edited by Kathy Rae Huffman and Dorine Mignot, (cat.) The Museum of Contemporary Art, Los Angeles, Stedelijk Museum, Amsterdam, 1987

The Biennale of Sydney. The Readymade Boomerang. Certain Relations in 20th Century Art, edited by René Block, (cat.) Art Gallery of New South Wales, Sydney 1990

The BiNational. American Art of the Late 80's, edited by David A. Ross and Jürgen Harten, (cat.) The Institute of Contemporary Art, Museum of Fine Arts, Boston, (DuMont) Cologne 1988 (see *BiNationale*)

The European Iceberg. Creativity in Germany and Italy Today, (cat.) Art Gallery of Ontario, Toronto, (Mazzotta) Milan 1985

The Postmodern Moment. A Handbook of Contemporary Innovation in the Arts, edited by Stanley Trachtenberg, Westport, Connecticut / London 1985

Tiefe Blicke. Kunst der achtziger Jahre aus der Bundesrepublik Deutschland, der DDR, Österreich und der Schweiz, (cat.) Hessisches Landesmuseum Darmstadt, (DuMont) Cologne 1985

Transformations in Sculpture. Four Decades of American and European Art, edited by Diane Waldman, (cat.) Solomon R. Guggenheim Museum, New York 1985

Turner, Victor: *From Ritual to Theatre. The Human Seriousness of Play*, New York 1982

U-ABC. Painting, Sculptures, Photography from Uruguay, Argentina, Brazil, Chile, (cat.) Stedelijk Museum, Amsterdam 1989

über flusser. Die Fest-Schrift zum 70. von Vilém Flusser, edited by Volker Rapsch, Düsseldorf 1990

Übrigens sterben immer die anderen. Marcel Duchamp und die Avantgarde seit 1950, (cat.) Museum Ludwig Köln, Cologne 1988

Uit het oude Europa. From the Europe of Old, (cat.) Stedelijk Museum, Amsterdam 1987

Un'altra obiettività. Another objectivity, (cat.) Centre National des Arts Plastiques, Paris, Museo d'Arte Contemporanea Luigi Pecci, Prato, (Idea Books) Milan 1989

Unerwünschte Monumente. Moderne Kunst im Stadtraum, edited by Walter Grasskamp, Munich 1989

Vattimo, Gianni: *La fine della modernità*, Milan 1985

Video-Skulptur. retrospektiv and aktuell. 1963–1989, edited by Wulf Herzogenrath and Edith Decker, Cologne 1989

Virilio, Paul: *Das öffentliche Bild*, Bern 1987

Virilio, Paul: *Guerre et cinema 1. Logistique de la perception*, Paris 1984

Virilio, Paul: *La machine de vision*, Paris 1988

Virilio, Paul: *L'Espace Critique*, Paris 1984

Virilio, Paul: *L'Horizon négatif*, Paris 1984

Von der Revolution zur Perestroika. Sowjetische Kunst aus der Sammlung Ludwig, edited by Martin Kunz, (cat.) Kunstmuseum Luzern, Lucerne (Hatje) Stuttgart 1989

von hier aus. Zwei Monate neue deutsche Kunst in Düsseldorf, edited by Kasper König, (cat.) Messegelände Halle 13, Düsseldorf, (DuMont) Cologne 1984

Vor der Jahrtausendwende. Bericht zur Lage der Zukunft, edited by Peter Sloterdijk, 2 vols, Frankfurt am Main 1990

Wechselströme, (cat.) Bonner Kunstverein, Bonn (Wienand) Cologne 1987

Wege aus der Moderne. Schlüsseltexte der Postmoderne-Diskussion, edited by Wolfgang Welsch, Weinheim 1988

Weibel, Peter: *Die Beschleunigung der Bilder. In der Chronokratie*, Bern 1987

Weitersehen (1980–1990 –), (cat.) Museum Haus Lange, Museum Haus Esters, Krefelder Kunstmuseum, Krefeld 1990

Wellmer, Albrecht: *Zur Dialektik von Moderne und Postmoderne. Vernunftkritik nach Adorno*, Frankfurt am Main 1985

Welsch, Wolfgang: *Ästhetisches Denken*, Stuttgart 1990

Welsch, Wolfgang: *Unsere postmoderne Moderne*, Weinheim 1987

Werckmeister, Otto K.: *Zitadellenkultur. Die schöne Kunst des Untergangs der achtziger Jahre*, Munich 1989

Westkunst. Zeitgenössische Kunst nach 1939, 2nd vol.: *heute*, edited by Laszlo Glozer, (cat.) Museen der Stadt Köln, Cologne 1981

Wiener Diwan. Sigmund Freud heute, (cat.) Museum des 20. Jahrhunderts, Vienna, (Ritter Verlag) Klagenfurt 1989

Wiener, Oswald: *Probleme der künstlichen Intelligenz*, edited by Peter Weibel, Berlin 1990

Wittgenstein, edited by Joseph Kosuth et al, 2 vols, (cat.) Wiener Secession, Haus Wittgenstein, Vienna 1989

Zeitgeist. Internationale Kunstausstellung Berlin 1982, edited by Christos M. Joachimides and Norman Rosenthal, (cat.) Martin-Gropius-Bau, Berlin 1982

Zeitlos, edited by Harald Szeemann, (cat.) Hamburger Bahnhof, Berlin, (Prestel) Munich 1988

Zielinski, Siegfried: *Audiovisionen. Kino und Fernsehen als Zwischenspiele in der Geschichte*, Reinbek near Hamburg 1989

Zugehend auf eine Biennale des Friedens, edited by René Block and Inge Lindemann, (cat.) Kunsthaus and Kunstverein in Hamburg, 1986

NOTES ON THE AUTHORS

ACHILLE BONITO OLIVA

Born Caggiano, near Salerno, 1939. Has organized numerous exhibitions since 1970. Broadcasts on Italian television (RAI) and contributes articles to the daily press and to international art periodicals. Professor of principles of art history at faculty of architecture, Roma University. Lives in Rome.

JEFFREY DEITCH

Born Hartford, Connecticut, 1952. Studied art history and business studies, and later worked as a full-time art dealer and part-time business adviser. Now works as writer, exhibition organizer, art critic, and (since 1986) principal of the International Art Advisory Firm. Lives in New York.

WOLFGANG MAX FAUST

Born Landstuhl, Palatinate, 1944. Studied literature, art history and sociology. Has taught in Berlin, San Francisco and New York and has contributed to numerous international periodicals. Author, catalogue editor, and exhibition organizer; editor of *Wolkenkratzer Art Journal* 1988–90, now works as lecturer and art critic. Lives in Berlin.

VILÉM FLUSSER

Born Prague, 1920. Studied philosophy there. Emigrated to London and then to São Paulo, where he continued his studies. Became director of a transformer factory in 1961. Taught at University of São Paulo from 1959, initially as lecturer in the philosophy of science and from 1963 as professor of the philosophy of communications. Returned to Europe in 1971. Has organized numerous exhibitions, contributed to international art and philosophy journals and written a number of books on questions of communications and aesthetics. Lives at Robion, Vaucluse, France.

BORIS GROYS

Born Leningrad, 1947. Studied mathematics and philosophy at Leningrad University. Associate of institute of structural linguistics, Moscow University, 1965–71. Moved to West Germany, 1981. Now lecturer in Russian intellectual history at institute of philosophy, Münster University; also active as author and journalist. Lives in Cologne.

DIETMAR KAMPER

Born Erkelenz, Lower Rhine, 1936. Formerly professor of education at Marburg University; now professor of sociology at Free University of Berlin and member of research centre for historical anthropology. Editor, with Christoph Wolf, of twelve-volume series on Logic and Passion; also co-editor of series on Historical Anthropology. Lives in Berlin.

CHRISTOPH TANNERT

Born Leipzig, 1955. Studied archaeology and art history at Humboldt University, East Berlin, 1976–81. Worked as art critic, organizer of events and exhibitions. Founded self-help publishing house, Ursus Press, 1985. Co-founder of Galerie Vier, 1990. Numerous publications in exhibition catalogues, anthologies, etc. Lives in Berlin.

PAUL VIRILIO

Born Paris, 1932. Founder of a new science of speed, to which he has given the name of dromology, and in which the history of technology, military strategy, town planning, aesthetics, physics and metaphysics overlap. He is director of the Ecole Spéciale d'Architecture, Paris, a member of the editorial board of *Traverses* and a regular contributor to *Libération*. Founder member of CIRPES (interdisciplinary centre for peace research and strategic studies). Lives in Paris.

PHOTO CREDITS

ARMLEDER: Courtesy Galerie Daniel Buchholz, Cologne; Victor Dahmen, Cologne; Portrait: Antonio Masolotti, Geneva – ARTSCHWAGER: Dorothy Ziedman, New York; Portrait: Richard Leslie Schulman, New York – BALKA: Courtesy Galerie Nordenhake, Stockholm; Courtesy Galerie Isabella Kacprzak, Cologne; Portrait: Wojciech Niedzielko, Warsaw – BARANEK: Claudio Franzini, Venice; Antonio Ribeiro, São Paulo; Portrait: Antonio Ribeiro, São Paulo – BASELITZ: Frank Oleski, Cologne; Portrait: Martin Müller, Cologne – BLECKNER: Ziedman/Fremont, New York; Portrait: Sebastian Piras, New York – BOROFSKY: Courtesy Paula Cooper Gallery, New York; Portrait: Megan Williams, California – BUSTAMANTE: Attilio Maranzano, Italy; Cary Markerink, Belgium; Portrait: anonymous – BYARS: Portrait: Heinz-Günter Mebusch, Düsseldorf – CABRITA REIS: Werner Zellien, Berlin; Portrait: Ines Gonçalves, Lisbon – CAVENAGO: Studio Blu, Turin; Portrait: Turi Rapisarda, Turin, Courtesy Galleria Franz Paludetto, Turin – CLEGG & GUTTMANN: Clegg & Guttmann, New York; Portrait: anonymous – DANIËLS: Peter Cox, Eindhoven; Courtesy Paul Andriesse, Amsterdam; Frans Grummer, bfn; Portrait: Courtesy Paul Andriesse, Amsterdam – DAVENPORT: Prudence Cuming Associates Limited, London; Portrait: Henry Bond, London – DOKOUPIL: Courtesy Galerie Bischofberger, Zurich, and Reiner Opoku, Cologne; Portrait: Nicola Angiolli, Bari – EICHHORN: Werner Zellien, Berlin; Gunter Lepkowski, Courtesy Galerie Wewerka & Weiss, Berlin; Portrait: Marius Babias, Berlin – FABRE: Courtesy Ronny Van de Velde Gallery, Antwerp; Courtesy Jan Fabre; Courtesy Jack Tilton Gallery, New York; Portrait: Robert Mapplethorpe – FERMARIELLO: Peppe Avallone, Naples; Portrait: Peppe Avallone, Naples – FINLAY: Courtesy Jule Kewenig Galerie, Frechen-Bachem; Portrait: Chris Felver, California – FISCHLI/WEISS: Fischli/Weiss, Zurich; Portraits: M. Bühler, Basle – FÖRG: Wilhelm Schürmann, Aachen; Portrait: Wilhelm Schürmann, Aachen – FRITSCH: Nic Tenwiggenhorn, Düsseldorf – GILBERT & GEORGE: Courtesy Gilbert & George, London; Portrait: Deborah Weinreb, London – GOBER: Joaquin Castrillo, Madrid; Portrait:

Zoe Leonhard, New York – GÖRLICH: Ulrich Görlich, Berlin; Portrait: E. Collavo, Berlin – GÖRSS: Werner Zellien, Berlin; Portrait: Andreas Rost, Berlin – GUZMÁN: Romualdo Segura, Madrid, Courtesy Galerie Ascan Crone, Hamburg; Romualdo Segura, Madrid, Courtesy Galería La Máquina Española, Madrid; Portrait: Victoria Gil, Seville – HALLEY: Nic Tenwiggenhorn, Düsseldorf; Portrait: Timothy Greenfield-Sanders, New York – HEISTERKAMP: Michael Detleffsen, Berlin; Ole Schmidt, Berlin; Portrait: Fritz Heisterkamp, Berlin – HEROLD: Wilhelm Schürmann, Aachen; Portrait: Wim Cox, Cologne – HILL: Courtesy Garry Hill; Portrait: anonymous – HOLZER: Courtesy Barbara Gladstone Gallery, New York; Portrait: Michaela Zeidler, Cologne, Courtesy Barbara Gladstone Gallery, New York – IGLESIAS: Portrait: Nanda Lanfranco – KAUFMANN: Salvatore Licitra, Milan; Portrait: Maria Pia Giarre, Milan – KELLEY: Fredrik Nilsen; Paula Goldman; Werner Zellien, Berlin; Portrait: Grant Mudford, Los Angeles – KENMOCHI: Masayuki Hayashi, Tokyo; Kazuo Menmochi, Tokyo; Portrait: Masaru Okazaki, Tokyo – KESSLER: Courtesy Luhring Augustine Gallery, New York; Peter Muscato, New York; Portrait: Loren Hammer, Paris – KNOEBEL: Nic Tenwiggenhorn, Düsseldorf; Portrait: Rosa Frank, Hamburg – KOONS: Jim Strong, New York; Fred Scruton, New York; Portrait: Riccardo Schicchi, Rome – KOUNELLIS: Courtesy Jannis Kounellis, Rome; Portrait: Benjamin Katz, Cologne – KOVÁCS: Courtesy Attila Kovács, Budapest; Portrait: Lenke Szilágyi, Budapest – KUITCA: Courtesy Annina Nosei Gallery, New York; Courtesy Barbara Farber Gallery, Amsterdam; Courtesy Galleria Gian Enzo Sperone, Rome; Portrait: Marta Fernandez, Buenos Aires – LAPPAS: Thanassis Pettas, Athens; Portrait: Thanassis Pettas, Athens – LAUBERT: Martin Marencin, Bratislava; Jan Sekal, Bratislava; Portrait: Martin Marencin, Bratislava – MERZ: Philipp Schönborn, Munich; Portrait: Frank Rümmele, Munich – METZEL: Olaf Metzel, Munich; Ulrich Görlich, Berlin; Portrait: Ulrich Görlich, Berlin – MORIMURA: Yasumasa Morimura, Osaka; Portrait: Courtesy Yasumasa Morimura – MUCHA: Reinhard Mucha, Düsseldorf; Portrait: anonymous – MUÑOZ: J. Declerc, Spain;

Courtesy Galería Marga Paz, Madrid; Portrait: anonymous – NAUMAN: Courtesy Leo Castelli Gallery, New York; Courtesy Art Institute of Chicago; Portrait: Donald Woodman, New York – NOLAND: Colin de Land, New York; Courtesy American Fine Arts, New York – ODENBACH: Courtesy Marcel Odenbach, Cologne; Portrait: Frank Roßbach, Cologne – OEHLEN: James Franklin, Los Angeles; Portrait: James Franklin, Los Angeles – PERRIN: Courtesy Philippe Perrin, Nice; Portrait: Simone Simon, Cagnes-sur-Mer, France – PRIGOV: Anno Dittmar, Berlin; Portrait: Renate von Mangoldt, Berlin – PRINCE: Larry Lame, New York; Portrait: Richard Prince, New York – RICHTER: Friedrich Rosenstiel, Cologne; Portrait: Benjamin Katz, Cologne – RUFF: Thomas Ruff, Düsseldorf; Portrait: Thomas Ruff, Düsseldorf – RUSCHA: Courtesy James Corcoran Gallery, New York; Portrait: Chris Felver, California – SARMENTO: Courtesy Galeria Cómicos, Lisbon; Jose Manuel Costa Alves, Lisbon; Portrait: anonymous – SCHNABEL: Phillips/Schwab, New York; Ken Cohen, New York; Portrait: Michael Heimann, Tel Aviv – SHERMAN: Courtesy Cindy Sherman, New York; Portrait: David Robbing 'talents', New York – STARN TWINS: David Familian, New York; Portrait: Timothy Greenfield-Sanders, New York – STEINBACH: David Lubarsky, New York; Portrait: Wolfgang Neeb, Hamburg – TROCKEL: Bernhard Schaub, Cologne; Portrait: Bernhard Schaub, Cologne – VIOLA: Kira Perov, Long Beach, California; Portrait: Kira Perov, Long Beach, California – WALL: Courtesy Jeff Wall, Vancouver; Portrait: Ian Wallace, Vancouver – WEST: Wolfgang Woessner, Vienna; Courtesy Galerie Peter Pakesch, Vienna; – WHITEREAD: Ed Woodman, London; Portrait: Marcus Taylor, London – WOODROW: Courtesy Bill Woodrow, London; Portrait: Chris Felver, California – WOOL: Courtesy Christopher Wool, New York; Portrait: Larry Clark, New York – ZAKHAROV: Courtesy Galerie Sophia Ungers, Cologne; Portrait: Vadim Zakharov, Moscow.

Text N. Rosenthal: Horst Luedeking, Berlin; Jürgen Müller-Schneck, Berlin, Courtesy Edition Block, Berlin

DATE DUE